Trinidad Ethnicity

Edited by

Kevin A. Yelvington

25 September 1994

To Iveris,

I hope your
studies take you
to Trinidad!

Kevin

The University of Tennessee Press

Knoxville 37996-0325

First published 1993

Published by The University of Tennessee Press,
Knoxville, Tennessee

ISBN 0 – 87049 – 779 – 0

Printed in Hong Kong

Library of Congress Cataloging-in-Publication Data
Trinidad ethnicity / edited by Kevin A. Yelvington.
    p.   cm.
Includes bibliographical references and index.
Contents: Social organisation and class: racial and cultural conflict
in nineteenth century Trinidad / Bridget Brereton – Notes on the
evolution of inequality in Trinidad and Tobago / Ralph M. Henry –
"Race" and "colour" in pre-independence Trinidad and Tobago /
Daniel A. Segal – Spatial pattern and social interaction among Creoles
and Indians in Trinidad and Tobago / Colin Clarke – Ethnic conflict
in Trinidad and Tobago: domination and reconciliation / Ralph
Premdas – Afro-Trinidadian identity and the Africanisation of the
Orisha religion / James Houk – What is "a Spanish"?: ambiguity and
"mixed" ethnicity in Trinidad / Aisha Khan – Structures of
experience: gender, ethnicity, and class in the lives of two East Indian
women / Patricia Mohammed – An evaluation of the "creolisation"
of Trinidad East Indian adolescent masculinity / Niels M. Sampath –
Ethnicity and social change in Trinidadian literature / Patrick Taylor
– Ethnicity and the contemporary calypso / Keith Q. Warner.
   ISBN 0 – 87049 – 779 – 0 (alk. paper)
   1. Trinidad and Tobago – Race relations. 2. Ethnicity – Trinidad and
Tobago. I. Yelvington, Kevin A., 1960 –
F2119.T73 1993   92 – 30207
305.8′00972983 – dc20   CIP

Series Preface

The Centre for Caribbean Studies at the University of Warwick was founded in 1984 in order to stimulate interest and research in a region which is now receiving academic recognition in its own right. In addition to the publication of the papers from annual symposia which reflect the Centre's comparative and inter-disciplinary approach, other volumes in the series will be published in disciplines within the arts and social sciences.

The present collection is one of a number of volumes in this series focusing on the question of ethnicity and problems of the multi-cultural societies of the Caribbean.

With both Spanish and French colonial legacies and with the influx of Asian indentured labour, as well as the presence of small comprador minorities, Trinidad is the most ethnically varied, religiously and culturally heterogeneous of all Caribbean islands. While this has been one reason for its creative vitality, tensions are now posing acute problems as evidenced by the rising of 1991 which exposed ethnic and class cleavages. Politics have too often been organised along ethnic group lines, during the colonial period, in the anti-colonial struggle and after independence. This collection studies recent developments in a new and original manner.

Trinidad's ethnic and cultural diversity has made it a laboratory for the study of the relationship between race and class, and for the ways in which ethnicity becomes politicised. The nature of the Trinidadian economy, with its oil wealth, has given an international dimension to this complexity which complicates the analysis still further. With its wide spread of contributors writing from different perspectives, this collection illustrates the importance of an approach transcending traditional disciplinary boundaries whilst the introduction is a significant addition to the theoretical study of complex societies. This book not only increases our understanding of Trinidadian society but has wider implications for the region as a whole, as well as making a valuable contribution to the burgeoning interest in ethnicity throughout the world.

Alistair Hennessy

Contents

The Contributors

Bridget Brereton is senior lecturer and head of the Department of History at the University of the West Indies, St Augustine, Trinidad. She is the author of *Race Relations in Colonial Trinidad 1870-1900* (1979) and *A History of Modern Trinidad 1783-1962* (1981).

Colin Clarke is a fellow of Jesus College, University of Oxford. A geographer, he has written a number of articles and books on the Caribbean. He is the author of *East Indians in a West Indian Town: San Fernando, Trinidad, 1930-1970* (1986), *Kingston, Jamaica 1692-1962* (1976) and the editor of *Caribbean Social Relations* (1978) and *Society and Politics in the Caribbean* (1991).

Ralph M. Henry is senior lecturer and head of the Department of Economics of the University of the West Indies, St Augustine, Trinidad. His main research interests lie primarily in human resource economics and the distribution of income and poverty. In both areas he has published widely and in recent years he has paid close attention to distributional problems in plural societies.

James Houk is an assistant professor in the Department of Geography and Anthropology at Louisiana State University. An anthropologist, he spent 15 months during 1985 and 1988-9 doing fieldwork in Trinidad.

Aisha Khan is a Ph.D. candidate in the Anthropology Program, City University of New York Graduate Center. She has published on her fieldwork among the Garifuna (Black Carib) in Honduras and among East Indians in Trinidad. She is also co-editor of the book *Women Anthropologists* (1989).

Patricia Mohammed is a research fellow at the Institute of Social and Economic Research, University of the West Indies, St Augustine, Trinidad, where she has been the course director for the Women and Development Studies programme. A sociologist, she has published a number of articles on gender, ethnicity, education, and development. She is the co-editor of *Gender in Caribbean Development* (1988).

Ralph Premdas holds a joint appointment with the Department of Government at the University of the West Indies, St Augustine, Trinidad, and with the Centre for Developing Area Studies, McGill

University, Montreal, Canada. He has written extensively on issues of Caribbean ethnicity and development.

Niels M. Sampath is a research student at the Institute of Social Anthropology at the University of Oxford. Between 1985 and 1989 he spent 21 months in Trinidad doing fieldwork on rural East Indian masculinity.

Daniel A. Segal teaches anthropology and world history at Pitzer College of the Claremont Colleges. He is the author (with Richard Handler) of *Jane Austen and the Fiction of Culture: An Essay on the Narration of Social Realities* (1990) and the editor of *Crossing Cultures: Essays in the Displacement of Western Civilization* (1992). He received his Ph.D. from the University of Chicago for a study of nationalism and state formation in Trinidad and Tobago. In 1989, he was guest curator for an exhibit of Caribbean art at Lang Gallery of the Claremont Colleges.

Patrick Taylor is an assistant professor in the Division of Humanities at York University, Toronto, Canada. He is the author of *The Narrative of Liberation: Perspectives on Afro-Caribbean Literature, Popular Culture, and Politics* (1989) and the co-editor of *Forging Identities and Patterns of Development in Latin America and the Caribbean* (1991). He has published widely on his research interests, which include social and political aspects of Indian and African identity, creolisation, and cultural pluralism in the Anglophone and Francophone Caribbean, including Haiti, as expressed in religion, popular culture and literature.

Keith Q. Warner was born in Port of Spain, Trinidad and studied French Literature at the University of Caen. He has taught at the University of Saskatchewan's Regina Campus, Howard University, the University of the West Indies at St Augustine, Trinidad, and is currently chair of Foreign Languages and Literatures, George Mason University. His varied publications include *Kaiso! The Trinidad Calypso: A Study of the Calypso as Oral Literature* (1982), and translations of two French Caribbean novels, *Black Shack Alley* by Joseph Zobel, and *The Bastards* by Bertène Juminer.

Kevin A. Yelvington is an assistant professor in the Department of Sociology and Anthropology at Florida International University. He received his D.Phil. in social anthropology from the University of Sussex in 1991 based on fieldwork among female factory workers in Trinidad. His research interests include ethnic, gender, and class relations, Latin American and Caribbean history and literature, urban anthropology, and development studies.

Acknowledgments

The efficiency and helpfulness – not to mention talents – of the contributors to this volume greatly facilitated its production. In every way they were models of co-operation and I want to thank each of them for making my job as editor a pleasant one.

A number of Trinidadians helped in one way or another during my stays there over the years. Besides those informants too numerous to mention, I would especially like to thank Cheryl Ali, Guy and Uckline Chan Poon, Dr Annette M.T. Ching, George, Teddy, Marina and Annette de Gannes, Roger and Aulrica McFalane, Tony Salandy, and the members of Maple Club.

Thanks are also owed to colleagues at Florida International University for their encouragement and advice. These include Professors Anthony P. Maingot, Mark B. Rosenberg, and John F. Stack, Jr and Drs Bàrbara C. Cruz and Richard Tardanico.

At the University of Tennessee Press I would like to thank Meredith M. Morgan. I would like to thank Barbara Croucher of Macmillan Caribbean who copy-edited the entire manuscript with precision. I would like to thank Professor Alistair Hennessy, editor of the Warwick University Caribbean Studies series. And finally, I would especially like to thank Macmillan Caribbean Publisher Shirley Hamber, whose competent hands guided the manuscript through all of the stages of the production process and who did so with kindness and patience.

To my brother Barry Yelvington

Erratum: on page 17, line 13
'Trinidadians' should read 'Trinidadianists'.

CHAPTER 1

Introduction: Trinidad ethnicity

Kevin A. Yelvington

'Colonials, we began with this malarial enervation: that nothing could ever be built among these rotting shacks, barefooted backyards and moulting shingles;...If there was nothing, there was everything to be made'. Derek Walcott, 'What the Twilight Says' (1972:4).

Introduction

As a significant dimension in the development of all contemporary societies, ethnicity has been an especially critical phenomenon in many of the social and political-economic events recently seen in Europe, Africa, Asia, and the Americas. Ethnicity is particularly salient in a number of post-colonial, underdeveloped states such as those in the Caribbean. As these countries strive for economic betterment they continue to grapple with the legacies of colonial labour schemes which devised the importation of peoples from different parts of the world to toil on plantations – before and after the formal end of slavery. Ethnicity became established as a critical variable that partially determined one's access to the means of production, wealth, political power and prestige. These states are now riven with factionalism and complexly divided loyalties based on ethnic allegiance.

Trinidadians[1] count among their number the descendants of people from West Africa, India, Europe, China, the Middle East, and those native to the Americas. In Trinidad, ethnicity permeates all of the society's social, cultural, political and economic institutions and practices because ethnicity is implicated in the power struggles of everyday life. A collection of original articles based on recent research and from a number of academic disciplines, this book represents a concentrated attempt to explicate the phenomenon of ethnicity as it exists in one of the most economically-developed and possibly the most ethnically-diverse and religiously heterogeneous Caribbean territory.

In seeking to understand the ways ethnicity is defined, evoked as social identity, and articulated with religion, class, and notions of 'culture', this volume also addresses larger issues that impinge on the rest of the post-colonial world and will therefore be useful for scholars whose regional interests are outside the Caribbean. These issues include communal politics with groups vying to wrest state power from an 'Other' (however defined); the vicissitudes of ethnicity and class as derived from both symbolic and material relationships; nationalist ideologies based on permutations of 'imagined communities' (Anderson, 1983) and the 'invention of tradition' (Hobsbawm and Ranger, 1983), a process implicated in the invention of ethnicity (Sollors, 1989a) and involving not only claims to legitimacy – and hence power – but notions of shared history and affinity which determine who is 'in' and who is 'out' of a group; transformations in the structures of dominance in 'cultures of colonialism' (Stoler, 1989) by the inheritors of colonial power; the international dimensions of ethnicity in a transnational world (Stack, 1981a, 1981b); and changes in the dialectic between labour relations and the meaning(s) attributed to them in the context of an ethnic division of labour, to name but a few. While they are distinctly expressed in Trinidad, the larger, global forces that continue to exert influence upon these societies are in many ways of a similar kind. Thus, students of these processes outside of the Caribbean will find this book useful not only for cross-cultural comparisons but for theory-building as well.

Based on her study of ethnicity and Trinidad's sugar industry, Ching (1985) describes ethnicity as 'the social construction of primordiality', a construction which, she argues, is achieved through the use of kinship metaphors. Theorising about ethnicity is particularly important at the present historical moment. With the withdrawal of the colonial powers, inter-ethnic rivalry has led to critical and intense levels of open and protracted inter-ethnic violence in such societies as Fiji, Malaysia, Nigeria, Sri Lanka and, in the Caribbean, in Guyana.[2] Indeed, inter-ethnic rivalry and violence has become entrenched within the boundaries of former colonial and neo-colonial powers. In Trinidad, by contrast, inter-ethnic relations have not – with the exception of a few notable events – had the same tenor. Writing on the nascent nationalist movements in the Caribbean during the 1940s, Howard University professor A.H. Maloney contrasted black-white relations in the United States with ethnic relations in the Caribbean. Whereas prejudice in the United States was in the 'active mood', in the Caribbean '...society is plagued with the disease of a psychology of self-interest' (1949:141).

This observation is not intended to play down the trends of prejudice in the 'active mood' in Trinidadian history and certainly not to claim that ethnic violence did not characterise the experience of slavery and indenture. Nor, for that matter, is it to suggest – as certain post-independence politicians and other Trinidadians have – that ethnic relations in the island are typified by a certain harmony. It is simply to emphasise what is unique in Trinidad compared to other multi-ethnic post-colonial societies. In some ways, this makes the study of ethnicity and ethnic relations in Trinidad even more challenging and compelling than in those societies characterised by more manifest forms of inter-ethnic violence. The studies in this volume, in sum, show the (often subtle) ways in which ethnicity is invented, constructed, defended, and presented as part of the 'natural' (i.e., timeless and above question) order of things. The contributors collectively emphasize the stratification and hierarchy behind these constructions. Writing of the invention of ethnicity, Sollors observes:

> It is always the specificity of power relations at a given historical moment and in a particular place that triggers off a strategy of pseudo-historical explanations that camouflage the inventive act itself (1989b:xiv).

Therefore people invent their ethnicity as they invent their history, but, to paraphrase Marx, not exactly in ways in which they please.

Trinidad ethnicity: historical themes

Any discussion of ethnicity in Trinidad must begin with a discussion of Trinidadian history, especially the formative years of the early-nineteenth century, although mine will be brief here[3] as several chapters in this volume pay close attention to ethnicity in Trinidadian history (e.g., the chapters by Brereton, Clarke, Henry, Khan, Mohammed and Segal). Trinidadian history is one of cleavages and fault lines running down not only ethnic, but class, cultural, national, religious, and sexual boundaries. The resulting competitive ethic is as much the consequence of colonial divide and rule policies as of an incomplete hegemony (whether by the holders of colonial power or their inheritors) that gave 'space' for group agency and strategies of ascendancy. However, the most ubiquitous and determinative feature in this history is the development of what has been called an ethnic/class social structure. This structure was characterised by a close correspondence of ethnic identity to class and power. In other words, the society was ethnically stratified. And although this structure has broken down in contemporary times, its pervasiveness continues to inform contemporary ethnic relations.

The ethnic/class structure was the result of colonial policies. For centuries before the advent of European colonialism the island had been visited, attacked and settled by Amerindian peoples of the Carib and Arawak groups. With the arrival of Christopher Columbus on the morning of 31 July 1498, the island would become incorporated into an expanding network of European 'great power' possessions. The imperatives of ethnicity came to permeate the ordering of the history of Trinidad (so-named by Columbus after sighting a 'trinity' of hills on the island's south-east coast).

Although Trinidad became a backwater colony in the Spanish Empire, being virtually ignored for 300 years after the arrival of Columbus, the Amerindian population was decimated by disease and warfare (with the Spanish and other indigenous groups). Many Amerindians were exported as forced labour to other Spanish possessions, and the Spanish engaged in Christianising efforts among them.[4]

Responding in the eighteenth century to an increasingly aggressive British imperialism and realising that Trinidad, lacking a productive base, had a stagnant economy, the Spanish attempted to transform Trinidad into a profitable agricultural slave colony by opening up the island to Catholic foreigners from friendly nations. The *Cedula de Población* in 1783 was directed at French planters in the French islands formally ceded to Britain and those resident in the French Antilles as well. The former were suffering from severe political and social discrimination at the hands of British administrators, the latter from exhausted soils and plagues of insects. These planters were given grants of land and other inducements, receiving an amount of land commensurate with the number of slaves they brought with them: the more slaves, the more land. Free coloureds[5] received half the amount of land as whites. This group, suffering from discrimination in the now-British islands, outnumbered the white immigrants and formed an important part of the plantocracy. More settlers arrived from French communities and from France itself once the reverberations of the French Revolution were felt. Trinidad soon developed a plantation economy roughly along the lines of the rest of the Caribbean, but besides sugar, cocoa and coffee were cultivated. 'French culture' in terms of language, religion, and ideology among the planters and, at least nominally, among their slaves, soon predominated.

Trinidad was captured by the British in 1797 and the island was formally ceded to Britain in 1802. This meant that, besides British administrators, British planters and their slaves added to the island's ethnic and national diversity. These planters came from other West Indian islands, in search of new opportunities, leaving behind less fertile conditions for agriculture. The sugar economy expanded and British-controlled merchant houses and industries that supported the plantation economy became established. Along with the British estate owners came estate overseers, and managers and clerks in the merchant houses. Typically, these were young men from Scotland and Ireland and, although white in a society that fetishised 'whiteness', they occupied a status far below that of the estate owners. They were resented by white and coloured Creoles who were denied access to these jobs. Coloureds, in fact, had to wage a campaign for equal rights under British law.

Divergent groups of free blacks came to populate Trinidad during slavery and afterwards. These included former American slaves, slaves freed from foreign slave ships by the Royal Navy, and immigrants from other Caribbean islands. At the same time, there was still another wave of immigration to Trinidad. Between 1810 and 1820 revolutionary upheavals in the Spanish colonies on the mainland caused a number of people to flee to Trinidad, including white and free coloured cocoa and cotton planters, blacks and *peon* labourers.

At the beginning of the nineteenth century, Trinidad was a society being built on slave labour. The slaves were a very diverse group, many were born in Africa, although there were about twice as many slaves who were born in the Caribbean. The Africans were of varied ethnic, cultural, linguistic and religious groups from along the West African coast (Warner-Lewis, 1991). By contrast, Creole slaves presumably spoke the language of their masters, that is a French or English creole, depending on their islands of origin. Besides ethnic and cultural diversity, Trinidad was characterised by linguistic diversity (Winer, 1984). While slaves and free blacks certainly differentiated between and among themselves in terms of ethnicity and culture, this past is difficult to reconstruct in the present (cf. Wood:39-40). Certainly, the African dynamic in Trinidad culture, to paraphrase Warner-Lewis (1991), extends beyond folklore, linguistics, music, dance, and oral and written literature.

From this time Trinidad exhibited an ethnic/class structure. There were three major socio-economic classes which corresponded very closely to the three main ethnic groups and with very little mobility between them. As planters, owners of merchant houses, and administrators, whites controlled most of the colony's resources; coloureds were in intermediate occupations, many were professionals; and the mass of blacks were slaves, agricultural labourers or peasants. In addition, ethnic differences *within* classes were important – unlike, say, in Barbados. There is evidence, though, that each ethnic/class influenced each other in terms of culture and values in the creation of 'creole society' (for Jamaica, see E. Brathwaite, 1971). Shortly after this period ethnic relations in Trinidad were to become even more complicated.

One consequence of British rule was an increased rivalry among the elite over such issues as language, religion, education and economics (Brereton, 1979, 1981; Wood, 1968). Trinidad was 'French' in temperament and the French Creoles saw themselves as Trinidad's aristocracy (cf. Maingot, 1962). However, there was a slow, if sure, 'Anglicisation' process occurring. One method of dealing with the multi-ethnic environment by the Imperial government was the institution of Crown Colony government (Millette, 1970).

At the end of slavery in 1834 and the apprenticeship system in 1838, the planters bemoaned the fact that they were losing a captive workforce and now would not be able to compete on the British market with slave-produced and beet sugar from outside the Empire. The planters wanted a docile and controllable workforce but what they got was a highly mobile one that refused to be bound by a work contract. However, the ex-apprentices did not withdraw completely from estate labour as it was one of the only sources of wage work. The ex-apprentices merely sought to find the best working conditions possible.

The planters looked to external sources of labour. Many ex-apprentices came from neighbouring islands as wages in Trinidad were comparatively high. In addition, recruitment efforts in West Africa and North America were tried, but had little success in attracting the numbers and, especially, the *kinds* of workers that the planters required, given Victorian notions of the 'suitability' of national and ethnic identities for a particular kind of labour. The planters searched further afield, encouraging Portuguese-speakers from Madeira and Chinese from the Cantonese ports of Whampoa and Namoa to come to Trinidad as indentured labourers. However, both the Portuguese and the Chinese were not suitable for estate work as defined by the planters' needs. Both groups became involved in the grocery and dry goods trades (for the Chinese, see Bentley and Henry, 1969; Johnson, 1987; Ho, 1989). The Chinese and Portuguese were joined by the Syrian/Lebanese after the First World War as Trinidad's 'trading minorities' (Nicholls, 1981:422-6).

The Chinese, Portuguese and Syrian/Lebanese groups complicated Trinidad's ethnic relations, with some members of these groups quickly becoming 'creolised' while others attempted to maintain a strict vigilance over what they perceived as the group boundary. But these groups paled in comparison to the demographic effects of the immigration of more than 144,000 indentured labourers from India between 1845 and 1917.

Indentured immigration from India was first tried in Mauritius in 1834 and, in British Guiana, the 'Gladstone coolies' (Love, 1982) were a test case in 1838. Soon after, European powers established a 'new system of slavery' (Tinker, 1974) in their colonies. Labourers were recruited and left from the ports of Calcutta and Madras. In general, they were given five-year contracts, they were promised housing, medical care, and clothing, and they were guaranteed a free passage back to India. What they met in Trinidad were squalid conditions in the estate barracks and gruelling, poorly-renumerated work.

The Indians brought with them their cultures, languages, and religious traditions. While Hinduism and Islam were 'allowed' to be practised – certainly more so than Africans were allowed to practise their religious traditions under slavery – it is probably correct to say that these religions were not encouraged by the power elite. In addition, the caste system tended to break down (Schwartz, 1967) although vestiges of caste remain in claims to high status and/or class and complicate intra-ethnic relations (Khan, forthcoming). Further, Hindu-Muslim divisions and, to a lesser extent, divisions between those from different regions in India (Calcutta vs. Madras), have been important at different points in Trinidadian history.

In the early years of the Indian indenture experience Indians were apart – geographically and culturally – from the rest of the society. This cultural difference has been evident in, for example, the differing family structures of East Indians and Creoles (cf. Roberts and Braithwaite, 1967; Bell, 1970; Angrosino, 1976; MacDonald and MacDonald, 1973; Abdullah, 1991). Thus, in a large part, their own value systems, practices, and social organisation were able to be transported intact in a significant way and they were able to 'resist' much longer than other groups the process of 'creolisation'. This phenomenon was later called 'cultural persistence' (Klass, 1961) and was given strength by the fact that there was a continuous stream of arrivals from the subcontinent up until 1917, when the scheme ended, and even in small numbers up until World War II. Many Indians intended on returning home. A small percentage did but the rest chose to forgo their return passage for land. This may have accounted partly for the substance of their cultural ideology.

Most studies of contemporary Trinidad have focused on black-East Indian relations, as these are the demographically dominant groups. It is instructive to look at the history of the way these two groups interacted because, as Brereton (1974) points out, the stereotypes formed during the nineteenth century inform contemporary relations. But in so doing, we must not see these groups in isolation from the other, more powerful, groups in Trinidad, namely the planter elite.

On the one hand, blacks and East Indians lived in nearly separate worlds in the mid-nineteenth century. There was a clear ethnic division of labour being created (see Table 1.1), with whites as plantation owners, Chinese and Portuguese in trading occupations, blacks and

Table 1.1:   Employment in Trinidad, 1891, of East Indians, non-East Indian natives of Trinidad, and natives of the United Kingdom.

Industrial category	East Indians	Native-born	British
Official and professional	0.4	2.5	24.1
Commercial	1.7	3.8	14.8
Industrial	14.2	40.7	28.1
Domestic	2.4	17.2	1.8
Agricultural	81.3	35.8	11.1
Indefinite and unoccupied	–	–	20.1
Totals	100.0	100.0	100.0

Source: Compiled from the 1891 *Census of Trinidad and Tobago.*
Note: The totals for the categories 'East Indians' and 'Native-born' are their 'working populations', or the number of people who are employed. The 'Indefinite and unoccupied' category is included for natives of the United Kingdom because, of the 181 so classified, 36 were listed as 'living on private means' and five were counted as proprietors. The 'East Indian' category includes individuals born in India and those born in Trinidad to Indian parents.

coloureds moving into the professions and skilled manual occupations, and East Indians almost completely in agricultural pursuits (e.g., Ramesar, 1976; Richardson, 1975, 1979; Ryan, 1991a). On the estates, blacks performed skilled occupations while East Indians performed labour-intensive tasks. This ethnic division of labour[6] henceforth tended to break down with blacks and East Indians coming to occupy more or less similar occupations (Yelvington, 1987b). This did not mean, though, that historically-privileged groups (whites and coloureds) or newly-privileged groups (Chinese, Portuguese and Syrian/Lebanese) experienced downward mobility.

In addition, in a large part, the two groups were separated geographically: many blacks were urban-based, especially in and around Port of Spain, while the East Indians were more numerous in the central and southern parts of the island (this trend continues to the present). And, even though there was an extreme shortage of women among the first migratory flows from India, there was no competition over women between black and East Indian men (Wood, 1968:138). Indeed, Brereton (1979:183) reports that the Protector of Immigrants wrote in 1871 that 'there is not probably at this moment a single instance of an indentured immigrant ... who cohabits with one of the negro race'.

Given this 'distance', each group developed negative stereotypes of the other, but we must ask how (and from where) these images were derived. Blacks were regarded by the planters – and later by Indians – as being lazy and irresponsible, as having a pencha_ drinking and conspicuous consumption, and being prone to profligacy (e.g., Ryan, 1991a:170). East Indians were seen by blacks and others as being miserly, being prone to domestic violence, acquiescent to authority, clannish, and 'heathen' for not adopting 'Western' ways.

Brackette Williams notes similar stereotypes for Guyana and argues that these first came from the elite and were later expanded upon by the subordinate groups (blacks and East Indians) (1991:127-8, 183). It is important here to consider historical evidence of the uses of elite ideology in Trinidad. Apparently, the planters were quick to point out the supposed 'suitability' and 'docility' of the East Indians, while, on the contrary, Samaroo (1987:27) emphasises that in reality blacks *and* East Indians actively resisted the plantation regime. Wood cites statements from pleased planters, recorded in the *Trinidad Royal Gazette* of 1848:

> For the most part the Indians seem to have given satisfaction ... Mr MacKenzie, the manager of Cedar Hill and Forest Hill, with more than 100 working for him, found them 'industrious, cheerful, contented, docile, obedient'; John Richardson, the coloured manager of Windsor Park, Savonetta, considered them to be better workers than the Creoles; and Horatio Nelson Huggins, proprietor of Union Hall, South Naparima, observed that the Indians were 'less easily offended, devoid of the savage, unruly disposition of the African' (1968:114).[7]

Wood concludes that:

> The first criterion of the whites in assessing the qualities of the Negroes was their industry, particularly on plantations. All else was subordinate ... The same Victorian yardstick of industriousness was used in judging the immigrants and they were naturally compared with the Negroes in this respect (*ibid.*:303).

The 'culture of ethnicity' in Trinidad

The roots of the 'culture of ethnicity' (viz. Alexander, 1977) in Trinidad lie, then, in the justifications of the colonial elite for the labour schemes which sustained them, their way of life, and the political oppression of subjugated groups. The culture of ethnicity also involves the forms of resistance to and acceptance of these forces on the part of subjugated groups. By claiming that blacks were poor workers and that East Indians were industrious and docile they rationalised a programme that involved, among other things, the taxation of working class blacks and other groups to subsidise the planters so they could import workers who would (at least indirectly) compete as labour. This lowered the price of labour, and, ultimately, divided the subjugated groups. The symbolisation process was and is, in a large part, monopolised by those who have had access to the 'symbolic capital' to perpetrate 'symbolic violence' (Bourdieu, 1977) against less-endowed groups.

In the colonial context, notions of history and the past can be used in a variety of instrumental ways (cf. Ranger, 1983). The persistence of colonial ethnic stereotypes in Trinidad during the present – when there is much concern over each group's access to society's economic, political and symbolic resources – is testimony to the way in which notions of history are implicated in the hegemonic struggles (see Brow, 1990), which often typify the construction of ethnicity. The past of 'the group' is embedded in 'the group's' historical interpretations. These interpretations are not idiosyncratic nor are they arbitrary. Certain symbols like the body, skin colour and 'culture', which are 'available' for use in certain circumstances, indicate 'groupness'.[8] Symbols are available to be interpreted; however, not just any symbol and not just any interpretation. The availability of certain symbols and of a certain symbolic universe is determined (though not in any simple or complete way) by the groups who hold political-economic power and those who are able to legitimate this power and the prestige that accompanies it (usually – but not always – these groups are one and the same) and it is contested by the subordinate groups. This is the conjunction of political-economic and symbolic resources in the construction of ethnicity.

Narratives of the past are not neutral, they are given value. Narratives of the relationship of ethnicity to the past are multivocal, but one 'determinant' of this value is the position of the ethnic group to the widely-construed division of labour (see Mintz, 1987 for the Caribbean; Bourgois, 1989 for Central America; and R. Williams, 1990 for the United States).

The process of ethnic identity formation involves 'sensing' likeness and differences and attaching meaning – and thus value – to those identities. This process in Trinidad has proceeded along the lines of what elsewhere has been referred to as the 'commoditisation process' (Kopytoff, 1986; see, also Appadurai, 1986). Ethnic identity formation in Trinidad has occurred in a context of an increasing commodification of labour, which has been intimately connected to the *objectification of ethnicity*. This objectification process involves for Trinidadians the reification of ethnicity whereby individuals and groups are weighted with cultural values and their identities are seen as having an essential existence. This leads to a *commodification of ethnicity*, a process most obvious in the allocation of places in the division of labour but which has far-reaching implications for the symbolisation process generally. While it has been noted that the ethnic division of labour has tended to break down in actual fact – and to lead to shared cultural practices – in certain aspects,[9] it has also been noted that aspects of the ethnic/class structure remain (cf. Parris, 1985; Hintzen, 1989). This has meant that the subordinate groups (blacks and East Indians) have not only been unable to manipulate easily their own ethnic symbols, but they have been effectively precluded from developing truly national images that give equal weight to all ethnic and cultural traditions in a meaningful way (cf. Stewart, 1991:162, 163). This is further complicated by the fact that the commodification of ethnicity occurs on an international scale and Trinidad ethnicity must be seen in the light of a transnational perspective on ethnicity.[10] In the case of a dependent, Third World society like Trinidad, what becomes noteworthy are images generated and transmitted via the international media, through the process of international migration, and through the 'cultural contact' of international tourism. And the rules of these games are set by more powerful groups of 'Others'.

Despite the cultural and geographic 'distance' between various groups during the nineteenth century, syncretisms and acts of cultural borrowing were occurring in the formation of what are seen today as typical Trinidadian cultural forms, such as religion (e.g., Khan, 1990), carnival (e.g, Pearse, 1956; Brereton, 1979), calypso (e.g., Warner, 1982; Rohlehr, 1990) and steelband (e.g., Stuempfle, 1990). These processes were punctuated by specific acts of co-operation, such as when blacks and Hindu East Indians began to participate actively in Hosein celebrations (Brereton, 1979:183).

Ethnicity and politics

Cultural and political depictions of such co-operation and cultural 'borrowing' were not only lost but actively suffocated by colonial administrators – and at times by post-independence politicians as well. As a number of studies have documented, politics have been organised along ethnic group lines, that is, political parties tend to include and represent one ethnic group and ethnicity tends to determine voting behaviour.[11] Ethnic politics in Trinidad have involved the use of ethnicity in the anti-colonial struggle, the anti-neo-colonial struggle, in the inter-group struggle, and the rise of nationalism. Trinidad's political topography did not 'invent' ethnic conflict, per se (cf. Eriksen,

1991a:134; Naipaul, 1985 [1962]:80). It is best instead to see ethnicity as politically-derived and to look at the ways in which ethnicity is *politicised*, a process which involves strategies of inter- and intra-group domination. This politicisation of ethnicity has responded to the imperatives of the (permutating) ethnic/class structure with the utilisation of colonial stereotypes in the struggle to control state resources.

The anti-colonial struggle, beginning in earnest at the turn of the century (cf. Magid, 1988), and culminating at independence in 1962, involved the manipulation of ethnic symbols. During the Caribbean-wide labour unrest and strikes of the 1930s, the predominantly-black oilfield workers protested about their harsh treatment and restricted upward mobility at the hands of expatriate white managers. For a time they linked up with East Indian sugar workers to generalise the protests, submerging ethnic conflicts and taking somewhat united class and anti-colonial stances (e.g., Basdeo, 1985; Cross, 1988; Phillips, 1990). Although the colonial authorities brought in troops to quell the disturbances, the trade union movement was born – a movement which, as the Barbadian novelist George Lamming (1985) points out, was the most democratising force in the Caribbean. Immediately after World War II politics took a different turn with the advent of universal suffrage in 1946,[12] and political candidates began making overt appeals to ethnicity in order to become elected. The institutionalisation of ethnic politics came with the institutionalisation of party politics.

In 1955, the black Oxford-educated historian Dr Eric Williams[13] and a group of urban, black and coloured middle-class intellectuals and professionals formed the People's National Movement (PNM). The PNM soon received strong support from working class blacks and became identified with the interests of blacks. The PNM was opposed in the 1956 elections by the People's Democratic Party (PDP) whose leader was also the head of the largest sugar workers' union (which had mainly East Indian members) and the head of the main Hindu religious organisation. The PNM and Williams – whom Oxaal (1968:100) called the 'racial messiah' – led the country to independence and dominated the PDP's 'Indian party' incarnations, the Democratic Labour Party (DLP), during the 1960s, and the United Labour Front (ULF), during the 1970s, each of which featured charismatic leaders of their own (see LaGuerre, 1991).

The PNM's brand of nationalism (cf., Oxaal, 1968; Segal, 1987, n.d.; Eriksen, 1991b, 1992) consisted of putative attempts at erasure of ethnic differences in the forging of a new 'nation'. Williams always maintained that the PNM was multi-ethnic and a few East Indians and other minorities were given prominent (but token) posts within the government. On the one hand, Trinidad was politically depicted as a melting pot. For example, the national anthem features the line describing Trinidad and Tobago as the country 'where every creed and race finds an equal place'. But, on the other hand, ethnicity became implicated in the PNM's nationalism as the symbols of this melting pot were constructed as 'national' symbols which were interpreted as Afro-Trinidadian-derived (cf. Eriksen, 1991b:270-1). These included steelband, calypso, and carnival.

Thus, Williams and the PNM took up the banner of 'creolisation', but this ideology constructed 'Trinidadian' and 'national' as Afro-Trinidadian-derived 'culture' and labelled practices (such as 'East Indian culture') which deviated from such a process as 'racist' and 'unpatriotic'. This was evident in Williams' allusion in 1958 to the East Indians as a 'recalcitrant and hostile minority', in the escalation of ethnic tensions to near violent proportions on the eve of the 1961 elections, and in Williams' refusal to allow the DLP opposition any say in the independence constitution – widespread ethnic violence only being averted when he finally compromised (cf. Ryan, 1972). The oft-repeated (by politicians and Trinidadians at large) notion that Trinidad is an ethnic democracy was emphasised during this era.

PNM dominance remained unchallenged until, ironically, the Black Power movement of the 1970s (cf. Nicholls, 1971; Oxaal, 1971; Sutton, 1983; Gosine, 1986; Bennett, 1989), in which urban blacks complained about continued multinational and local white domination of the economy. The movement tended to alienate East Indians because it used 'African' symbols and referred to the politically and economically disadvantaged as 'black', because its leadership was mostly black, and because it tended to concentrate its activities in urban areas. But the movement did eventually force the PNM into a redistributive stance, which was made possible by the oil boom of the early 1970s. The vast economic changes associated with the oil boom did *not* have the effect of submerging ethnic identity (Vertovec, 1987). Further, the economic gains to the state (Sandoval, 1983) facilitated the growth of the state enterprise sector. This often at times translated into state patronage, which apparently tended to favour blacks (Craig, 1974).

In Trinidad there is a preoccupation with the economic 'gains' made by different groups (Ryan, 1991a) – which are always seen as detrimentally affecting others. Research by Henry and others (Henry and Harewood, 1985; Henry, 1988, 1989, this volume) suggests that society-wide income distribution was worse in 1971 than in 1958, that the income disparity between blacks and East Indians is now insignificant, but that the disparity between blacks and East Indians, on the one hand, and 'others' (Syrian/Lebanese, Chinese, whites, and 'mixed' individuals), on the other hand, while becoming less so, is still salient. This is consistent with the arguments of Hintzen (1989), who shows that the white-dominated commercial elite have been the major recipients of international capitalist penetration (cf. also, Parris, 1985).

At the same time, and despite discrimination in state and private sector employment (Harewood, 1971; Camejo, 1971), blacks and East Indians benefited from the PNM's expansion of educational opportunities (cf. Reddock, 1991) and from the expansion of state sector employment. The argument is made in Trinidad that blacks dominate the state sector and that East Indians have a veritable monopoly on entrepreneurial activities. It is argued that this situation has East Indians poised to 'take over' the economy as, in the context of the oil 'bust', the state sector is contracting. Certainly a number of blacks were appointed to prestigious posts on the boards of state enterprises and continue to dominate strategic entities like the police and army. Recent research suggests that while East Indians are still not prevalent in the upper echelons of the public sector, they are now significantly represented in public sector employment (Ryan, 1991a:70).

In 1986 the PNM was finally defeated in landslide style by the multi-ethnic National Alliance for Reconstruction (NAR), an amalgam of ethnic- (including the ULF) and class-based parties. Optimists felt at the time that overt appeals to ethnicity in a political context would now be over. However, the NAR, led by the black Tobagonian A.N.R. Robinson, splintered along ethnic lines (cf. Yelvington, 1987a, 1991; Ryan, 1990; Premdas, this volume). As the country's economic crisis deepened, appeals for state patronage were made on the basis of ethnicity and class from within and from outside the NAR. When the in-fighting reached its apogee, Robinson fired four cabinet ministers, including former ULF leader Basdeo Panday, a charismatic Hindu East Indian. Panday and others formed the East Indian-based United National Congress in 1989 to challenge the NAR, which is seen by a large segment of society as representing the interests of the Creole and, to an extent, East Indian middle class. Meanwhile, in 1990 Robinson and his cabinet were held hostage in a coup attempt by a black Muslim group (Ryan, 1991c; Yelvington, forthcoming), an event that exposed, among other things, the ethnic and class cleavages of the society.

Certainly, 'ethnic politics' are not restricted to institutional parliamentary democracy at a national or local level (Vertovec, 1990), but are evident in such activities as beauty contests (Trinidad and Tobago, 1973), cricket (Yelvington, 1990a), calypso (Rohlehr, 1988, 1990; Trotman, 1991; Warner, this volume), and carnival (Miller, 1991; Ahye, 1991; Lee, 1991).

Competing theories of ethnic and cultural diversity

The interest in cultural and ethnic diversity and the issue of power has made Trinidad a social science laboratory for more than 40 years.[14] In the 1950s and early 1960s a debate ensued in the social science literature on the nature of the multi-ethnic society in Trinidad. The disagreement was centred basically on the following question: Do the different cultural and ethnic groups in Trinidad maintain the same set of values and cultural institutions? In order to answer this question and others, at least three competing theoretical approaches were brought to bear on the nature of ethnic and cultural diversity in Trinidad, and versions of these models are still employed.

The three competing theories used to explain Trinidadian society can be called the stratification school, the plural society school, and the plantation society school. The theorists of the stratification school (e.g., Braithwaite, 1954, 1960, 1975 [1953]; R.T. Smith, 1956; Nevadomsky, 1982, 1984) took a structural-functional approach and held that, despite obvious cultural and ethnic diversity, the society was held together by a consensus on norms and values. The emphasis of the plural society school (e.g., M.G. Smith, 1965, 1967, 1971, 1974, 1984; LaGuerre, 1976, 1982, 1988, 1991) was different. These theorists posited that there was no such consensus and that each cultural section maintained its own social institutions, distinct and separate from the others institutions. The theorists of the plantation society school (e.g., Mintz, 1959; Wagley, 1960; Rubin, 1960; Williams, 1960; Best, 1968; Girvan, 1975) emphasise that the society's social relations were shaped by the plantation economy and argue that those relations have not really changed since the days of slavery and indenture.

It may be argued that, in their original form, these theories shared a common weakness: that of not being able to account for social change.[15] These theorists tended to see society according to their own static constructs and models and therefore looked for behaviour that served to meet the needs of those constructs. They tended to attribute causation to those structures, thus reifying social action. Unfortunately, social science in the Caribbean seems to be locked into these competing paradigms. For example, M.G. Smith's latest statement promises to resolve issues '... in the light of recent developments in the theory of pluralism' (Smith, 1991:3), but these 'recent developments' turn out to be a re-hashing of the changes Smith's theory went through from the 1950s up to the early 1970s (cf. Robotham, 1991). Equally unfortunate is the fact that many studies of ethnicity in Trinidad tend to focus on one ethnic group in isolation from other groups, thus implicitly supporting one or another theoretical viewpoint. While many of the contributions to this voiume are informed by some of these theoretical models, they transcend these models with an attention both to changing empirical and historical contexts and to ethnic group relations.

Trinidad ethnicity: a multidisciplinary approach

The complexities of Caribbean societies dictate an approach (or approaches) that transcends traditional disciplinary boundaries. As one Caribbean scholar put it:

> Caribbeanists, regardless of their chosen discipline, realized that an area of such linguistic, cultural and political diversity could be studied only through interdisciplinary or at least multidisciplinary paradigms ... It was quite evident that anyone attempting to study Haiti, Cuba or, say, the West Indies without a multidisciplinary approach was merely skimming the surface of his selected country's reality. In an area where the poet, novelist and, indeed, the song writer, have very often provided the best descriptions of social reality, Caribbeanists learned early to incorporate their work not merely as data but as worthy conceptualizations of their societies (Maingot, 1983:3-4).

This book, therefore, is multidisciplinary in nature. Contributors to this volume are drawn from the disciplines of anthropology, economics, geography, history, literature and literary criticism, political science, and sociology. In addition, many of the contributors are avowedly interdisciplinary in their orientation. From the varied insights offered by such research strategies, the contributors bring a wide range of empirical data and analytic concepts to bear in a collective challenge to the received wisdom on ethnicity in Trinidad – whether this wisdom is transmitted as theories promulgated in academia or as 'folk models' among Trinidadians themselves.

In recent years, practitioners from a number of established academic disciplines have become concerned with the power, politics and bias involved in their depiction of disempowered 'others', be they women, the poor, ethnic minorities, or citizens of Third World territories. For the most part, this awareness has been affected by the objections and resistance of the 'subjects' themselves, rather than from an egalitarian impulse on the part of upholders of the traditional academic canon. These 'subjects' (in both senses of the word) rise to challenge not only the accuracy but the socio-economic and political effects of the way they are being depicted and, by implication, the motives and ideology behind academic discourse. In Caribbean studies the jury is still out as to whether the accounts of native versus foreign scholars are more accurate, more sensitive, and more bias-free. This issue is particularly problematic in the study of ethnic group relations, where the native scholar can be especially impassioned by a web of class, ethnic, regional, and religious affiliations so as to inhibit an effective distance from the issues at hand. Many native scholars are extremely distant from the masses in their societies, coming from the upper classes, educated abroad, and imbued with North Atlantic culture. The contributions to this book purposively do not represent one 'national' viewpoint; they are drawn from Trinidadians living and working in Trinidad, Britain, Canada and the United States.

The book begins with Bridget Brereton's discussion of nineteenth century Trinidad and the cultural, class and ethnic conflict inherent in the society. Brereton modifies the classic three-tiered ethnic/class model of post-emancipation Caribbean societies. She shows how, given its historical uniqueness and ethnic complexity, Trinidad deviated from classic slave societies on a number of grounds. She utilises a four-tiered model not only to analyse the efforts of domination on the part of the elites and strategies of resistance on the part of the masses, but, in explicating the complexities of Trinidadian history, to show how differentiation *within* these tiers was affected. She shows how, for example, ethnicity, language, religion, and occupation were used both to differentiate and to bind distinct groups in the process of political, economic and, perhaps above all, cultural struggle in the colonial context.

Ralph M. Henry takes up the theme of economic inequality between ethnic groups. Tracing the historical foundation of inequality and the permutations in this structure, he argues that much of the neo-classical and Marxist economic paradigms are inadequate for the analysis of the economics of 'plural societies'. Attention to the economics of plural societies is especially crucial, he asserts, in a post-colonial order characterised by inter-group inequality. Imperfect markets, discrimination, and 'gate keepers' are the norm in such settings where labour is valued by a number of subjective criteria. He concentrates on the question of income distribution in post-independence Trinidad, not only showing how changes in the overall economic situation – like the oil boom and bust – have affected group income, but also showing changes in the traditional ethnic/class relations, pointing at the same time to barriers and setbacks in the way of greater inter-group equality.

Daniel A. Segal, in departing from the received paradigms of Caribbean ethnicity, presents a semiotic analysis of the culture of 'race' and 'colour' in pre-independence Trinidad. He shows the ways in which ethnicity was socially constructed during this period. He examines the meanings embedded in terms for 'race' and 'colour', including both terms for 'pure races' and for various 'mixed' kinds, all the while demonstrating the relations of hierarchy implicit in the political semiotics of ethnicity. He explores the symbolism of ethnicity, arguing that such factors as genealogy, descent, phenotype, gender, class, education, and others all contribute to ethnicity's meaning and serve to define the limits of its malleability.

In his chapter, Colin Clarke, a geographer, outlines the contours of social distance among Creoles and East Indians in Trinidad's second city, San Fernando, and in a neighbouring, predominantly East Indian, village, Débé. He shows the changes, between 1960 and 1980, of spatial segregation between major ethnic groups at the national and local levels. Clarke traces residential segregation in rural and urban settings, and at the national level, compares its incidence to intermarriage between blacks and East Indians in these settings. In his discussion of the complex data he challenges the received wisdom that there exists in Western urban settings a close correlation between class (or social group), residence and endogamy. Once again, the Trinidad data provide counter-examples.

The chapter by Ralph Premdas is one of the latest instalments in the saga of ethnic politics in Trinidad. However, unlike many of his contemporaries who comment on Trinidadian politics in an anecdotal way, Premdas employs a theoretical perspective in his analysis. He uses Lijphart's (1977) ideas of 'consociational democracy' in his examination of the case of the formation and breakup of the multi-ethnic National Alliance for Reconstruction party, which was in power from 1986 until 1991. Premdas argues that while communal domination is not inevitable, the legacy of ethnic rivalry encouraged and bequeathed by Britain has meant a certain 'momentum' for inter-ethnic zero-sum reckoning in the political realm.

James Houk's chapter on black identity and the *Orisha* religion addresses and revives a number of classical issues in Caribbean anthropology. After earlier work by the Herskovitses (1947), F. Mischel (1958), Simpson (1965) and, more recently, Glazier (1983) and Warner-Lewis (1991), Houk shows from his recent participant-observation research how cultural forms, like religion, are imbued with meanings essential to the formation and reproduction of ethnic identity and consciousness. He points to an 'Africanisation' of the *Orisha* religion as a response to, among other things, an increased presence of East

Indians and what are regarded as East Indian religious artifacts within the realm of this Afro-Christian form of worship (cf. also, Henry, 1983 and Mahabir and Maharaj, 1989). Houk, then, does not reify the *Orisha* religion nor imbue it with a 'timeless' and 'pure' character, but, instead, shows it as a site and process of inter-ethnic relations.

Aisha Khan's chapter is an example of the possibilities of an approach that unites history and anthropology. She unpacks the political-economic and symbolic processes behind the social construction of 'Spanish' identity in Trinidad, heretofore unexamined in the Trinidadian literature. Indeed, the construction of 'mixed' ethnic identities has received little attention in the literature on ethnicity in general. Rather than a discreet and bounded entity, 'Spanish' identity is ambiguous and amorphous. In her chapter Khan traces the contingent meanings of 'Spanish' to contexts of hierarchy and stratification, showing that why, when and how ethnicity is sensed, promulgated, and contested is dependent on a wider network of relations of power.

The next two chapters point to the importance of examining the intersections of gender and ethnicity in Trinidad (cf. also Mohammed, 1988; Miller, 1991; Yelvington, 1990b). Sociologist Patricia Mohammed uses the techniques of oral history to explore the 'structures of experience' of two East Indian women in order to investigate how the dynamics of ethnicity, class and gender operate in their lives. Mohammed shows how such issues as class and caste serve to structure and mitigate the social reality of those who ostensibly share the same ethnic identity. Mohammed's chapter is important not only because it rescues 'people's history', but because it shows that, despite its power, ethnicity is a qualifying and contingent variable and to concentrate on it alone is to miss the substance of the real life experiences of men and women.

In his chapter Niels M. Sampath presents a sustained analysis of masculinity which, somewhat ironically, is sorely missing from the literature on Trinidad (but, for example, see Lieber, 1981). Based on his intensive fieldwork in a small East Indian village in south Trinidad, Sampath examines the local context of 'creolisation' and 'modernisation' and how these terms are used in meaningful ways by the villagers themselves to define masculinity. Sampath demonstrates the inherent tension in the identities of male East Indian adolescents and shows how they grapple with what they construe as their ethnic heritage, their position in the local, national and international political-economic and cultural hierarchy, and their progress into male adulthood. All the while Sampath is sensitive to the various levels and contexts of inter-ethnic interaction.

The book's final two chapters examine how ethnicity is manifested in Trinidadian popular culture. Patrick Taylor shows the interplay of ethnicity and nationalism in the evolution of the Trinidadian literary tradition. He examines, through the novelist's art, the way in which different ethnic groups are depicted and the content that is given to 'ethnic' characters. He uses the works of the East Indian writer Samuel Selvon and the black writer Earl Lovelace, and their respective views of nation-building, to contrast with the views of other Trinidadian authors whose perspectives, Taylor argues, are limited because they remain trapped within narrow, colonial, world views regarding ethnicity. Taylor argues that the literature either simply takes ethnic conflict as a 'given', or, more hopefully, examines the whys and wherefores of ethnic conflict, simultaneously making sense of this conflict and pointing the way to a more democratic future. Taylor's analysis of the literature can be seen as a cultural analysis of the discourse of ethnicity.

Finally, Keith Q. Warner examines the ethnic politics of the contemporary calypso, formerly the almost exclusive preserve of black men and still regarded by Trinidadians as a 'national' cultural form. Warner delves into the complexity of the musical tradition, outlining its origins and how its tradition of political commentary reflected change in the social structure of the post-independence era. Warner explores the political and ethnic consciousness of calypsonians in the context of the 1970 Black Power movement and how they assumed self-appointed spokespersons' roles for the black masses. The themes of black redemption emerge, but not in any simple or straight-forward way, and Warner tells us just when calypsonians are saying what they mean and when they are meaning what they say. He also points to changes in the traditional presentation of calypso, changes in how East Indians are depicted, and, importantly, changes in the ethnic identity of calypsonians and the subjects of their songs in today's Trinidad.

Recent research has convincingly pointed to the ways in which social science has been complicit in the ideology, justification, and rationalisation of domination in the colonial and neo-colonial contexts. For example, Thomas (1989) shows how early representations of Fijian material culture were used by settlers and administrators in the subordination of native Fijians at the onset of British colonialism; Ekeh (1990) argues that social anthropology was employed by colonial administrators in the creation and depiction of 'tribes' in Africa; and Hanson (1989) examines the role of anthropologists in the invention of New Zealand Maori culture. It is hoped that this book, as a whole representing a multidisciplinary and multinational approach, will suggest the ways in which ethnicity is constructed and the contexts of power and domination in which it acquires meaning and is expressed. Rather than serving the ends of the dominators, if this books suggests to Trinidadians and others that ethnicity, despite its ubiquity, *need not* be the basis upon which individuals and groups have access to society's rewards and are valued, it will have succeeded.

Acknowledgements

I would like to thank Aisha Khan, Daniel A. Segal and John F. Stack, Jr. for their comments on this chapter. They are not responsible for any shortcomings. I would also like to thank Professor Stack for facilitating the institutional support which made the completion of this project possible.

Notes

1 Trindad is part of the twin-island Republic of Trinidad and Tobago. The focus of the book is on the island of Trinidad, which is far more ethnically heterogeneous than Tobago and which has developed along very different lines from Tobago.
2 On comparisons of ethnic relations between Trinidad and Guyana, see, for example, Wood (1968:4 – 10) and Cross (1978).
3 Although the history of Trinidad is still under-researched (compared to, say, Jamaica), there are a number of published book-length studies that deal with a number of themes, including the works of Brereton (1979, 1981), Brereton and Dookeran (1982), John (1988), LaGuerre (1985 [1974]), Naipaul (1969, 1985 [1962]), Trotman (1986), and Wood (1968).
4 For a description of the early conquest period and Spanish colonialism, see Newson (1976).
5 A word on ethnic terminology is important here. In the Caribbean, 'coloured' people are the descendants of black-white sexual unions. Originating in the context of slavery, this group has traditionally distanced itself from the black masses while at the same time being somewhat excluded from the privileges of white society. In Trinidad the term 'Creole', from the Spanish *criollo* (meaning 'of local origin'), has traditionally referred to those of European, African and Euro-African ancestry. Thus, Creole does not refer to other ethnic groups, such as East Indians. Creole is also used as a modifier to refer to various local 'white' groups such as the French Creoles.

   The terms Trinidadians use for different ethnicities are complex indeed (see the chapters by Brereton, Khan and Segal, this volume). One is in a quandary as to whether to use 'emic' or 'etic' terms. I have chosen in this Introduction to fall somewhere in between by using the terms used in the 1980 *Census of Trinidad and Tobago* (but see Reddock 1991:212 for the effect of ethnicity on reporting in the census). Different contributors to this volume handle the situation in various ways, however.
6 For fictional depictions, see Mittleholzer (1974 [1950]) and Naipaul (1967).

7   Similar stereotypes exist between East Indians putatively from northern India and those putatively from Madras. Stereotypes of Madrassis held by northern Indians are similar to those of blacks. As Wood notes (1968:139 – 40), this is traced to the planters' evaluation of Madrassis as poor workers. Acutally, indentured workers from Madras were urban slum-dwellers, and thus not used to agricultural labour, as opposed to the number of agriculturalists from the north.

8   We are thus away from the tautological position that it is a 'group' because it is a 'group'.

9   The process of occupational diversification over time has led to the sharing of workplace space (especially in the state sector) and this has led to a sharing of cultural assumptions among blacks and East Indians. Eriksen (1991:135 – 8), calling on Wittgenstein's concept of 'language-games', argues that the context of wage work institutes commensurability in language-games between blacks and East Indians (cf. also, Yelvington, 1987b). At the same time, however, ethnic differences regarding the suitability of a certain group for a certain type of work remain important.

10 Nye and Keohane define transnationalism as 'the movement of tangible or intangible items across state boundaries when at least one actor is not an agent of government or an intergovernmental organization' (1971:xii, cited in Stack, 1981b:42, fn. 7).

11 These studies include Rubin (1962), Bahadoorsingh (1968), Harewood and Henry (1985), Malik (1971), Oxaal (1968), Ryan (1972, 1981, 1989, 1991b, 1991c), Segal (1987), Hintzen (1989), Yelvington (1987a, 1990a, 1991), and Yelvington (forthcoming), among others.

12 The local franchise committee recommended that voters should be able to understand spoken English – a recommendation seen to deprive many East Indians of the voting right. This qualification was rescinded after protests were made to London.

13 Besides his autobiography (Williams, 1971 [1969]) and collected speeches (Sutton, 1981), see works regarding Williams, including Oxaal (1968) and Boodhoo (1986).

14 Early published research on various aspects of ethnicity includes the work of Baksh (1979), F. Brathwaite (1976a, 1976b, 1980), Goodenough (1978), Green (1964, 1965), Lengermann (1971), W. Mischel (1958, 1961), Niehoff and Niehoff (1960), and Rubin and Zavalloni (1969).

15 These theorists all emphasised aspects of the social structure that they felt maintained order in the society. Braithwaite, for example, in his adherence to structural-functionalism, was too concerned with factors in the social structure that prevent conflict and maintain order between ethnic groups and he ignored the role of conflict. More importantly for a theory that purported to explain the whole society, Braithwaite's analysis ignored the East Indians; this is a critical omission for a theory (structural-functionalism) that supposedly predicts behaviour on the basis of common values. Braithwaite's uncritical emphasis on the value of 'whiteness' and 'white values' could not account for the Black Power movement, for example. Nor does it apply to the Trinidad of the 1990s. As Ryan writes, 'The stratification system which Braithwaite described has now largely disappeared, though ... its shadows still linger in many areas of the social and economic life of the community' (1991a:60).

The plural society theory was used as a counter to structural-functionalism, but, as Cross (1968:381) pointed out, they are alike in many ways, mainly because Smith's early theory was a static one (Hoetink, 1967:36; Cross, 1971:484). Social change was not adequately accounted for because Smith applied a 'first moment' of creation view to plural societies, no matter what their development (Hoetink, 1967:40). This is possibly because Smith's understanding of the plural society concept was based on a misunderstanding (Cross, 1971:480). Smith drew on the work of J.S. Furnivall (1944, 1956). For Furnivall, a plural society came into existence because of colonial economics. For Smith in his early works, though, differentiation along racial lines was a function of cultural diversity. Since this cultural determinism could not explain social change, Cross was correct to point out that this was more a classificatory system than a theory proper (Cross, 1971:482 – 4).

When he did turn his attention to social change in later works (1971, 1974) Smith engaged in a monocausal analysis and political determinism. Smith believed that social change was only possible when groups who were denied access to meaningful political institutions finally gained access to them. The society may be transformed from plural to heterogeneous only when these groups go from being 'subjects' to 'citizens'. Then, and only then, can their cultural institutions be transformed from incompatible to compatible (1971:59). But if, as Smith wrote in *Corporations and Society* (1974), they are excluded on the basis of different culture, how does this happen? Smith gave no answer (see Robotham, 1991).

The theories of the plantation society school can be criticised for lumping all plantation societies into a single type, when, as one bibliography on the plantation worldwide suggests, there was considerable variation among 'plantation societies' (Kirk, 1987). These theories can also be criticised for not accounting properly for social change. Namely, there is the changing empirical situation – the plantation system and agricultural employment have declined and the mining, communications, service and government sectors have gained in importance (although economic dependency will not be debated here). This new reality demonstrates the need for new conceptualisation (Craig, 1982:149). In addition, it is incorrect to assert, as many neo-Marxists do, that Caribbean cultural forms are really manifestations of class consciousness. It is certainly true that certain ethnic identities have been indicative of certain class positions in the Caribbean. But the point is to see how ethnicity and class are constructed together, rather than submerging one in favour of another concept.

References

Abdulah, N., 1991, 'Ethnicity, Mating Patterns and Fertility', in Ryan, S. (ed.), *Social and Occupational Stratification in Contemporary Trinidad and Tobago*, St Augustine: Institute of Social and Economic Research, University of the West Indies, pp. 454-72.

Ahye, M., 1991, 'Carnival, the Manipulative Polymorph: An Interplay of Social Stratification', in Ryan, S. (ed.), *Social and Occupational Stratification in Contemporary Trinidad and Tobago*, St Augustine: Institute of Social and Economic Research, University of the West Indies, pp. 399-416.

Alexander, J., 1977, 'The Culture of Race in Middle-Class Kingston, Jamaica', *American Ethnologist*, Vol. 4, No. 3, pp. 413-35.

Anderson, B., 1983, *Imagined Communities: Reflections on the Origins and Spread of Nationalism*, London: Verso.

Angrosino, M.V., 1976, 'Sexual Politics in the East Indian Family in Trinidad', *Caribbean Studies*, Vol. 16, No. 1, pp. 44-66.

Appadurai, A., 1986, 'Introduction: Commodities and the Politics of Value', in Appadurai, A. (ed.), *The Social Life of Things: Commodities in Cultural Perspective*, Cambridge: Cambridge University Press, pp. 3-63.

Bahadoorsingh, K., 1968, *Trinidad Electoral Politics: The Persistence of the Race Factor*, New York: Oxford University Press.

Baksh, I.J., 1979, 'Stereotypes of Negroes and East Indians in Trinidad: A Re-Examination', *Caribbean Quarterly*, Vol. 25, Nos. 1 and 2, pp. 52-71.

Basdeo, S., 1983, *Labour Organisation and Labour Reform in Trinidad, 1919-1939*, St Augustine: Institute of Social and Economic Research, University of the West Indies.

Bell, R.R., 1970, 'Marriage and Family Difference Among Lower-Class Negro and East Indian Women in Trinidad', *Race*, Vol. 12, No. 1, pp. 59-73.

Bennett, H.L., 1989, 'The Challenge to the Post-Colonial State: A Case Study of the February Revolution in Trinidad', in Knight, F.W. and Palmer, C.A. (eds), *The Modern Caribbean*, Chapel Hill: University of North Carolina Press, pp. 129-46.

Bentley, G. and Henry, F., 1969, 'The Chinese in Trinidad', in Henry, F. (ed.), *McGill Studies in Caribbean Anthropology*, Montreal: Centre for Developing Area Studies, McGill University, pp. 19-33.

Best, L., 1968, 'Outline of a Model of Pure Plantation Economy', *Social and Economic Studies*, Vol. 17, No. 3, pp. 283-326.

Boodhoo, K.I. (ed.), 1986, *Eric Williams, the Man and the Leader*, Lanham, MD: University Presses of America.

Bourdieu, P., 1977, *Outline of a Theory of Practice*, Translated by R. Nice, Cambridge: Cambridge University Press.

Bourgois, P.I., 1989, *Ethnicity at Work: Divided Labor on a Central American Banana Plantation*, Baltimore: The Johns Hopkins University Press.

Braithwaite, L., 1954, 'The Problem of Cultural Integration in Trinidad', *Social and Economic Studies*, Vol. 3, No. 1, pp.82-96.

– 1960, 'Social Stratification and Cultural Pluralism', in Rubin, V. (ed.), *Social and Cultural Pluralism in the Caribbean*, Annals of the New York Academy of Sciences, Vol. 83, Art. 5, pp.816-31.

– 1975 [1953], *Social Stratification in Trinidad*, Mona: Institute of Social and Economic Research, University of the West Indies.

Brathwaite, E., 1971, *The Development of Creole Society in Jamaica, 1770-1820*, Oxford: Clarendon Press.

Brathwaite, F.S., 1976a, 'Upward Mobility and Career (Value) Orientation: An Empirical Test of the Embourgeoisiement Thesis', *International Journal of Comparative Sociology*, Vol. 17, Nos. 1 and 2, pp. 73-83.

– 1976b, 'Race and Class Differentials in Career (Value) Orientation', *Plural Societies*, Vol. 7, No. 2, pp. 17-31.

– 1980, 'Race, Social Class and the Origins of Occupational Elites in Trinidad and Tobago', *Boletin de Estudios Latinoamericanos y del Caribe*, No. 28, pp. 13-30.

Brereton, B., 1974, 'The Foundations of Prejudice: Indians and Africans in 19th Century Trinidad', *Caribbean Issues*, Vol. 1, No. 1, pp. 15-28.

– 1979, *Race Relations in Colonial Trinidad 1870-1900*, Cambridge: Cambridge University Press.

– 1981, *A History of Modern Trinidad 1783-1962*, London: Heinemann.

Brereton, B. and Dookeran, W. (eds), 1982, *East Indians in the Caribbean: Colonialism and the Struggle for Identity*, New York: Krauss International Publications.

Brow, J., 1990, 'Notes on Community, Hegemony, and the Uses of the Past', *Anthropological Quarterly*, Vol. 62, No. 1, pp. 1-6.

Camejo, A., 1971, 'Racial Discrimination in Employment in the Private Sector in Trinidad and Tobago: A Study of the Business Elite and Social Structure', *Social and Economic Studies*, Vol. 20, No. 3, pp. 294-318.

Ching, A.M.T., 1985, 'Ethnicity Reconsidered, with Reference to Sugar and Society in Trinidad', unpublished D.Phil. thesis, University of Sussex.

Craig, S., 1974, 'Community Development in Trinidad and Tobago: 1943-1973: From Welfare to Patronage', *Working Paper No. 4*, Mona: Institute of Social and Economic Research, University of the West Indies.

– 1982, 'Sociological Theorizing in the English-Speaking Caribbean: A Review', in Craig, S. (ed.), *Contemporary Caribbean*, Maracas, Trinidad: Susan Craig, pp. 143-80.

Cross, M., 1968, 'Cultural Pluralism and Sociological Theory: A Critique and Re-Evaluation', *Social and Economic Studies*, Vol. 17, No. 4, pp. 381-97.

– 1971, 'On Conflict, Race Relations, and the Theory of the Plural Society', *Race*, Vol. 16, No. 3., pp. 477-94.

– 1978, 'Colonialism and Ethnicity: A Theory and Comparative Case Study', *Ethnic and Racial Studies*, Vol. 1, No. 1, pp. 37-59.

– 1988, 'The Political Representation of Organised Labour in Trinidad and Guyana: A Comparative Puzzle', in Cross, M. and Heuman, G. (eds), *Labour in the Caribbean*, Warwick University Caribbean Studies series, London: Macmillan, pp. 285-308.

Ekeh, P.P., 1990, 'Social Anthropology and Two Contrasting Uses of Tribalism in Africa', *Comparative Studies in Society and History*, Vol. 32, No. 4, pp. 660-700.

Eriksen, T.H., 1991a, 'The Cultural Contexts of Ethnic Differences', *Man*, Vol. 26, No 1, pp. 127-44.

– 1991b, 'Ethnicity versus Nationalism', *Journal of Peace Research*, Vol. 28, No. 3, pp. 263-78.

– 1992, *Us and Them in Modern Societies: Ethnicity and Nationalism in Mauritius, Trinidad and Beyond*, Oslo: Norwegian University Press.

Furnivall, J.S., 1944, *Netherlands India*, Cambridge: Cambridge University Press.

– 1956, *Colonial Policy and Practice*, New York: New York University Press.

Girvan, N., 1975, 'Aspects of the Political Economy of Race in the Caribbean and in the Americas', *Working Paper No. 7*, Mona: Institute of Social and Economic Research, University of the West Indies.

Glazier, S.D., 1983, *Marchin' the Pilgrims Home: Leadership and Decision-Making in an Afro-Caribbean Faith*, Westport, CT: Greenwood Press.

Goodenough, S., 1978, 'Race, Status and Ecology in Port of Spain, Trinidad', in Clarke, C.G. (ed.), *Caribbean Social Relations*, Liverpool: Monograph Series No. 8, Centre for Latin-American Studies, University of Liverpool, pp. 17-45.

Gosine, M., 1986, *East Indians and Black Power in the Caribbean: The Case of Trinidad*, New York: African Research Publications.

Green, H.B., 1964, 'Socialization Values in the Negro and East Indian Subcultures of Trinidad', *Journal of Social Psychology*, Vol. 64, No. 1, pp. 1-20.

– 1965, 'Values of Negro and East Indian School Children in Trinidad', *Social and Economic Studies*, Vol. 14, No. 2, pp. 203-16.

Hanson, A., 1989, 'The Making of the Maori: Culture Invention and Its Logic', *American Anthropologist*, Vol. 91, No. 4, pp. 890-902.

Harewood, J., 1971, 'Racial Discrimination in Employment in Trinidad and Tobago', *Social and Economic Studies*, Vol. 20, No. 3, pp. 267-93.

Harewood, J. and Henry, R., 1985, *Inequality in a Post-Colonial Society: Trinidad and Tobago 1956-1981*, St Augustine: Institute of Social and Economic Research, University of the West Indies.

Henry, F., 1983, 'Religion and Ideology in Trinidad: The Resurgence of the Shango Religion', *Caribbean Quarterly*, Vol. 29, Nos. 3 and 4, pp. 63-9.

Henry, R.M., 1988, 'The State and Income Distribution in an Independent Trinidad and Tobago', in Ryan, S. (ed.), *Trinidad and Tobago: The Independence Experience 1962-1987*, St Augustine: Institute of Social and Economic Research, University of the West Indies, pp. 471-93.

– 1989, 'Inequalities in Plural Societies: An Exploration', *Social and Economic Studies*, Vol. 38, No. 2, pp. 69-110.

Herskovits, M. and Herskovits, F., 1947, *Trinidad Village*, New York: Alfred A. Knopf.

Hintzen, P.C., 1989, *The Costs of Regime Survival: Racial Mobilization, Elite Domination and Control of the State in Guyana and Trinidad*, Cambridge: Cambridge University Press.

Ho, C., 1989, ' "Hold the Chow Mein, Gimme Soca": Creolization of the Chinese in Guyana, Trinidad and Jamaica', *Amerasia*, Vol. 15, No. 2, pp. 3-25.

Hobsbawm, E. and Ranger, T., (eds), 1983, *The Invention of Tradition*, Cambridge: Cambridge University Press.

Hoetink, H., 1967, 'The Theory of the Plural Society as Envisaged by M.G. Smith', *Caribbean Studies*, Vol. 7, No. 1, pp. 36-43.

John, M., 1988, *The Plantation Slaves of Trinidad 1783-1816: A Mathematical and Demographic Inquiry*, Cambridge: Cambridge University Press.

Johnson, H., 1987, 'The Chinese in Trinidad in the late Nineteenth Century', *Ethnic and Racial Studies*, Vol. 10, No. 1, pp. 82-95.

Khan, A., 1990, 'Sipari Mai', *Hemisphere*, Vol. 2, No. 2, pp. 40-1.

– forthcoming, ' "What Don't Kill Does Fatten": Food, Pollution, and the Indian Diaspora in Trinidad', in Dabydeen, D. and Samaroo, B., (eds), *Across the Dark Waters: Indo-Trinidadian History and Culture*, London: Macmillan.

Kirk, C., 1987, *People in Plantations*, Brighton: Institute of Development Studies Research Report No. 18, University of Sussex.

Klass, M., 1961, *East Indians in Trinidad*, New York: Columbia University Press.

Kopytoff, I., 1986, 'The Cultural Biography of Things: Commoditization as Process', in Appadurai, A. (ed.), *The Social Life of Things: Commodities in Cultural Perspective*, Cambridge: Cambridge University Press, pp. 64-91.

LaGuerre, J.G., 1975, 'Afro-Indian Relations in Trinidad: An Assessment', *Social and Economic Studies*, Vol. 25, No. 3, pp. 291-306.

– 1982, *The Politics of Communalism*, 2nd. ed., Port of Spain: Pan-Caribbean Publications.

– 1988, 'Race Relations in Trinidad and Tobago', in Ryan, S. (ed.), *Trinidad and Tobago: The Independence Experience 1962-1987*, St Augustine: Institute of Social and Economic Research, University of the West Indies, pp. 193-206.

– 1991, 'Leadership in a Plural Society: The Case of the Indians in Trinidad and Tobago', in Ryan, S. (ed.), *Social and Occupational Stratification in Contemporary Trinidad and Tobago*, St Augustine: Institute of Social and Economic Research, University of the West Indies, pp. 83-112.

LaGuerre, J.G. (ed.), 1985 [1974], *Calcutta to Caroni*, 2nd. ed. St Augustine: Extra-Mural Unit, University of the West Indies.

Lamming, G., 1985, 'The Role of the Intellectual in the Caribbean', *Cimarrón*, Vol. 1, No. 1, pp. 11-22.

Lee, A., 1991, 'Class, Race, Colour and the Trinidad Carnival', in Ryan, S. (ed.), *Social and Occupational Stratification in Contemporary Trinidad and Tobago*, St Augustine: Institute of Social and Economic Research, University of the West Indies, pp. 417-36.

Lengermann, P.M., 1971, 'Working-Class Values in Trinidad and Tobago', *Social and Economic Studies*, Vol. 20, No. 2, pp. 151-63.

Lieber, M., 1981, *Street Scenes: Afro-American Culture in Urban Trinidad*, Cambridge, MA: Schenkman.

Lijphart, A., 1977, *Democracy in Plural Societies*, New Haven: Yale University Press.

Love, H., 1982, 'The Gladstone Coolies of British Guiana', unpublished M.A. thesis, Florida Atlantic University.

MacDonald, J.S. and MacDonald, L.D., 1973, 'Transformation of African and Indian Family Traditions in the Southern Caribbean', *Comparative Studies in Society and History*, Vol. 15, No. 2, pp. 171-98.

Magid, A., 1988, *Urban Nationalism: A Study of Political Development in Trinidad*, Gainesville: University Presses of Florida.

Mahabir, N. and Maharaj, A., 1989, 'Hindu Elements in the Shango/Orisha Cult of Trinidad', in Birbalsingh, F. (ed.), *Indenture and Exile: The Indo-Caribbean Experience*, Toronto: Toronto South Asian Review, pp. 191-201.

Maingot, A.P., 1962, 'Nineteenth Century Trinidad, A Discussion of the Relative position of the French Creole Group in the Society', unpublished M.A. thesis, University of Puerto Rico.

– 1983, 'Caribbean Studies as Area Studies: Past Performances and Recent Stirrings', *Caribbean Educational Bulletin*, Vol. 10, No. 1, pp. 1-14.

Malik, Y., 1971, *East Indians in Trinidad*, New York: Oxford University Press.

Maloney, A.H., 1949, *After England – We: Nationhood for Caribbea*, Boston: Meador.

Miller, D., 1991, 'Absolute Freedom in Trinidad', *Man*, Vol. 26, No. 2, pp. 323-41.

Millette, J., 1970, *The Genesis of Crown Colony Government: Trinidad, 1783-1810*, Curepe, Trinidad: Moko.

Mintz, S.W., 1959, 'The Plantation as a Socio-Cultural Type', in *Plantation Systems of the New World*, Social Science Monographs No. 7, Washington, D.C.: Pan American Union, pp. 42-9.

— 1987, 'Labor and Ethnicity: The Caribbean Conjuncture', in Tardanico, R. (ed.), *Crises in the Caribbean Basin*, Beverly Hills: Sage, pp. 47-57.

Mischel, F.O., 1958, 'A Shango Religious Group and the Problem of Prestige in Trinidadian Society', unpublished Ph.D. dissertation, Ohio State University.

Mischel, W., 1958, 'Preference for Delayed Reinforcement: An Experimental Study of Cultural Observation', *Journal of Abnormal and Social Psychology*, Vol. 56, No. 1, pp. 575-61.

— 1961, 'Father Absence and Delay of Gratification: Cross-Cultural Comparisons', *Journal of Abnormal and Social Psychology*, Vol. 63, No. 1, pp. 116-24.

Mittelholzer, E., 1974 [1950], *A Morning at the Office*, London: Heinemann.

Mohammed, P., 1988, 'The "Creolization" of Indian Women in Trinidad', in Ryan, S. (ed.), *Trinidad and Tobago: The Independence Experience 1962-1987*, St Augustine: Institute of Social and Economic Research, University of the West Indies, pp. 381-97.

Naipaul, V.S., 1967, 'The Baker's Story', in *A Flag on the Island*, London: Andre Deutsch.

— 1969, *The Loss of El Dorado*, London: Andre Deutsch.

— 1985 [1962], *The Middle Passage*, New York: Vintage.

Nevadomsky, J., 1982, 'Social Change and the East Indians in Rural Trinidad: A Critique of Methodologies', *Social and Economic Studies*, Vol. 31, No. 1, pp. 90-126.

— 1984, 'Economic Organization, Social Mobility and Changing Social Status Among the East Indians in Rural Trinidad', *Social and Economic Studies*, Vol. 33, No. 3, pp. 31-62.

Newson, L., 1976, *Aboriginal and Spanish Colonial Trinidad*, New York: Academic Press.

Nicholls, D.G., 1971, 'East Indians and Black Power in Trinidad', *Race*, Vol. 12, No. 4, pp. 283-326.

— 1981, 'No Hawkers and Pedlars: Levantines in the Caribbean', *Ethnic and Racial Studies*, Vol. 4, No. 4, pp. 415-31.

Niehoff, A. and Niehoff, J., 1960, *East Indians in the West Indies*, Milwaukee: Milwaukee Public Museum.

Nye, J.S., Jr. and Keohane, R.O., 1971, *Transnational Relations and World Politics*, Cambridge, MA: Harvard University Press.

Oxaal, I., 1968, *Black Intellectuals Come to Power*, Cambridge, MA: Schenkman.

— 1971, *Race and Revolutionary Consciousness*, Cambridge, MA: Schenkman.

Parris, C., 1985, 'Power and Privilege in Trinidad and Tobago', *Social and Economic Studies*, Vol. 34, No. 2, pp. 97-109.

Pearse, A., 1956, 'Carnival in Nineteenth Century Trinidad', *Caribbean Quarterly*, Vol. 4, Nos. 3 and 4, pp. 175-93.

Phillips, D., 1990, 'Race and Role it Plays in National Life', *Caribbean Affairs*, Vol. 3, No. 1, pp. 186-98.

Ramesar, M.D., 1976, 'Patterns of Regional Settlement and Economic Activity by Immigrant Groups in Trinidad: 1851-1900', *Social and Economic Studies*, Vol. 25, No. 3, pp. 187-215.

Ranger, T., 1983, 'The Invention of Tradition in Colonial Africa', in Hobsbawm, E. and Ranger, T., (eds), 1983, *The Invention of Tradition*, Cambridge: Cambridge University Press, pp. 211-62.

Reddock, R., 1991, 'Social Mobility in Trinidad and Tobago 1960-1980', in Ryan, S. (ed.), *Social and Occupational Stratification in Contemporary Trinidad and Tobago*, St Augustine: Institute of Social and Economic Research, University of the West Indies, pp. 210-33.

Richardson, B.C., 1975, 'Livelihood in Rural Trinidad in 1900', *Annals of the Association of American Geographers*, Vol. 65, No. 2, pp. 240-51.

– 1979, 'Plantation Infrastructure and Labor Mobility in Guyana and Trinidad', in Browman, D.L. and Schwarz, R.A. (eds), *Peasants, Primitives, and Proletariats: The Struggle for Identity in South America*, The Hague: Mouton, pp. 389-406.

Roberts, G.W., and Braithwaite, L., 1967, 'Mating Among East Indian and Non-Indian Women in Trinidad', *Research Papers*, Port of Spain: Central Statistical Office, pp. 148-85.

Robotham, D., 1991, 'A Further Critique of M.G. Smith's Corporation Theory', in Ryan, S. (ed.), *Social and Occupational Stratification in Contemporary Trinidad and Tobago*, St Augustine: Institute of Social and Economic Research, University of the West Indies, pp. 36-48.

Rohlehr, G. 1988, 'Images of Men and Women in the 1930s Calypsoes: The Sociology of Food Acquisition in a Context of Survivalism', in Mohammed, P. and Shepherd, C. (eds), *Gender in Caribbean Development*, St Augustine: Institute of Social and Economic Research, University of the West Indies, pp. 232-306.

– 1990, *Calypso and Society in Pre-Independence Trinidad*, Port of Spain: Gordon Rohlehr.

Rubin, V., 1960, 'Cultural Perspectives in Caribbean Research', in Rubin, V. (ed.), *Caribbean Studies: A Symposium*, 2nd. ed., Seattle: University of Washington Press, pp. 110-22.

– 1962, 'Culture, Politics and Race Relations', *Social and Economic Studies*, Vol. 11, No. 4, pp. 433-56.

Rubin, V. and Zavalloni, M., 1969, *We Wish to be Looked Upon*, New York: Teachers College Press, Columbia University.

Ryan, S., 1972, *Race and Nationalism in Trinidad and Tobago*, Toronto: University of Toronto Press.

– 1989, *Revolution and Reaction: Parties and Politics in Trinidad and Tobago 1970-1981*, St Augustine: Institute of Social and Economic Research, University of the West Indies.

– 1990, *The Disillusioned Electorate: The Politics of Succession in Trinidad and Tobago*, Port of Spain: Imprint Caribbean.

– 1991a, 'Social Stratification in Trinidad and Tobago: Lloyd Braithwaite Revisited', in Ryan, S. (ed.), *Social and Occupational Stratification in Contemporary Trinidad and Tobago*, St Augustine: Institute of Social and Economic Research, University of the West Indies, pp. 58-79.

– 1991b, 'Social and Ethnic Stratification and Voting Behaviour in Trinidad and Tobago: 1956-1990', in Ryan, S. (ed.), *Social and Occupational Stratification in Contemporary Trinidad and Tobago*, St Augustine: Institute of Social and Economic Research, University of the West Indies, pp. 113-44.

– 1991c, *The Muslimeen Grab for Power: Race, Religion and Revolution in Trinidad and Tobago*, Port of Spain: Imprint.

Samaroo, B., 1987, 'Two Abolitions: African Slavery and East Indian Indentureship', in Dabydeen, D. and Samaroo, B. (eds), *India in the Caribbean*, London: Hansib/University of Warwick, pp. 25-41.

Sandoval, J.M., 1983, 'State Capitalism in a Petroleum-Based Economy: The Case of Trinidad and Tobago', in Ambursley, F. and Cohen, R. (eds), *Crisis in the Caribbean*, New York: Monthly Review Press, pp. 247-68.

Segal, D., 1987, 'Nationalism in a Colonial State: A Study of Trinidad and Tobago', unpublished Ph.D. dissertation, University of Chicago.

– n.d., 'Nationalism and Its Consequences in Trinidad and Tobago', unpublished manuscript.

Schwartz, B., 1967, 'The Failure of Caste in Trinidad', in Schwartz, B. (ed.), 1967, *Caste in Overseas Indian Communities*, San Francisco: Chandler Publishing Co.

Simpson, G.E., 1965, *The Shango Cult in Trinidad*, Rio Piedras: Institute of Caribbean Studies, University of Puerto Rico.

Smith, M.G., 1965, *The Plural Society in the British West Indies*, Berkeley: University of California Press.

– 1967, 'Forword', in Despres, L., *Cultural Pluralism and Nationalist Politics in British Guiana*, Chicago: Rand McNally, pp. vii-xxi.

– 1971, 'Institutional and Political Conditions of Pluralism', in Kuper, L. and Smith, M.G. (eds), *Pluralism in Africa*, Berkeley: University of California Press, pp. 27-65.

– 1974, *Corporations and Society*, London: Duckworth.

– 1984, *Culture, Race and Class in the Commonwealth Caribbean*, Mona: Extra-Mural Unit, University of the West Indies.

– 1991, 'Pluralism and Social Stratification', in Ryan, S. (ed.), *Social and Occupational Stratification in Contemporary Trinidad and Tobago*, St Augustine: Institute of Social and Economic Research, University of the West Indies, pp. 3-35.

Smith, R.T., 1956, *The Negro Family in British Guiana*, London: Routledge and Kegan Paul.

Sollors, W. (ed.), 1989a, *The Invention of Ethnicity*, New York: Oxford University Press.

– 1989b, 'Introduction: The Invention of Ethnicity', in Sollors, W. (ed.), *The Invention of Ethnicity*, New York: Oxford University Press, pp. ix-xx.

Stack, J.F., Jr., 1981a, 'Ethnicity and Transnational Relations: An Introduction', in Stack, J.F., Jr. (ed.), *Ethnic Identities in a Transnational World*, Westport, CT: Greenwood, pp. 3-15.

– 1981b, 'Ethnic Groups as Emerging Transnational Actors', in Stack, J.F., Jr. (ed.), *Ethnic Identities in a Transnational World*, Westport, CT: Greenwood, pp. 17-45.

Stewart, J., 1991, 'Ethnic Image and Ideology in Rural Trinidad', in Ryan, S. (ed.), *Social and Occupational Stratification in Contemporary Trinidad and Tobago*, St Augustine: Institute of Social and Economic Research, University of the West Indies, pp. 149-65.

Stoler, A., 1989, 'Rethinking Colonial Categories: European Communities and the Boundaries of Rule', *Comparative Studies in Society and History*, Vol. 31, No. 1, pp. 134-61.

Stuempfle, S., 1990, 'The Steelband Movement in Trinidad and Tobago: Music, Politics and National Identity In a New World Society', unpublished Ph.D.

dissertation, University of Pennsylvania.

Sutton, P. (ed.), 1981, *Forged From the Love of Liberty: The Selected Speeches of Eric Williams*, London: Longman.

– 1983, 'Black Power in Trinidad and Tobago: The "Crisis" of 1970', *Journal of Commonwealth and Comparative Politics*, Vol. 21, No. 2, pp. 115-32.

Thomas, N., 1989, 'Material Culture and Colonial Power: Ethnological Collecting and the Establishment of Colonial Rule in Fiji', *Man*, Vol. 24, No. 1, pp. 41-56.

Tinker, H., 1974, *A New System of Slavery: The Export of Indian Labour Overseas, 1830-1920*, London: Oxford University Press.

Trinidad and Tobago, 1973, 'Report of the Commission of Enquiry into the Miss Trinidad and Tobago Beauty Contest 1971, and the Organization of Such Contests and Competitions in Trinidad and Tobago', report presented to the Acting Governor-General, Sir Arthur H. McShine, Port of Spain: Government Printery.

Trotman, D.V., 1986, *Crime in Trinidad*, Knoxville: University of Tennessee Press.

– 1991, 'The Image of Indians in Calypso: Trinidad 1946-1986', in Ryan, S. (ed.), *Social and Occupational Stratification in Contemporary Trinidad and Tobago*, St Augustine: Institute of Social and Economic Research, University of the West Indies, pp. 385-98.

Vertovec, S.A., 1987, 'Hinduism and Social Change in Village Trinidad', unpublished D.Phil. thesis, University of Oxford.

– 1990, 'Religion and Ethnic Ideology: The Hindu Youth Movement in Trinidad', *Ethnic and Racial Studies*, Vol. 13, No. 2, pp. 225-49.

Wagley, C., 1960, 'Plantation America: A Culture Sphere', in Rubin, V. (ed.), *Caribbean Studies: A Symposium*, 2nd. ed., Seattle: University of Washington Press, pp. 3-13.

Walcott, D., 1972, *Dream on Monkey Mountain and Other Plays*, London: Jonathan Cape.

Warner, K.Q., 1982, *Kaiso! The Trinidad Calypso: A Study of the Calypso as Oral Literature*, Washington, D.C.: Three Continents Press.

Warner-Lewis, M., 1991, *Guinea's Other Suns: The African Dynamic in Trinidad Culture*, Dover, MA: Majority Press.

Williams, B.F., 1991, *Stains on My Name, War in My Veins: Guyana and the Politics of Cultural Struggle*, Durham, NC: Duke University Press.

Williams, E., 1960, 'Race Relations in the Caribbean', in Rubin, V. (ed.), *Caribbean Studies: A Symposium*, 2nd. ed., Seattle: University of Washington Press, pp. 54-60.

– 1971 [1969], *Inward Hunger: The Education of a Prime Minister*, Chicago: University of Chicago Press.

Williams, R., 1990, *Hierarchical Structures and Social Value: The Creation of Black and Irish Identities in the United States*, Cambridge: Cambridge University Press.

Winer, L., 1984, 'Early Trinidadian Creole: The *Spectator* Texts', *English World-Wide*, Vol. 5, No. 2, pp. 181-210.

Wood, D., 1968, *Trinidad in Transition: The Years After Slavery*, London: Oxford University Press.

Yelvington, K.A., 1987a, 'Vote Dem Out: The Demise of the PNM in Trinidad and Tobago', *Caribbean Review*, Vol. 15, No. 4, pp. 8-12, 29-33.

– 1987b, 'Occupational Diversification in Trinidad, 1891-1980: A General Review', unpublished manuscript.

– 1990a, 'Ethnicity "Not Out": The Indian Cricket Tour of the West Indies and the 1976 Elections in Trinidad and Tobago', *Arena Review*, Vol. 14, No. 1, pp. 1-12.

– 1990b, 'Ethnicity, Class, and Gender at Work in a Trinidadian Factory', unpublished D.Phil. thesis, University of Sussex.

– 1991, 'Trinidad and Tobago, 1988-89', in Malloy, J.M. and Gamarra, E.A. (eds), *Latin American and Caribbean Contemporary Record*, Vol. 8, New York: Holmes and Meier, pp. B459-77.

– forthcoming, 'Trinidad and Tobago, 1989-90', in Malloy, J.M. and Gamarra, E.A. (eds), *Latin American and Caribbean Contemporary Record*, Vol. 9, New York: Holmes and Meier.

CHAPTER 2	**Social organisation and class, racial and cultural conflict in 19th century Trinidad**
	Bridget Brereton

The legacy of slavery

Throughout the Caribbean the end of formal slavery, achieved after a long drawn out and agonising ordeal lasting from the 1790s (in Haiti) to the 1880s (in Cuba), left the region's societies deeply divided. Race, ethnicity and phenotype; socio-economic interest and class position; national origin, culture and religion constituted fissures that profoundly affected Caribbean social relations. Slavery, of course, had played a role of widely differing significance in the various islands and mainland colonies, and the effects of its abolition were consequently far from uniform or simple to predict. Yet, with few exceptions, Caribbean societies were largely shaped in the post-abolition era by the legacy of the slave system and its twin, the plantation mode of production.

   In the classic slave and plantation societies, the large-scale production of export staples had dominated economic life and the enslavement of Africans had been established as the fundamental system of labour organisation ever since the seventeenth and eighteenth centuries. Here, Africans and their locally-born descendants formed the overwhelming majority of the population and economic resources were concentrated (though never exclusively) in the hands of relatively few capitalist landowners. These societies, including all the larger British and French islands and the mainland colonies of Surinam and the Guianas, inherited from the slave/plantation system a fairly simple three-tier social and ethnic structure. At the top were the elites, predominantly of European descent (British, French, Dutch), landowners and ex-slaveowners, allied to groups of metropolitan bureaucrats and merchants. In the middle was a mixed-race stratum of people who were descended mainly from unions between white men and slave women. Before the end of slavery these 'free coloureds' (including, always, some 'free blacks', people who were wholly or predominantly of African descent but who were legally free) had been largely excluded from civil and political rights and were economically marginal to the plantation system. Yet their legal status as free men and women, their access to

educational opportunities and their ability to carve out certain occupational niches, especially artisanal trades and small-scale commerce, gave
them significant advantages over the multitudes freed by legislative
enactments in the 1830s (Britain), 1840s (France) and 1860s (Holland).
The bottom tier comprised the ex-slaves and their descendants, the great
majority of the population. Entering free society with all the massive
disadvantages which flowed from two centuries of enslavement, the
ex-slaves would find their opportunities for economic, social and
cultural improvement harshly limited and always difficult, yet nowhere
entirely absent.

Trinidad, a Spanish colony conquered by Britain in 1797, certainly
conformed broadly to the three-tier model, but it differed in some
important respects from the classic slave societies such as Jamaica or
Martinique. First, it was late to enter into its phase of plantation
development: it was not until the late 1780s that the island became a
significant producer of West Indian export crops and that, as a result,
African slaves became an important part of its labour force. When
Trinidad became a British colony in 1797, slaves constituted just
over half of the total population, another way of saying that this was
still an immature slave colony at the end of the eighteenth century.
Moreover, slave imports from Africa and the Caribbean took place
at a significant level only between the late 1780s and 1806-7, when
Britain abolished the African trade and placed restrictions on the
inter-island traffic. Consequently, the African population was always
fairly small and the ratio of slaves to free people in the society was
low in comparison to the mature slave colonies. In 1838 only 20,656
apprentices (i.e., former slaves) were set free (Brereton, 1981:13-31,
52-62; Wood, 1968:44).

Second, Trinidad's experience of plantation slavery was brief,
about fifty years (1780s to 1830s), perhaps the shortest of any significant
ex-slave society in the New World. The legacy of slavery, though
critically important for the island's development over the 'long'
nineteenth century, was probably less overwhelming than it was for
many other Caribbean societies.

Finally, Trinidad entered the post-abolition era with an unusually
large 'middle tier' of free coloureds and free blacks. In 1838 this group
numbered around 12,000. It included estate owners and former slave-
holders who (with their families) formed part of the economic elite (the
top tier) by virtue of their status as landowners and employers. Yet they
often encountered discrimination and prejudice based on their race from
resident whites. All this is to indicate that the three-tier model, though
broadly descriptive of Trinidad in the nineteenth century, must be
applied with a proper sensitivity to the nuances.

Large-scale immigration to Trinidad, a direct result of the end of slavery, transformed the three-tier model by introducing new ethnic groups. Many came from the smaller islands of the Eastern Caribbean, especially Barbados, St Vincent, Grenada and Tobago. These people brought distinct ethnic, cultural, linguistic and religious identities which complicated social relations. Many (especially those from Barbados, St Vincent and Tobago) spoke an English creole instead of French creole *(patois)*, were Protestant rather than Catholic, and cherished a strong sense of attachment to their islands of origin: 'neither C'rab (Carib) nor Creole (i.e., Trinidadian) but true Barbadian born', as the saying went (*Port of Spain Gazette*, 24 October 1894). Another group of post slavery immigrants were the 'liberated' Africans, people freed by the British Navy from foreign slave ships and persuaded or forced to emigrate as indentured labourers to the West Indies. Some 6,600 arrived in Trinidad between 1841 and 1861. They preserved their special ethnic and cultural identities well into the twentieth century, with the Yorubas exercising an especially important influence on Trinidadian culture and religion (Wood, 1968:73-80; Brereton, 1981:97-8; Brereton, 1979:134-7).

Venezuelans settled in Trinidad right through the nineteenth century, both before and after the end of slavery. Though some were prosperous, relatively well-educated, and 'white', like the De Limas, and soon assimilated into the local white elite, most were labourers and peasants, illiterate and of mixed antecedants (Amerindian-African-European). These so-called *'peons'* became an important part of the island's rural population: they were Spanish-speaking, Catholic, and were identified with cocoa cultivation and a Spanish/Venezuelan cultural complex which absorbed and reinforced the island's original Amerindian heritage (Wood, 1968:32-4; Brereton, 1979:130-3).

Among the smaller groups of Europeans arriving in the nineteenth century were the Portuguese from Madeira. Although only a few came as labourers in the middle decades of the century, the 'Portuguese' group was increased by later arrivals coming to join relatives or help in family businesses. As we shall see, the Madeirans were certainly not considered part of the elite, though they were Europeans, but by the 1920s some prosperous and educated Trinidadians of Portuguese descent were moving up into the top tier. From around 1890 a few immigrants from Syria and Lebanon arrived to form a small but upwardly mobile community of entrepreneurs and traders which kept much to itself and seemed (up to the 1920s) hardly a part of the local society.

From Asia came immigrants from China and India. About 2,500 Chinese came as indentured labourers between 1853 and 1866, and in the later-nineteenth century and in the first half of the twentieth, more came as voluntary, free immigrants. Shopkeeping became their special niche in the colonial economy. The Chinese brought their language and culture, and influenced the host society, particularly with respect to cuisine and games of chance (Johnson, 1987; Brereton, 1981: 99-100; Wood, 1968: 160-7).

But the Indians, coming to Trinidad as indentured labourers between 1845 and 1917, constituted by far the largest group of new arrivals (Brereton, 1981:100-5). Because of their large numbers, and because they brought religions (Hinduism, Islam), languages and cultural forms which were new to the island and the region, they greatly complicated as well as enriched the society. As early as 1870 Indians (including those born locally of Indian parents) constituted about a quarter of Trinidad's population, and by the 1920s perhaps one third. They came to form a large and separate sector, separated from the other three tiers or groups of ex-slave society by culture, religion, language, ethnicity and (until 1917) legal restrictions. Because they were relatively late-comers, they entered the society at a time when the basic three-tier system had already been established. Though their economic or 'class' position, at least in the nineteenth century, would have categorised them with the third tier, the differences between them and the descendants of the ex-slaves were too great. In Trinidad, as in Guyana and Surinam, Indians constituted a fourth distinct tier in the social structure. Soon, as socio-economic differentation got under way among the Indians, that 'fourth tier' would lose its initial homogeneity.

Socio-economic differentiation after slavery

In nineteenth century Trinidad, the upper tier, the elite, consisted mainly of persons of European descent or birth who controlled much of the colony's resources as landowners, ex-slaveowners and employers of labour, merchants and bureaucrats. But this white elite was not monolithic. There were significant tensions, even conflicts, between different elements, and divisions along lines of national origin, language, religion, economic interests and political positions. At least three groups may be discerned in Trinidad at this period: the 'expatriates', those born in Europe, especially Britain, the colonial power; the 'French Creoles', those born in the island descended from mainly French, but also Spanish, Irish, Italian or German immigrants; and the 'English Creoles' locally-born and descended from English or Scottish immigrants. The first, the 'expatriates', were both the most and the least important: most important because among them were politically powerful officials including the governor and most of his top advisers and some of the wealthiest and most influential planters, plantation managers and businessmen; and least important because, with few exceptions, they were 'birds of passage' staying only for a few years until a promotion came along or until it was time to return home. For them, Trinidad was only a way station. Their orientation remained essentially British or Imperial, they left hardly any imprint on the society. But there were always some tensions between the expatriates and the white Creoles, who resented the former's snobbery and arrogance, and felt excluded from the top jobs in 'their' island.

Because Trinidad had been a Spanish colony with significant French immigration in the eighteenth century, the Creole elite was divided into the 'French' and 'English' groups, each with a strong sense of identity and separateness. The French Creoles were more numerous, they were proud of their ancestors – noble in fact or in family myth – who had pioneered 'civilisation' in Trinidad, and they saw themselves as the island's true local aristocracy. Roman Catholic, usually devoted to the France of the *ancien régime* rather than the Republic, speaking French at home (as well as creole to their servants and labourers) but increasingly forced to learn English, they were landowners rather than businessmen. The French Creoles had reconciled themselves to British rule but resented the attacks mounted after 1838 on their church, their language, their culture and their economic and political position – attacks which amounted to a full-scale policy of 'Anglicisation'. Many of them whose families had owned small, marginal sugar estates since the late-eighteenth or early-nineteenth centuries were squeezed out of production by around 1870 as the sugar industry fell increasingly into the hands of British firms or individual Englishmen. At about the same time, expatriates or English Creoles came to occupy most of the important posts in the Legislative Council and in the civil service. The English Creoles, consisting of a few local families of English descent, Protestant (the majority Anglican) and of course English-speaking, benefited from the campaign to Anglicise Trinidad between the 1830s and the 1860s, which was spearheaded by one of their nineteenth century leaders, Charles Warner, Attorney-General from 1844 until 1870 (Wood, 1968:171-237).

Relations between French and English Creoles were uneasy for most of the nineteenth century, but towards its end an *entente* developed, which was pragmatic rather than cordial. The French Creoles bowed to the realities by toning down their 'Frenchness'. They stopped sending their children to France for their schooling, educating them instead either in British Catholic institutions or at home at St Mary's College, and they gradually phased out the use of the French language. The rapid growth of the cocoa industry after about 1870 gave the French Creoles the economic base for social and political resurgence. On the other side, the colonial government dropped its aggressive policy of Anglicisation, relying on the passage of time to effect this still-desired result, and took care to appoint prominent French Creoles to positions in the legislature and the public service. Moreover, by 1900 or so, and only too obviously by 1920, the traditional elite was under challenge from middle stratum coloureds and blacks, even from sections of the black masses. It was time to close ranks. The French Creoles continued to cherish a sentimental feeling for old France, they hung on for dear life to their aristocratic traditions, their 'old blood'. But increasingly they combined with the English Creoles and the expatriate representatives of Imperial power and Imperial capital to maintain their control over the commanding heights of the colonial economy and their hegemony over the society (Wood, 1968:265-301; Brereton, 1979:34-63).

By the end of the 'long' nineteenth century, however, individuals from outside the traditional elite were knocking on the doors for entry. Among them were families from three of the post-slavery immigrant groups, the Portuguese, the Chinese, and the Syrian/Lebanese.

The immigrants from Madeira came as penniless labourers from simple peasant backgrounds, spoke little or no English and possessed a distinctively Portuguese culture, so their ethnicity alone could not win for them upper class status. They were marked off as a separate group, and Trinidad censuses of the period had a category 'Portuguese' which was distinct from 'Europeans'. In the 1890s, the 'Portuguese jobber', or market gardener, was considered to be a 'low type', and the humble 'Potogee' shopkeeper doling out his rice and saltfish to poor black customers was not much better. But by the 1920s, some Portuguese families had become prosperous through successful wholesale and retail commerce. They had sent their children to secondary schools and even universities abroad, and their lifestyle was much the same as the traditional elite. This group is vividly portrayed in the novel *Pitch Lake* (first published in 1934) by Alfred Mendes, himself a Trinidadian of Portuguese descent (Mendes, 1934; see also, Gomes, 1974). Their ethnicity, now, would help these well-off Portuguese families to enter the upper tier.

By the 1920s some Chinese families, like the Lee Lums, had also achieved prosperity through shopkeeping and related businesses. Edward Lee Lum became Randolph Rust's partner in the first successful oil prospecting in the Guayaguayare district at the turn of the century. Some prosperous Chinese families had adopted Christianity, intermarried with Creoles, and taken Western names. Close business, sporting and other links certainly developed between these Chinese Trinidadian families and the old elite, but the social and ethnic barriers which separated them – erected on both sides – would not be easily dismantled.

The small Syrian/Lebanese immigrant community was clearly upwardly mobile by the 1920s or 1930s. Most were Catholics (many had been Maronite Christians in the Middle East) and quickly acquired English. By about 1930 they had carved out a secure niche as a closed ethnic group involved almost exclusively in retailing cloth, clothes and household goods. Some families prospered, laying the foundations for their post-World War II emergence as an important element in Trinidad's economic elite – but the social distance between them and the traditional elite was still vast.

Closer to the traditional elite, in some important respects, were the upper echelons of the mixed-race middle stratum, especially the descendants of Trinidad's long-established 'free coloured aristocracy'. During and long after the slave period, a numerically small but important group of free coloured families formed a sort of brown elite parallel to the white Creoles. These families were mostly founded by emigrants from Grenada or the French islands. They were Catholic, French and creole-speaking, and with a French Antillian cultural orientation. They educated their boys (though not their girls) sometimes even to university level, they were estate owners, slaveowners, merchants, and occasionally professional men. Like the white French Creoles, they cherished the past with the same nostalgic feeling for family traditions and the same respect for birth and breeding. Like the French Creoles, too, they tended to intermarry and to be obsessed with family connections. Two leading families of this group were the Philips and the Romains of the Naparimas. When Marie Romain, née Philip, died as a very old lady in 1894, her obituary stressed that she belonged to 'one of the oldest and most aristocratic coloured families in the island . . . . She was polite to her inferiors, but never familiar . . . . Even in her old age her aristocratic training clung to her in the highest degree' (*San Fernando Gazette*, 14 February 1894).

P.G.L. Borde, the French Creole historian of Spanish Trinidad who wrote his books in the 1880s, thought that the free coloured aristocracy formed a *parallel* elite, separate but equal, as it were, and that the caste-like barriers which guarded the traditional elite from encroachment by the upwardly mobile browns remained almost impervious all through the 'long' nineteenth century (Borde, 1982: 308-10). Nevertheless, by the 1920s, some families at the top of the mixed-race middle tier were poised to cross the barriers. Generally, they were light-complexioned, perhaps descended from the old 'aristocracy', prosperous, and headed by prominent, well-educated professional men such as Sir Lennox O'Reilly, Gaston Johnson, or T.M. Kelshall, to name three men conspicuous in legal and public life in the 1920s and 1930s.

Much more significant than this small-scale, agonisingly difficult, movement up into the top tier was the gradual increase in the size of the middle stratum after the end of slavery. Indeed, this is one of the most important developments in Trinidad's social history in the 'long' nineteenth century.

As I have noted, this middle stratum had its origins in the free coloured/black 'second tier' of slave society. By the 1830s this stratum was led in Trinidad (as elsewhere) by a small group of educated men, generally though not exclusively light-complexioned, relatively well-off and European in their cultural orientation. But this middle stratum, predominantly urban, grew significantly in the century after emancipation. The growth in the size and importance of Trinidad's towns, especially Port of Spain and San Fernando, opened up new employment opportunities for educated coloureds and blacks as clerks, store assistants, civil servants and minor professionals, teachers, pharmacists, nurses and journalists. The towns were the base for coloured and black small business people and a growing intelligentsia which would eventually challenge white ascendancy.

After the end of slavery there was considerable movement from the black masses into the middle stratum. First, through independent farming or the skilled trades, ex-slaves might accumulate some capital and/or land which would give them a social and economic position above that of the mass of labourers and poorer peasants. Second, exposure to elementary education in church or government schools might lead to white collar jobs and enhanced status. Of course, these two paths were interrelated: the child of a relatively secure peasant farmer or artisan was far more likely to be chosen as a pupil teacher or to get a place in a secondary school. Third, the churches played a role in social mobility for blacks and coloureds. The church-oriented 'respectable' labourer or peasant families were again more likely to secure access to the schools for their children and to occupy leadership positions in the community. Mainly through these routes the original core of the pre-1838 free coloureds and free blacks was greatly augmented by upward mobility on the part of relatively large numbers of ex-slaves and their descendants.

Of course, the middle stratum was itself stratified along lines of economic position, colour (shade), educational levels and occupation. At the top were persons who enjoyed all or most of these advantages: fairly high incomes, prestigious occupations such as law, medicine, clergy, secondary school teaching, a secondary or tertiary education, and light complexion. At the bottom were persons with lower incomes, less prestigious jobs as minor clerks and civil servants, store assistants, nurses, rural elementary school teachers, with no secondary education and with darker skins. However, all members of this stratum were distinguished from the masses by their white collar jobs, their literacy, their command (in varying degrees) of 'good' English and their adherence to European cultural norms. The economic base of this stratum was typically salaried, urban or semi-urban, white collar occupations such as teachers, clerks, shop assistants, druggists, printers, journalists, nurses, civil servants, professionals, skilled artisans and policemen – the last two being on the borderline. Virtually none owned large business concerns though some ran small shops, pharmacies or printing presses. These men and women were of crucial importance to the social and political development of Trinidad after the end of slavery.

The 'bottom' tier of slave society had been formed, logically enough, by the slaves, African or Creole, overwhelmingly black but always including people of mixed African-European heritage. After abolition, this sector – the Creole 'labouring population', to use a nineteenth century phrase – became even more heterogeneous. Its nucleus comprised the Trinidad ex-slaves and their descendants, mostly Catholic, at least nominally, and creole-speaking. But it also included immigrants from the Eastern Caribbean, mainly Protestant and English or English-creole speaking; liberated Africans from many different nations and regions of West Africa; black ex-soldiers of the West India Regiment disbanded after 1815 and settled in eastern Trinidad; ex-slaves from the United States who had fought for Britain in the War of 1812 and had been settled in southern Trinidad; the descendants of free coloureds and free black peasants and labourers; and *peons* of Spanish-Amerindian-African descent who had come from Venezuela. There were wide cultural, linguistic and religious differences between them, though something approaching a common 'Creole culture' was certainly developing in this stratum during the 'long' nineteenth century. There was also an urban-rural divide, with most of the West Indian immigrants and many of the Creole ex-slaves settling in the towns while the other groups were predominantly rural.

If the large Indian population may be thought of as constituting a 'fourth tier' in nineteenth century Trinidad society, then its internal stratification began quite early. All the adult immigrants were indentured on arrival, men and women, and had the same legal status, performed roughly the same jobs and earned the same wages, depending on strength, age and gender. But the immigrants were differentiated by religion (most were Hindus but Muslims were a significant minority), area of origin, language, caste, family background and previous occupations. By 1870, if not earlier, some immigrants had emerged from the mass and the process of socio-economic differentation within the Indian community had begun, though this process is still inadequately understood.

Many immigrants who were appointed *'sirdars'* or foremen on the estates used this office to great advantage. In one way they accumulated cash, and *sirdars* were often money lenders and shopkeepers on the plantations. The money thus acquired might be invested in land or shops. Caste advantages almost certainly played a role in upward mobility, though the sirdars were not as a rule chosen from upper caste immigrants (Haraksingh, 1981). Indians who had served out their indentures were able, after 1869, to acquire land either by Crown grants in lieu of repatriation to India or by purchasing Crown lands or parcels sold by estates or by leasing land from planters. The formation of new, mainly Indian villages and settlements after 1870 opened up opportunities for craftsmen, farmers and shopkeepers. Moreover, schooling became increasingly available in the later-nineteenth century when the Canadian Presbyterian Mission established a network of primary schools mainly intended for the children of Indian immigrants (Brereton, 1979:180-5).

By the 1920s a distinct middle stratum within the Indian community had emerged. It was itself divided into two sectors. First, there was a group whose status rested on the possession of land, businesses (shops, contracting operations, transport, cinemas) and cash. These relatively wealthy families often controlled networks of dependants, clients and employees in what was known as a *'praja'* (patron-client) relationship. They were mostly Hindus or Muslims, might have had little formal education (indeed, wealthy Indian landowners might be illiterate in this period), and were often largely uninfluenced by Westernisation. The second group emerged through education and absorption of Western culture. Essentially the product of the Canadian Mission primary schools, their secondary schools (Naparima College and Naparima Girls' High School) and their teacher training college, these men and women were typically Christian (Presbyterian), Western in cultural orientation, and employed in white collar, salaried occupations – above all teaching. They were certainly less prosperous than most people in the first group, but their education, their new religion, their familiarity with Western ways, their 'modernity', gave them great prestige and, at least up to 1920, the political leadership of the whole Indian community tended to rest in their hands.

The elite and post-slavery hegemony

The end of formal slavery presented a significant challenge to the traditional elite which attempted to preserve its control over society at large and to maintain its dominance over the ex-slaves and their children, without the buttress of slave ownership. Of course, continued control of economic resources, especially land, and manipulation of the political and legal systems, were critical to this effort. But social and cultural weapons were important too. Social distance could be preserved, and hegemony could be reasserted – and here we see the legacy of slavery with special clarity – through a profoundly racist conviction of the superiority of the European 'race' and its civilization and the irremediable inferiority of Africans and their culture, linked to an obsession with colour and phenotype and with racial 'purity' (defined as the absence of any known African ancestor) as the key index of elite status. In former slave societies like Trinidad, where the traditional elites were overwhelmingly of European descent (whether locally-born Creoles or immigrants), the upwardly mobile middle strata were predominantly European-African mixtures and the masses were of African origin. This racism was directed against blacks and coloureds and preoccupation with colour or shade were especially salient in the post-abolition nineteenth century as elite mechanisms for social control.

It would not be an exaggeration to state that post-emancipation society in Trinidad was based on racism and sensitivity to colour and shade, even though no formal apartheid system existed and in law all were equal. Institutionalised discrimination against non-whites existed everywhere despite the absence of official segregation policies, a situation especially galling to upwardly mobile, educated and often cultured coloureds and blacks. In general, resident whites maintained a marked social aloofness both from the coloured middle stratum and from the blacks. Their private life was a closed world; exclusive social clubs were established and much of white social life was conducted within them and in family gatherings. Interaction with non-whites was confined to stereo-typed relationships in which social distance and superiority/inferiority were clearly demarcated. The Creole whites in particular showed great sensitivity to social relations with blacks and coloureds: they felt even more acutely than European immigrants the need to maintain distance and to preserve and 'prove' their purity, and they had imbibed Caribbean prejudices since infancy. But most white immigrants soon adjusted, whatever their liberal intentions, and few ever broke out of the white enclave. Fear as well as racism was at work, fear of the masses and their potential for 'revenge' – the Haitian bloodbath was never far from the minds of Creole whites in the nineteenth century.

The French Creoles preserved their 'purity' by a strict policy of endogamy. Marriage with someone suspected of having 'coloured blood' was impossible. In *A Handful of Dust*, first published in 1934, Evelyn Waugh described a fictional French Creole young woman going home to Trinidad from school in Paris to get married. She explains to someone on board the ship: 'There are so few young men I can marry.

They must be Catholic and of an island family ... there are two or three other rich families and I shall marry into one of them.' The poor girl was limited to seven possible candidates, and one of them was ruled out because, although very rich, 'he isn't really a Trinidadian. His grandfather came from Dominica and they say he has coloured blood' (Waugh, 1945 [1934]):163, 166). And apart from the crucial question of marriage, French Creoles did not mix with non-white Trinidadians on an equal basis. Non-whites would not be invited to private gatherings in French Creole homes, and even more public contacts in political and official life, in business and the professions, or in church activities, were quite limited.

If racism and social exclusiveness seemed to be indispensable mechanisms for the maintenance of hegemony by the white elite after the end of slavery, they were hardly sufficient to achieve this end. Control of economic resources as landowners and employers continued to be the basis of its position. But, in addition, the elite formed or controlled numerous organisations – political, social, professional, cultural or religious in orientation – to advance its interests, to minimise threats from upwardly mobile groups or to lobby with metropolitan authorities for advantages. Both political and non-political strategies were pursued to these ends.

After the end of slavery the white elite sought to maintain its grip over the colony's political system. 'White power' here meant manipulating the institutions of the colonial government so that the ex-slaves were largely excluded from them and the leaders of the coloured middle stratum were co-opted or controlled. Trinidad was a Crown Colony: there were no elected members in the Legislative Council and the governor at least in theory possessed autocratic powers. But in practice powerful elite whites exercised considerable influence over legislation and policy-making. Throughout the 'long' nineteenth century, most members of the Council were white, nominated to represent the traditional propertied interests of sugar, cocoa, commerce and, later, oil. Whites also held most of the senior positions in the government and the civil service. Despite the myth of Crown Colony government protecting the people against the entrenched oligarchy, the local elite successfully manipulated the governor and the British officials in its own narrow interests, and the Colonial Office in London rarely intervened. It is not surprising that the white elite strongly defended the retention of the Crown Colony system when it came under increasing attack after 1918 (Brereton, 1981:136-70; Ryan, 1972:28-69).

Outside the realm of formal politics the elite established organisations to defend its interests. Planters established the Agricultural Society; owners of cocoa estates (mainly French Creoles) set up the

Cocoa Planters Association. Located in London was the West India Committee, a venerable and influential pressure group which lobbied the British government on behalf of West Indian sugar producers. It harassed the Colonial Office, persuaded Members of Parliament to ask questions in the Commons, and 'wined and dined' governors before they took up office in the Caribbean or when home on leave. The Committee often intervened in Trinidad politics, for example in 1890 they attacked the governor's efforts to diversify the local economy in a letter which generated considerable public controversy. Merchants in Port of Spain set up the Chamber of Commerce in 1878. Its members were mainly white Creoles of French and English descent and British immigrants, all engaged in the import/export trade with Europe, North America and Venezuela. It routinely petitioned the local government on matters connected to taxes, tariffs, harbour facilities and the like.

A number of social or recreational associations were established by the Trinidad white elite to express group solidarity and to maintain distance from the 'lower orders'. Masonic lodges were important in the social life of elite men in the period, and it seems that Trinidad lodges were informally segregated. Some were more or less exclusively white, while others were controlled by middle stratum coloureds and blacks. Prominent Catholics, as well as Protestants, belonged to lodges and the church apparently did not object to masonic rituals at Catholic funerals. In Port of Spain, the Queen's Park Hotel was a favoured elite meeting place. The Union Club counted among its members around 1900 'nearly all the influential citizens', exclusively whites and predominantly Britons or Creoles of English descent. The Savannah Club was equally select. The Queen's Park Cricket Club controlled cricket in the colony and its membership was largely but not exclusively white and so were most of the teams it fielded in this period – definitely 'gentlemen players' from the 'respected' white families. Elite men and women ran charitable societies like the Anglican Daily Meal Society or the Trinidad Home Industries Association (to enable gentlewomen in distressed circumstances to add to their incomes). Societies devoted to discussions of scientific issues and to investigations in Trinidad's natural history, and literary, theatrical and musical groups, were dominated by elite whites though educated coloureds and blacks certainly participated in them.

In the nineteenth century the Catholic Church was an important elite organisation and a significant mechanism for social control. Trinidad was predominantly Catholic despite British control since 1797, and the church was very closely identified with the island's French Creole elite at least until the 1920s. The Church was staffed mainly by Frenchmen, French West Indians or local French Creoles, and French was the language normally used for sermons. Indeed, most priests did not speak English. French Creoles were the leading laypeople and dominated all the church's institutions. The Church authorities were often accused of discriminatory acts against coloureds and blacks, and Trinidad's small coloured and black educated group came to include a few outspoken anti-clericals who wished to reduce the ecclesiastical influence on education and society in general. But the Church remained an entrenched organisation still largely dominated by the French Creole elite. It did, however, bow to the realities by gradually replacing the French priests with Irish Dominicans, by appointing Englishmen as archbishops of Port of Spain, and by phasing out the use of French in its schools. Trinidad's Catholic Church was certainly less 'French' by 1900, reflecting shifts within the elite between 'French' and 'English' sectors of the island's white community, but it was still very much in the hands of the white French Creoles. The Anglican Church was much smaller, but influential because the governor and other top British officials – and many important sugar planters and businessmen – usually adhered to it. Even though it was 'disestablished' in 1870, it retained its prestige as an elite organisation (though of course many coloureds and blacks belonged to it). Most of its clergy in the nineteenth century, and all its bishops, were English.

Secondary education, in the nineteenth century, was largely the preserve of the white elite, though this was changing by its end. The three leading institutions in this period were St Joseph's Convent, a school for girls established by French nuns, Queen's Collegiate School, later Queen's Royal College, a government-funded and controlled boys' school which opened in 1857, and St Mary's College, set up in 1863 by a French teaching order. The majority of the pupils at St Joseph's and at St Mary's, up to about 1920, were white French Creoles. At Queen's Royal College most pupils were the sons of expatriate English Protestants, or English Creoles. Fees at all three schools were high, and they were modelled on French Catholic institutions or, in the case of the government college, English public schools. Though the children of the better-off brown middle stratum families were from the start admitted to all three schools – for no formal segregation existed – they often encountered subtle discrimination and hostility became more overt when black lower middle-class children began to penetrate them in small numbers in the later part of the century.

The middle stratum: strategies for social mobility

Middle stratum coloureds and blacks began to enter formal politics in Trinidad, as elsewhere in the Caribbean, just before the abolition of slavery. In the 1820s, they had campaigned successfully for legal equality with whites, achieved in 1829, and then for a 'fair share' of posts in the civil service. Non-whites were effectively barred from entry to the wholly nominated Legislative Council, set up in 1831, as well as suffering discrimination in appointments to the more attractive positions in the bureaucracy. It is not surprising, therefore, that educated brown (and later black) men joined in movements to reform Crown Colony government by admitting elected members to the Legislature. In the 1840s and 1850s coloured leaders such as Thomas Hinde agitated for an elected legislative assembly and against discrimination in the civil service. In the period between 1880 and 1914, the anti-Crown Colony movement gathered considerable momentum and its leadership passed from 'liberal' white Creoles and Englishmen to brown and black professional men like Henry Alcazar, C.P. David and Edgar Maresse-Smith. Though the immediate goal of the movement – the admission of elected members to the Legislature – was not achieved until 1924-25, it represented a significant challenge by the middle stratum to the political ascendancy of the traditional elite.

Municipal politics were also important to the middle stratum leadership. Elected town or borough councils existed in the nineteenth century for Port of Spain, San Fernando and (in the 1880s) Arima, and seats on these bodies, elected by ratepayers, were eagerly sought after by brown and black would-be politicians. The first mayor of San Fernando, Louis Romain, was from an 'old' coloured family. M.M. Philip, a brown lawyer, became the first non-white mayor of Port of Spain in 1867. The virtual exclusion of the brown and black middle stratum from the colonial legislature and from top posts in the bureaucracy made municipal politics all the more crucial to its leaders, who were predominantly urban-based. And this explains why the abolition of the elected Borough Council of Port of Spain by the British government in 1898 was such a burning grievance. Indeed, this action led directly to the 'Water Riots' of 1903 – when Trinidadians protested against the Crown Colony government's authoritarian nature as evidenced by its water policy – and to lengthy agitation for the restoration of the elected council which was finally successful in 1914 (Brereton, 1981:142-52; Magid, 1988:*passim).*

Entry into legislative and other political bodies, and access to posts in the bureaucracy, were key strategies for advancement on the part of the coloured and black middle stratum. Its members also formed or controlled cultural, social, recreational and professional organisations, much like the white elite. In Trinidad they established literary and debating societies intended to prepare young persons for leadership, to encourage self-education, to help develop political agendas and to 'prove' their equality with (if not superiority to) local whites in all matters pertaining to culture. A good example is the Trinidad Athenaeum, formed in the 1870s by J.J. Thomas, the self-educated linguist, educator and writer who wrote *Creole Grammar* (1869) and *Froudacity* (1889) and was a source of great pride to the coloured and black intelligentsia in the late-nineteenth century (Wood, 1969; Campbell, 1976; Brereton, 1977). The Masonic lodges and proliferating Friendly Societies were very important to men of the middle stratum, giving them organisational experience and scope for leadership, and promoting group solidarity. Because so many middle stratum men and women were teachers, the Trinidad and Tobago Teachers' Union, first formally registered in 1919, played a significant role in these same areas.

The colonial newspaper press was always important to middle stratum strategies for mobility. From at least the middle of the nineteenth century brown or black men owned or edited one or two papers, even if the lives of their publications were often short and their circulation painfully small. Among the Trinidad papers which articulated the views of the middle stratum in this period were *New Era*, the *Trinidad Press*, the *Trinidad Colonist*, the *Telegraph, Public Opinion, Truth, The Mirror*, and several rather more ephemeral publications. Proprietors, editors and contributors like Joseph Lewis, Samuel Carter, J.J. Thomas, William Herbert and Edgar Maresse-Smith used these papers to air the grievances of their group, to develop political agendas, and to move towards an ideology with which to confront the pervasive racism of colonial society.

Inevitably, a race-conscious ideology was slowly developed by Trinidad's brown and black intelligentsia in the second half of the century, and articulated in the newspapers controlled by this group. Its most distinguished spokesman was undoubtedly J.J. Thomas, who put forward a fully developed Pan-Africanism in *Froudacity*. The celebration of the jubilee of Emancipation in 1888 was the occasion for considerable public debate on issues of identity and consciousness, preparing the ground for the more broadly-based movements of the next century. H.S. Williams, a black Trinidadian teacher who qualified as a lawyer, founded the Pan-African Association in London in 1897. When he visited his homeland in 1901 he was enthusiastically received and branches of the Association were formed in Port of Spain, San Fernando and several smaller towns and villages. It found its supporters mainly from the black and coloured middle stratum, whose members by then had evolved a distinctly race-conscious worldview, which co-existed more or less comfortably with a determination to 'prove' that blacks and browns could master European or Western culture as competently as whites, a determination to 'vindicate the Race' (Mathurin, 1976).

Survival, co-operation, resistance: the masses

Everywhere in the Caribbean after the end of slavery the materially impoverished multitude of the people devised formal and informal institutions and strategies for mutual co-operation, both to ensure their physical survival and to defend their religious and cultural forms. These institutions often drew inspiration from ancestral Africa. Afro-Christian sects, Afro-Catholic brotherhoods, Afro-Creole artistic and cultural forms were at the heart of the efforts of Trinidadian labourers and peasants to survive and even to triumph over material deprivation and cultural oppression.

Afro-Christian religion became fundamentally important to lower-class blacks in Trinidad. Because of poverty and ill health, poor communications in the rural areas, and generally a lack of leisure, schooling and self-confidence, these men and women were unable to develop the wide range of social and political associations which we have noted in the case of the elite and the middle stratum. Moreover, the African worldview was essentially spiritual, seeing no distinction between the sacred and the worldly. Hence the crucial importance of religion, as interpreted by the people themselves, as a social institution holding communities together and focusing popular resistance to elite hegemony. These syncretic faiths typically merged traditional West African beliefs and practices with those of Christianity, whether in its Protestant or Catholic variety. In Trinidad as elsewhere, Afro-Christian religions may be seen as a continuum moving from almost 'pure' African religions like Shango (or the *Orisha* religion) or the Rada cult to the Shouter/Spiritual Baptists who were clearly Christian but whose rites and cosmology included African elements. It need hardly be said that all these faiths had much in common.

Shango, or the *Orisha* religion, Trinidad's most important neo-African faith in the nineteenth and twentieth centuries, was derived from Yoruba immigrants. The *orishas* (deities or spirits) were worshipped through spirit possession and animal sacrifice and were identified with Catholic saints. Yoruba was preserved as the ritual language for the '*orisha* work' well into the present century. In fact, the Yoruba immigrants were the core of a unified African tradition which lent cultural dynamism to the whole black Trinidadian population. Significantly, one white Creole, writing in 1858, noted that 'the whole Yoruba race of the colony may be said to form a sort of social league for mutual support and protection' (de Verteuil, 1858:175) – and this tradition of self-help would be as important as their religious and cultural influence. Another neo-African faith practised up to the 1950s was the Rada cult. It was based in Belmont, outside Port of Spain, where a flourishing religious community was founded by a liberated African immigrant from Dahomy in the middle of the nineteenth century (Carr, 1953). Towards the end of the same century, the Shouter or Spiritual Baptist faith was established in Trinidad. It may have been brought by immigrants from St Vincent and merged with Baptist beliefs and practices found among the 'Merikens', the settlements of former American slaves in the Company villages of southern Trinidad. Unlike the *Orisha* and Rada faiths, the Baptists combined African with Protestant, not Catholic, traditions.

The defence and preservation of Afro-Christian or neo-African religious forms became important to black Trinidadians in their struggle to carve out a life for themselves on their own terms. They were up against persistent efforts to denigrate, even to persecute, those forms. Devotees of the *Orisha* or the Rada faiths were often imprisoned and even flogged under an 1868 law which made the practice of 'Obeah' a criminal offence. The Shouter/Spiritual Baptists were forbidden by ordinance from holding public services of worship between 1917 and 1951. To preserve the faith, therefore, was an act of resistance. And this was also the case when it came to secular Afro-Creole cultural forms, especially festivals, music and dance. Excluded as lower-class blacks generally were from most other aspects of social and institutional life, the preservation and defence of their unique culture helped them to develop group cohesion and a sense of self-worth.

After emancipation the whole cultural complex associated with the pre-lenten carnival – stickfighting or Kalinda, calypso, tamboo-bamboo percussion music, drumming, Afro-French dances like the Bele or Belair – came to be central to Afro-Trinidadians' sense of identity. Some were ready to resist the authorities if they tried to meddle with it, as happened more than once in the 1880s. Despite partially successful efforts to repress those aspects of carnival felt to be dangerous to law and order or culturally alien and 'uncivilised', it never lost its liveliness nor its anarchic folk spirit, and some of the features suppressed in the late-nineteenth century re-emerged in the steelband movement of the 1940s and 1950s. The folk also cherished their language, creole, an integral part of the Afro-French or French Antillian culture which they shared with Martinique, Guadeloupe, Haiti, St Lucia and Dominica. Creole remained the *lingua franca* of Trinidad all through the nineteenth century, despite the offical attitude that it was a barbarous gibberish and an obstacle to progress. Not until the early-twentieth century did creole give way to English and English creole (Brereton, 1979: 163-6).

It was characteristic for the Afro-Trinidadian people, especially the rural folk, to develop co-operative institutions; it was not only the Yorubas who stuck together for 'mutual support'. The *gayap* was an informal arrangement by which villagers helped their neighbours without pay to perform certain tasks like clearing a piece of bush or building a house. The 'host' provided food and drink for the rest, and the occasion became a social and festive gathering. Of course, it worked only in a cohesive village society where reciprocal obligations were binding. No doubt the *gayap*, which is found under different names everywhere in the Caribbean, had African antecedents, though similar arrangements can be found in most cash-poor peasant economies. In both rural and urban communities, Friendly Societies played an important role in providing people with funeral and sickness benefits, at a time when neither governments nor employers made any provision for such matters and wages were too low and irregular to make large saving possible. The *sou sou*, African in origin, was an informal saving club by which people regularly contributed small sums to a common pool; each contributor in turn took the total sum collected (the 'hand') at stated intervals.

The strategies adopted by Afro-Trinidadians after slavery to defend their religions and culture and to survive material poverty were paralleled in some respects by the adaptations of the Indian immigrants and the locally-born children. Faced with a generally unwelcoming host society, and unwilling to interact with Creoles to any considerable extent because of their own prejudices of religion, caste and race, the Indians tried to re-create 'traditional' cultural and social institutions to cushion themselves from the wider society. Both Hinduism and Islam took a firm hold in Trinidad and the Hindu pundits and Muslim imams became influential leaders of the Indo-Caribbean community even if they were accorded scant respect by the wider society. When large numbers of Indians left the plantations after about 1870 and settled as independent cultivators either on the margins of the estates or in remoter villages, it was possible to re-create some of the 'traditional' institutions of rural India, including the *panchayat*, the council of high caste community elders who kept people in line and ensured that traditional mores were observed. The Indian family, with its strongly patriarchal cast and its subordination of women (except for the older matriarch) and children, was re-established after the dislocations experienced on the plantations. The Indo-Caribbean community was characterised by its intense family cohesiveness and loyalty. Though caste could not be fully re-established in the Caribbean, it did re-emerge in the post-1870 Indian villages and played a role in their stratification system. So did the Hindu-Muslim division, though relations between people of the two great faiths were never anything as troubled as in India (Haraksingh, 1988).

For most of the period of indentured Indian immigration to Trinidad (1845-1917), there was relatively little social or other interaction between Indians and the rest of the population. This was reinforced by a pervasive pattern of residential and occupational segregation. Indians were concentrated on the plantations and in rural settlements, Creoles were in the towns or semi-urban areas; Indians were estate labourers or peasants, most Creoles were employed in services, industries and commerce, urban jobs or in the oil industry. Even where Creoles were involved in agriculture, it tended to be in different areas. For example, Trinidad's black peasantry after 1870 was concentrated along the north coast whereas Indian farmers were mostly in the central and southern parts of the island. Mutual misunderstandings and even contempt for each other's culture and way of life strengthened this low level of interaction (Brereton, 1974). It was not until the 1890s that we find Indians in Trinidad establishing formal organisations to defend their interests and beginning to venture into the political arena. The East Indian National Association was founded in 1897, and the East Indian National Congress (named after the Congress in India) in 1910. Most of the early leaders of each body were Christians who had been educated in the Canadian Mission schools and (in some cases) at universities abroad. It was not until the 1920s or 1930s that a significant Hindu or Muslim leadership emerged and formal organisations representing the various Hindu and Muslim denominations were established. In general, Indians took relatively little part in colonial politics until after 1918, although a few Indian ratepayers began to vote in the San Fernando Municipal Council elections as early as the 1870s, and an Indo-Trinidadian lawyer (a Christian) was nominated to sit on the Legislative Council in 1914.

But like their Afro-Trinidadian counterparts, 'grassroots' Indians persisted in their cultural traditions and defended them against the indifference, hostility or outright persecution of the colonial elite and the host society in general. The very fact that after decades of effort by the Canadian Presbyterians, the Catholics and the Anglicans, only 11.8 per cent of the Indian population had accepted Christianity by 1921, is also testimony to cultural resistance and to the absolutely crucial role of Hinduism and Islam as psychological protection, a source of self-worth with which to face the society's contempt. The Indians tried to maintain their religious festivals despite discouragement or actual coercion. The Madrasi Hindu festival of 'fire-pass', for instance, was banned in the 1870s, and the traditional open air Hindu cremation of the dead was made difficult to carry out until the 1940s. In 1884, the colonial government attempted to put restrictions on the by-then traditional Muslim festival of Muhurram or Hosay as it was celebrated in and around San Fernando. The unarmed celebrants tried to carry on as before and were fired on by troops and police, leaving at least 12 dead and over 100 injured. It is no coincidence that the Muhurram massacre took place just after rioting, in 1881 and again earlier in 1884, by Afro-Trinidadians protesting against similar attempts to restrict carnival (Singh, 1988). Indian estate labourers, putting lie to the myth of their 'docility', were also prepared to organise strikes and on occasion riots to defend their rights and to protest against any deterioration of their always rigorous working conditions. There was a wave of strikes and riots among estate-resident Indians in the 1880s, for instance, when planters attempted to reduce earnings and increase the size of daily tasks.

For the Indians who settled in new peasant villages after 1870, the most important strategy for survival, self-help and mobility (in addition to religion), was the family. The large extended family, usually based on the ownership of land even if only a small plot, and on the peasant mode of production, was the core institution for the Indo-Trinidadians. Traditions of mutual help like the *gayap*, and an informal co-operative borrowing institution like the *sou sou*, and the *chaiteyi* from north-east India, did develop in these Indo-Trinidadian peasant villages. But it was the strong, cohesive, patriarchal family structure which was crucial.

Conclusion

Trinidad society after the end of slavery was divided by race, ethnicity and skin colour, by class and by national origin, culture, language and religion. Yet there were forces which mitigated or softened these divisions. Rural society was still deeply affected by traditional paternalistic relations between estate owners and their labourers. White Creole planters regarded their black workers (the descendants, perhaps, of their parents' or grandparents' slaves) as 'their people', who were entitled to protection and charity in exchange for deference and respect. Of course, traditional patriarchal relations between resident planters from old Creole families and their long established labourers were breaking down in Trinidad, as elsewhere in the Caribbean, by the early-twentieth century as the forces of modernisation, capitalisation and technological change advanced. But they still profoundly shaped rural society.

Language, culture and religion could be unifying as well as divisive forces. We have seen that the white elite often tried to impose versions of European culture on the whole population and that the people, especially those of African descent, struggled to preserve and defend Afro-Creole forms. Yet the possession of a common linguistic and cultural heritage might also unite people of different ethnicities and class positions. The creole language, for instance, was shared by the elite and masses insofar as the French Creoles were concerned, and so was a whole world of folklore and magico-religious beliefs expressed in that language, as well as Catholicism. There is no doubt that, as a result of their shared heritage, Trinidad's French Creoles were far closer to the Afro-Trinidadians than the whites of English or Scottish origin. It is no accident that Trinidad's premier labour leader of the 1920s and 1930s was a white French Creole. Moreover, Christianity and European culture were accepted as normative by the middle stratum in general and also by many members of the 'respectable', upwardly mobile peasants and workers, even though large numbers of them resisted their imposition.

Finally, we should note that deeply divided though it undeniably was, Trinidadian society in the nineteenth century was not static. It was hierarchical and authoritarian, based on ancestry and racial origin, ethnicity and skin colour, economic position and family status, but the lines were not frozen nor were they sanctioned by religion or by universal consensus as in contemporary India. Indeed, hierarchy and ascription were coming under challenge from 'modern', egalitarian values which derived both from Christianity and from Enlightenment views about merit depending on personal achievement. The former set of values was clearly ascendant in the nineteenth century, but the latter was gaining in strength particularly among the middle stratum, upwardly mobile workers and liberal, modernising sectors within the elite. Trinidadians born after the end of slavery were certainly limited in their opportunities for socio-economic advancement, above all if they were born into poor black or Indian families, but they were not doomed to total immobility and there was, in fact, considerable degree of movement. People were not inexorably trapped for life in their 'orders' or 'estates' and there was no universal consensus on the legitimacy of the social hierarchy.

These forces helped to soften the deep divisions that existed, and also to ensure that the masses of the people were not totally and irrevocably alienated from society as had probably been the case with enslaved Africans. They ensured that Trinidadian society was held together by more than mere force, and was capable of movement and change. This was made possible by the end of slavery and the decades of slow and painful evolution which followed that momentous event.

References

Borde, P.G.L., 1982, *The History of the Island of Trinidad under the Spanish Government*, Vol. 2, Port of Spain: Paria Publishing Co. (originally published in two volumes, Paris, 1876 and 1882).

Brereton, B., 1974, 'The Foundations of Prejudice: Indians and Africans in Nineteenth Century Trinidad', *Caribbean Issues*, Vol. 1, No. 1, pp. 15-28.

– 1977, 'J.J. Thomas, an Estimate', *Journal of Caribbean History*, Vol. 9, pp. 22-42.

– 1979, *Race Relations in Colonial Trinidad 1870-1900*, Cambridge: Cambridge University Press.

– 1981, *A History of Modern Trinidad 1783-1962*, London: Heinemann.

Campbell, C., 1976, 'J.J. Thomas of Trinidad', *African Studies Association of the West Indies Bulletin*, Vol. 8, pp. 4-17.

Carr, A., 1953, 'A Rada Community in Trinidad', *Caribbean Quarterly*, Vol. 3, No. 1.

de Verteuil, L., 1858, *Trinidad*, London.

Gomes, A., 1974, *Through a Maze of Colour*, Port-of-Spain: Key Caribbean.

Haraksingh, K., 1981, 'Control and Resistance among Overseas Indian Workers: A Study of Labour on the Sugar Plantations of Trinidad 1875-1917', *Journal of Caribbean History*, Vol. 14, pp. 1-17.

– 1988, 'Structure, Process and Indian Culture in Trinidad', *Immigrants and Minorities*, Vol. 7, No. 1, pp. 113-22.

Johnson, H., 1987, 'The Chinese in Trinidad in the late-nineteenth Century', *Ethnic and Racial Studies*, Vol. 10, No. 1, pp. 82-95.

Magid, A., 1988, *Urban Nationalism: A Study of Political Development in Trinidad*, Gainesville: University Presses of Florida.

Mathurin, O., 1976, *Henry Sylvester Williams and the Origins of the Pan-African Movement, 1869-1911*, Westport, CT: Greenwood Press.

Mendes, Alfred, 1934, *Pitch Lake*, London: Duckworth.

Ryan, S., 1972, *Race and Nationalism in Trinidad and Tobago*, Toronto: University of Toronto Press.

Singh, K., 1988, *The Bloodstained Tombs: The Muharram Massacre in Trinidad, 1884*, London: Macmillan.

Waugh, E., 1945 [1934], *A Handful of Dust*, New York: New Directions.

Wood, D., 1968, *Trinidad in Transition: The Years After Slavery*, London: Oxford University Press.

– 1969, 'John Jacob Thomas', in *Froudacity*, London: New Beacon Books, pp. 9-22.

CHAPTER 3

Notes on the evolution of inequality in Trinidad and Tobago

Ralph M. Henry

Introduction

Discussion in the economics literature on inequality and distribution in Third World countries and even generally has centred on the validation of the Kuznets Curve. In earlier empirical work, Kuznets (1955) discovered that there seemed to be a relationship between the level of inequality, as measured through an index like the Gini Coefficient, and the level of per capita income. At low levels of per capita income, the Gini tended to be low but would rise sharply as a country achieved middle-level income and would taper off and fall as growth in income brought the country among the high per capita income group. Thus, both high-income and very low-income countries would display low levels of inequality while middle-income countries tended to be character-ised by much higher levels of inequality. This relationship between per capita income and the level of inequality was reflected in the 'Inverted U' (Kuznets, 1955; Paukert, 1973).

The preoccupation with per capita income has tended to ignore inequality among groups. In recent work on income inequality, it has been argued that inter-group disparities have a much larger societal relevance than the individual differences in income in non-homogeneous societies (Henry, 1989). Thus, while it is useful to examine such measures as the Gini Coefficient which may reflect differences among households or individuals, it is even more important to examine the degree of inter-group inequality since the first basis for engendering higher levels of equity in a plural society is to ensure that there are no differences among groups in their access to the resources of the country. Indeed, in the case of Trinidad and Tobago, this is implied in its national anthem. The work on inequality in this latter country suggests that while inequality both within and among groups has tended to fall as per capita incomes increase, reverses are not impossible nor unknown (Harewood and Henry, 1985; Henry, 1989; Henry, Nicholls and Melville, forthcoming).

The two major paradigms in economic analysis have tended to be deficient in the analysis of the economics of plural societies. On the one hand, neo-classical economic analysis asserts the primacy of free markets in the elimination of discrimination and the presence of inter-group differences. Further, it limits its attention to the labour market operations and the factors therein which allow for or erode segmentation (Hutt, 1964; Becker, 1971; and Roback, 1988). On the other hand, the Marxian paradigm tends to treat group inequalities as simply epiphenomena in a larger class analysis which may, at worst, frustrate attempts by the exploited class to solidify and to recognise the 'true' basis of their exploitation. In this chapter I shall explore the entirely different approach provided by institutional economics in examining inequality and its basis in Trinidad and Tobago, a country with a plural social order.[1]

Institutional economics

In recent work I have argued against the weakness of both the neo-classical and Marxian approaches and have sought to widen the terrain of analysis to embrace the work and insights provided by other areas of social science which, together with economic analysis, are far more helpful in the understanding of changes in the distributional picture in so-called plural societies (Henry, 1989, 1991). The events of eastern Europe and the re-emergence of issues of ethnicity in countries like Yugoslavia, the former Soviet Union and Czechoslovakia have served to emphasise that the presumed eradication of class has not solved the problem of group inequalities in societies that had experienced a socialist revolution.

Nabli and Nugent (1989) have discussed the role of institutional factors in economic development and have argued cogently that what they call the New Institutional Economics provides a far more useful theoretical framework for analysis of economies and for examining developmental issues. They attribute certain qualities to social institutions:

> The first such characteristic is the rules and constraints nature of institutions ... Their second ... is their ability to govern the relations among individuals and groups ... the third is their predictability (Nabli and Nugent, 1989:1335).

Moreover, and very much apropos the discussion that follows, they note that:

... markets, be they stock exchanges, labour markets, credit markets, wholesale markets, or traditional bazaars *(suqs)*, are institutions because they embody rules and regulations, formal or informal, which govern their operation (Nabli and Nugent, 1989:1335).

The analysis of distribution and economic inequality is hardly complete until we examine the economic, social and political base of the society and economy which are the focus of attention. In other words, the works of the sociologist, the anthropologist and the political scientist are ignored at their peril by economists. This is particularly the case in the study of plural societies. M.G. Smith (1965), borrowing from Furnivall, was the first to apply the pluralism concept to the analysis of societies in the Commonwealth Caribbean. Unfortunately, it is only in recent years that economists have imported this framework into the discussion of certain features of countries like Trinidad and Tobago, Guyana and Surinam.

On the other hand, there is another stream of thought which, while not built on the plural society model, recognises the role of historical forces in the nature, structure and functioning of these economies. The work of Best (1968) and Best and Levitt (1968) could be regarded as the earliest attempts by economists to reckon with the peculiar social institutions of Caribbean-type economies. Indeed, the pure plantation economy was defined as a 'total economic institution', operating as an extension of a metropolitan economy.

In an earlier article an attempt was made to examine the factors that have influenced the distribution in 'post-colonial' plural societies (Henry, 1989). There, the emphasis was directed at the distributional changes in such countries like Guyana, Fiji, Malaysia, Trinidad and Tobago, and Sri Lanka, all of which have become nations in the post-World War II period and in which inherited group inequalities (political, social and economic) – or at the very least poor inter-group distribution – have remained high on the agenda in the political economy of these new nation-states.

Four primary factors were identified as instrumental in the attainment of greater equity in these new nation-states which in their establishment during the colonial period would have had certain inequities among groups directly built in to their political and social processes. These four factors that have an immediate contemporary relevance are:

(i) the nature of the state sector *vis-à-vis* the organisation and control of primary income-earning activities in the economy;
(ii) the degree of ethnic segmentation of the economy and of the

labour market inherited from the colonial period, and the degree to which universalistic criteria are observed in the various sectors; (iii) the relative rates of growth among sectors; and
(iv) the constraints on, and the efficiency and efficacy of, the fiscal re-distributive process.

More recently, in addressing the problem of equity enhancement in so-called plural societies it has been argued that policy formulation has to recognise that the presence of market forces presumed to exist in the economies of these societies does not automatically lead to the elimination of barriers and structures that might have been established in the colonial period or that might have emerged since as a result of earlier inequalities (Henry, 1991). Moreover, contrary to Hutt (1964), it is argued that imperfect competition is far more normal than the perfect market model and even if perfect markets were synonymous with the elimination of discrimination, the fact that they seldom exist means that discrimination and inequity among groups could subsist unless other factors intervene to push a plural society along a path of greater inter-group equity. In other words, in the imperfection of markets inherent power factors may be exercised on a group basis depending on the degree of internal solidarity of the group.

In the context of plural societies much depends on the control exercised by 'gate keepers' – those strategically-placed individuals, groups and/or institutions with the ability to control access to society's rewards or resources – over the income generation process (Henry, 1991). Following Nabli and Nugent (1989) it can be suggested that institutional factors determine the operations of the gate keepers to the various markets (labour, land, credit, wholesale, retail, etc.) and therefore, by implication, impact on 'the division of labour, rules for entry, exit, decision-making and external relations' (Nabli and Nugent, 1989:1335). Given that the very foundation of many plural societies was based on social and economic inequality among groups, it can be readily accepted that the 'gate keeping institution' will show conflict as some would want to change the status quo to correct for inequalities while others would want to maintain the status quo. It would be rare, for example, to find all the gate keepers espousing and abiding by rules that promote rapid reduction of inequality within, and more particularly, among groups.

In a market economy inequality is reflected not only in the ownership of assets but also in income flows. These derive from: (a) wages and salaries; (b) fees; (c) profits, rents and dividends; and (d) transfers.

The first constitutes labour income from the labour market; fees may come from an independent professional practice, or from the provision of a service. Profits, rents and dividends derive from the ownership of assets that contribute to the production process. Transfers, however, come from the redistribution process either among private individuals or from provisions of the state. The gate keepers can be identified and their performance assessed at critical points in the income flows with a view to determining the extent to which they promote or reduce inequality among groups and individuals.

Stewart (1983), in a review of the problem of inequality reduction in developing countries, has suggested that there are three factors that contribute to inequality in primary income: technology, population growth and the payments system. If one imports into the discussion the presence of political and socio-cultural factors that influence each of these, the difficulty posed in assessing any particular situation of inequality in time and space is understandable. One may be forced to seek the safety of *ceteris paribus* (other things being equal) assumptions, but these are hardly appropriate for informing policy in countries like Yugoslavia and Sri Lanka where ethnic and nationalist issues threaten the very foundation of the nation-state. Indeed, a proper understanding of the issues may help to protect some plural societies from the tendency to social explosion that seems to characterise many such countries. It is necessary, therefore, to relax as many assumptions as resources permit even if the analytical frame becomes complicated to manage.

The rest of this chapter explores the evolution of inequality in Trinidad and Tobago starting with a description of the country in its foundation stage. However, it is only in respect of the period since 1956 that the data exist for a more quantitative assessment of the structure of inequality in the country, especially since 1971/72 when the Central Statistical Office increased the periodicity by conducting *Household Budgetary Surveys*. An attempt will be made to identify some of the issues that lie on the periphery of formal economics but which cannot be ignored in examining inequality in a country like Trinidad and Tobago. In effect, I shall attempt to look at the role and performance of the gate keepers in the operation of the payments system at different points in time.

A fundamental thesis of this study is that the structure and trend in inequality among groups would be responsive to a number of institutional variables and would be a function of factors that extend beyond the mere growth and change in the economy as hypothesised in the 'Inverted U' hypothesis. Moreover, in explaining the present, it is necessary to retrace to snapshots at different periods in the past to comprehend fully the factor or factors that are responsible for what exists currently. A much larger effort is being undertaken to review the distributional structure over time borrowing, in part, from the approach of *'histoire raisonnée'* employed by Best (1968) but with the focus more narrowly directed to the distributional question. The present paper merely presages this more ambitious effort.

The unequal foundation

The year 1937 marks a watershed in the political history of Trinidad and Tobago and indeed of the Commonwealth Caribbean. In June 1937, there erupted general disturbances in Trinidad which helped provide a spark for the rest of the region as the mass of people rose up against conditions that they considered intolerable. Almost one hundred years after emancipation the descendants of the ex-slaves and the ex-indentured workers were decrying their lot and were prepared to take matters into their own hands against the colonial system under which they had lived.

Lewis (1977 [1939]) and the Moyne Commission have documented the atrocious social conditions of the period. Lewis quotes two sentences of a Professor Macmillan:

A great many of the people everywhere show independence on a modest competence; but the masses are poor or very poor, with a standard of living reminding one of the native and coloured communities of the Union of South Africa even more than of the peasants of West Africa .... A social and economic study of the West Indies is therefore necessarily a study of poverty (Lewis, 1977 [1939]:17).

As we saw in Chapters 1 and 2, above this mass of poverty of people of African descent, and in Trinidad and British Guiana also of East Indian descent, stood a small white aristocracy. A succinct statement on the nature of distribution is given by Lewis:

But this tiny white element dominates every aspect of West Indian life. Economically and politically the white man is supreme: he owns the biggest plantations, stores and banks, controlling directly or indirectly the entire economic life of the community (1977 [1939]:11).

On average, some 50 per cent of the population was engaged directly in agriculture throughout the region, many of them landless agricultural labourers, dependent on seasonal employment on the sugar plantations, and living on the periphery of the plantations or on the plantations in barracks, 'constructed on the same principle as stables' (Lewis, 1977 [1939]:15). The other 50 per cent was engaged in commerce, transport, light industry and domestic service. Trinidad, even at that time, enjoyed a 'higher' standard of living but its superior status could be more aptly characterised as having a lower level of poverty than the other countries mainly because of the presence of a burgeoning oil industry.

The structure of poverty and inequality of the late 1930s, and the structure of the economy then could be traced to the very foundation of the country as a colony of Britain toward the end of the eighteenth century (see Chapter 2). Following its conquest by the British from the Spaniards in 1797, Trinidad became the ideal-type plantation economy – the tropical extension of a metropolitan economy. One could portray the society of the day. Firstly, there was the superordinate segment of colonial officials representing the British Crown, in whom resided the power and authority of the British overlord, with the governor at the top of this hierarchy. Within this segment must also be included the planters and merchants who had come out in search of fortunes to be built around the establishment of sugar plantations in the new colony.

There was also a sub-segment of French settlers whose presence pre-dated the coming of the British by just a few years. Most had fled from Haiti with their slaves and had sought the refuge afforded them by the Spaniards who were then eager to increase the population. There were also other French *émigrés* from Guadeloupe, Martinique and other French dependencies for whom the reverberations of the revolution in France posed particular discomfiture and even a threat to their existence.

While there were substantial differences and initially much hostility between this group and the British overlords, and a wide divide in terms of culture and of language, they were indeed a rather solid group *vis-à-vis* the other major segment of the population – the African slaves. Most of these were French-speaking but others, new inputs into the plantation system, or imports from other British islands after the end of the slave trade, spoke an English creole. They were definitely all subordinate to whites, who technically held the power of life and death over them. There was also a small coloured group, the result of liaisons between white men and slave women. While many were free they were subjected to numerous disabilities both formally and informally and wielded little influence on the basic two-caste structure of slavery.

What is significant for present purposes is that the major productive assets of the period, land and slaves, were owned and controlled by one group, the whites. The early French settlers, joined subsequently by English settlers as overlords, had control over all the resources under private ownership. This base was to prove fundamental to their adjustment to economic changes over time. Indeed, as trite as the statement may seem, the structure of ownership and of control in the economy of Trinidad today has its base in, and still partly reflects, the influence of the foundation period at the end of the eighteenth century. The description provided by Lewis (1977 [1939]) shows how much the structure remained intact for over a century. The last 50 years might have been the period of greatest change but there are more than traces of the past in the current structure – the specifics of the change process is being examined elsewhere.

Upon emancipation in 1838, most of the Africans sought to establish themselves in communities off the plantations. The planters were faced with an immediate shortage of labour, and adopted a number of approaches to correct for this. Firstly, the colonial authorities restricted the availability of land to the emancipated Africans. While Trinidad had over one million acres of undeveloped Crown Land, immediately on emancipation in August 1838, legislation was introduced to prevent squatting and 'vagabondry' and to control petty trading. Even before the actual event but in anticipation of it, the colonial authorities had adopted the policy of restricting the alienation of Crown Lands to parcels of no less than 340 acres initially and then later raised the figure to 680 acres. In this way ex-slaves, even in large groups, were hard-put to organise the necessary financial capital, let alone to bring virgin forests on such a scale into productive use. They immediately resorted to squatting.

Another mechanism that the planters resorted to was, of course, the encouragement of immigration and they tried a number of arrangements and experiments with other Africans, including other West Indians, Americans and Europeans. But Brereton reminds us that the basic colonial strategy of 'developing a tropical colony that Europeans owned and managed while the coloured races did the manual labour' would have been corroded by any large-scale entry of Europeans, and would have undermined the notion of white hegemony associated with the caste-like structure of the society (Brereton, 1981:99). East Indian immigration was to fill the vacuum created by the shortage of labour and within a decade of the end of slavery Indian immigration had become the natural labour reservoir for the plantation system in Trinidad.

In August 1838 the planters were required by law to relinquish all claims to their erstwhile property in slaves. For this they received 'full' compensation. The slaves, on the other hand, received their freedom. Williams has captured the sentiment of the period:

No account was to be taken of the former slaves. *The metropolitan governments had emancipated them and paid compensation not to them but to their owners* (Williams, 1964:95, emphasis in original).

Their emergence out of property and the official barriers immediately erected in August 1838 to staunch access to land, the major economic resource of the period, were to have an effect that reverberates on the economic pyramid up to the present time.

With the shortage of labour that soon emerged on emancipation and with the resort to Indian indentured labour, the social and economic structure of the country was to change. The planters from then on were concerned to create an excess supply of labour by encouraging a continuing influx, whatever the situation in the sugar industry. Land was used as an enticement to induce indentees to remain in the colony on the periphery of the plantation on the completion of their indentureship, a factor of immense dimensions in the establishment of an Indian peasantry in the last century.

Over the first 50 years of colonial occupation the British created an experimental colony which was built on slave labour first and then on indentured labour. The first was characterised by total exploitation of slaves as chattel property, the second was based on the incorporation of a people suffering the ravages of colonial exploitation in their own country, and periodic famines deriving from crop failures and from landlessness. They moved from one system of exploitation and poverty in the hope that less exploitation with a more secure future awaited them in a distant land. For much of the early period hope rather than reality justified the move.

An hypothesis that is deserving of investigation with the use of the historical data is the differential access to land between African ex-slaves and Indian ex-indentees and also their differential propensities, firstly in overcoming barriers to access and secondly in retaining ownership of their land acquisitions. It is my hypothesis as well that there were intervening social and cultural factors beyond the political decision to prevent or allow access to land by the authorities, that have had an influence on the structure of land ownership today.[2]

One hundred years after slavery Trinidad and Tobago remained a highly unequal society, with race and colour being very much determinants of social status, and approximation to the caucasoid phenotype having a high association with income and wealth as had applied even before emancipation. The sociological study by Braithwaite (1975 [1953]) was the first scientific corroboration of what was the popular perception of the order of things. Of course, radical elements drawn from the trade union movement, and a small but increasingly vocal educated bourgeoisie of African ancestry, and to a more limited extent of Indian ancestry, were prepared to challenge this 'natural' order.

Power and authority in Trinidad and Tobago in 1937 resided squarely in the hands of colonial officialdom, with the governor in charge. A small 'nominated' element of the Legislative Council that shared in this power indirectly held sway, together with an influential white elite with a plantation and commercial base; later this base was extended to include the oil and asphalt sectors. All these interests determined the economic and commercial development of the country, and dictated over a majority comprised of an African and East Indian under-caste. The aggressively mobile among the Africans sought educational advancement to escape the trap of lower income and status by entry into the low orders of mainly the public service and teaching, and a few through embarking on the learned professions. The East Indians sought escape either through control over an expansive agriculture, entry into the professions or by broaching a few limited areas of commerce and distribution in the domestic economy. In the final analysis, however, the white colonial elite dictated the rules on gate keeping.

Self-government and independence

The report of the Commission appointed to investigate the causes of the riots and disturbances that started in the Caribbean in the 1930s provides a rich testimony to the decadence of the colonial period after the prosperity of sugar had vanished and the oldest and once most highly-prized of British possessions had faded into obscurity. The Commission's report (the Moyne Report) was made public after World War II and was the basis of the ameliorative measures introduced by the British government in the British West Indian colonies. One important element was the introduction of universal suffrage and the revamping of constitutions to allow for the representational principle in the running of the affairs of the old Crown Colony. The years of World War II were, to some extent, a distraction, but at its end demobilised troops returned with new ideas to add to the ferment and the discussion of nationalistic issues. The advent of suffrage in the mid-1940s meant that at last the popular will would henceforth count in the allocation of public expenditure, and attention was directed at upgrading social services like education, health and housing.

From 1956 onward the political order in Trinidad and Tobago could have been described as that of a unitary state with formal democracy and with a government observing the rule of law and abiding by the major constitutional provisions – free speech, equality of all citizens before the law, rights of individuals to private property, and to elect and to be elected as representatives of the people. In respect to its social order, it continued to be a plural society comprised of different ethnic, racial and religious groups but all sharing elements of a Trinidad and Tobago culture, enough to allow mutual understanding and relative social peace among the various groups and to permit intermarriage and other forms of voluntaristic social interaction among groups.

By 1956 when Eric Williams formed the first broadly-based political party, the country was set on course to undertake fundamental changes to its social and economic structure. The success of the new party at the polls ushered in an administration prepared to explore all the limits of an evolving constitutional status to correct some of the inequalities of the past. At the same time, it attempted to create new poles of growth through opening up the economy to foreign investment in manufacturing production, and by encouragement of the local commercial elite to copy the model of the foreign investor.

This was at centre stage of the early development strategy codified in its first 'Development Programme'. The thrust was economic expansion with light manufacturing, with distributional objectives being tackled through the opening up of educational opportunity, improvements in health and housing, as well as through the provision of jobs in the expansion of infrastructural works and in the upgrading of governmental administration.

From 1956, then, it could be argued that the people of the country started fully on the road to self-government and to the administration of their own affairs. The extent of change in inequality in income and in wealth could therefore be attributed in part to the functioning of the political process, to the commitment of government administrations since then to modify the distributional structure and to the capacity of the groups, classes and even individuals that constitute the society, to thwart the process or to help it along by dint of collective or individual efforts.

The years that preceded the oil windfall in 1973 were difficult ones for the administration. Its strategy can be broadly characterised as an attempt to perform a balancing act. On the one hand, in keeping with the adopted Puerto Rican model, interpreted for the rest of the Caribbean by Lewis (1950), the government was disposed to rely on private domestic and foreign capital to transform the economy and to create badly needed employment:

> The government cannot guarantee that all jobs needed will be created. Direct government employment is relatively small. What the government has to do is to create a framework which is favourable to investment and to try to persuade as many persons as possible, here or overseas, to create new opportunities (Government of Trinidad and Tobago, 1958:4).

While the government enjoyed large-scale support, especially from the urban masses, it recognised that a very small country could not embark on any large-scale socialist experiment, a position which created conflict with Marxian supporters like C.L.R. James, the famous socialist intellectual. But, anyway, Williams was not inclined to be another Fidel Castro.

On the other hand, the government had to address the distributional question which was a key concern to its major constituency. Lacking the resources to attempt to promote development and diversification by the entry of the state into directly productive activity, it needed to rely on the private sector. But it had to be seen to be changing the colonial inheritance of white privilege and African and Indian economic and social subordination.

The balancing act had inherent problems at the political level, well exemplified in the introduction of the Industrial Stabilisation Act in 1965 that sought to regulate industrial relations and to establish a moderating effect on wage determination in the country, a policy which immediately had it pitted against the more radical trade unions. Only a rapid rate of growth in the economy might have helped to reduce tensions and open conflict.

The rate of growth, which was encouraging for a relatively brief period in the 1950s, settled to a very slow rate of increase in the 1960s mainly because of less buoyant conditions in the export sector. The growth rate in the 1960s maintained a low average 3 per cent to 3.5 per cent for most of the period. The hoped-for jobs in manufacturing did not materialise on the scale anticipated. Export agriculture could not absorb workers and needed to shed labour to improve efficiency. The reforms in domestic agriculture (e.g., land distribution programmes) did increase capacity in chicken, pork, fruit, milk and root crop production, but not on a scale to make a dramatic change in the dependence on imported food nor to absorb a quickly growing labour force.

Meanwhile, unemployment remained high at about 14 per cent, much of this concentrated among the youth. The period of self-government and independence, and of political mobilisation for the process, prompted a rising tide of expectations and aspirations which actual economic and social changes could scarcely satisfy. Advances took place particularly in secondary and tertiary education, with a much larger number in the appropriate age cohort benefiting respectively from free secondary education (fee paying in government schools had ended by 1957) and from the establishment of a campus of the University of the West Indies (UWI) at St Augustine. Other social services were being upgraded – health, water supply, sewage, public housing, and the physical infrastructure of roads, port facilities and communications. In spite of these ameliorative factors, the poor record in job creation, the slow rate of economic growth, and the conflict in industrial relations provided a highly combustible combination. The perception of a continuing deep-seated inequality and of discrimination against people of African descent in the established commercial and banking enterprises produced the spark that led to the 'Black Power' riots of 1970 and the near toppling of the government by a mutiny within part of the Defence Force.

The perception of discrimination was validated in statistical and sociological research that was undertaken by the Institute of Social and Economic Research at the UWI. Harewood (1971), utilising the data of the 1960 census, found that when education was held constant, people of African and Indian descent earned lower incomes than persons who deemed themselves to be white. Camejo (1971) surveyed the business elite in the late 1960s and found that there was evidence to suggest serious under-representation of people of African descent and to a lesser extent of Indian descent. In another study on the returns to education, I used dummy variables to find highly significant and much larger coefficients for whites in equations that related the level of education and race to the level of income (Henry, 1974).

As a result of the Black Power disturbances, the government was forced to shift policy and committed itself to the development of a 'People's Sector' consisting of small-scale agriculture, small-scale industry, distribution and transport, small hotels and guest houses, credit unions, co-operatives and trade union enterprises. All of this was targeted at addressing

> ... the historical and sociological factors influencing the attitude of the people of African descent, and in the light of the many economic and social liabilities affecting numerous under-privileged people of Indian descent (People's National Movement, 1970:24).

While the government did undertake redistributive policies (including the reform of the tax system) and put in place a number of measures designed to improve the quality of life and standard of living of the lower income groups, there was a deep sense of resentment about perceived inequalities. The statistical evidence suggests that the perception coincided with the reality. In spite of the measures adopted by the government, inequality increased in favour of the traditional elite, some of whom, linked to the commercial sector and the new manufacturing establishment, undoubtedly benefited from the tariff and other protection accorded to domestic industry. Indirect state sponsorship was meant to provide jobs, but its impact might have done more to increase inequality than to increase employment.

Meanwhile there was already in the making a middle class who, by dint of educational performance, could accede to the widening of occupational opportunities that arose in the expansion of the public services of a newly-independent country. The increase in school places required an enlargement of the teaching body as well. The expansion of the state would have served to mute some of the tensions, and while a larger percentage of people of African descent entered the public services, it was clear that universalistic rules in hiring and in promotion were far more widely observed in the public service than elsewhere.

During this period too, a substantial number of people of East Indian ancestry embarked on commercial and manufacturing activity, usually with the collateral base that had been established in land assets. Further, family, religious and other support structures were in place to provide a solid base for launching into competitive endeavours. Thus, while many East Indians remained trapped in the poverty of seasonal employment in plantation agriculture, there was visible evidence of new contracting firms and distribution chains in food, dry goods, and building supplies that were under the control of East Indian families. Indeed, some of these areas were no longer the sole preserve of the elite of the colonial period. This partly explains the finding by Camejo (1971) that East Indians were better represented in the business elite than were people of African descent. Their internal group organisation had allowed some of them to mobilise resources and to escape past traditional gate keepers, whether these were the white-dominated banks, or the commercial houses involved in large-scale importation. That base and example were to stand them in good stead in the time of plenty, which came with the rise in oil prices partly occasioned by the Arab-Israeli conflict of the early 1970s.

The oil windfall

The change in the fortunes of Trinidad and Tobago over the last two decades could only be described as dramatic. A rapid increase in income for almost ten years has been followed by a precipitous decline thereafter with the rate of decline tapering off and probably finally being arrested in 1990. The period witnessed changes in the direct role of the state sector in the productive process. There were also changes in the ethnic segmentation of parts of the labour market, in growth rates among sectors and in fiscal redistributive measures. In the much enlarged mixed economy of the late 1970s and early 1980s, one could also analyse the degree of change or persistence of gate keeping institutions determining income flows in the form of wages, salaries, fees, profits, rents, dividends and transfers. In this chapter I shall only touch on some of these.

Trinidad and Tobago had an oil-based economy long before the price of oil increased in 1973. Oil provides much of the government's revenue, most of the foreign exchange earnings and is a substantial share of Gross Domestic Product (GDP). Obviously then, a small country with a population of just more than a million people and blessed with oil and natural gas supplies much in excess of its domestic requirements, would benefit immensely from the economic rents that emanated from the initial quadrupling of the price of oil in the wake of the oil crisis of 1973. Over the period 1973 to 1982, GDP at constant prices increased by 58 per cent – a most respectable rate of growth by any standard – and the country approached the upper levels of the World Bank's list of middle-income countries, simply because of the buoyant oil market.

This high rate of growth in the economy afforded the government of Trinidad and Tobago an enormous increase in its revenues and, with this, the opportunity to address a number of problems which fiscal stringency could not previously accommodate. One such problem was the distributional goal. Not only did it increase social expenditures, but in its attempts at quickening the pace of economic diversification by modernising and expanding the physical infrastructure, it created a large number of jobs directly and indirectly. New forms of social expenditures emerged and pre-existent forms received increased real allocations. Old age pensions and social welfare assistance were systematically increased. Free public transport to the elderly was introduced, as well as a free school bus service in many areas of the country. A school meals service was also introduced, along with a school book grant for primary and secondary school children.

At the same time as this widening of subsidies took place, employment was increasing, led in particular by the construction industry which attracted almost one-quarter of the labour force. The expansion of port facilities and other infrastructure (e.g., roads and highways), the building of secondary schools, of hospitals, and other major public buildings, the establishment of new housing in the public and private sectors, and the construction of a number of mega-projects in keeping with the government's plan to diversify the economy by going downstream of oil, all put enormous pressure on the labour power resources of the country and led to a rapid increase in wage compensation. Indeed, wage rates in construction led the way in general wage increases. At the same time, unemployment fell to under 10 per cent and there were clear signs of 'Dutch Disease' effects, especially on domestic agriculture as output from the sector became uncompetitive with imports (Hilaire, 1989). The real standard of living of workers improved immensely and approximated to that of a developed country, including the pattern of expenditure, such that high-income durables like private automobiles became part of wage goods (Henry and Melville, 1989).

While the hard evidence is not yet available it can be hypothesised that, as direct employment by the state grew, the greater observance by the state of universalistic criteria in the hiring of workers would have made the public service less segmented in ethnic terms than other sectors. Ryan (1991) has provided some data that show that East Indians, who traditionally were not well represented in the public service, have improved their share at this level. Moreover, in an expanding economy, even private employers that display preferences in hiring from one or other ethnic group would have been forced to look outside the preferred group as shortages developed in some areas of the labour market.

The relative absence of Africans in the ownership and control of private business, and especially of large and medium-sized operations, meant that they were the one group that did not have 'discretion' in observing ethnic selection rules in hiring for the private sector.[3] On the other hand, the growth of a state enterprise sector, and the propensity of this sector to rely heavily on public servants transferred from the public services, would have allowed a relatively larger percentage of people of African descent to enter the competitive environment than was the case in the higher echelons of the private sector. There are, unfortunately, no known studies of this period that have sought to replicate the effort of Camejo (1971) on the experience of the late-1960s.

The growth in the economy would have opened up some opportunities that were under the control of traditional gate keepers, e.g. access to credit, to distributorships, to the prime real estate market, etc. In other words, a much larger group and a mixed group could have earned incomes by way of fees, profits, rents and dividends. On the other hand, in an economy where monopoly and oligopoly control has been dominant in much of the private sector, the previously-established firms would have had a major head-start in seizing opportunities offered by a boom. Williams (1979), prime minister at that time, was sensitive to the fact that his efforts to democratise the private sector through the creation of a 'People's Sector' had not been a resounding success: the traditional businesses had become conglomerates and, as the 'local sharks', they were consuming the 'local sardines'.

The oil price fall

From 1983 the economy of Trinidad and Tobago went into decline as immediately as the price of oil fell. By 1988 GDP per capita in constant dollars had declined by 36 per cent on the level achieved in 1982. The revenue base of the government was seriously eroded and it was forced into shifting its base, and adjusting or cutting subsidies to restore some degree of balance between revenue and expenditure. The price of oil plummeted further in 1986 and confidence in the party that had been in power for 30 years collapsed and with that a new party was ushered into power in the general elections at the end of 1986.

The new administration had little initial success in arresting the decline and its popularity and cohesion suffered immensely as it was forced into taking unpopular decisions to arrest the slide. It shifted the tax base to indirect taxes, cut salaries of public servants, froze posts, eliminated some subsidies, imposed user charges on some of the utilities, privatised some state enterprises and shut down a few others.

While only preliminary estimates of inequality are available, it seems that by 1988 the Gini index had approached 0.5. Unemployment can be used as a proxy for what happened in the economy. The unemployment rate, which stood at 9.9 per cent in 1982, rose very quickly to 15.6 per cent in 1985 and climbed even further to 22.4 per cent by 1989. Even in the difficult years of the late-1960s and early-1970s, the unemployment rate never reached this level.

The decline in incomes set off immediate tensions and open conflicts in industrial relations. Some splintering at the political level also took place against a background of charges of racial and ethnic discrimination. Whatever might be the bases for these conflicts, perceived and/or real, there is every reason to hypothesise that the process of downward adjustment would not retrace the path followed when average incomes were rising, an eventuality that tends to be ignored in the discussion of the 'Inverted U'. Furthermore, the rules followed by the various gate keepers could further exacerbate inequality among groups, given the original tendency to segmentation of economic participation.

While the data do not exist as yet to validate various hypotheses on composite causes and effects, it is still useful to explore a few probable outcomes. In the first place, the cutback on employment in the public sector has been broadly based and therefore would have impacted on all workers. To the extent that the state observes universalistic criteria, all groups that depend on employment from the state sector will be hurt 'equitably'. Likewise, the reduction in salaries that had been imposed on all public servants would have had a general impact on all groups. In other words, inter-group equity within the public services would not have been influenced by public service pay cuts and by reduction in employment, even though the net effect can be inequitable in the total context.

On the other hand, since in the private sector there is less of a commitment to the observance of equity among groups in hiring and firing, a decline in incomes in this sector might not have been as equitable in its inter-group effects as applied in the public service. Incomes earned from profits, rents and dividends – the rewards to capital – would have declined for most of those who derive their income from this source. There have been bankruptcies, liquidations and giant take-overs. Here again one can identify the impact of gate keepers: their effort as creditors or otherwise in the system is not to democratise ownership and control but rather to strengthen the viable and weed out the unviable in the throes of an economic decline. Groups that were relatively under-represented in business are likely to find the going rougher. The conflict within capital is more likely to take on the appearance of a 'clash of the giants' as oligopolies battle for market space. If anything this creates a tendency towards greater concentration of capital and there is even less space for dwarfs, with consequential implications for the distribution of business income among groups.

There is another development that seems to emerge during recessionary times that runs counter to the disequalising tendency of capital concentration just noted. The collapse of paid employment sends many workers to the breadline. Some enter the informal sector where the harsh facts of life often generate entrepreneurship in what are seen to be the most unlikely of places. Girvan (1988) has referred to the aggressive hard-nosed business acumen of the higglers of Jamaica. A similar phenomenon could indeed be emerging in Trinidad and Tobago with new entrepreneurs, many of them of African ancestry, embarked on ventures which in time could challenge the old centres of business power. In other words, they may operate in ways to escape traditional gate keepers, bending rules on foreign exchange and customs procedures, and even breaking established laws in the process. If they are prepared to flout the rules of the state and the Central Bank, in respect of foreign exchange etc., they are not likely to be any more reverential to monopolists as licensed sole distributors, etc. In the Guyanese case they have created an underground economy that has bypassed much of the formal economy with the established players. It is too early to make any pronouncement on their efficiency in democratising ownership and control in the Trinidad and Tobago case. The new informal business entrepreneurs would have to be assessed against the beneficiaries of new state-directed programmes like the Small Business Development

Company that has been set up by the government to encourage new entrepreneurs.

Measured inequality

In Table 3.1, I present data on measured inequality with the use of the Gini Coefficient calculated for the *Household Budgetary Surveys* conducted since 1957-58. While the latest survey (the *Household Budgetary Survey 1988*) has been analysed, the Gini Coefficient has not been made public as yet but there are preliminary estimates suggesting that it might have increased for the country as a whole (Henry, Nicholls and Melville, forthcoming).

Table 3.1:   Gini Ratios, Trinidad and Tobago 1957/58 – 1981/82

Race	1957/58	1971/72	1975/76	1981/82
Black	n.a.	0.48	0.44	0.47
Indian	n.a.	0.49	0.46	0.43
Other	n.a.	0.56	0.47	0.48
Overall	0.43	0.51	0.46	0.45

Source: Henry (1989:Table 3).
n.a. = not available

Table 3.1 shows that inequality as measured by the Gini index increased between 1957/58 and 1971/72, fell by 1975/76, but showed only a marginal change by 1981/82. Over the period 1975/76 to 1981/82, Trinidad and Tobago enjoyed one of its fastest rates of growth because of the oil price increases. In other words, the fall in the Gini ratio over the period 1975/76 to 1981/82 was somewhat disappointing. On the other hand, when one examines disparity ratios, important changes took place between the two major ethnic groups in the country in spite of what appears to have been a marginal decline in inequality and this is reflected in Table 3.2.

The data show that the Indian community was a major beneficiary of the boom period and that the mix of socio-political and economic factors had brought about a convergence in the level of incomes of blacks and Indians in contradiction of prognostications drawn from earlier analyses (Dookeran, 1985 [1974]). All groups shared in the wealth, but relative to their earlier position, the East Indian community made the greatest advance in correcting any negative status they had

Table 3.2: Disparity ratios, Trinidad and Tobago 1971/72 to 1981/82.

Year	Black/Indian	Other/Indian
1971/72	1.16	1.84
1975/76	0.91	1.39
1981/82	1.00	1.21

Source: Henry (1989: Table 4).

vis-à-vis other groups. What is also interesting is that this improvement in the relative distribution and in the equality between Indians and Africans was achieved with a consistent decline in inequality within the Indian community, which suggests that the lowest income groups among the Indian community benefited considerably in the economic changes that took place in the 1970s and early 1980s.

Table 3.3: Distribution of the population by ethnic origin and religion, 1960-80.

Characteristics	Census Data		
	1960	1970	1980
I. Ethnic origin			
African	43.3	42.8	41.0
Indian	36.5	40.1	40.8
European	1.9	1.2	0.9
Mixed	16.3	14.2	16.4
Other	2.0	1.7	0.9
II. Religion			
Roman Catholic	36.2	35.7	32.9
Anglican	21.1	18.1	14.7
Presbyterian	3.9	4.2	3.8
Methodist	2.2	1.7	1.4
Seventh-Day Adventist	1.5	1.8	2.5
Hindu	23.0	24.7	24.9
Muslim	6.0	6.3	6.0
Other	5.5	7.6	11.7
None and not stated	0.5		2.0

Source: Abdulah (1988: Table 4).

Table 3.3 gives the ethnic origin and religious affiliation of the population for census years 1960, 1970 and 1980. We see there that the African and Indian populations were in relative parity in 1980 and together constituted over 80 per cent of the population. Europeans were a very small minority, just under one per cent in 1980, but were recognised as socially and economically more significant than their numbers would suggest.

With a population so composed and with government observing formal democratic institutions, it could be argued that the distributional conflicts would have been contained and would have abated since all groups in the society, including the most dispossessed, experienced some improvement in their real standard of living, either directly, through the growth in employment, and/or through the wide array of subsidies and transfers. Once all incomes are growing there would be less social and political concern over the share of the cake.

The achievement of relative parity between the two major groups by 1981/82 suggests that the growth in the economy, and the nature of political and social processes, allowed equalising factors to operate positively in the economy. If the preliminary data suggesting an increase in inequality since then are indeed corroborated, it is not unlikely that this would have resulted in some changes in the parities, possibly at the expense of the African element in a segment of society that is more solidly dependent on wage employment. The major problem here relates to those who occupied the middle and upper-income brackets in this ethnic group. They would have less latitude as a group than the middle and elite elements in other groups given that their incomes would have derived more from salaried income. Here we have both contradictions and convergences of caste and class impacting on distribution, a factor anticipated by Hall (1977) and by Harewood and Henry (1985). The less secure base of the elite of African ancestry had prompted the speculation in the early 1980s that any recession in the fortunes of the oil economy would have devastated this group.

> While this entire group became an elite parallel to the traditional elite in terms of lifestyle and income, their relationship to the means of production was still discretely different and their condition was more directly tied to the resources of the state sector (Harewood and Henry, 1985:74).

Meanwhile the lower orders of society, composed of people of African and Indian ancestry, have all suffered equally from the substantial fall in gross output over the period. Preliminary evidence suggests that, at the lower levels, Africans and Indians may be sharing equitably in the poverty that has afflicted the society. There may, however, be substantial differences in the way the downturn has impacted on their respective elites.

Conclusion

This chapter has sought a preliminary evaluation of the factors that have contributed to the evolution of inequality in Trinidad and Tobago. I have argued the need to examine the dynamics of change in the social and political processes of society and not only against the background of the changes in the economic structure. As a plural society, the country has been relatively successful in moderating tensions and conflicts over ethnic distribution. On the one hand, all groups are being exposed to homogenising forces in their cultures, and rules of ethnic endogamy are increasingly difficult for any group so disposed to observe. Intermarriage is creating an increasingly mixed population. On the other hand, ethnic economic segmentation can be used as a mobilising force to exacerbate ethnic tensions and rivalries. Continuing success in maintaining relative peace is not guaranteed. But it is the task of researchers to map out the realities as distinct from the perceptions, so that policymakers could avoid paths that would sharpen divisions. Better information and analysis would allow them instead to keep society on track to dissolving the link between initial status of ancestors as slave, indentee and planter with their position on the economic and social pyramid today. Social equity in a post-colonial society is essentially about correcting the effects of history at the same time as one mobilises for growth and transformation of the economy.

Acknowledgements

The helpful comments of Lou Anne Barclay on an earlier draft are hereby acknowledged. The author remains responsible for all remaining errors.

Notes

1   The population of Trinidad reflects a higher degree of ethnic and cultural pluralism than Tobago. Only 4 per cent of the population of 1.23 million was resident in Tobago at the last census in 1990. Tobago, however, is far more homogeneous, with the population being mainly of African ancestry. For present purposes, we shall use the nation state of Trinidad and Tobago.

2   One important factor here is the fact that in spite of caste and religious differences among the East Indians, their common and distinctive culture and the absence of solidarity with the other major exploited group provided the base for intra-group solidarity. The East Indian National Congress was the visible formal vehicle of mobilisation. The clear group position on land acquisition was asserted by F.E.M. Hosein in an address to the Congress on 5 May 1913, when he argued that with a higher birth rate and the rapid increase in land acquisition, East Indians would 'drive out' the other races from Trinidad (Tikasingh, 1982).

3   There is evidence that some of the larger firms which derive their base from the elite of the colonial period, having converted themselves to public companies, have been less particularistic in their hiring and aggressively seek talent and skills wherever these exist, irrespective of race and ethnicity. The old and new, large and medium-sized private companies are another matter.

References

Abdulah, N., 1988, 'Structure of the Population: Demographic Developments in the Independence Years', in Ryan, S. (ed.), *Trinidad and Tobago: The Independence Experience 1962-1987*, St Augustine: Institute of Social and Economic Research, University of the West Indies, pp. 437-69.

Becker, G., 1971, *The Economics of Discrimination*, 2nd. ed., Chicago: University of Chicago Press.

Best, L., 1968, 'A Model of Pure Plantation Economy', *Social and Economic Studies*, Vol. 17, No. 3, pp. 283-326.

Best, L. and Levitt, K., 1968, 'Externally Propelled Industrialization and Growth in the Caribbean', Montreal: McGill University, Centre for Developing Area Studies (mimeo).

Braithwaite, L., 1975 (1953), *Social Stratification in Trinidad*, Mona: Institute of Social and Economic Research, University of the West Indies.

Brereton, B., 1981, *A History of Modern Trinidad 1783-1962*, London: Heinemann.

Camejo, A., 1971, 'Racial Discrimination in Employment in the Private Sector in Trinidad and Tobago: A Study of the Business Elite and the Social Structure', *Social and Economic Studies*, Vol. 20, No. 3, pp. 294-318.

Dookeran, W., 1985 [1974], 'East Indians and the Economy of Trinidad and Tobago', in LaGuerre, J. (ed.), *Calcutta to Caroni: The East Indians in Trinidad*, 2nd. ed. St Augustine: Extra-Mural Unit, University of the West Indies, pp. 63-73.

Girvan, N., 1988, 'C.Y. Thomas and the Poor and the Powerless', *Social and Economic Studies*, Vol. 37, No. 4.

Government of Trinidad and Tobago, 1958, *Five Year Development Programme*, Port of Spain: Government Printery.

Hall, S., 1977, 'Pluralism, Race and Class in Caribbean Society', in *Race and Class in Post-Colonial Society: A Study of Ethnic Group Relations in the English-Speaking Caribbean, Bolivia, Chile and Mexico*, Paris: UNESCO.

Harewood, J., 1971, 'Racial Discrimination in Employment in Trinidad and Tobago', *Social and Economic Studies*, Vol. 20, No. 3, pp. 267-93.

Harewood, J. and Henry, R., 1985, *Inequality in a Post-Colonial Society: Trinidad and Tobago 1956-1981*, St Augustine: Institute of Social and Economic Research, University of the West Indies.

Henry, R.M., 1974, 'Earnings and Education in Trinidad and Tobago: Some Evidence for 1970', *Central Statistical Office Research Papers*, No. 7, Port of Spain: Central Statistical Office.

– 1989, 'Inequality in Plural Socieities: An Exploration', *Social and Economic Studies*, Vol. 38, No. 2, pp. 69-110.

– 1991, 'In Search of Equity: The Plural Society Problem', St Augustine: University of the West Indies, Department of Economics, mimeo.

Henry, R.M. and Melville, J.A., 1989, 'Private Automobiles and the Boom in Trinidad and Tobago: Positional Goods or Wage Goods?', St Augustine: University of the West Indies, Department of Economics, mimeo.

– forthcoming, 'Poverty Revisited: Trinidad and Tobago in the late 1980s', St Augustine: University of the West Indies, Department of Economics.

Henry, R.M., Nicholls, S. and Melville, J.A., forthcoming, 'Inequality: Its Fall and Rise in Trinidad and Tobago', St Augustine: University of the West Indies, Department of Economics.

Hilaire, A.D.L., 1989, 'The Effects of Trinidad and Tobago's Oil Boom on Relative Prices, Wages and Labour Flows', a paper presented to the Trinidad and Tobago Economics Association General Meeting, May 1989.

Hutt, W.H., 1964, *The Economics of the Colour Bar: A Study of the Economic Origin and Consequences of Racial Segregation in South Africa*, London: Andre Deutsch.

Kuznets, S., 1955, 'Economic Growth and Income Inequality', *American Economic Review*, Vol. 45.

Lewis, W.A., 1977 (1939), *Labour in the West Indies: The Birth of a Workers' Movement*, London: New Beacon Books.

– 1950, 'Industrialisation of the British West Indies', *Caribbean Economic Review*, Vol. 2, No. 1, pp. 1-61.

Marshall, W., 1968, 'Notes on Peasant Development in the West Indies Since 1838', *Social and Economic Studies*, Vol. 17, No. 3.

Nabli, M.K., and Nugent, J., 1989, 'The New Institutional Economics and its Applicability to Development', *World Development*, Vol 17, No. 9.

Paukert, Felix, 1973, 'Income Distribution at Different Levels of Development: A Survey of Evidence', *International Labour Review*, Vol. 108, August-September.

People's National Movement, 1970, *The People's Charter Revised*, Port of Spain: P.N.M. Publishing Company.

Roback, J., 1988, 'W.H. Hutt's *The Economics of the Colour Bar*', *Managerial and Decision Economics*, Winter, 1988.

Ryan, S., 1991, 'Social Stratification in Trinidad and Tobago: Lloyd Braithwaite Revisted', in Ryan, S. (ed.), *Social and Occupational Stratification in Contemporary Trinidad and Tobago*, St Augustine: Institute of Social and Economic Research, University of the West Indies, pp. 58-82.

Smith, M.G., 1965, *The Plural Society in the British West Indies*, Berkeley: University of California Press.

Stewart, F., 1983, 'Inequality, Technology and Payments Systems', in Stewart, F. (ed.), *Work, Income and Inequality: Payments Systems in the Third World*, London: Macmillan.

Tikasingh, G., 1982, 'Toward a Formulation of the Indian View of History: The Representation of Indian Opinion in Trinidad, 1900-1921', in Brereton, B. and Dookeran, W. (eds), *East Indians in the Caribbean: Colonialism and the Struggle for Identity*, New York: Krauss.

West India Royal Commission, 1945, *Report of the West India Royal Commission* (Moyne Report), London: HMSO.

Williams, E., 1964, *History of the People of Trinidad and Tobago*, London: Andre Deutsch.

– 1979, 'Address at Formal Opening of Small Business Consultation', organised by the Industrial Development Corporation, Port of Spain.

Wood, D., 1968, *Trinidad in Transition: The Years after Slavery*, London: Oxford University Press.

CHAPTER 4

'Race' and 'colour' in pre-independence Trinidad and Tobago

Daniel A. Segal

> Americans ... tend to accord race a transhistorical, almost
> metaphysical, status ... The first false move in this direction
> is the easiest: the assumption that race is an observable fact
> .... Barbara Fields (1982:144)

Introduction

Racial categories and identities have increasingly been analysed as
socially constructed, or historically invented, phenomenon. This
approach holds that there is no inherent affinity between people sharing
a common racial identity; rather, racial identities are seen as historical
products which shape social affinities and antipathies, and thereby
precipitate various social groupings and boundaries. Such groupings
are fundamentally contingent, though this is precisely what is obscured
when they are called 'races', for these denominations represent
historically contingent groupings as facts given to us by an objective
reality.[1] The discourse of race is thus a regulating discourse: it both
organises social relations and disciplines our understanding of them.

The social constructionist view adopted here departs from much
of the social scientific and historical literature on the Caribbean. For
the most part, accounts of Caribbean societies describe the interaction
of transhistorical, collective selves – the existence of which are taken
as a given. Thus, for example, studies of Trinidad often assume the
existence of 'whites' 'East Indians', and 'Afro-Trinidadians' and
describe these as collective individuals, composed of numerically definite
populations, which occupy particular social strata and compete for
political power and economic resources. One indication of the
inadequacy of this approach is that at any moment in Trinidadian
history one finds persons who – on a variety of criteria – do not fit neatly
within the boundaries of these groupings. This chapter explores
this and other such indications below. What is important to observe
initially is that approaches which take races to be transhistorical actors

reproduce, rather than work through, the most fundamental premise of post-Columbian racism – specifically, that races have a reality independent of human invention.

By contrast, the social constructionist approach takes the existence of racial groupings as something to be explained and interrogated. In part, this involves the study of the historical emergence and ongoing reproduction of racial groupings in particular social contexts (Dominguez, 1986; Fields, 1982; Segal, 1991). And in part it involves the study of racial idioms as systems of representation, that is, as semiotic systems which presuppose and affirm regulating typifications or stereotypes. Such a semiotic study in turn makes possible a study of the social pragmatics of racial idioms, that is, a study of what racial distinctions do to society and what people purposefully do with them.[2] The primary purpose of this chapter is to study the semiotics of 'race' and 'colour' terms in Trinidad during the half century or so prior to 1962.[3] Beyond this, the chapter suggests some avenues for the study of the social pragmatics of 'race' and 'colour' in this period of Trinidadian history.

The 'races' of pre-independence society

As we have seen in earlier chapters, in pre-independence Trinidad the history of conquest and colonisation was understood to have virtually eliminated the indigenous population, and to have populated the island with three distinct, immigrant 'races' – 'Europeans', 'Africans' and 'East Indians'. As all three denominations indicate, these 'races' were identified in terms of an ancestral territory, that is, a delimited area belonging to and occupied by its own 'race'. Trinidad's 'Europeans', 'Africans' and 'East Indians' were therefore associated with other lands from which they were said to have 'originated'. We should note, however, that in the case of 'East Indians' the connection with an ancestral territory was modified: though they had come from 'India' their ancestral land received the added specification of being of 'the East'.

Two of these three races – the 'European' and 'African' – were also denominated by colour terms, specifically the binary opposition of 'white' and 'black'. There was, however, no conventional colour correspondence for 'East Indians', which is not to say such persons were without pigmentation.[4] Finally, for 'Africans' or 'blacks' we find yet a third referential synonym, 'Negroes', a term of phylogeny. In sum, we have an asymmetrical set of eight terms used referentially for three distinct 'racial' kinds.[5]

There were, in addition, other 'races' – also from other lands –

which, as they were counted, were less significant components of Trinidad's twentieth-century population. These included the 'Portuguese', the 'Chinese', and the 'Syrian', all of which were distinguished from 'whites', 'blacks' and 'East Indians'. 'Race' – variously represented in terms of ancestral lands, colour, and phylogeny – was, among other things, an inherited property that was passed on by both parents. A person was racially 'pure' only if both parents were of the same 'race'. A person born to parents of different 'races' was 'mixed', and was regarded as being outside of the 'racial group' of both parents. Trinidad's 'races' were thought to have lived in geographic isolation in their ancestral territories prior to their emigration, and to have 'mixed' – a term which denoted the production of offspring by parents of different 'races' – only after their arrival in the Caribbean. Indeed, the 'mixing' of disparate 'races' was identified as being emblematic of both Trinidad and, more generally, the West Indies. As Crowley observed:

> [In Trinidad,] a number of individuals know of six or more racial ... strains in their ancestry ... Such people are proud of their mixed origins, and boast that they are 'a real mix-up,' or 'a West Indian callallu' (a crab stew with many other ingredients mixed by a swizzle stick ...) (Crowley, 1957:819-20).

Here the use of a dialect word which must be explained to a non-Trinidadian audience emphasises the symbolic local-ness of being 'mixed'. 'Pure races', by contrast, were what had arrived in Trinidad from other places.

An important dimension of the meaning of racial distinctions can be unpacked by examining the distinctively Caribbean contrast between 'white' and 'Portuguese'.[6] In Trinidad, 'the Portuguese' were 'identified as dirty shopkeepers' (Braithwaite, 1975 [1953]:44; see also Mendes, 1980 [1934]:*passim;* Williams, 1971 [1969]:18; Ryan, 1972:19). The stigma of 'the Portuguese' was not dark pigmentation, but sufficiently unclean economic behaviour – shopkeeping – as to render them 'dirty' – that is, un-white. In short, the contrast between 'whites' and 'Portuguese' inscribed a distinction of the colonial political economy.

Yet, though class positions were both imaged and ascribed in terms of 'race', racial distinctions were only roughly coincident with class distinctions: not all 'Portuguese' were shopkeepers and not all shopkeepers were deemed 'Portuguese'. Racial categories were not so pliable as to be determined by the political-economic order, nor so determining as to be the sole basis of a person's class position. Indeed, had either been the case, the idiom of race would have been semiotically empty: rather than representing and configuring the political economy, it would simply have mirrored the political economy. Contrary to such a view, the set of racial categories was shaped both by their use in reference to class positions and by significations of race that were independent of class.[7]

In particular, the belief that each race entered as a 'pure' kind meant that each race was thought to possess a singular point of entry into colonial society. The category 'white' included three 'nationalities' – 'the French', 'the Spanish', and 'the British'[8] – and each of these was understood as having entered colonial Trinidad as 'masters' and 'rulers'. 'The Portuguese', by contrast, were understood as having entered colonial society as dependent labourers who quickly and successfully entered into small trade. The distinction between 'white' and 'Portuguese' thus gave each grouping an emblematic history, one defined by a singular point of entry into the colonial social order. Indeed, each of Trinidad's 'races' was conceived of as having a distinct beginning in the colonial order. To be 'white' was to have been a 'master'; to be 'black' was to have been a 'slave'; to be 'East Indian' was to have been an 'indentured labourer'; and to be 'Portuguese' was to have been a dependent labourer with a propensity for profitable trading. In sum, the idiom of 'race' memorialised particular pasts and connected those pasts to contemporary social groupings (cf. Alexander, 1977:431; 1984:77).

Racial accounting

The lexicon of 'race' was not, however, limited to a list of 'pure races'. Rather, the concept of 'pure races' served as the foundation for an elaborate vocabulary of 'mixing', which, in turn, figured and memorialised interactions among 'races' in the West Indies. Given the socially constructed presence of three main 'races' ('Africans', 'Europeans' and 'East Indians'), it follows that there were six possible types of sexual unions:

    (i) 'African'-'European';
   (ii) 'African'-'East Indian';
  (iii) 'European'-'East Indian';
  (iv) 'African'-'African';
   (v) 'European'-'European';
  (vi) 'East Indian'-'East Indian'.

As previously mentioned, offspring from unions of the last three types were identified as 'pure' and as members of a particular 'race'. By contrast, offspring from unions of the first three types were 'mixed'. Yet, while 'mixed' persons were not of any one 'race', they were none the less identifiable in racial terms, either with an idiom of genealogy ('his father is white, his mother East Indian') or an idiom of fractions ('he half white and half black'). Thus, though 'mixing' combined 'races' it did not alter, eliminate or create them. Or to put the matter slightly differently, races were figured as immutable elements (cf., Alexander, 1977). Indeed, racial elements could be accounted for regardless of the degree of 'mixing'. The offspring of, say, a 'half white, half Negro' and a 'half East Indian, half white' could be identified as 'half white, one fourth Negro, and one fourth East Indian'. And the same 'mixture' could be expressed genealogically by specifying the 'races' of the four grandparents. In either terms, however, 'mixing' was traced until all racial elements were accounted for.

These rules for classifying 'mixed' persons were formal and unambiguous. To know a person's racial genealogy, or their racial composition, was to know something 'factual'. There were still other ways of representing 'mixing', but racial accounting was the foundation of social truth upon which Trinidad's discourse of 'mixing' rested.

Within the idiom of racial accounting, 'mixing' quickly gave rise to a plethora of racially distinguishable 'kinds'. After one generation there were, as we have seen, six permutations, after two generations

Table 4.1:   Racial accounting in Trinidad.

'Pure races'	white
	Negro
	East Indian
'Mixed' offspring of first generation	½ Negro – ½ East Indian
	½ white – ½ East Indian
	½ white – ½ Negro
'Mixed' offspring of second generation	¼ Negro – ¾ East Indian
	¼ Negro – ¾ white
	¼ Negro – ¼ East Indian – ½ white
	¼ Negro – ½ East Indian – ¼ white
	½ Negro – ¼ East Indian – ½ white
	¾ Negro – ½ East Indian
	¾ Negro – ½ white
	¼ East Indian – ¾ white
	¾ East Indian – ¼ white

Fifteen possible permutations in the system of racial accounting from two generations of unions between Trinidad's three major 'races'.

the number increased to fifteen, nine of which were 'mixed' kinds that needed to be specified in terms of 'fourths' (see Table 4.1). Such genealogical detail was, however, employed in few interactional contexts in pre-independence Trinidad.[9] Rather, a person's racial composition was conventionally identified through a more condensed set of colour terms, a set which encoded myriad meanings – notably distinctions between local and foreign identities, and distinctions of status.

The origins of 'coloured' people

All persons with a 'mixture' of European and African ancestors could be designated 'coloured' (Braithwaite, 1975 [1953]:87). This included not only the offspring from 'black'-'white' unions, but also the offspring of unions between a 'coloured' person and either a 'black', a 'white', or another 'coloured' person. In effect, these principles of descent implicitly recorded the aggregate extent of all white-black 'mixing', for they constituted a category of persons with any degree of white-black 'mixing' in contrast to persons who were 'pure black' or 'pure white'.

Unlike the pure 'races', the 'coloured' population was understood to have been produced in the 'West Indies'. Specifically, it was said to have 'stemmed from the miscegenation of some of the landowners and certain of the slave women to whom they were attracted' (Wooding, 1960:145; see also Braithwaite, 1975 [1953]:86-7; Powrie, 1956:224). This 'mixing' was thought to have produced not simply a 'coloured' population, but more complexly, a 'coloured middle class': 'a new and recognisable social group had been established. The mixed or coloured population filled, without truly bridging, the social gap between the upper and lower class' (Powrie, 1956:224).

This highly conventionalised tale of the origins of 'the coloured middle class' located natural male desire and dominance as the cause of 'mixing', and memorialised this 'mixing' as the beginning of a distinctively West Indian social order. In this origin tale, colour and status were imaged as neatly coincident. Indeed, terms of status were rendered equivalents of terms of race – and vice-versa: the 'coloured population' was said to be 'between the upper and lower class' (see also Braithwaite, 1975 [1953]:*passim*). This telling of history thus imbued each 'race' with a singular status and hierarchical value. In addition, it affirmed that the 'mixed' children of 'African' mothers could be recognised, that is, that they could be distinguished from children with two 'African' parents. Genealogy was, in short, assumed to have an observable concomitant in bodily appearance. Terms of bodily appearance ('white', 'coloured' or 'black') were thus made symbols of the knowable, but not always known, 'facts' of racial ancestry.[10]

The Creole scale of 'colour'

Whereas the category 'coloured' included all persons with a mixture of 'white' and 'black' ancestors, particular 'colour' terms ('white', 'red', 'brown', 'light black', 'black', 'black-black') identified the relative proportion of 'black' and 'white' in a person's make-up. A person's 'colour' or 'shade' was not, however, reducible to their pigmentation; rather:

> skin-colour, hair and facial characteristics (the straight nose, the thick lip) are used [to form] an over-all composite judgment of the individual .... Hence arises the extreme concern over the quality of the hair, the possession of 'good hair' being universally desired ...

Understood as this complex constellation of bodily features, 'colour' was a finely graded continuum ordered hierarchically by the valorisation of the 'European' ('white') over the 'African' ('black'):

> ... By 'good' hair is not meant the aesthetically pleasing; or rather the aesthetically pleasing is identified as the 'straight hair' of the European .... The closer the approximation to European features the more likely is the individual ... both to get acceptance ... and to achieve mobility (Braithwaite, 1975 [1953]:91-2).

Thus, in addition to being a category of all persons with 'white' and 'black' ancestors, 'colour' was a scale with a continuous range of values, defined by the endpoints of 'black' and 'white'.[11]

That 'white' and 'black' were connected, as well as opposed, was also revealed by the use of the term 'Creole' – a word meaning 'local' or 'West Indian' (Crowley, 1957; Brereton, 1979: 2-3). Used as a noun, 'Creole' standardly referred to persons; as an adjective it was used commonly to describe persons, foods, language, dress, and culture. For a person to be 'a Creole', it was necessary that she or he be either 'coloured' or one of the 'racial' constituents of the 'coloured' population – that is, either 'black' or 'white'. The term was applied to all 'blacks' and 'coloureds', but only to a segment of the 'whites', distinguishing 'local whites' from 'expatriates' on assignment in Trinidad.[12] It was within this set of 'Creoles', extending continuously from 'local whites' to 'blacks', that persons were distinguished by 'colour' or 'shade'.

In Trinidad 'local whites' were identified not only as 'Creole whites', but more specifically, as 'French Creoles'. While the term encoded the distinction between 'French' plantation owners and 'British' governmental administrators, its referential use was not confined to persons of 'French' descent. Rather, the term was applicable to any 'white' who was truly 'local', regardless of 'nationality'. For example, in 1985, a 'whitish' man born in the 1920s told me that 'the McClellans' were one of the most prominent 'French Creole families' in the Trinidad of his youth.[13]

Yet despite its broad referential use, the term 'French Creole' retained the connotations suggested by a 'French'/'British' distinction: 'French Creoles' were regarded as 'warmer' than the 'cold British'. Indeed, Lowenthal reports that this was a matter of pride for 'Creoles', who

> like to consider themselves French in temperament – volatile, imaginative, fun-loving, artistic, generous – by contrast with the more decorous, phlegmatic, dowdy English . . . (1961:88)

It is significant that we find a similar contrast between the 'volatile' and 'decorous' in comparisons of 'Africans' and 'Europeans', though with the valuation of the adjectives reversed.[14] Thus, through the term 'French Creoles,' 'local whites' were represented as being unlike 'the British' in the same way that 'Africans' were represented as being unlike 'whites' in general. In short, these terms established an analogic series in which 'local whites' and 'Africans' were paradigmatic substitutes, and thus, implicitly, were likened and linked to each other:

$$\frac{\text{local whites}}{\text{expatriate whites}} \quad : \quad \frac{\text{French Creoles}}{\text{the British}} \quad : \quad \frac{\text{Africans}}{\text{whites}}$$

The connection between 'local whites' and 'non-white Creoles' was indicated as well by a pair of additional terms of racial classification: 'Trinidad white' and the more derogatory 'so-called white'. As represented by these figures of speech, the 'whites' of Trinidad were not 'white Trinidadians', but a marked and modified variant of 'whiteness'. They were, in short, 'so-called whites' – that is, persons who, though they may have looked 'white', had at least some non-white ancestors. To quote Braithwaite:

The term 'Trinidad white' is ... used not merely as a means of identifying place of origin of the individual being described, but frequently, too, as indicating that the person is not really white but passes for white ... (1975 [1953]:83).

In sum, for a 'white' to be 'local' was to be 'mixed' with, and connected to, 'blacks'.

Dividing 'colours', personally

Though 'colour' was considered an observable sign of 'racial ancestry', colour terms were not governed strictly by genealogical principles. As something observable, 'colour' diverged from ancestry in being an individual trait of persons: full siblings, for instance, could be different in their 'colour' identities.

To cite one example, a very dark-skinned Trinidadian, born in the 1930s and now a senior executive of a bank, told me of his experiences growing-up with 'lighter' siblings:

My brother had been to St Mary's College[15] ..., and based on the experiences there, I saw the racial overtones. For example, my brother had kind of softish hair and was lighter than me, so that was a little all right, but with my kind of hair, my kind of colour, I know I would have had a problem. ... My sister, for example, she was much lighter than me, and I had the experience where if she were in the road with her school friends, you know, she would pass me straight[16] because of colour and so on. So I was sensitive to all of those innuendoes. They were not open and aggressive, but if you were alert, you knew and you felt and you sensed them ...

And the recollections of a very light-skinned Trinidadian, of roughly the same age, indicate that this inter-familial fragmentation was also present at the lighter end of the colour scale:

[My mother's grandfathers] were English and Irish, and they married local girls, who by that time would be regarded as white, but who would have had an admixture of coloured blood already. In these instances, one child was blond and blue eyed, and the other quite dark skinned – straight hair, straight nose and everything else, but dark-skinned. They would be two brothers. This would create a difference within the family, and the fair brother would invariably marry a white girl either locally or foreign, and his side of the family would remain fair skinned and he would avoid too much contact with his darker skinned brother ...

Similarly, both James (1933:8) and Braithwaite (1975 [1953]:101) report that 'colour' divisions within families were a widespread sociological phenomenon in pre-independence Trinidad. That siblings could be divided by 'colour' demonstrates that the idiom of colour diverged from the idiom of racial accounting upon which it rested. Since 'colour' was taken as a sign of ancestry even though it was not determined by it, 'colour' was inherently ambiguous. Ancestry and appearance could give the same individual different colour identities: persons with an 'admixture' of blood could none the less be 'regarded as white'. This doubling of colour identity meant that lived experience involved a dialectic of visible appearance and a knowable reality. 'Those who are endeavouring to pass for white are anxious to shed kinship connections with people of darker hue .... Candidates for positions in the public service have been known to prefer to jeopardise their chances of obtaining a job to producing their birth or baptismal certificates' (Braithwaite, 1975 [1953]:96).

'Colour' as a shifter

There were yet additional ambiguities of 'colour', for observable 'colour' and 'racial accounting' diverged in other ways. The Creole scale of 'colour' lacked the clear and fixed divisions inscribed by the fractions of genealogical accounting. 'Shades' blended into contiguous 'shades', and even more importantly, their referential use shifted with observers and context.

In a discussion of the British West Indies census of 1946, for instance, Cumper noted the difficulty of obtaining a count of the 'coloured' population given the absence of fixed boundaries between 'white', 'coloured' and 'black' (n.d. [1978]:26-7). Examining figures for all of the British West Indies, Cumper noted 'shift[s]' in these classificatory boundaries between (i) different colonies, (ii) the counting of males and females within particular colonies, and (iii) the census of 1946 and its predecessors.[17]

Similarly, Braithwaite reports shifting that hinged upon the social status of the observer: 'The dark-skinned person makes distinctions which white or fair-skinned people do not make' (1975 [1953]:155). And in an extensive discussion of Trinidad's social clubs, he presents evidence of the vice-versa—that 'lighter' persons made distinctions which 'darker' persons did not. Throughout this discussion Braithwaite presupposes the equivalence of terms of 'race' and 'status', precisely as chartered in the origin tale of 'the coloured middle class':

> the upper sections of the coloured group ... would stress ... the mixed nature of ... clubs such as the Union Club and the Country Club. To the member of the lower middle class and the lower class these are all 'white clubs', however; and indeed symbolic in many cases of white domination or superiority (1975 [1953]:65).

A person's 'colour' or 'shade' was determined, then, not simply by his or her bodily appearance, but by the relationship between the observer and the observed. 'Colour', in short, was a shifter (Silverstein, 1976).

Here is an additional ambiguity of the idiom of colour. Given the absence of regimented boundaries of reference, persons of 'colour' could seek to downplay the significance in 'shade' between themselves and relatively 'lighter' persons, and to emphasise the difference between themselves and relatively 'darker' persons. As C.L.R. James wrote in 1933:

> There are the nearly white hanging on tooth and nail to the fringes of white society, and these, as is easy to understand, hate contact with the darker skin far more than some of the broader-minded whites. Then there are the browns, inter-mediates, who cannot by any stretch of the imagination pass as white, but who will not go one inch towards mixing with people darker than themselves. And so on, and on, and on. Associations are formed of brown people who will not admit into their number those too much darker than themselves, and there have been heated arguments in committee as to whether such and such a person's skin was fair enough to allow him or her to be admitted, without lowering the tone of the institution (1933:8).

In sum, within the Creole scale of 'colour', we find a recurring pattern of upward identification and downward distancing, pragma-tically pursued from a plethora of interested positions by a plethora of interested social actors.

Achieved lightness: 'respectability'

In addition to serving as a distinction of both 'ancestry' and 'physi-ognomy', the opposition between 'white' and 'black' commonly operated as an idiom of valuation for comportment and lifeways.

A person's speech could be 'white' (LePage, 1956:40; Braithwaite, 1975 [1953]:124-5); and both 'education' and 'church weddings' had a 'colour' identity – both were 'white'.[18] For a 'non-white Creole' to acquire such 'white' traits and biographical features was to gain 'respectability'. Indeed, Powrie's discussion of 'the coloured middle class' explicitly presents 'respectability' as a synonym for patterns of living *identified* as 'white':

> Respectability is the keynote of coloured middle class existence. The ideal person and form is ... 'white' and life is patterned to conform as closely as possible to all that is felt to be contained within this ideal (1956:225; cf. Braithwaite, 1975 [1953]:138).

Terms of colour were thus applied to achieved as well as ascribed characteristics. As a result, terms of colour established a correspondence – or paradigmatic substitutibility – between achievements and features of ascription. This substitutibility meant that a person's bodily 'colour' could be altered by 'achievements':

> Hence it arises that obviously coloured people are referred to as being white, on occasions. ... Usually the coloured person who is called 'white' is classified thus with full awareness of the *actual* colour of the individual. Occasionally, in borderline cases the classification blinds the individual to 'obvious' signs of colour (Braithwaite, 1975 [1953]:155, emphasis added).

Braithwaite's text tells us that though acquired 'respectability' could substitute for bodily 'lightness', the latter remained what was socially 'actual'. Thus 'respectability' masked, rather than removed, bodily 'darkness', and as a result, 'respectability' needed to be continuously re-established. To quote James:

> My grandfather went to church every Sunday morning at eleven o'clock wearing in the broiling sun a frock-coat, striped trousers and top-hat, with his walking-stick in hand, surrounded by his family, the underwear of the women crackling with starch. Respectability was not an ideal, but an armour (1983 [1963]:17-18).

'Respectability was not an ideal, but an armour' – that is, an outer layer of protective gear preventing bodily exposure.[19]

'Respectability' was thus not 'whiteness', but the vulnerable, substitute 'whiteness' of 'non-whites', and, at the same time, a measure of *approximation* to 'whiteness'. It placed 'whites' beyond valuation,[20] and measured 'mixing' as a variable degree of a single value ('being white'), rather than as a complex relation between two qualities ('Africanness' and 'Europeanness'). Thus, the 'whiteness' that could be acquired was constituted upon a scale in which 'whiteness' was the only positive term. 'Blackness' could be 'lightened up' because it was an absence – a blank slate upon which to inscribe 'respectability'. 'Respectability' extended the idiom of 'colour' beyond physiognomy to all aspects of personhood, but at the same time, it defined 'blackness' solely as the absence of 'whiteness'.[21]

In sum, as a third dimension of 'colour', 'respectability' offered yet another interpretation of 'mixing'. While this interpretation made a person's 'race' something alterable, it none the less insisted that the alterations were not the creation of something new but the adoption of the valorised element of the 'white'-'black' opposition. It thus made mobility in social practice contingent upon both the 'factual' reality of 'race' and the acceptance of the proposition that 'whites' defined 'respectability' and were by definition 'respectable'.

The classificatory erasure of 'mixing' between 'Europeans' and 'East Indians'

Like offspring from unions between 'Europeans' and 'Africans', offspring from unions between 'Europeans' and 'East Indians' were deemed 'mixed'. And the same system of fractional and genealogical accounting could be employed to describe such persons: 'she half white, half Indian' or 'her father white, her mother Indian'. Yet in marked contrast to the elaborate distinctions of 'colour', we find no lexical items for persons of 'East Indian' and 'European' ancestry other than the terms of racial accounting. There was no 'kind' which included all persons of 'East Indian' and 'European' descent, and similarly, no idiom in which 'East Indians' and 'Europeans' were the endpoint values of a single, continuous variable. 'East Indians' were never placed on a 'colour' scale with 'whites'.[22]

This lexical absence cannot, however, be regarded as mimetic of social relations: there was, as we say, 'mixing' between 'East Indians' and 'whites'. Indeed, Singh reports that on nineteenth century plantations unions between the white 'supervisory staff' and indentured 'East Indian' women were 'not infrequent', and were a continuation of 'the tradition of concubinage that had been associated with plantation life since the days of slavery' (1974:45). Mendes' short story, 'Boodhoo', which is set early in the twentieth century, also indicates that unions between 'white' male bosses and 'East Indian' female workers were commonplace (1978 [1932]). And by 1928 we find evidence of 'mixing' between 'East Indian' males of achievement and 'white' females. In that year, the barrister F.E.M. Hosein denounced 'the growing tendency of cultured Indian gentlemen . . . to seek as suitable life partners ladies of a higher . . . race' (quoted in Ramesar, 1976:65; cf. Braithwaite, 1975 [1953]:45). Finally, using data from the 1946 census, Cumper provides a numerical estimate of the 'mixing' between 'East Indians and coloured or white', reporting that in Port of Spain such 'mixed' persons were 'one fifth as numerous as the [East Indian] group' (n.d. [1978]:32-3; cf. Ramesar, 1976:64).

   Yet Cumper's estimate is as interesting for what it leaves out as for its report of ongoing 'mixing'. The census figures he relies upon include only the first generation offspring of unions between 'whites' and 'East Indians'. Thus in the official practice of counting persons, the second generation of descendants from 'mixed' unions involving 'Indians' were erased rather than memorialised. In the absence of a lexicalised space for this 'mixing', the 'mixing' itself was neither kept track of nor constituted. What, in classificatory terms, became of these persons? On the basis of oral histories taken in the mid-1980s, I suspect that in pre-independence Trinidad and since, such persons were identified, on a contingent and pragmatic basis, as being within lexicalised identities of race and colour – with 'white', 'East Indian', 'near white' and 'coloured' being possible results.

Two principles of subordination

We have seen that whereas the 'mixing' of 'Africans' and 'Europeans' was profusely represented, the 'mixing' of 'East Indians' and 'Europeans' was not. Thus, though 'Africans' and 'East Indians' were both deemed inferior to 'Europeans', their subordination differed in semantic structure. This is not to suggest that one instance of racism was any less vicious than the other. It argues only that 'racism' had multiple forms.

   As we have already seen, 'blacks' could most fully become 'white' in terms of 'respectability', for this idiom extended 'colour' identities to 'achievements'. Represented by this idiom, 'blackness' was not a positive term but an absence: 'mixing' with 'blacks' was not a matter of combining two elements, but of filling a void. It is precisely in these terms that we find very different images of 'African' and 'East Indian' inferiority. The immigrants from India and their descendants were thought to possess their own, albeit inferior, 'civilisation' as evidenced by their text-based religions (Hinduism and Islam) and corresponding, literate languages Hindi and Arabic[23]. The presence of this (inferior) alternative made the relationship between 'East Indians' and 'whites' a matter of 'either/or': from the perspective of the colonial order, a person was either a Hindu or a Christian. By comparison, there was little, if any, sense of 'African' alternatives that could occupy the place of Christianity. If the 'African' could be partially *évolué*, to borrow a term from the French colonial order, it was because he had nothing of his own. Possessed of languages, religions, and customs which were regarded as inferior cases of what 'Europeans' possessed, the immigrants from India and their descendants could not similarly be partially 'European'.

These contrasting images of the 'African' and 'East Indian' were accepted even by those who explicitly rejected claims of European superiority. 'Negro' deracination and 'East Indian' embeddedness in ancestral 'culture' were presuppositions not only of the hegemonic discourse of 'European' superiority, but equally of the nationalist contestation of that discourse. For example, in a text championing independence for Trinidad, Hugh Wooding wrote:

> West African Negroes ... had been uprooted from their homes and translated into slavery to cultivate the fertile fields ...

But:

> ... the Indians were permitted under the terms of indenture to bring with them their own religion, language and customs ... (1960:145).

Here the contrast is two-fold: between a slavery that 'uprooted' and an indenture that permitted ancestral retention, and between 'homes' (that were lost) and 'religion, language and customs' (that were retained). It was not only that indenture allowed cultural retention while slavery did not, but apparently that 'Indians' had a more elaborate 'culture' to begin with.

Tito P. Achong, one of the most avowedly radical critics of metropolitan rule, similarly illustrates the implicit acceptance of this contrast between 'Africans' and 'Indians' in anti-colonial discourse. Writing in his 1942-43 *Mayor's Annual Report* for Port of Spain, he recounted his own attack on a visiting representative of the British Council:

> The function of Mr Stannard, obviously, was to push down his brand of British culture into the willing, or unwilling, throats of the people of this land .... I told him in as clear

a manner as I could that his notion of a ... British culture
for the Trinidad community must be ruled out .... It would
be unwise for the Chinese and Indian sections of the people
of Trinidad, I said, to forsake the past glory of their ancestral
homelands and to be unmindful of their future generations
for British propagandist 'culture'. As for Afro-West Indians
it was their solemn mission, I emphasised, to gather as far
as practicable, the learning and culture of all lands and to
synthesise them into an organic whole, harmonising the end
product with their social history ....

This was too much for the British Council's professional
propagandist ... (Achong, n.d.:28-29).

In Achong's anti-imperialism we have very different prescriptions
for 'Afro-West Indians', on the one hand, and 'the Chinese and
Indian[s]', on the other. The former, specified as a type of West Indian,
are charged with absorbing 'culture' from 'all lands', and no mention
is made of a culture of their own. By contrast, the latter groups – who
are identified as persons of their 'ancestral homelands' and not as types
of West Indians – are enjoined to preserve their 'past glory', and
'forsake' the culture of all others, specifically 'British propagandist
"culture" '.

The 'mixing' of 'Africans' and 'Indians'

I have argued that the presence of terms for 'mixing' between 'whites'
and 'blacks', in contrast to the relative absence of terms for 'mixing'
between 'whites' and 'East Indians', figured 'Africans' as culturally
naked, in opposition to both 'whites' and 'East Indians'. But if this
typification of 'Africans' was encoded by the presence of a lexicon for
their 'mixing' with 'whites', it follows that it should also have been
encoded by the presence of a lexicon for their 'mixing' with 'East
Indians'. Or rather, if the absence of a lexicon for 'mixing' between
'East Indians' and 'whites' implied that both 'races' possessed a 'culture'
of their own, then the absence of a lexicon for 'mixing' between 'East
Indians' and 'Africans' would contest, rather than affirm, the figure
of 'African' cultural nakedness. Consistent with this argument, we find
the term *'dougla'* for the 'mixed' offspring of 'black' and 'East Indian'
parents.[24]

'Dougla' did not, however, operate fully in the same way as the
term 'coloured' did. To begin with, though *'dougla'* was employed as
a descriptive term identifying individuals, it was rarely used to designate

a collective grouping. Moreover, there seems to have been little inheritance of the *'dougla'* identity. If a *'dougla'* had a child with an 'East Indian', the child could, on a pragmatic and contingent basis, be assimilated to the category 'East Indian', though at various times and places it might be relevant that the person 'have a bit a Negro blood in she'. Similarly, a child produced by a union of a *'dougla'* and a 'black' or 'coloured' could, on a pragmatic and contingent basis, be placed along the Creole scale of colour, though again, in various contexts his 'Indian' ancestry might be relevant.

As with 'mixing' between 'whites' and 'blacks', then, there was some recognition of an intermediate 'kind'. However, as with 'mixing' between 'whites' and 'East Indians', this 'mixing' was ultimately erased, rather than recorded. If 'mixing' between 'East Indians' and 'blacks' was strictly analogous to the mixing between 'whites' and 'blacks', there would be no reason for this erasure. However, these two cases of 'mixing' differed in that the former, unlike the latter, did not involve Trinidad's colonisers. The 'mixing' of 'East Indians' and 'blacks' was of little note to the colonial order as hegemonically constituted and perceived, and though it was acknowledged in linguistic convention, it was not elaborately inscribed there.

Immigrants from South Asia and their descendants were neither a part of a locally-created 'white-Indian' continuum nor a part of a locally created 'black-Indian' continuum. In the socially constructed absence of local connections 'East Indians' never became 'Creoles', and had no place on the Creole scale of colour: they were emphatically 'East' and not 'West Indians' (see also Braithwaite, 1975 [1953]:4 and V.S. Naipaul, 1973 [1965]).

The social construction of cultural preservation

The image of the 'East Indian' as an unassimilated ancestral kind did not mean that 'Indian culture', 'religion' or 'language' had been effectively preserved. Indeed, there is ample evidence of both loss and syncretism. Both Vidia and Shiva Naipaul write of the vacuity of Hindu rituals in mid-twentieth century Trinidad. And speaking in 1956, Eric Williams could dismiss a proposal for introducing Hindi into Trinidad's schools by noting that Hindi was no longer spoken in East Indian homes.[25] The figure of the unassimilated 'East Indian' did not mean that an ancestral culture had been preserved; rather, it meant that cultural diffusion, like genealogical 'mixing', had been placed under erasure. 'We were steadily adopting the food styles of others', V.S. Naipaul writes, but 'everything we adopted became our own' (1964:35).

This figure meant, as well, that Indian languages and rituals had become emblems of difference within the colonial order. Indeed, even the most ostensibly 'traditional' practices were performed to configure social relations within Trinidad. As R.T. Smith and Chandra Jayawardena observed in their analysis of Hindu marriages in British Guyana:

> The fact of performing this marriage ceremony at all is in itself symbolic of the participants' position in the Guyanese social system. The strict performance of all ritual actions involved in an orthodox wedding has its own value for the participants because it is thought to be the proper 'Hindu' way of doing things, irrespective of whether each element has meaning itself (1958:191).[26]

The terms of 'race' and 'colour': a summary

I have argued that distinctions of race and colour in pre-independence Trinidad were patterned by and expressive of two distinct principles of subordination. Tables 4.2 and 4.3 present a summary of the lexical evidence I have analysed. Table 4.2 presents conventional terms for the six possible permutations from unions between Trinidad's three major races, and Table 4.3 shows the terms for the descendants from unions between all five of the lexicalised 'kinds' in Table 4.3. In simple terms Table 4.2 shows the lexical, or classificatory, results of one generation of unions between Trinidad's three main 'races', and Table 4.3 shows these results after two generations. Since there is no lexical element for an 'East Indian-white', this 'kind' is not carried over from Table 4.2 to Table 4.3, and their absence in the production of second

Table 4.2:   Terms for descendants of unions within and between Trinidad's 'pure races'

	Parent 1		
	'European'	'African'	'East Indian'
'East Indian'	{ }	*'Dougla'*	'East Indian'
'African'	'coloured'	'African'	—
'European'	'European'	—	—

Brackets indicate that an entry is not lexicalised. Dashes indicate a redundant entry.

Table 4.3:   Terms for descendants of unions between the five lexicalised 'kinds' produced by unions between Trinidad's three major 'races'

		Parent 1			
Parent 2	'white'	'black'	'dougla'	'coloured'	'East Indian'
'East Indian'	{ }	'dougla'	{'East Indian'}	{'dougla'}	'East Indian'
'coloured'	'coloured'	'coloured'	{'coloured'}	'coloured'	'East Indian'
'dougla'	{'coloured'}	{'coloured'}	{'dougla'}	—	—
'black'	'coloured'	'black'	—	—	—
'white'	'white'	—	—	—	—

Brackets indicate that an entry is not lexicalised. There is thus uncertainty about what term would have been used for such persons. Where appropriate, I have indicated a likely choice for these entries by placing a term within the brackets. Whereas in Table 4.2 I identified each 'kind' by ancestral territory, I have here made use of 'colour' terms, if they exist. This switch in my own usage encodes the distinction between ancestral immigrants to Trinidad (the parents in Table 4.2) and persons born in Trinidad (the parents in Table 4.3). In reading this table it is helpful to note the following contrast: whereas 'descent' is closed for the set of 'Creoles' (i.e, a child of two Creoles, whatever their 'colour', is also a 'Creole'), the offspring of a 'dougla' will in most cases be something other than a 'dougla'.

generation 'racial kinds' illustrates one of my basic points: the system of lexical terms effectively imposed a silence on the results of 'mixing' between 'whites' and 'East Indians'. By contrast, all 'mixing' between 'whites' and 'blacks' was recorded within the category 'coloured', a term that motivated detailed specification through the use of p rticular 'colours' (e.g., 'fair', 'red', and 'brown'). The 'mixing' of 'East Indians' and 'blacks' offers an intermediary case. Such 'mixing' was represented lexically by the term *'dougla'*, but in practice the term did not preserve a record of such 'mixing' over time. Furthermore, the different degrees of 'mixing' that could be produced over many generations were similarly absent from the lexical system. In sum, we have one case where 'mixing' is systematically erased, indicating an either/or relation between 'civilisations'; one where it is fetishised, providing a measure of 'improvement'; and one where it is acknowledged, but not elaborated upon.

This same pattern of meaning can be found in a different register if we return to the set of eight terms employed for Trinidad's main ancestral 'races'. To recall this basic data: persons who were imported as slaves were commonly identified as 'African', 'black', and 'Negro'; persons who arrived as masters were identified as 'European' or 'white'; and those who came as indentured labourers from South Asia were identified by the term 'East Indian' (see Table 4.4). Examining this set of terms we find that each grouping was situated within the discourse of isolable, ancestral kinds. In short, each was rendered a 'race'. In addition, the 'African' and 'European' were placed within a system of 'colour' which imaged them as physiological opposites and, at the same time, as the defining endpoints of a continuum of locally produced 'mixing'. Thus the idiom of 'colour' affirmed the 'natural' difference of these kinds, even while expressing their shared 'localness'. There was,

Table 4.4:   Terms for major 'racial kinds' in Trinidad

Ancestral term	Colour term		Phylogenetic term	
'African'	'Black'		'Negro'	
'European'	'white'		{	}
'East Indian'	{	}	{	}

Brackets indicate the absence of a lexical term. The absence of phylogenetic terms for 'East Indians' and 'Europeans' is only a relative absence: 'Caucasian' and 'Oriental' appear occasionally in the available historical records. Certainly, in the global discourse of Imperialism, these 'scientific' terms are readily available. This comparison hints at the complexity of the relationship between local and global instances of racial classification.

however, no similar term indicating the localness of 'East Indians'. Finally, the 'African' or 'black' was also identified as a 'Negro'. This 'kind' was located neither in a land of origin nor in the colonial order, but in a scientistic typology – that is, in a system of difference represented as an objective fact of nature. *Qua* 'Negro', the African differed absolutely and abstractly. This difference was both in the 'nature' of things and, dialectically, so detached from social context that it was alterable, though this plasticity was contingent upon accepting the absolute value of 'whiteness' (see Table 4.5 for a summary of this analysis of the semantic features of these racial terms).

Table 4.5: Semantic features of the three types of terms for 'racial kinds'

		Semantic feature		
		Natural	Foreign	Local
Type of term	Ancestral	+	+	−
	Colour	+	−	+
	Phylogenetic	+	−	−

The chart illustrates a general thesis of Saussurian semiotics. If 'local' and 'foreign' were simply opposites, it would be redundant to include both columns. Yet, since a phylogenetic term indicates neither a local nor a foreign attachment, but deracination, it has the same value (−) for these two columns. This is because, 'local' and 'foreign', in addition to their evident opposition, share a feature of similarity, specifically 'attachment to a place'.

Some observations on the pragmatics of 'race' and 'colour'

I have stressed that 'race' and 'colour' distinctions had a plethora of meanings that were extraneous to, and undetermined by, class distinctions. Yet, while relations to production were not determinative of this system of difference, the ordering of such relations was their pragmatic purpose: to practise racism was to constitute a hierarchy of relative independence and dominance in production. To put the matter slightly differently, racism was a model *of* ancestry, but a model *for* the subordination of labour. In consequence, for a 'non-white' to contest Trinidad's racial order meant seeking social mobility away from subordinate positions in the system of production. This much was shared by 'East Indians' and 'non-white Creoles' as persons deemed racially inferior to 'whites'. Yet the different semantic structures of the two 'non-white races' inflected the patterns of mobility characteristic of 'East Indians' and 'non-white Creoles'.

As we have already seen, for 'Negroes' and 'coloured persons' there were idioms of degrees of 'being white'. Indeed, in one dimension of the Creole scale of colour, achievement could replace physiognomic 'darkness', for achievements were 'light'. Achieved social status was thus registered in the ascribed idiom of 'race'. This had a number of important consequences. To repeat an earlier point, it meant that the 'achievements' of a 'dark' person had a contingent status relative to her or his 'true colour'. It meant, in addition, that 'achievements' were regulated by proximity to imaged 'whiteness', and as such, were a matter of 'respectability', rather than unfettered economic 'utility'. In short, the idiom of 'respectability' circumscribed a drive for 'profit' pure and simple. This point is well illustrated by the recollections of a president of a management consulting firm concerning the values of 'the black middle class',[27] within which he was raised in the 1930s and 1940s:

> We grew up in a situation in which one's [status] was related to one's academic knowledge. Success in academia was important – that was the black middle class. So most teachers were black; a lot of the doctors you went to were black; a lot of the lawyers .... One's vision ... was one of black people who were upright .... One didn't have a perception of businessmen being black .... It was so marked that I remember distinctly that when I was growing up there was a fellow who is now a multi-millionaire, who owns that bakery .... He is a multi-millionaire. He has several properties all over the place, but he was a deviant .... Smith was a deviant because he was into business ... and one didn't regard him as a quote unquote very respectable sort of person.

Finally, since 'achievements' were 'white', their accomplishment by relatively 'dark' persons contested the view that 'the Negro' was inherently inferior, but precluded the affirmation of 'Africanness' or 'blackness'. 'Africans' who 'achieved' were neither 'African' nor 'black'. 'Achievements' could not, then, be represented as the collective property of 'Negroes'; rather, their accomplishment by 'non-white Creoles' was an individual feat. Moreover, just as 'achievements' precluded the valorisation of things 'African', the affirmation of 'Africanness' implied a rejection of ('white') 'achievements'.

By contrast, the 'race' of 'East Indians' was configured as something autonomous from the colonial order, for their racial identity maintained a constant value as a term solely of ancestry: 'achievements' did not make an 'East Indian' anything other than an 'East Indian'. As something fixed and constant, this ancestral identity was set apart as 'a culture', and 'achievements' could be conjoined to affirmations of this 'culture'. Because 'achievements' did not alter 'Indian identity', 'Indian identity' could possess 'achievements' – which was precisely what the idiom of 'respectability' and the referential shifting of colour terms denied 'Africans'. 'Achievements' could thus be imaged as the property of the collectivity of 'East Indians', and not merely of exceptional individuals. Finally, the autonomy of 'Indianness' and 'achievement' meant that the latter could be constituted in purely economic terms as a matter of 'profit' and 'utility' unencumbered by the ideal of 'respectability'.

This schematic comparison can be illustrated and made more specific by comparing instances of the public representation of 'achievements' by 'East Indians' and 'non-white Creoles'. Here I look at one of each.

On 30 May 1945 some 20,000 Indians gathered in San Fernando, Trinidad's second largest city, to celebrate the centenary of Indian domicile in the colony, and this celebration was subsequently recorded in the *Indian Centenary Review: One Hundred Years of Progress* (Kirpalani, 1945:119).[28] The 'mammoth crowd', according to the *Review*, was an 'orderly' gathering reviewed by the British governor, who watched from 'a specially prepared stand'. Here we see that the mass mobilisation of 'East Indians' was conjoined to a recognition of British authority. In addition, the amassed collectivity of 'Indians' was explicitly detached from any one class position. The crowd was said to represent the 'unity ... of Indians from every walk of life' (p. 120); and 'Indians', as a collectivity, were lauded both as 'the sterling peasantry – the backbone of the country' (p. 120), and as a 'people [who had] permeated every cell of business life in this colony' (p. 103). Their distinctive essence was not a particular class position, but their 'habits of steady and regular work' (p. 49).[29] Similarly, individual 'Indians' were praised for a range of achievements, the diversity of which effaced any class specificity of the collectivity. For example, in the *Centenary Review*'s 'Who's Who' of Trinidad's 'Indians', the 223 entries included 11 barristers-at-law, 33 merchants, 10 contractors, and single cases of persons in such varied occupations as 'chief cashier', 'hairdresser', and 'cane farmer and peasant proprietor' (pp. 131-69). In sum, the centenary celebration represented 'Indians' as a solidary group distinctive in 'industry', and as a set of individuals varied in their achievements and class positions, (p. 45).

There is, by contrast, no evidence of any comparable amassing and celebration of 'Africans' or 'non-white Creoles' as a solidary group of diverse achievers. 'African' domicile was not identified with an initial moment from which anniversaries were counted. And while the centenary of emancipation was celebrated, the form of its celebration figured emancipation as evidence of the beneficence of British rule, not as a triumph of 'African' resistance. For example, on 30 July 1934 some 5,000 schoolchildren were brought together in Port of Spain to hear these words from the Acting-Governor:

> Now, children, more than 100 years ago people in England gave serious thought to the question of slavery. They asked themselves – 'Is it right? Is it Christian?'

> Wilberforce and his friends took up the question and they told all England that this must stop (*Trinidad Guardian*, 31 July 1934, p. 8).

The centenary celebrations also systematically de-emphasised the historical and racial specificity of West Indian enslavement, representing it as an element of universal history brought to an end by British Christianity. To quote again from the Acting-Governor's address to the amassed schoolchildren:

> Slavery seems to have been an institution which affected every country in the world.
> The Israelites got a bad time from their Egyptian masters.
> The ancient Greeks kept slaves and did not treat them well ...
> ... On August 1, 1834 ... [s]omething happened ... right through the British Empire which set the way through the Christian countries all over the world to remove the blot of slavery from our civilization.

Similarly, a series of 'historical pageants', open to the public at large, began 'with a tableau depicting the Court of Egypt' and ended with 'the rejoicing of slaves' in reaction to 'Wilberforce's fight for freedom ... in the House of Parliament' (*Trinidad Guardian*, 31 July 1934, p. 1, and 1 August 1934, p. 1). In sum, the centenary of emancipation – as celebrated by the colonial state – eschewed the celebration of 'Negroes' as a solidary race of achievers.[30]

'Negro' achievements were celebrated not in mass objectifications of ancestral identity, nor in catalogues of diverse accomplishments, but in the exemplary biographies of scholarship winners – most fully, in the biographies of the very few individuals who won Island Scholarships for university education in Great Britain and thereby achieved great 'respectability' as professionals.[31] In these accounts, achievement was attributed not to an ancestral disposition shared by persons of 'any walk of life', but to individual talent and striving. Moreover, achievement was specifically a matter of becoming (what was deemed) 'British' and more diffusely, 'white'. As a process that 'civilised' and 'elevated' students, education was a privileged means to this end. This meant both that 'being British' was imaged as 'being educated', and that education was shaped by the telos of making students (what was identified as) 'British'. As such, the celebration of 'achievements' by 'dark Creoles' was not an affirmation of their 'African' ancestry, but a valorisation of the metropolitan 'civilisation' which tutored them.

Eric Williams' autobiographical essay, 'A Colonial at Oxford', offers an important illustration of this configuration of 'Negro' achievement. Originally published in 1958 in *The Nation*, the organ of Williams' People's National Movement (PNM), the essay was subsequently incorporated into his *Inward Hunger: The Education of a Prime Minister* (1971 [1969]).[32] Though Williams wrote as the leader of the PNM, and though he decried the metropolitan bias of his colonial education, he none the less imaged his 'achievements' in terms of 'becoming English'.[33]

In this essay Williams repeatedly conjoins valorisations of Oxford's 'civilisation' and claims that he had been incorporated within it. For instance, as his narration reaches the point of his arrival at Oxford, he writes: 'I was, for seven years, to be a part ... of noble and inspiring traditions which have no equal anywhere in the world' (Williams quoted in Oxaal, 1982:38, and Mahabir, 1975:220). As Gordon Rohlehr has noted, this 'lyrical description of ... Oxford's heritage' reads like 'a fulfilment of self, the true discovery of ... identity' (1974:77). This impression is sustained as the narrative presents an extensive litany of favourable evaluations of Williams' scholarship from the Oxford faculty, including the compliments paid him for 'the regularity of my handwriting'. Indeed, he relates this particular commendation twice, and after the second time draws the following conclusion about his undergraduate years: 'I had come, seen and conquered – at Oxford!' (1971 [1969]:43). In sum, employing a 'classical' allusion, Williams claims to have been accepted into the Britain of Oxford.

Following this exclamatory celebration, Williams' text relates how his future unfolded after he earned his honours degree at Oxford. Here the narration does seem informed by Williams' subsequent position as an anti-colonial nationalist – though primarily by its silences and ellipses. The text tells of the steps Williams took to pursue a career as an academic historian – an aspiration which, in 1935, would have meant expatriation. Williams does not, however, adopt his own voice in relating his pursuit of a career that would have taken him away from Trinidad; rather, he presents these events through his mentors:

> What next? My tutor and my college principal, enormously pleased and vastly impressed – it was the first college First in history over a long period of years – were agreed that for me to proceed to a diploma in education as preparation for a secondary school career in Trinidad was a sheer waste of time (p. 43).

As additional evidence of his success, Williams then inserts in its entirety 'a testimonial for the Trinidad Government [from] the Authorities in Oxford' which urged that Williams be released from the obligation of returning to Trinidad to teach in a secondary school. Following this quite lengthy quotation, Williams' text continues in the voice of his mentors, and presents the strategies they suggested for pursuing an academic career in England. Continuing its reticence on Williams' own desires and hopes at the time, the text shifts into a critique of his mentors' social Imperialism:

> The first phase of my educational career had thus come to a dramatic close. My twenty-four years preparation for an English University had ended by unfitting me totally, in the eyes of those best qualified to judge, for life in Trinidad! The Trinidad people's investment in me was to bring dividends to England! (p. 44).

This is the first passage which explicitly acknowledges the possibility that Trinidad's nationalist prime minister might have spent his life in England, and the text carefully eschews any indication that the 24-year-old Oxford scholar himself sought such a life. Yet, though the text conveys views appropriate for the future nationalist leader, it also conveys an almost boastful pleasure at the possibility that the younger man might have been sufficiently valuable to have been kept by – and hence, incorporated into – 'England'!

This reading, which finds conflicting voices in Williams' narrative, is supported by the subsequent narration of a painful dinner interview with the Fellows of All Souls, Oxford. As the text relates the details of Williams' encounter with the entrenched snobbery of All Souls College, the authorial voice expresses its anger at the 'Warden of the College', who advises, 'in a paternal tone', that:

> ... the greatest service I could render my people who stood so sorely in need of it was to return to Trinidad.

The passage then ends with this conclusion:

The entire episode, capped by the Warden's advice, convinced me that I would never get an All Souls Fellowship, and that the racial factor would dispose of me in 1936 .... I was very angry. It was not that I felt that I had won the fellowship. I knew that I had not.

But I knew that I could never win one.

This is one of these difficulties that whites can never understand (p. 46).

It is, of course, fully credible that Imperialist condescension underlay both the view that the successful colonial should stay in England and the view that he should return to Trinidad. Similarly, there is no reason to doubt Williams' judgment that racism led to his rejection by All Souls. Yet, if these claims are realistic, then Williams' claim to have 'come, seen, and conquered – at Oxford!' must be recognised as unrealistic, and hence as the product of unavowed desire. From this perspective the voice of anti-colonialism ('This is one of these difficulties whites can never understand') provides a mask for a colonialist desire to be incorporated into, rather than severed from, the Empire's metropolitan apex. Indeed, in a revealing phrase, Williams himself proceeds to describe his rejection by All Souls as the 'blasting of my English career' (p. 47) – that is, in the reading proposed here, of his career 'being English'.

Concluding observations

In comparing the collective celebration of East Indian achievements and the celebratory autobiography of Eric Williams, I have sought to illustrate some of the social consequences of the two different principles of subordination I found by analysing Trinidad's system of race and colour distinctions. My point is not that these two principles determined the course of Trinidadian history, but rather that they structured a range of socially intelligible actions which have shaped subsequent patterns of social mobility. Racial classifying, in this view, is intimately involved with the forming of classes and the en-classing of persons.

More generally this chapter has attempted to demonstrate the fruitfulness of an approach which doubts the givenness and absoluteness of racial distinctions. To analyse racial distinctions as social constructs requires unpacking the social meanings such distinctions presuppose and affirm. The goal of this approach is to work through, rather than reproduce, the meaningful distinctions of race and colour which have regulated so much of Trinidadian history – and indeed, so much of post-Columbian history in the Americas and beyond.

Acknowledgements

Portions of this chapter were presented to the Department of Anthropology at the University of Virginia, and to a colloquium at the Shelby Cullom Davis Center for Historical Studies at Princeton University. The analysis presented here benefited greatly from the discussion on both occasions, and I owe particular thanks to John Comaroff, Natalie Zemon Davis, Richard Handler, George Mentore and Brackette Williams. Others who have helped me clarify this argument include Don Brenneis, Harry Liebersohn, Laurie Shrage, Raymond T. Smith, George Stocking, and Kevin Yelvington. In addition to the sources cited below, this analysis relies extensively upon oral histories I collected during field research in Trinidad and Tobago from September 1984 through August 1985. This research was supported by a fellowship from the Organization of American States. While I was in Trinidad, the Institute of Social and Economic Research at the University of the West Indies provided me with an office and valuable logistical support. For both, I am most grateful.

Notes

1   This remains true, if in a more subtle way, when groupings are deemed 'ethnic' or 'national', for these forms of objectification also affirm that members of a social grouping share a bundle of essential features. In the case of 'nations' and 'ethnic kinds', however, the essential features are generally said to be social rather than biological. But though the traits are 'social', their existence is none the less treated as a given rather than a social construct. For social constructionist approaches to 'race' see Cowlishaw (1987), Dominguez (1986), Fields (1982), Martinez-Alier (1989 [1974]), Morgan (1972), Saxton (1991); Segal (1991) and Stoler (1989). For related work on 'nations' and 'ethnic kinds', see Handler (1988), Höbsbawm and Ranger (1983), McDonald (1986), and Segal (1988, 1991).

2   For this approach to social pragmatics, see Handler and Segal (1990:53-8).

3   In defining this 'period' I do not claim that there are not ruptures, or points of discontinuity, at the beginning and end of this time span. Rather, this period of time is an analytic construct designed to establish a baseline for a subsequent examination of how nationhood and its institutional concomitants altered the meanings of race and colour terms (Segal, n.d.). This interpretive problem motivates the use of 1962 as the endpoint of my analysis – though terms of race and colour were, of course, effected by nationalism before independence actually occurred. Since post-independence meanings of race and colour are fundamentally predicated upon the presence of 'East Indians', I have not, as a rule, considered material from much earlier than the end of immigration by indentured South Asians in 1917 – hence my starting point roughly five decades before independence. All of this is to emphasise that a different

interpretive problem would require a different periodisation of Trinidad's history.

4   It was possible to use colour terms to describe the pigmentation of an East Indian, but such descriptive uses of colour terms are not evidence that there was a standardised colour term for 'East Indians'. Similarly, though 'East Indians' could be identified by the colour term 'non-white', this was a residual category and not a referential synonym for 'East Indian'.

5   This list of eight terms is, of course, a selection from a larger set. There were, for instance, numerous terms of abuse, and these certainly deserve of fuller attention than I have given them in this essay.

6   Though I have selected this contrast as an entrée to the symbolic meanings of racial difference, it is worth emphasising that from the social constructionist perspective adopted here, the distinction between 'European' and 'African' is no more real than that between 'Portuguese' and 'white'. The first distinction is more globally distributed than the second, but their ontological status as social constructs is the same. The tendency to treat the more global of these distinctions as somehow more real than the specifically local distinction is well illustrated by Brereton's generally admirable *Race Relations in Colonial Trinidad 1870 – 1900* (1979). In discussing the composition of Trinidad's 'white' population, she reports that this category did not include 'the Portuguese immigrants from Madeira, who of course were white ...' (p. 31). The final clause tells us that 'the Portuguese' were truly 'white', even if they were not recognised as such. Similarly, in the conclusion to her book Brereton reminds the reader that her account of Trinidad's 'whites' does not apply to 'the Portuguese', since they 'were not 'sociologically white' ...' (p.211). This last phrase appears to recognise the social ontology of colour groupings, but the recognition is not even-handed: the distinction between 'whites' and 'Portuguese' is described as sociological, but not the distinction between 'whites' and 'blacks'. Indeed, in Brereton's analysis, these two distinctions are two quite different phenomenon: in her writing the distinction between 'white' and 'black' is a difference in 'race', and the distinction between 'white' and 'Portuguese' is a difference in 'class' (p.211).

7   Here and in much of what follows, my analysis proceeds from a distinction between reference and signification as two components of meaning. Consider the phrase 'busy bee'. The person who is called a 'busy bee' is the term's referent. What is being said about this person by this figure of speech is the term's signification. Both are components of the term's meaning.

8   On the Trindidadian meaning of 'British', Braithwaite reports: 'English is used as equivalent of "British". Nice distinctions between English, Scottish, Welsh and even Irish are for the most part ignored' (1975 [1953]:72).

9   At other times and places in Caribbean history we find an elaborate vocabulary for the combinatorial possibilities of genealogical 'mixing'. Craton (1978:235), for instance, reports that in the records of the Worthy Park plantation in Barbados, 'the child of a union between a black and a white was styled a mulatto; of the miscegenation of mulatto and white, a quadroon; of a quadroon and white, a mestee or octaroon' (1978:235). Terms such as these had limited use in pre-independence Trinidad and their meaning is not considered here.

10   My analysis of histories of sexual relations between male masters and enslaved women as tales of the origin of colonial society follows closely the approach of Alexander (1977). The texts I have used as sources – Braithwaite's *Social Stratification in Trinidad* (1975 [1953]), Wooding's 'The Constitutional History of Trinidad and Tobago' (1960), and Powrie's 'The Changing Attitude of the Coloured Middle Class Toward Carnival' (1956) – present such identical accounts of the origin of 'the coloured middle class' that I treat them here as variants of a single, highly formalised mythic-historic. All three essays are instances of Trinidad's pre-independence, nationalist literature, and in the context of Trinidadian nationalism the origin tale of plantation 'mixing' has at least one additional meaning. Just as this tale assigns a status to each 'racial kind' (as noted above), it also figures race as the determinant of status. In effect, this attributes social stratification in the emerging nation to the race prejudice of the old order, and not, say, to the contemporary mode of production. Indeed, Braithwaite emphatically denies that Trinidad's colour-class groupings have a contemporary cause: the 'coloured middle class is not of recent origin either biologically or socially'. Significantly, Braithwaite insists upon this conclusion even though his text contains substantial evidence to the contrary, for he documents in detail a contemporary 'system of mobility' through 'mixed' marriages and sexual unions (pp. 43, 88-94, 134-5).

11   By contast, since the late-seventeenth century the dominant racial system of North America has insistently classified 'the mulatto as a Negro' (Jordan, 1962:200). For a comparison of the North American and Caribbean systems of racial classification, see Segal (1991).

12   That all 'blacks' were 'Creoles' expressed the view that all were locally born. This usage apparently arose after the end of immigration from Africa (cf. Brereton, 1979:2).

13   Similarly, Brereton reports that in the late-nineteenth century, 'French Creole' included 'people of English, Irish, [and] Spanish descent. Two prominent examples in this period are L.M. Fraser, English born ... and Sylvester Devenish, Irish born ...' (1979:35).

14   Braithwaite writes: 'There is the tendency to associate all bad traits with the Negro ancestry. Hence comments such as: "It is the nigger blood I have in me", *"Typicale! De quelle couleur?"* And other traits such as "hot-headedness" are attributed to "Spanish blood"; that is, when "hot-headedness" is viewed in a tolerant manner' (1975 [1953]:97; see also, 158).

15   In Trinidad a 'college' is a secondary school. As the name 'St Mary's' suggests, this is a Catholic School. My informant commented that as a Catholic he should have gone to St Mary's. Instead, he enrolled in Queen's Royal College, the non-denominational government school which had a reputation for being less racially exclusive.

16   In other words the sister walked by her brother as she would a stranger – that is, without turning to look at him. The phrase is idiomatic in Trinidadian English.

17   The most dramatic of these shifts occurred between the 1931 and 1946 censuses of Dominica. Cumper writes: 'The census would have us believe that the majority of Dominicans (75 per cent) are not black but coloured. At the previous census, however, the proportions were coloured, 30 per cent; black, 70 per cent. It is plain therefore that in 1946 Dominica drew the line between black and coloured at a point rather different from that

chosen by the other colonies, or by herself 15 years before' (p. 26). This suggests that any counting of West Indians is as much a function of those doing the counting as of those being counted (cf. Ardener, 1975).

18 On the 'colour' of Church weddings, see Powrie (1956:24) and Braithwaite (1975 [1953]:103, 105). On the 'colour' of education, see the discussion below of Williams (1971 [1969]).

19 That 'respectability' has been a form of 'masking' has been a matter for much serious play in carnival (Segal, 1990).

20 Examining nineteenth-century sources Brereton reaches a similar conclusion: 'Whites were by definition respectable. ... It was assumed that they were respectable ...' (1979:211).

21 Proceeding from psychology rather than semiology, Fanon reaches a similar conclusion: 'The Negro is comparison .... Whenever he comes into contact with someone else the question of value, or merit, arises. The Antilleans have no inherent value of their own, they are always contingent on the presence of the other' (1967:211).

22 An absence resists proof but we can note that though Cumper (n.d. [1978]), Mendes (1978 [1922]), and Singh (1974) discuss sexual 'mixing' between 'whites' and 'East Indians', none of these sources identify a conventional lexeme for the offspring of such unions. Ramesar (1976) uses the term 'Creole Indian', but her text indicates that this was a term she had adopted for her analysis and not a conventional expression. This reading of Ramesar is supported by Brereton, who reports that 'Creole Indian' was used to distinguish 'Indians' born in the West Indies from Asian immigrants (1979:2). Finally, in response to an earlier draft of this chapter, Kevin Yelvington reports a possible exception to my claim. He informs me that the term 'Canefield Indian' may have been used, if infrequently, as a term for persons with a 'mixture' of 'white' and 'East Indian' ancestry. My argument does not, of course, require that no such term was ever spoken or understood in pre-independence Trinidad, but only that there was no conventional element of speech with this meaning. While collecting oral histories in Trinidad in the mid-1980s, I never came across such a term.

23 Wood (1968:143) adds Tamil and Telugu as languages used by the indentured labourers from South Asia. Hindi and Urdu were predominant as spoken languages.

24 Etymologically, *'dougla'* was derived from the Hindi word meaning bastard. I do not know, however, the extent to which this meaning was present for Trinidadians during the period discussed in this chapter.

25 For example, Shiva Naipul writes: 'I had no knowledge of the meaning or significance of these rituals. Religion so far as it impinged on me, consisted of the protracted drone of a pundit chanting a language I did not understand from sacred texts, the clouds of incense ascending from the flower-strewn *puja* mound, the ringing of bells and the tuneless trumpeting of conch-shells. Beyond this my comprehension did not penetrate' (1985:26). For Eric Williams' comments about language see Ryan (1972:143). On the absence of a system of 'caste' in Trinidad see Schwartz (1967), Niehoff (1967), and Clarke (1967). Though these publications are from after 1962 much of the research was conducted before independence. In the academic literature which discusses this time period only Klass (1961) claims the existence of a coherent and largely intact culture from and of India.

26   Shiva Naipaul's rich, fictional account of the performance of Hindu tradi-
     tions in Trinidad (1971:88-9) nicely illustrates Smith and Jayawardena's
     point. For related arguments about the performance of 'tradition' within
     societies constituted as multi-ethnic see Handler (1988).

27   The use of the phrase 'black middle class' – as opposed to 'coloured middle
     class' – should, I think, be placed in the context of the historical moment
     these recollections were spoken, rather than the historical moment being
     recollected. I have never found this phrase in a document from the pre-
     independence period, and its identification of 'black' with a status other
     than 'lower' fits with the politics of meaning of the post-independence
     period, and in particular, of the period following the Black Power
     movement of 1970.

28   The *Review* consistently uses the term 'Indian', rather than 'East Indian'.
     This suggests that the elements of the referentially synonymous pair 'East
     Indian'/'Indian' were also in meaningful opposition, with the former
     emphasising that such persons were not 'West Indians', and the latter, that
     such persons were connected to their 'homeland'. In generally using 'East
     Indian', then, this chapter has implicitly – and regrettably – subscribed to
     a 'Creole' perspective.

29   The *Review* explicitly contrasts these 'habits of steady and regular work'
     to the habits of the emancipated, African slaves.

30   This analysis is supported further if we consider the year selected
     as the centenary of emancipation. 1934 is specifically the centenary
     of the Parliamentary Act which began the period of 'apprenticeship'
     prior to emancipation. Emancipation actually came in 1838, some
     two years prior to the date legislated by Parliament due to continued
     resistance to slavery. To make 1934 the centenary, rather than 1938,
     was, in effect, to recognise the agency of British abolitionists, while
     denying the agency of enslaved 'Africans'. See Segal (1992) for a
     discussion of similar issues in debates about the year of the centenary of
     Trinidad's carnival.

31   'East Indian' achievements could also be celebrated in exemplary
     biographies (see Shiva Naipaul, 1985:16), but the achievements of 'Indians'
     were not figured exclusively in these terms. By contrast, the achievements
     of 'non-white Creoles' were, in principle, incompatible with the sort of
     collective affirmation of the racial collectivity found in the Centenary Day
     celebrations.

32   It would have been preferable to use the 1958 version here, but I was unable
     to obtain a copy. I have, however, made use of the excerpts from the 1958
     version that are quoted in Oxaal (1982) and Mahabir (1972).

33   In previous paragraphs I have written about the valorisation of being
     'British' rather than 'English'. The switch from one to the other may bother
     readers who identify as either, but such concerns are foreign to the
     Trinidadian system being considered here. To repeat a quotation from
     Braithwaite: ' "English" is used as equivalent of "British". Nice
     distinctions between English, Scottish, Welsh and even Irish are for the
     most part ignored' (1975 [1953]:72).

References

Achong, T. P., n.d., *The Mayor's Annual Report: Municipal Year 1942-43*, Boston: Meador Publishing Co.

Alexander, J., 1977, 'The Culture of Race in Middle-Class Kingston', *American Ethnologist*, Vol. 4, No. 3, pp. 413-35.

– 1984, 'Love, Race, Slavery, and Sexuality in Jamaican Images of the Family', in Smith, R.T. (ed.), *Kinship Ideology and Practice in Latin America*, Chapel Hill: University of North Carolina Press.

Ardener, E.W., 1975, 'Language, Ethnicity, and Population', in Beattie, J. and Lienhardt, G. (eds), *Studies in Social Anthropology: Essays in Memory of E.E. Evans-Pritchard*, Oxford: Oxford University Press, pp. 333-53.

Braithwaite, L., 1975 [1953], *Social Stratification in Trinidad*, Mona, Jamaica: Institute of Social and Economic Research, University of the West Indies.

Brereton, B., 1979, *Race Relations in Colonial Trinidad 1870-1900*, Cambridge: Cambridge University Press.

Clarke, C., 1967, 'Caste Among Hindus in a Town in Trinidad: San Fernando', in Schwartz, B. (ed.), *Caste in Overseas Indian Communities*, San Francisco: Chandler Publishing Co.

Cowlishaw, G., 1987, 'Colour, Culture and the Aboriginalists', *Man*, Vol. 22, No. 2, pp. 221-37.

Craton, M., 1978, *Searching for the Invisible Man*, Cambridge, MA: Harvard University Press.

Crowley, D., 1957, 'Plural and Differential Acculturation in Trinidad', *American Anthropologist*, Vol. 59, No. 5, pp. 817-24.

Cumper, G. n.d. [1978], *The Social Structure of The British Caribbean*, Millwood, N.Y.: Krauss Reprint Co.

Dominguez, V., 1986, *White by Definition*, New Brunswick, N.J.: Rutgers University Press.

Fanon, F., 1967, *Black Skin, White Masks*, Trans. by C. Markman, New York: Grove Press.

Fields, B., 1982, 'Ideology and Race in American History' in Kousser, J. and McPherson, J. (eds), *Region, Race and Reconstruction*, Oxford: Oxford University Press, pp. 143-77.

Handler, R., 1988, *Nationalism and the Politics of Culture in Quebec*, Madison: University of Wisconsin Press.

Handler, R. and Segal, D., 1990, *Jane Austen and the Fiction of Culture*, Tucson: University of Arizona Press.

Hobsbawm, E. and Ranger, T. (eds), 1983, *The Invention of Tradition*, Cambridge: Cambridge University Press.

James, C.L.R., 1933, *The Case for West-Indian Self Government*, London: Hogarth Press.

– 1983 [1963], *Beyond A Boundary*, New York: Pantheon.

Jordan, W., 1962, 'American Chiaroscuro: The Status and Definition of Mulattos in the British Colonies', *William and Mary Quarterly*, 3rd Ser., Vol. 19, No. 2, pp. 183-200.

Kirpalani, M. (ed.), 1945, *Indian Centenary Review: One Hundred Years of Progress*, Port of Spain.

Klass, M., 1961, *East Indians in Trinidad*, New York: Columbia University Press.

LePage, R.B, 1956, 'The Language Problem in the British Caribbean', *Caribbean Quarterly*, Vol. 4, No. 1, pp. 40-9.

Lowenthal, D., 1961, 'The Social Background of West Indian Federation', in Lowenthal, D. (ed.), *The West Indies Federation: Perspectives on a new Nation*, New York: The American Geographical Society.

McDonald, M., 1986, 'Celtic Ethnic Kinship and the Problem of Being English', *Current Anthropology*, Vol. 27, No. 4, pp. 333-47.

Mahabir, W., 1985, *In and Out of Politics*, Port of Spain: Inprint Caribbean.

Martinez-Allier, V, 1989 [1974], *Marriage, Class and Colour in Nineteenth-Century Cuba*, Ann Arbor: University of Michigan Press.

Mendes, A., 1978 [1932], 'Boodhoo', in Sander, R.W. (ed.), *From Trinidad*, London: Hodder and Stoughton.

— 1980 [1934], *Pitch Lake*, Port of Spain: New Beacon Books Ltd.

Morgan, E., 1972, 'Slavery and Freedom: The American Paradox', *Journal of American History*, Vol. 59, pp. 5-29.

Naipaul, S., 1971, *Fireflies*, London.

— 1985, *Beyond the Dragon's Mouth*, New York: Viking.

Naipaul, V.S., 1973 [1965], 'East Indian', in *The Overcrowded Barracoon*, New York: Alfred A. Knopf.

Niehoff, A., 1967, 'The Function of Caste among the Indians of the Oropuche Lagoon, Trinidad', in Schwartz, B. (ed.), *Caste in Overseas Indian Communities*, San Francisco: Chandler Publishing Co.

Oxaal, I., 1982, *Black Intellectuals and the Dilemmas of Race and Class in Trinidad*, Cambridge, Ma.: Schenkman Publishing Company.

Powrie, B., 1956, 'The Changing Attitude of the Coloured Middle Class Towards Carnival', *Caribbean Quarterly*, Vol. 4, Nos. 1 and 2, pp. 224-45.

Ramesar, M., 1976, 'The Integration of Indian Settlers in Trinidad after Indenture, 1921-1946', *Caribbean Issues*, Vol. 11, No. 3, pp. 52-69.

Rohlehr, G., 1974, 'History as Absurdity: A Literary Critic's Approach To *From Columbus To Castro*', in Coombs, O. (ed.), *Is Massa Day Dead?*, Garden City: Anchor Books.

Ryan, S., 1972, *Race and Nationalism in Trinidad and Tobago*, Toronto: University of Toronto Press.

Saxton, A., 1991, *The Rise and Fall of the White Republic*, New York: Verso.

Schwartz, B., 1967, 'The Failure of Caste in Trinidad', in Schwartz, B. (ed.), *Caste in Overseas Indian Communities*, San Francisco: Chandler Publishing.

Segal, D., 1988, 'Nationalism, Comparatively Speaking', *Journal of Historical Sociology*, Vol. 1, No. 3.

— 1990, 'The Politics of Colour, the Politics of Masking in Trinidad's Carnival', invited lecture at College Art Association annual meeting, New York, N.Y., 17 Feb.

— 1991, ' "The European": Allegories of Racial Purity', *Anthropology Today*, Vol. 7, pp. 7-9.

— 1992, 'Carnival and the Absence of Nationalist Substantiation in Trinidad and Tobago', in Ottenberg, S. (ed.), *Nationalism and the Arts*, forthcoming.

— n.d., 'Nationalism and Its Consequences in Trinidad and Tobago', unpublished manuscript.

Silverstein, M., 1976, 'Shifters, Linguistic Categories, and Cultural Description', in Basso, K. and Selby, H. (eds), *Meaning in Anthropology*, Albuquerque: University of New Mexico Press, pp. 11-56.

Singh, K., 1974, 'East Indians and the Larger Society', in LaGuerre, J. (ed.), *Calcutta to Caroni*, Port of Spain: Longman Caribbean, pp. 39-68.

Smith, R.T. and Jayawardena, C., 1959, 'Marriage and the Family amongst East Indians in British Guiana', *Social and Economic Studies*, Vol. 8, No. 4, pp. 321-75.

Stoler, A., 1989, 'Rethinking Colonial Categories: European Communities and the Boundaries of Rule', *Comparative Studies in Society and History*, Vol. 31, No. 1, pp. 134-61.

Williams, E., 1971 [1969], *Inward Hunger*, Chicago: University of Chicago Press.

Wooding, H.O.B., 1960, 'The Constitutional History of Trinidad and Tobago', *Caribbean Quarterly*, Vol. 6, Nos. 3 and 4, pp. 143-59.

CHAPTER 5

Spatial pattern and social interaction among Creoles and Indians in Trinidad and Tobago

Colin Clarke

Trinidad and Tobago – a two-island unitary state with 1,056,000 inhabitants in 1980 – is outstanding among the territories of the Caribbean archipelago for the segmented nature of its social structure. Creoles accounted for 58 per cent of the population in 1980 – whites for 0.9 per cent, mixed people (mostly mulatto) for 16.3 per cent, and blacks for 40.8 per cent, while the remainder were almost entirely Indian – 40.7 per cent, the descendants of indentured labourers imported from Imperial India. Although this Indian segment is, unlike the Creole, racially homogeneous, it is subdivided by religion, the vast majority being Hindu (24.9 per cent of the state's inhabitants), the minority either Muslim (5.9 per cent) or Christian (9.7 per cent), the latter being largely Presbyterian in the south or Catholic in the north.

This chapter examines the changing racial proportions and patterns of residence among Creoles and Indians in Trinidad and Tobago during the period 1960 to 1980, essentially the first twenty years of independence. It does so by recording the size and mapping the generally stable spatial pattern of the major racial and colour groups according to the censuses of 1960 and 1980. Attention is then concentrated on the only sizeable, socially mixed settlement, San Fernando. Statistical measures of segregation are set forth for 1960 and 1980 to detail residential change in the town over time, a change which has been substantially in the direction of greater segregation. Finally, this chapter provides a numerical basis for comparison with similar measures calculated for the entire state.

The main focus, however, is on changes in one key aspect of social interaction – intermarriage – among Creoles and Indians during the same time period, 1960 to 1980. Urban data drawn from the marriage registers for San Fernando are examined and compared with those for a neighbouring, and predominantly Indian, village, Débé. The evidence shows small increases in urban exogamy by race, yet Indian rural endogamy has scarcely altered over the years.

Discussion then follows of the relationship between racial segmentation and segregation at the national level, and of the lack of Creole-Indian segregatoin (whites excepted), despite segmentation in San

Fernando. The interrelationships between all these features, as aspects of Trinidad's plural society, are briefly reviewed. So, too, are the implications of the San Fernando results for Beshers' (1962) hypothesis that, in Western urban societies, there is a close link between class (or social group), residence and endogamy. My research shows that the supposed association between low racial segregation and high racial endogamy does not work for San Fernando. Indeed, the San Fernando data run counter to Beshers' hypothesis. Over time, Creole-Indian segregation has generally increased, but so too has Creole-Indian exogamy. Nevertheless, high segregation and low exogamy certainly characterise Indians – and therefore Indian-Creole relations – at the national scale.

Society and space

The outstanding feature of the social structure of Trinidad and Tobago is the dichotomy between Creole and Indian. As we have seen in previous chapters, the term 'Creole' has a distinctive local meaning in Trinidad. It excludes the Indian population, together with the small Syrian, Portuguese, Chinese and Carib minorities. Creoles may be white, brown or black, and genotype correlates broadly with socio-economic status. Stratification of the Creole segment was established during slavery, though the post-emancipation and post-independence periods have witnessed accelerating non-white social advance through access to education, the bureaucracy, and the expanding, and increasingly oil-based, economy.

Within barely more than a decade of British slave emancipation in 1834, Trinidad's white-brown-black social hierarchy was complicated by the arrival of Indian indentured labourers – mostly from the Ganges Plain – brought in by the planters to work on the newly-established sugar estates. This influx of workers, who were engaged on five-year contracts, continued until 1917 when the 'new system of slavery' (Tinker, 1974) was outlawed by the Indian government.

At first, white Creole society viewed the Indians as transients, who would leave Trinidad once their contracts had expired. In 1853, however, the planter-legislators decided that, although indenture should remain a five-year term, Indians would have to work on the island for a further five years before they were eligible for repatriation; after 1895, immigrants had to contribute to their return passage. Many Indians remained in estate employment – as the planters hoped – for the period of their 'industrial residence', but some cultivated plots acquired on former Crown Lands during and after the 1860s, while

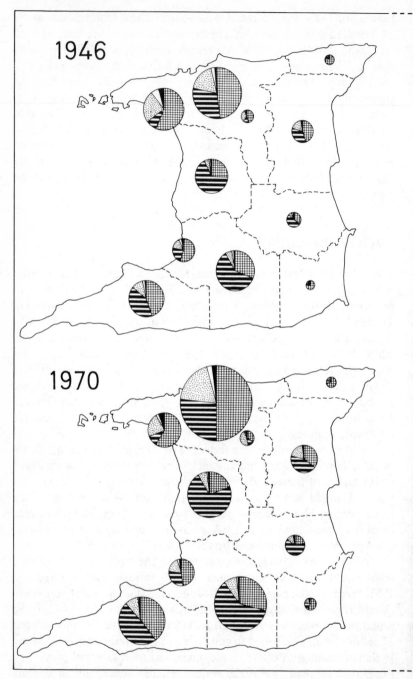

Figure 5.1:   Distribution of racial groups in Trinidad in 1946, 1960, and 1970.

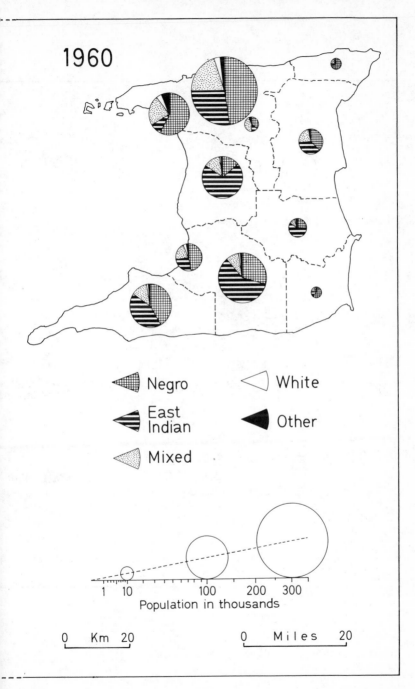

1960

Negro
White
East Indian
Other
Mixed

Population in thousands

0   Km   20   0   Miles   20

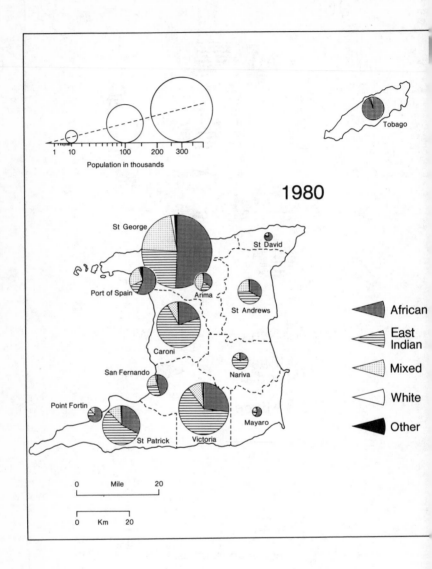

Figure 5.2:   Distribution of racial groups in Trinidad and Tobago in 1980

others turned to the crafts and trades they had once practised in India (Wood,1968).

During the 70 years of indentured immigration, 144,000 Indians came to Trinidad – scarcely any to overcrowded Tobago – and only 33,000 returned to India. As a result, the Indian element in Trinidad's population increased from 27,000 in 1871 to 70,000 in 1891 and its proportion of the colony's total expanded from 22 to 32 per cent. Natural increase ensured the permanence of the Indian community. By 1871 more than one-in-seven of the Indians had been born in Trinidad, and in the early 1900s the local-born outnumbered Indian immigrants. Thus, for the native Indians, India would never be home (Clarke, 1986).

Simultaneously, racially homogeneous Indian enclaves of estate labourers and peasants arose in the sugar belt south of Port of Spain and in the Naparima plains around San Fernando. They were consolidated by the high rate of Indian reproduction, which outstripped that of all other groups after 1920. In Creole eyes the Indians changed from sojourners to settlers, from 'Coolies' into 'East Indians'. Indian class structure changed too, and while their location tied the majority to rural tasks, some converted to Christianity, urbanised, entered retailing, joined the professions, and, after independence, moved in droves into secondary education, from which white-collar employment was accessible on a substantial scale in both the private and public sectors.

At the end of the colonial period the two contraposed and class-stratified racial segments – Creole and Indian – were locked in electoral struggle to take command of the state: electoral politics, based on adult suffrage, ensured Creole domination for almost a quarter of a century after 1962. It is hardly surprising, therefore, that racial salience – originally based on white bias, but after 1950 on Creole-Indian tension – was projected from colonial times into the post-colonial period; that the proportion of Indians in the society continued to increase against the tide of accumulated Creole political power; or that the distribution of Creoles and Indians at the national level remained stable overall, though, in detail, segregation between the major racial components increased.

Out of a population of just under one million in 1960, Creoles accounted for 61 per cent. The breakdown by colour groups was: whites 2 per cent, browns 16 per cent and blacks 43 per cent. Indians made up 37 per cent of the total, among whom Hindus comprised 23 per cent, Muslims 6 per cent and Christians 8 per cent. Two decades later two noteworthy shifts had taken place in racial and religious proportions: the racial majority of Creole over Indian had been cut by 3 per cent, and the proportion of Indians who were Christian increased from 8 to 9.7 per cent under the proselytising influence of American evangelical sects. It ought also to be added that while the number of Hindu adherents increased proportionately (to 24.9 per cent of citizens) and Islam remained stable, both religions underwent revitalisation through the dual impact of foreign missionary activity and the Indian identity crisis associated with being the rump of the permanent political opposition in the post-colonial state (Vertovec, 1987).

Comparison of the map showing census-based racial distributions for 1946, 1960 and 1970 (Figure 5.1) with the map for 1980 (Figure 5.2) suggests that, on the basis of the 13 boroughs and counties, the pattern remained remarkably stable over time. National segmentation between Creoles and Indians was reflected spatially in the enduring contrast between town-dwelling Creoles and rural Indians. However, this simple division hides a much more complex pattern of sub-regional racial dominance which gives rise to six major racial zones.

The western sugar belt and its subsidiary rice-growing areas (1) lying between Port of Spain and San Fernando, together with the Naparimas around San Fernando, were predominantly Indian. Port of Spain and its associated conurbation (2) stretching along the east-west corridor towards Arima, contained over 250,000 inhabitants in 1980, more than 75 per cent of whom were Creole. San Fernando (3), with a population of over 60,000, was the only other town of note, and it too recorded a large but, by 1980, declining Creole majority. The north and east of Trinidad (4) were rural and sparsely populated, largely by blacks, except for Nariva, where there was a pocket of Indians. By far the racially most mixed locality was the central uplands on the borders of Caroni, Arima, St Andrews and Nariva (Figure 5.2)(5), where communities containing blacks and Indians have traditionally subsisted by small-scale cultivation supplemented with cocoa farming. In contrast to Trinidad, Tobago (6), a partially self-governing island, had an almost totally black peasantry, but with some diversification into tourism.

This superficially static pattern breaks down if the framework of the 13 boroughs and counties is set aside and census data are used for the boroughs – Port of Spain, San Fernando, Arima and Point Fortin – and wards, a total of 38 spatial units in 1960 and 39 in 1980 (when Point Fortin was added). This material is far finer grained, and shows that at the end of the colonial period, whites, coloureds and blacks were only weakly segregated from one another at the national level, largely because these groups were strongly urban in location (Table 5.1). All three indices of dissimilarity were between 18 and 31 on a scale of from 0 to 100, where 0 represents no segregation and 100 indicates complete separation.

Table 5.1: *Trinidad: Indices of dissimilarity in 1960 and 1980.*

1960 1980	White	Mixed	Negro (Black)	Hindu	Muslim	Christian Indian
White	—	26.0	30.2	58.4	54.5	40.2
Mixed	34.5	—	18.2	53.3	42.1	28.4
African (Black)	40.2	22.8	—	52.9	41.3	38.8
Hindu	62.4	48.1	56.9	—	16.1	32.5
Muslim	54.2	40.5	46.1	13.0	—	22.3
Christian Indian	46.7	29.5	36.9	20.8	16.3	—

Source: Data for boroughs and wards, *Census of Trinidad and Tobago,* 1960 and 1980.

In short, only 30.2 per cent of whites would have had to move to another borough or ward to reproduce the spatial distribution of blacks, and vice versa. The three Indian religious groups – Hindu, Muslim and Christian – recorded indices of the same order of magnitude among one another as the Creole groups did among themselves. But the Creole colour categories achieved moderately high scores with each of the three East Indian religious groups (four out of nine indices were over 50), the highest indices being with the Hindus and least with the Christians. Christians were more urbanised than Hindus and Muslims.

Post-independence decolonisation (1960-80) did not bring about desegregation at the national scale. Indeed, segregation increased between whites, browns and blacks, decreased between Hindus, Muslims and Christians, but increased between whites and blacks on the one hand and Hindus on the other (Table 5.1). Additional reduced segregation involved comparatively small groups – coloureds (with Hindus and Muslims), Muslims (with whites and coloureds) and Christian Indians (with blacks). Increased spatial separation between black and Hindu (from 52.9 to 56.9) was significant, because these two populations were the key elements – demographically and attitudinally – in Creole-Indian confrontation. Young, educated Hindus stayed in their parents' villages, and commuted to white-collar jobs in the towns. Black penetration of the sugar belt through suburban sprawl from Port of Spain remained a minor phenomenon of little significance nationally. Unlike in Trinidad as a whole, however, suburbanisation had a marked impact upon the social geography of the towns, as San Fernando demonstrates.

San Fernando

San Fernando lies on the Gulf of Paria 56 kilometres south of Port of Spain. Creoles were numerically dominant, though the East Indian population increased from 17.4 per cent of the total in 1931 to 23.6 per cent in 1946 and 25.7 per cent in 1960. Whites comprised just over 3 per cent of San Fernando's population in 1960, the mixed or coloured group 21 per cent, and blacks 47 per cent. An unusual feature of San Fernando's social structure was the preponderance of Christians among Indians – 32.8 per cent Presbyterian, 8.2 per cent Catholic and 3.6 per cent Anglican, compared to the comparatively small size of the Hindu (29.2 per cent) and Muslim (22.1 per cent) groups. By 1960 nearly all Presbyterians were Indian, converts or the descendants of converts of the Canadian missionaries. In addition there were 340 Presbyterians of mixed race, predominantly of black-Indian origin called *'douglas'* (bastards) in Hindi (see also Chapter 4).

Differences between the *de facto* and *de jure* town boundaries of San Fernando present some difficulties for statistical analysis, especially since the gap between the two definitions, though close in 1960, widened since then. In 1960 San Fernando borough had a population of 39,800, which, according to the census, dropped to 36,900 in 1970 and 33,400 in 1980. In reality, city-centre decline coupled with suburbanisation occurred quite rapidly during the 1960s and 1970s, so that the combined populations for the urban and suburban areas of San Fernando, recognised by the census, were 49,200 in 1970 and 62,500 in 1980.

In 1960 San Fernando had 47 enumeration districts – the smallest spatial units into which the town was divided. They remained identical in 1970, though the census added 12 suburban districts to make a total of 59. By 1980 the original 47 enumeration districts comprised the core of the town, but suburban extensions required the addition of 26 suburban units, making a total of 73. These enumeration districts, 47 in 1960, 47 (urban) and 59 (urban and suburban) in 1970, and 73 (urban and suburban) in 1980 form the matrix of spatial units for which indices of dissimilarity have been calculated at different points in time.

Compared to Trinidad as a whole in 1960, segregation among Creole colour groups was higher in San Fernando, while the indices of dissimilarity for the Indian religious groups were lower (Table 5.2). White segregation was the most prominent feature in the town, together with the generally low degree of segregation between coloured and black Creoles on the one hand, and the various Indian elements on the other.

Table 5.2: San Fernando: Indices of dissimilarity in 1960 and 1970.

	White	Mixed	Negro (Black)	Hindu	Muslim	Oriental religion	Presbyterian
			1960				
White	—	59.5	57.6	61.6	63.8	nd	59.0
Mixed	(65.6)						
	56.9	—	21.6	31.5	30.5	nd	24.2
Negro (Black)	(75.8)	(28.6)					
	68.5	24.1	—	32.2	34.5	nd	27.4
Hindu	nd	nd	nd	—	30.3	nd	28.0
Muslim	nd	nd	nd		—	nd	30.5
Oriental religion	(68.8)	(31.8)	(31.5)				
	59.0	26.9	32.7	nd	nd	—	
Presbyterian	(73.8)	(27.8)	(36.1)			(20.0)	
	67.6	22.5	34.1	nd	nd	20.4	—
			1970				

The urban and suburban indices of dissimilarity for San Fernando in 1970 are given in parentheses.

Source: Enumeration district data, *Census of Trinidad and Tobago*, 1960 and 1970. The 1970 data are unpublished, but were made available by the Central Statistical Office.

nd = no data

Whites were marginally closer to blacks (57.6) and Presbyterians (59.0) than to the mixed group (59.5). Among Indians, the distribution of whites was slightly more nearly approximated by Presbyterians (59.0) than by Hindus (61.6) and Muslims (63.8); these Indian groups were much more segregated from whites than they were from one another. The anomalous position of the Presbyterian Indians is emphasised by their small indices of dissimilarity with the mixed group (24.2) and with blacks (27.4), the figures being even lower than their indices with Hindus (28.0) and Muslims (30.5). However, Muslims were no more dissimilar from Hindus (30.3) than from Presbyterians (30.5).

A continuum can be proposed that provides a summary of the socio-spatial situation in San Fernando at the end of the colonial period. Whites constituted a segregated minority located at the apex of the socio-residential scale and distanced spatially from all other categories. The black and mixed populations who comprised the greater part of Creole society were closer to one another than to any other category. Hindus and Muslims formed distinct elements, in aggregate terms ranking at the bottom of the social scale with blacks. Between them and the Creoles, but spatially closer to the Creoles, were the Presbyterian Indians. Though by no means acculturated to the Creole community, they stood closer – culturally if not geographically – to Hindus than to Muslims in the continuum. Most Presbyterians retained Hindu names as surnames.

Evidence for segregation expresses the increased salience of race in the period after independence, exemplified in ever larger indices of dissimilarity. In 1970, for example, the census was taken in the aftermath of the Black Power disturbances of that year and the statistics are redolent of, and possibly flawed by, the tensions that then prevailed. The pattern for the first decade of independence was for Hindus and Muslims together – for they cannot be separated in the small-area statistics – to maintain their segregation *vis-à-vis* coloured people (26.9) and blacks (32.7), while reducing their distance from Presbyterians (20.4). The pattern was also for whites and browns to locate closer together (56.9), and for blacks to be increasingly separated not only from Presbyterians (34.1), but also from white (67.6) and brown Creoles (22.5).

Inclusion of the suburbs around San Fernando in 1970 (Table 5.2) reveals even greater white segregation from all other categories. Indeed, in every instance that pairs of categories are compared, the urban and suburban data together produce larger indices of dissimilarity than the urban data alone. This result is partly an artefact of spatial growth, but Creole-Indian stress, together with black disaffection from brown Creole government, undoubtedly played a part.

Although the impact of Black Power dissolved during the oil-boom which began in 1973, the other factors behind increased segregation – notably Creole-Indian stress – continued after 1970. By 1980 the Creole portion of San Fernando's population (in the urban and suburban area) had dropped to 64.9 per cent, with the white proportion decreasing to 1.8 per cent, coloureds to 17.8 per cent and blacks to 45.3 per cent. Indians increased commensurately to 34.1 per cent, divided between Christians (45.6 per cent), Hindus (38.1 per cent) and Muslims (16.3 per cent). Hindus grew at the expense of the Muslims, in part as a result of the incorporation of former Indian villages on the town's periphery. Evangelical missionary activity among American-based sects made it more appropriate to think in terms of Christian Indians rather than Presbyterians.

Comparison of the data sets for urban and suburban San Fernando in 1970 (Table 5.2) and 1980 (Table 5.3) shows enhanced white segregation from all other groups, increased polarisation between coloureds and Hindus (46.9), Muslims (37.0) and Christian Indians

(29.0), and between blacks and Hindus (44.0) and Muslims (36.5). Hindus and Muslims grew even closer together than they had been in 1960, but Christian Indians gravitated further away from them towards the black Creoles – perhaps as a result of the racially mixed nature of congregations among the American sects.

It seems safe to conclude that San Fernando became, generally, more segregated by race (Indians against black and brown Creoles) and religion (Oriental religions against Christians) after independence, the very opposite of what one might have predicted with the passing of white Imperialism. In some measure this was due to suburban expansion and the political tension between Creole and Indian political parties. But proportional white population decline and the incorporation of pre-existing settlement enclaves were important factors in San Fernando, where the formerly expatriate residential compound next to the oil refinery at Pointe-à-Pierre was added to the suburbs by 1980.

Similar processes and patterns existed at the national scale, and the indices of dissimilarity for Trinidad and San Fernando were much closer in 1980 than they had been 20 years earlier. By Trinidad standards whites were excessively segregated in San Fernando, but black and brown Creole-Indian separation remained modest by US standards of black *vis-à-vis* white immigrant segregation (Lieberson, 1963:126, Table 41), where scores in the 80s were common. The generally low level of segregation between San Fernando's black and brown Creoles and Indians is to be explained by the similarity in their occupational structures and their capacity to compete for residential space in a non-segregated housing market (Clarke, 1971).

What were the implications of increased segregation in San Fernando between blacks and coloureds, on the one hand, and Hindus and Muslims, on the other? To transcend these spatial data and examine social interactions at the most intimate interactional scale, information on marriage and intermarriage is analysed, based on official data for San Fernando.

The urban mosaic and settlement exogamy

The situation described so far for San Fernando is the antithesis of the assimilationist scenario, in which newcomers – in this case Indians – are, over time, integrated spatially through desegregation into the 'host' society (Lieberson, 1963). Black and brown Creole segregation with Indians has never been high in San Fernando, but it is currently increasing not decreasing. On the basis of Beshers' hypothesis it might be expected that residential mixing would lead to intermarriage between black and brown Creoles and Indians, but my previous publications on San Fernando have shown this does not apply (Clarke, 1971, 1986).

Fewer than 5 per cent of Hindu and Muslim households sampled in 1964 recorded Creole spouses, and only 10 per cent of Creole households contained Indian spouses, a figure matched by Christian Indian households with Creole spouses (11 per cent) (Clarke, 1971:212, Table III). As Creoles are non-exclusive of others, endogamy on this scale must be due largely to Indian volition. Socialisation of Indian youth of all religions into hostility to intermarriage (or any other interaction of lesser significance) with Creoles, the role of Indian parents in the choice of marriage partner – once strong, particularly among Hindus – and the existence of non-urban marriage 'fields', are all likely to play a part.

It is argued that the increased age at marriage of the bride and groom will provide some evidence for the declining role of parents in choice of partner, and this is examined together with the changing pattern of settlement exogamy. For, if Indians marry out of San Fernando, following the village-exogamous tradition of their North Indian forebears, their spatial proximity to Creoles in San Fernando will be of little significance for intermarriage.

The following analysis is based upon data for all couples, extracted with the permission of the Registrar General of Trinidad and Tobago, from the *Hindu Marriage Register* and the *Muslim Marriage Register* for 1960 and 1980, and for 1 in 3 samples taken from the *General Marriage Register* for 1980. The Hindu and Muslim registers include only endogamous unions performed by a licensed marriage officer; exogamous unions and civil unions are recorded in the *General Marriage Register*, together with the marriages which take place within and between all other groups. Fortunately, Indians can be distinguished from Creoles in the *General Register* by their surnames, and the combination of

Table 5.3: San Fernando: Indices of dissimilarity in 1980

	White	Mixed	African (Black)	Hindu	Muslim	Christian Indian
White	—	72.9	84.7	80.4	71.1	77.1
Mixed		—	27.1	46.9	37.0	29.0
African (Black)			—	44.0	36.5	31.8
Hindu				—	25.6	33.6
Muslim					—	22.3
Christian Indian						—

Source: Enumeration district data for 1980, unpublished, but made available by the Central Statistical Office.

Table 5.4: Settlement exogamy and average age of brides and grooms at marriage for San Fernando and Débé

	1960				1980		
	Settlement exogamy	Av. M	age F		Settlement exogramy	Av. M	age F
San Fernando							
Hindu (19)	78.9%	24.2	17.8	(147)	69.5%	26.6	22.1
Muslim (5)	60.0%	28.8	22.4	(85)	65.9%	28.8	23.2
Débé							
Hindu (41)	92.5%	22.1	19.4	(73)	69.9%	25.6	21.8
Muslim (3)	100.0%	25.3	19.3	(10)	70.0%	23.0	18.8
San Fernando (1:3 sample)					*1980*		
Creoles marrying Creoles				(101)	21.8%	31.5	26.9
Indians marrying Indians				(60)	45.0%	31.4	23.8
Indians marrying Creoles				(24)	29.2%	33.1	30.3
Débé (1:3 sample)							
Indian marriages				(34)	64.7%	26.7	23.0

Source: Hindu and Muslim Marriage Registers, Trinidad and Tobago, 1960 and 1980. Samples taken from *General Marriage Register*, Trinidad and Tobago, 1980.

forenames and surnames permits the tentative separation of Hindu, Muslim and Christian Indians. In all cases, one or both partners were living in San Fernando or Débé at the time of their marriage.

Very high settlement exogamy in 1960 was recorded for Débé, located in the sugar and rice belt south of San Fernando, both by Hindus (92.5 per cent) and Muslims (100 per cent) (Table 5.4). The rate was lower in San Fernando but still impressive for Hindus (78.9 per cent). By 1980 exogamy had declined everywhere, except among urban Muslims, whose rate was low to start with. Most urban and rural groups, including Débé's Indians, recorded 65 to 70 per cent. Of course, these latter Indians, drawn from the *General Marriage Register*, may be Hindu, Muslim or Christian.

When compared to the rate of settlement exogamy among Creoles marrying Creoles in San Fernando in 1980 (21.8 per cent), the Indian figures are even more impressive, and point to their cultural tradition of village exogamy, as well as to the availability of mates at a regional rather than a local scale. Settlement exogamy is a more marginal factor when Indians marry (unspecified) Indians (45 per cent), but is of negligible significance when Indians marry Creoles (29.2 per cent),

Table 5.5:   Racial endogamy and intermarriage in San Fernando and Débé

	1:3 sample	Estimate	Percentage
San Fernando			
Creoles marrying Creoles	101	303	53.0
Indians marrying Indians	60	180	31.4
(Possibly Hindu marrying Muslim)	(15)		
Creoles marrying Indians	24	72	12.6
Chinese marrying Chinese	3	9	1.5
Chinese marrying Indians	1	3	0.5
Chinese marrying Creoles	2	6	1.0
TOTAL	191	573	100.0
Débé			
Indian marrying Indian	33	99	97.1
Indian marrying Creole	1	3	2.9
TOTAL	34	102	100.0

Source: General Marriage Register, Trinidad and Tobago, 1980.

though this figure, appropriately, lies midway between the Creole and Indian rates for settlement endogamy. It must also be remembered that Creole endogamy is likely to be confined sharply to San Fernando, because the field of eligibles is restricted by the town's isolation within an encompassing rural Indian ghetto.

Among all the groups analysed, irrespective of year, the average age of brides was lower than for grooms, but the marked rise in the age at marriage between 1960 and 1980 correlated with increasing settlement endogamy. At Débé in 1980, even more remarkably than in San Fernando, where marriages were always later, young people delayed marriage until their early-to-mid 20s and married more locally – probably at their own initiative. Once more the distinctions between rural and urban Hindus, taken together, and Creoles were marked, Creoles and Indians marrying at later ages, but not as late as couples engaged in Creole-East Indian exogamy. Racial intermarriage involved adults of mature age, but an additional factor was at play among black Creoles, where a tendency to initiate mating by visiting and serial polygamy produced an older age at marriage for endogamous unions as well (Clarke, 1986:Table C.l).

Race endogamy and exogamy

Setting aside the Hindu and Muslim marriage registers, which by definition are devoted solely to endogamous unions, an attempt is made to estimate the proportion of endogamy and exogamy in the *General Marriage Register* for 1980, making distinctions between the three identifiable categories of Creole, Indian and Chinese (Table 5.5). For Débé, 97 per cent of unions involved Indians marrying Indians, the remainder being exogamous unions with Creoles. It is likely that 33 per cent of the cases of Indian endogamy involved mixed religions – mostly Hindus and Christians – with a further 15 per cent accounted for by Hindu-Muslim exogamy.

San Fernando's pattern was slightly different. Creole endogamy (53.0 per cent of all cases), Indian endogamy (31.4 per cent) and Chinese endogamy (1.5 per cent) together amounted to over 85 per cent of unions, with Creole-Indian exogamy (12.6 per cent) accounting for almost all the rest. Interestingly, the small creolised Chinese group married as exogamously as endogamously.

Table 5.6: Estimates of all marital unions, San Fernando and Débé 1980

San Fernando weddings, 1980		
	No.	%
Hindu marrying Hindu	147	18.3
Muslim marrying Muslim	85	10.6
Creole marrying Creole (est)	303	37.6
Indian marrying Indian (est)	180	22.4
Creole marrying Indian (est)	72	8.9
Chinese marrying Chinese (est)	9	1.1
Chinese marrying Indian (est)	3	0.4
Chinese marrying Creole (est)	6	0.7
TOTAL	805	100.0

San Fernando and Débé Indian weddings, 1980, compared				
	Débé		San Fernando	
	No.	%	No.	%
Hindu marrying Hindu	73	39.5	147	30.3
Muslim marrying Muslim	10	5.4	85	17.6
Indian marrying Indian (est)	99	53.5	180	37.2
Indian marrying Creole (est)	3	1.6	72	14.9
TOTAL	185	100.0	484	100.0

Source: Tables 5.2 and 5.3.

Among the 24 sampled cases of Creoles marrying Indians, 12 of the grooms were Creole and 12 East Indian; more than 75 per cent of these unions involved Christian Indians, with the rest split equally between Hindus and Muslims. There was also surname evidence for Hindus marrying Muslims in 15 out of the 60 sampled cases (25 per cent) where Indians married Indians in unions that were neither wholly Hindu nor Muslim. The vast majority of the 60 cases were, almost certainly, Christian Indians, though some of the name evidence is equivocal in this instance.

Estimates derived from the *General Register* sample (by multiplying the sample scores by three) have been added to the populations extracted from the *Hindu* and *Muslim Marriage Registers* (Table 5.5) to calculate the total body of weddings in San Fernando in 1980 (Table 5.6). Crucially, Creole-Indian exogamy accounted for only 8.9 per cent of all unions recorded. Comparison of East Indian exogamous experience in San Fernando and Débé (leaving the Creole and Chinese out of the reckoning) illustrates the town's greater experience of exogamy. Indian-Creole marriages accounted for 14.9 per cent of all East Indian weddings in San Fernando, but for only 1.6 per cent in Débé. The racially more heterogeneous town was notably more intermarrying than the Indian village by 1980, but what were the changes between 1964 and 1980?

Indian-Creole exogamy as a percentage of all Indian unions in San Fernando and Débé, and Creole-Indian exogamy as a percentage of all Creole unions in San Fernando, have been calculated for 1980 and compared with sample household data in 1964 (Table 5.7). The data reveal a more than doubling of the rate of Indian exogamy as a percentage of all Indian unions, and a similar, but marginally lower, increase among Creoles. In neither instance does out-of-race marriage account for 20 per cent of unions, but the speeding up of the process –

Table 5.7: Measures of racial endogamy for San Fernando and Débé 1964 and 1980

	1964	1980
San Fernando		
Indian-Creole exogamy as % of all Indian unions	6.1	14.9
Creole-Indian exogamy as % of all Creole unions	11.9	19.2
Débé		
Indian-Creole exogamy as % of all Indian unions	0	1.6

Source: 1964 – sample survey of households; 1980 – Table 5.4.

almost entirely due to the Christian Indians – will be appreciated when it is noted that the 1964 figure is an accumulated percentage derived from sampled households, whose date of formation may have been at any point in the previous half century or so, whereas the 1980 data refer to a single year.

If the 15 Hindus and Muslims who intermarried in the 1:3 sample are multiplied up by a factor of three to estimate their actual number, the rate of exogamy for all marriages of Hindus (192) and Muslims (130) can be calculated as 23.4 and 34.0 per cent, respectively. These, too, are far higher than the figures recorded in 1964 (Hindus 14 per cent exogamy with all Indian non-Hindus, and Muslims 11.5 per cent exogamy with all Indian non-Muslims), and once more the composite nature of the 1964 sample must be noted.

At Débé, the shift towards exogamy between Indian and Creole was from non-existent to minimal (Table 5.7). This clearly augured ill for intermarriage at the national scale, where Indian-black and Indian-brown Creole segregation was increasing. San Fernando's racial and religious separation was becoming more similar to the level for Trinidad and Tobago as a whole, but its recent history of intermarriage was quite atypical.

Conclusion

Trinidad and Tobago provides an excellent example of a society, segmented by race and religion, where post-colonial rivalry has led to increased segregation at the national level, though within a stable regional framework of racial dominance. In San Fernando, the principal multi-racial town, Creole-Indian segregation – whites excepted – has been low in the past (for 1931 see Clarke, 1986:51), but has increased substantially since 1960.

Trinidad and Tobago exemplifies social pluralism and demonstrates how this segmentation can be elaborated through the use of space, not formally, as in South Africa under *apartheid*, but informally, via the labour market and social values to create and reinforce social worlds under Creole or Indian control. Racial enclaves occur at national and urban levels and have intensified in response to post-colonial pressures, though increased segregation among whites appears as a throwback to colonial elitism.

The main thrust of the argument, however, has been to show that Beshers was too narrow in hypothesising a link between social group, residence and endogamy, with parental choice of marriage partner in the Far East being replaced by parental choice of neighbourhood in the

West – neighbourhood eventually influencing the selection of a desirable partner. More important than the specific role of parental choice is the more general influence of group socialisation. Hindus and Muslims do not marry blacks, despite their proximity in San Fernando, partly because of (slackening) parental control, partly because of the persistence of settlement exogamy which nullifies the impact of the urban mosaic, and partly because everything young people hear, from being born into their home to leaving their largely race-segregated school, informs them that blacks are beyond the pale.

Ceri Peach (1980) has demonstrated for New Haven, Connecticut, a close correlation between ethnic residential desegregation and ethnic exogamy. So high is the association between the two processes over time, that rates of intermarriage can be predicted accurately from changes in the indices of dissimilarity. In San Fernando such prediction is impossible. From the low pattern of black and brown Creole-Indian segregation, only intermarriage could be forecast. But the reality is otherwise and spatial mixing together with racial endogamy is the norm.

Moreover, the two processes in San Fernando are intensifying. Segregation is increasing between Indians and Creoles, but so too is Creole-Indian intermarriage. The 1964 sample revealed the key role of Christian Indians in Creole-Indian intermarriage, and there is ample evidence for 1980 to show that their broker role has been maintained and has probably intensified, despite increased Creole-Christian Indian segregation between 1960 and 1980. Additional factors encouraging race exogamy have been the older age at marriage and the shift in spouse selection to the couple themselves, even among Hindus. This has led to enhanced intermarriage between Hindus and Muslims in step with the reduction in their mutual segregation.

San Fernando is becoming more typical of Trinidad society as its racial segregation increases, but commensurately more atypical in that Indian-Creole intermarriage is increasing quite quickly. Exogamy is prevalent largely because 45 per cent of the East Indians are Christian, a proportion recorded in no other settlement of note in Trinidad and Tobago. Débé is a more faithful reflection of the national scene. Set deep in the sugar belt, racial ghettoisation and almost total endogamy correlate. Here, parental choice of marriage partner has traditionally weeded out not only Creoles – who were never seriously in contention – but Muslims and undesirable Hindu castes as well. In Débé, even today, the more modern regime of mate selection, which tolerates unions with Christian and Muslim Indians, effectively rules out black and brown Creoles.

Acknowledgements

I am indebted to the Nuffield Foundation, which funded fieldwork in Trinidad in 1985 and enabled me to collect most of the material analysed in this chapter. I am also grateful for the hospitality and assistance offered me by the Extra-Mural Studies Unit, University of the West Indies, St Augustine, during this visit. Warmest thanks go to my wife, Gillian Clarke, and to Dr Steven Vertovec, my former research student, who helped me to copy the marriage data kindly made available by the Registrar General of Trinidad and Tobago.

References

Beshers, J., 1962, *Urban Social Structure*, New York: The Free Press of Glencoe.

Clarke, C.G., 1971, 'Residential Segregation and Intermarriage in San Fernando, Trinidad', *Geographical Review*, Vol. 61, No. 2, pp. 198-218.

– 1986, *East Indians in a West Indian Town: San Fernando, Trinidad, 1930-1970*, London: Allen and Unwin.

Lieberson, S., 1963, *Ethnic Patterns in American Cities*, New York: The Free Press of Glencoe.

Peach, C., 1980, 'Ethnic Segregation and Intermarriage', *Annals of the Association of American Geographers*, Vol. 70, No. 3, pp. 371-81.

Tinker, H., 1974, *A New System of Slavery: The Export of Indian Labour Overseas, 1830-1920*, London: Oxford University Press.

Wood, D., 1968, *Trinidad in Transition: The Years After Slavery*, London: Oxford University Press.

Vertovec, S.A., 1987, 'Hinduism and Social Change in Village Trinidad', unpublished D.Phil. thesis, University of Oxford.

CHAPTER 6

Ethnic conflict in Trinidad and Tobago: Domination and reconciliation

Ralph Premdas

Ethnic politics in the Third World has been marked by pervasive societal malaise and often at times open communal violence. Frequently, this has led to the establishment of *de facto* ethnically-based regimes in which one group dominates the lives of others. In Trinidad and Tobago this eventuated from 1956 to 1986 when the predominantly Creole-backed People's National Movement (PNM) governed the twin-island state. The institutional bequest from Britain encouraged open and unrestrained competition for votes and pitched one communal group against another, resulting in ethnically-polarised party politics and a deeply divided state. In a context of inter-ethnic distrust and fears of ethnic domination, and above all the absence of over-arching national consensual values over fundamental issues and institutions, one ethnic group practically seized power to assure its self-preservation. In Trinidad ethnic dominance was not a crude and cruel event characterised by systemic oppression and acts of physical genocide. Creole ascendancy and dominance were executed through free and fair elections in a democratic framework. All the same, it left in its wake a deeply divided society in which ethnic exclusion bred enduring resentment and a crippled public will.

Ethnic domination was neither necessary nor inevitable, as the plural society theorists would have us believe. For both J.S. Furnivall and M.G. Smith, maintaining order and stability in multi-ethnic plural societies required an ethnic group to seize power and dominate the rest (see Smith, 1969). Furnivall's 'ethnic domination model' of the plural society, which Smith uncritically imitated, was justified and legitimised on the proposition that the ethnic sections in the colonial state constituted 'a medley, for they mix but do not combine' and that this segmented condition would inevitably degenerate into chaos without an 'umpire' to maintain elementary order. Nothing was said about the institutional system of political life bequeathed by Britain that encouraged zero-sum uncompromising conflict and competition among the ethnic groups for the limited resources and values of the society. The multi-ethnic mosaic in Trinidad was itself the creation of colonialism in which

Imperial control was effected through a policy of divide and rule. Colonial institutions kept the immigrant groups residentially, occupationally and culturally apart. A body of shared values did not emerge to weld the disparate peoples into any sort of coherent community.

That chaos would ensue at independence from this legacy was really a case of prophetic fulfilment in the light of antecedent colonial policy. Was it inevitable that colonial politics and communally divided society be succeeded at independence by inter-ethnic and internecine conflict leaving one group in control of the rest? Clearly, from the results of the 1986 general elections in Trinidad when a multi-ethnic party, the National Alliance for Reconstruction (NAR), won overwhelmingly, the answer is in the negative. There are alternatives to uncompromising inter-ethnic competition and resultant ethnic domination as suggested not only by the 1986 Trinidad experience but by the cases of several other Third World countries which at one time or another had experimented with new institutions for regulating ethnic strife. In this chapter I examine the case of Trinidad in 1986 to see what factors led to overcoming the spell of ethnic rivalry and the evolution of a formula for ethnic accommodation. In particular, I examine the 1986 story against the larger theoretical claims of the viability of consociational systems of inter-ethnic accommodation designed at once to maintain stability and democracy.

The problem of finding a formula for inter-ethnic coexistence

Multi-ethnic societies in the Third World throw up special problems for political accommodation. The variety of ethnic combinations in these societies ranges from preponderantly polarised bifurcation to intense segmentation. Trinidad and Tobago (Trinidad hereafter) describes a case of bifurcation as discussed in Chapter 5 and shown in Table 6.1.

The pre-eminent political problem in every case of ethnic segmentation turns on the issue of inter-ethnic coexistence within an accepted framework that protects the fundamental interests of each community. This has been a very elusive problem. Inter-ethnic peace, when it has been attained by general consent, tends to be fragile, rarely enduring for long periods of time without being shattered, throwing the society once more into processes of both domination and reconciliation. In the midst of long stretches of oppression, harmonious solutions have been found even for short durations. This incidence of short-term inter-ethnic coexistence suggests that a systematic analysis may yield insights towards formulae for more enduring accommodation. The utter

Table 6.1:   The ethnic composition of Trinidad and Tobago's population

Group	Numbers	% of total
Africans	430,862	40.8
Indians	429,187	40.7
Mixed	172,265	16.3
Europeans	9,987	0.9
Chinese	5,562	0.7
Others	4,055	0.6
TOTALS	1,055,763	100.0

Source: 1980 *Census of Trinidad and Tobago.*

destructiveness of inter-ethnic strife thrown up by the metaphor of a 'Lebanised future' compels the search for solutions. In this chapter I look at the Trinidad 1986 case to see why it succeeded and failed against the backdrop of the solution proposed by 'consociational democracy' (Lijphart, 1977). It will be useful at the outset to offer a brief sketch of the consociational formula.

The major disagreement with the 'domination' or 'control model' has come from the consociational school spearheaded by Arend Lijphart. While conceding that integration in plural societies is problematic, the consociational democracy proponents do not accept as inevitable government by communal domination (Lijphart, 1977: 1-20; see also, Daalder, 1974). Lijphart argues that both stability and democracy can be retained under certain circumstances where elites from the various communal groups coalesce to form a government. Lijphart rejects the parliamentary model with its competitive and adversarial zero-sum implications in the distribution of power which many Third World countries have inherited on independence. Instead, pointing to the experience of certain continental European countries with communal divisions, such as Austria, The Netherlands and Belgium, Lijphart proposed governing regimes constituted through the process of inter-elite bargaining to promote sharing of power and the benefits and burdens of government. Under this formula the coalescent elites must retain the confidence of their respective communal constituents, be endowed with powers to veto any proposal which they view as inimical to their sectional interests, participate proportionately in the government at the level of representation, civil service posts, allocation of funds, etc., and maintain relative autonomy in the governance of their respective communities. To be sure, this formula for political peace and democracy can only take place under a set of circumstances such as where a multiple balance of communal sections exists, where cleavages are not too extreme, and where some cross-cutting cleavages and over-arching loyalties exist. Nevertheless, the consociational democracy alternative stands as a positive challenge to the prescribed inevitability of domination found in the literature on plural societies.

Critics of consociational arrangements point to the special conditions which hedge this sort of grand coalition as too structured and too infrequent to be of much use. Bargaining theorists David Rothchild and Brian Barry seem to agree that there are alternatives to domination in plural societies, but in rejecting consociational democracy they stress the need for bargaining between communal elites as the requisite foundation for sharing power and maintaining stability (Rothchild, 1986; see also Barry, 1975). They reject the consociational model mainly on the grounds that its structure is too elaborate, rigid and formalistic to be viable or operable (Premdas, 1986:157-9).

Many of the features of the consociational model – coalition, mutual veto, proportionality, and segmental autonomy – have at one point or another been incorporated in many Third World governments' attempts to reconcile communal adversaries. But for the most part these concessions have not been consistent, sincere or unqualified to entire communal sections to persuade them to relinquish opposition to governing regimes. The upshot has been that consociational arrange-ments are few and far between, while communal domination has been the prevalent norm. In the few cases in the Third World where consociational devices have been applied, they have tended to be transitory and quickly superseded by domination regimes (Milne, 1982:176; see also Premdas, 1981).

Most recently, the control model has received finer elaboration by Ian Lustick in his study of Arabs in Israeli society (Lustick, 1979). Other authors have also applied a variant of the control model to study Third World states (Premdas and Hintzen, 1983). Lustick's model and Smootha's application to Israel and Northern Ireland have been very useful but I believe deficient in some important respects, limiting its general applicability to a few cases (Smootha, 1980:256). In any event, my focus is mainly on the consociational formula.

Trinidad in December 1986: voting for the multi-ethnic NAR

In this part of the chapter I look at the momentous event in December 1986, when the multi-ethnic party, the NAR, won the general elections overwhelmingly in Trinidad. In particular, I examine the NAR party for its composition and structure against the background of the formation and performance of the PNM.

The PNM was formed in 1956 with a nationalist programme under an exceptionally talented leader, Eric Williams (see Ryan, 1972). Its multi-racial projection, however, was a facade for it was *de facto* preponderantly a mass-based Creole party, but led by an educated Creole middle class. It was launched as a separate party at a time when East Indians were already mobilised and organised around the Peoples' Democratic Party (PDP) led by Bhadase Maharaj. White Europeans (sometimes collectively called French Creoles even though descended from French and English settlers), off-whites and many middle-class coloureds were also organised as a separate political formation under the Party of Political Progress Groups (POPPG). In effect, despite its rhetorical claims to being nationalist and multi-racialist, when the PNM was launched it effectively completed the organisation of most of the colony's peoples into ethnically compartmentalised parties.

From 1956 to 1961 the tripartite party system underwent fundamental transformation into a polarised two-party system. The Indian-based PDP, which later became the Democratic Labour Party (DLP), at one point succeeded in gaining the support of the POPPG element. But it lost this support to the PNM by the 1961 general election. Much ethnic bad blood was let between the 1958 federal election and the 1961 general election. When the new Indian party leader, Dr Rudranath Capildeo was harassed by unruly behaviour of some PNM Creole activists at his party meetings, he called for the use of counter-ethnic violence. This was a critical point when the system practically disintegrated, for inter-ethnic civility between Indians and Creoles was severely tested. At the time when this happened the internal civil government was under PNM governance. That systematic violence and civil war did not follow is of secondary importance to the view imparted to Indians that they were not offered security to conduct free political campaigns at election time. The PNM government under Creole leadership was accused of failing to provide elementary protection to the preponderantly Indian-based opposition party. It is, however, fair to point out that Indians expressed as much ethnocentric chauvinism as Creoles, each threatening the other with domination.

If the PNM government failed to provide for law and order, then the Indian-based opposition was equally irresponsible in calling for violence. What was significant in these events was the destruction of a common basis for inter-ethnic coexistence. Elections in plural societies are not moments for debating and clarifying issues by different parties. Nor are they integrative events when citizens limit their discourse to procedural issues. Rather, because of the zero-sum structure of the contest conducted in a context where consensual values shared by all citizens are lacking, elections are fought over fundamental stakes. Each ethnic bloc views this event in semi-military terms in which the victor literally defeats and punishes the vanquished. Winners in a zero-sum competitive game take all the benefits of government and may even re-define the rules of the game to perpetuate their power. The stakes are thus total and long-term. In the end, avoidance of ethnic domination becomes the most salient underlying issue in these elections. When, for instance, the Indian-based DLP won the election in the now defunct Federal West Indian election in 1958, this was seen to signal Indian superiority and dominance of Creoles. Similarly, the 1961 general election in Trinidad was cast in total terms as Indian conquest by Creoles.

The PNM under Williams inherited a deeply divided state that it had partly assisted in creating as it sought to win power. If the Indian-based DLP under Capildeo had won, its terms of reference in governing a wholly shattered society would have been the same. In the 1961 general election, although French Creoles, mixed races and Chinese sought refuge under the umbrella of the Creole-dominated PNM, the exclusion of the significant Hindu section was a body blow to regime legitimacy and effectiveness.

The political and social wounds of the 1961 election were partly healed for a few years thereafter when Williams and the DLP seemed to have decided to bury the hatchet. A measure of inter-party amity, consultations and compromise characterised this period as Capildeo, a University of London physics lecturer, sought to run the party from London. The weakening of the militancy of the DLP under the absentee Capildeo encouraged the PNM to withdraw from consulting the opposition. Progressively, the PNM grew not only in strength but in arrogance as it dictated the terms of political life in Trinidad.

The emergence of a virtually dominant one-party system in Trinidad and Tobago following the eclipse of a perpetually divided Indian-based opposition from 1961 to 1986, invited the discriminatory practice of ethnic preference in government allocation of jobs and resources. First, though, the PNM decided to secure and consolidate its power by a policy of non-reconciliation with the Hindu segment of the Indian population. This was done in three ways. First, no Hindu throughout its 30-year hold on power was allowed to enter the PNM cabinet. Representing nearly a third of the population, the Hindus construed their exclusion from the highest decision-making council of the land as a deliberate instance of political revenge. Hindus had, however, consistently voted en bloc for the Indian-based party. Dr Williams and the PNM retaliated by appointing only a few Hindus to the Senate and none to the Cabinet throughout their 30-year tenure of office. The same policy was followed without thought for its social consequences at the level of appointments to ambassadorial positions in the diplomatic corps. It was ironic that this blatant and thorough-going policy of ethnic exclusion was pursued even when increasingly many middle-class Hindus had decided to vote for the PNM. To squash the Hindu vote was more important to the PNM than to build a united nation.

The second deliberate policy of isolating the Hindus was the systematic over-representation of Muslims (who constituted about 15 per cent of the Indian population) not only in the Cabinet but in all public positions. Again, this short-sighted political policy was aimed at maximising electoral gain. Knowing that Hindus and Muslims have traditionally maintained a relationship of malaise, to continue to cultivate and capitalise on the cleavage, even when its electoral paramountcy had become unassailable, was plainly a case of gross overkill. The wedge used to maintain and exploit Hindu-Muslim religious differences was partly effective in gaining substantial Muslim electoral support. Yet in no constituency was the Muslim vote so distributed that it was needed by the PNM to win a seat. Moreover, only about half of the Muslims tended to support the PNM, in any case. The gains of cultivating Hindu-Muslim antipathy were not significant enough to offset the damage that was deliberately inflicted on the social and cultural national fabric. The PNM polity of religious discrimination did, however, prevent the Indians from forming a coherent electoral bloc.

The third deliberate policy against Hindus in particular by the PNM government pertained to appointments to the public service. Through-out its rule, the size of the public service grew to some 60,000 persons. The number of state corporations rose to 65. In both of these segments of the public bureaucracy practically all the top and senior positions were assigned to non-Hindus, especially to Creole and mixed races. The blatant discrimination was visible for all to see and was similar to racism in the colonial bureaucracy. Less visible, until recently, were the precise figures of each ethnic group's presence in the public service. In 1989 one researcher revealed that the results of a survey of the public service showed that Indians held only about 25 per cent of all the posts. By 1988 Indians had come close to numbering 50 per cent of the population.

The racially discriminatory policies of the PNM also extended to government allocation of expenditure in relation to regions, neighbour-hoods and projects designed to benefit particular ethnic segments. For 30 years then a systematic policy of ethnic preference was openly practised against Indians and mainly Hindus in Trinidad. The result was the evolution of a middle-income government-employed black bourgeoisie who politically and administratively had come to dominate a government in the multi-ethnic plural society. Indian response consisted mainly of socially withdrawing and economically cultivating the private sector where many slowly prospered at the periphery of the political system. It is clear that for the most part this ethno-nationalist discriminatory policy was motivated less by personal hate than by collective fear of an ethnic group that was as narrow in its national vision as the short-sighted chauvinists who led the PNM for 30 years.

To many non-Indian citizens, the discriminatory treatment meted out to the Hindus in particular was not only unjust but was destructive to Trinidad's political and economic development. This was emphatically registered on the national consciousness as the PNM regime dragged the country and all ethnic groups into deep recession following the dramatic collapse of oil prices. PNM racism was compounded by public corruption and bureaucratic inefficiency to such an extent that everyone, Hindu and Creole alike, became victims, engendering a national outcry which led to the eviction of the PNM from power.

Mode of control in PNM-Creole dominance

The PNM hold on power followed a particular mode of control or dominance. It would be useful to identify the pillars of dominance which the PNM had chosen to utilise in maintaining itself in power. It should be recognised here that there are several 'control' or 'repression' models available by which to subjugate a group of people. For example, as noted earlier, Ian Lustick devised a model of control which evolved in relation to Israeli-Jewish control of Arabs in Israel (Lustick, 1979). The Arab-Israeli conflict can be conceived as an international ethnic conflict that went completely out of control. The superordinate group (the Jews) have systematically repressed the subordinate group (the Arabs). The *modus operandi*, according to Lustick depended on three strategies:

(1) *Segmentation:* This refers to the isolation of the subordinate group while at the same time fostering internal schisms in the subordinate group to be manipulated for future use;

(2) *Dependence* refers to the method by which the subordinate group is made to rely on the resources of the superordinate group for survival; and

(3)   *Co-optation* is the process by which members of one side are recruited openly or surreptitiously to serve the interest of the dominant group.

Unlike Israeli control of the Arabs, the PNM control of the Indians had to take place within a democratic framework, albeit one that was under a corrupt, dominant, one-party dictatorial personalistic ruler. The PNM strategy did stress *segmentation* in its effort to isolate and discriminate against Hindus. Pointedly, Muslims, who are also Indians, were omitted from these discriminatory practices. This heightened the isolation of the Hindu community which in turn forced them into disciplined habits of harder effort and self-reliance for their economic welfare. There are some who say that over a period of time this moulded the Indians into legendary, self-sacrificing workhorses compared with their more pampered Creole compatriots.

Dependence was only partly achieved since Indians withdrew within the private sector which they assiduously cultivated as their own realm. But this apart, Hindus depended heavily on government contracts to do business and because of their virtual dominance over medium and small contracting businesses, they were depended upon by the government to execute official programmes. Hence, while dependence for government jobs was achieved, a system of interdependence evolved between government expenditure and Hindu private enterprise. However, overall, a psychology of dependence developed coexisting simultaneously with a sense of satisfying defiance.

Co-optation was also utilised by the PNM so that a few Hindus were recruited to the PNM and offered conspicuously high positions. Among these were a number who were appointed to the Senate. These strategies of control were not as total or comprehensive as would be found in a totalitarian order. Indians were not put under surveillance nor made to report regularly to state officials, nor required to carry identity cards, nor compelled to live in specific neighbourhoods, nor restricted to particular occupations, etc., such as exist in Lustick's 'total control' system. However, the Indian was made to feel politically inferior, as a second-class citizen, by discriminatory practices and by preference to English and Creole culture.

Clearly 'control' mechanisms are radically different from 'consociational' devices. The former stresses ethnic dominance and exclusivity in the use of resources, the latter depends on sharing and balance for its success. Further, the former ultimately depends on a backdrop support of coercion. The PNM maintained almost total control over the armed forces and police, organisations to which few Indians were recruited. The consociational structure is not funded on coercion but co-operation. Finally, a system based on control operates in the shadow of illegitimacy, inviting rebellion and subversion by excluded sections. It may be under attack by an underground movement. Eventually it will be replaced. We must now turn and look at the evolution of a semi-consociational system that replaced the PNM.

Victory by the NAR in December 1986

When the PNM's redoubtable leader Dr Eric Williams died in 1981, everyone expected the personalised machine through which he governed to collapse in cataclysmic fashion. The PNM did fall, but it collapsed gradually over a period of five years. The new PNM Prime Minister, George Chambers, reshuffled his cabinet, terminated a few extravagant projects such as the horse-racing complex, settled a number of important industrial disputes, made himself accessible to the press, visited and held consultations with the people, and promised, in a persuasive slogan, that 'what's wrong must be put right'. Together, this public relations assault created the illusion of a new PNM with a new hope. The PNM knew, however, that this was a camouflage concealing the undercurrent of multiple problems which had beset the population. They desperately wanted to win, to spend the following four or five years in salvaging the economy and averting the popular wrath that was bound to bury them in future elections.

The Chambers' honeymoon with the public notwithstanding, the death of Williams saw the blossoming of forces once suppressed by his awesome personality. New parties were formed and old parties revitalised. Foremost among the new parties was the Organisation for National Reconstruction (ONR) led by the former PNM stalwart, Karl Hudson-Phillips. The ONR attacked the Williams' legacy of dependence and corruption and attracted large multi-racial crowds. Another group that emerged was called the National Alliance composed of a loose alignment of the old Tobago-based Democratic Action Congress (DAC) led by A.N.R. Robinson, another ex-PNM stalwart, and the United Labour Front (ULF), led by Basdeo Panday. The ULF was the new Indian-based party and it was led by a lawyer activist who was the head of the All Trinidad Sugar Estates and General Workers Trade Union, the main sugar union. The ULF's victories in past general elections were confined to certain Indian-dominated constituencies only but together they always constituted a minority.

The PNM minus Williams won the 1981 elections in what superficially was a resounding victory, taking 26 out of 36 seats. However, voter turnout was only 54.7 per cent. The opposition parties fared well. Although the ONR did not win a seat, it gathered an astounding 22.1 per cent of the votes cast. The National Alliance won 10 seats, eight in the sugar belt and two in Tobago, taking 21 per cent of the votes. In effect, while the PNM continued to control the Parliament, its popular victory represented only 29.8 per cent support from the entire electorate.

Chambers was no Williams. Not only did he lack charisma but he had to face the full meaning of the decline in oil prices. What severely restricted Chambers' capacity to restructure the economy was the fact that he faced new county council elections in 1983. The result of these elections was interpreted as being indicative of a party's popular acceptance. The Chambers' regime wanted desperately to win. The results of the county elections stunned the PNM. In an historical arrangement, the ONR and National Alliance had joined forces against the PNM. The PNM obtained a total of 54 council seats to the opposition 66. The ruling regime was now mortally wounded.

The end of 30 years of PNM rule came in the December 1986 general election. The successful ONR-National Alliance collaboration in the county council elections led to a new formal political coalition incorporating the Tapia House party led by Lloyd Best and designating itself the National Alliance for Reconstruction. The NAR was a formidable alignment of ethnic groups, classes and regions in Trinidad and Tobago. It was *de facto* that elusive multi-ethnic formation that had so far failed to appear in Trinidad's politics. It called itself the 'rainbow party' proclaiming a philosophy of 'one love'. Robinson was chosen to lead the NAR.

A new general election was scheduled for December 1986. A poll just prior to the election showed that 41 per cent of Creoles, 82 per cent of Indians, and 47 per cent of mixed races supported the NAR. It was also known that the French Creole elite had shifted its support to the NAR and provided much of its financing and public relations propaganda. The PNM lost to a resoundingly victorious NAR which obtained 67.3 per cent of the votes and won all but three seats in the 36-seat House of Representatives. The day of the NAR's victory witnessed unprecedented multi-ethnic celebrations across the country. The NAR assumed power in the spirit of cross-communal reconciliation, promising a new day of dignity and justice to all (Yelvington, 1987). In particular, the previously excluded Hindus had great hopes for fair play in the new regime.

Although it proclaimed it was a unitary party, the NAR in fact was a loose confederal combination of its four unintegrated parts. The differences were temporarily submerged during the electoral battle against the PNM. When the common enemy was eliminated, internal fissures surfaced. How they were handled determined the NAR's future as a unified movement for change. When Robinson was appointed leader no concession was made to his superiority in any way over his co-leaders, Panday, Hudson-Phillips and Best. He was chosen because electorally he was most likely to maximise votes for a NAR victory. The leaders, especially Panday, Hudson-Phillips and Robinson, who previously had independent electoral parties, worked closely together during the election campaign. Although Best had mentioned the need for it, no formula for sharing power, in the event of victory, was devised. In fact the NAR did not expect to win until the final weeks of the campaign, and by then a spirit of common purpose made a power-sharing formula appear unnecessary. It was anticipated that the spirit of 'one love' and consultation prior to the election would continue afterwards. As time would tell, this was not true and it was a fatal mistake not to have designed a formula for power-sharing. In terms of the Lijphartian consociational formula, only one of the four factors was present in the NAR, that is, a grand coalition. Absent was proportionality in the sharing of cabinet appointments and civil service jobs. Hence, there was no possibility of mutual veto in decision making. In fact, a collective decision-making system with its participants and procedures was not designed and there was no system of decentral-isation. The entire new government rested on a coalition of diverse interests without any system of sharing and accountability specified.

Almost as soon as victory was obtained, internal strife entered this power vacuum. Prime Minister Robinson took it upon himself to name his cabinet without consulting his partners in victory. Strictly speaking, Robinson followed protocol as in Westminster parliamentary systems. The ethnic structure of the new cabinet shocked Indians who had voted overwhelmingly (82 per cent) for the NAR. Of 19 cabinet posts, only five were allocated to Indians, two to whites, one to a person of a mixed race, and 11 to Creoles. Although the NAR's overwhelming 33-seat victory was a 'combinational' event, each ethnic group interpreted its cabinet share by reference to its imagined input in the victory. By their ethnic arithmetic, Indians felt grievously short-changed in cabinet posts.

Panday and his old ULF faction in the NAR decided against challenging Robinson immediately, but a wedge of distrust had been driven into the very heart of the hydra-headed NAR leadership. Indian chagrin was suppressed. Robinson continued to separate himself from his erstwhile electoral co-leaders and retreated behind a cadre of personal staff and technocrats from the public service. The small handful of ULF Indian ministers claimed that they were deliberately excluded from Robinson's inner circle of ex-PNM technocrats. Panday was not amused and he openly reminded the public that he had not dedicated his life to destroy PNM-ism only to see it slip back into power through the back door. The 'rainbow' multi-ethnic feature of the NAR was progressively being eroded and eclipsed by the internal leadership schism. Panday, deputy leader of the NAR and Foreign Minister, and his loyal group of ULF ministers, alleged that they continued to suffer exclusion from decision making. In anger, Panday went so far as to compare Robinson's open formal commitment to multi-racialism to the rhetoric of Williams who 'used to make similar speeches and then went on to set up the most racist society that we ever had' (Ryan, 1988:77). However, before this dispute blew the NAR apart, about nine months after its December victory, the party was engaged in county council elections. The NAR closed ranks, forgot its internal squabbles, and won the September 1987 county council elections. The margin of victory was, however, less than in the 1986 general election. The NAR lost three of the 11 councils to the PNM. The internal ethnic struggle had re-stimulated ethnic polarisation so that many Creoles were returning to the PNM.

The internal ethnic schism that the NAR experienced was matched in magnitude by the external economic situation that the party faced in assuming office. They assumed a deficit of TT$ 2.8 billion left by the PNM, an empty treasury, a debt service obligation that required TT$ 1.7 billion annually, or 39 per cent of all anticipated revenues, and the exhaustion of the legal limits of public borrowing. Robinson, serving in the capacity of Finance Minister, remarked that 'it was as though the PNM was determined to sink the country before being voted out'. The PNM had engaged in an orgy of overspending to save themselves from defeat at the polls.

The NAR had underestimated the depth of the economic crisis that the country confronted. During its election campaign it optimistically promised to 'roll back the recession'. Lacking a plan or strategy to cope with the crisis, it fought desperately to rescue Trinidad, in Robinson's words, 'from the jaws of three financial dragons – an unbridgeable budget deficit, a continuing balance of payments crisis, and the debt trap'. To survive, the NAR had to administer bitter medicine to its own supporters who voted it into power. In its first budget the many and varied forms of subsidies which the PNM had built into the economy were swiftly eliminated. The annual Cost of Living Allowance (COLA) was unceremoniously dropped. The two-tier currency exchange system which subsidised food and drug imports to the tune of TT$ 700 million was scrapped. Taxes were put on gasoline, airline tickets, and other items, while old taxes were increased. A national recovery levy was imposed on all persons with income above TT$ 70,000 annually. These measures and many others had the desired effect of substantially reducing the annual deficit. Yet the problem remained formidable for oil prices continued to fall. Unemployment passed the 20 per cent mark. The International Monetary Fund was approached. More and new drastic measures had to be imposed in 1988.

After one year in office then, the NAR was buffeted by internal crises and threatened to tear the new multi-ethnic party apart at its ethnic seams. Continued public criticisms by Panday's faction about Robinson's leadership style, the alleged lack of consultation, and the existence of 'an invisible government' of Creole technocrats and big business finally reached a crescendo on 26 November 1987 when Robinson asked the entire cabinet to submit its resignation. The country was in total shock; racial conflict appeared ready to engulf the society. For 48 hours Robinson agonised and finally fired John Humphrey, the (white) Pandayite Minister of Housing. Panday's own Ministry of External Affairs was shrunk by the removal from it of immigration and citizenship. Kelvin Ramnath, who had vocally criticised the PNM technocrats around Robinson, was transferred from the powerful Energy Ministry to Public Utilities, which in turn was shorn of several critical utilities. Emmanuel Hosein, the Minister of Health, lost Welfare and Women's Affairs.

The Pandayite faction was not expelled but found itself with reduced responsibilities and power. At the same time Robinson added three new ministries and assigned all of them to Creoles. Robinson's message to the NAR was that he was the Prime Minister and that intra-party complaints must be handled through established procedures. But the Panday group was not about to be silenced or intimidated. In turn, the Panday faction was accused in one famous news story of wanting more power to secure Indian domination. The internal crisis reached a head when Panday proceeded to negotiate for the building of the Indian Cultural Centre, a gift from the Indian government to Trinidad, only to be thwarted by a racially-divided cabinet. When Panday and his faction spoke out again, on 8 February 1988, they were expelled from Robinson's cabinet. The core of the ULF contingent – Panday, Trevor Sudama, Ramnath and Humphrey – was now gone. Panday, the hero of the Indian people, was no longer with the government. The internal bickering in the NAR was resolved but at the expense of dividing Trinidad's population once more along Creole-Indian polarised lines.

Underlying causes of the NAR's leadership schisms

When the NAR, which had stimulated so much hope for a racially unified country in coming to power, suffered the unfortunate blow of internal disharmony, the repercussions were ominous. The division was open along the fundamental ethnic cleavage that separated the two largest communal groups in Trinidad. Few inter-communal institutions had evolved during the colonial period to weld Indians and Creoles together into any sort of harmonious community. Colonial politics were marked by ethnic distrust and rivalry. At independence, sectionally-based institutions such as political parties organised and mobilised the ethnic groups into separate compartments. The PNM, for the first 24 years after independence, did little to build bridges of co-operation and trust between Indians and Creoles. When the NAR acceded to power it appeared at last that institutionalised ethnic disunity would be brought to an end. The internal schism in the NAR one year after it acceded to power killed that prospect of inter-ethnic co-operation between Indians and Creoles. There was so much high expectation attached by the population to the NAR's unifying symbolism that when its leaders stumbled on the rocks of ethnic competition, one shocked woman declared: 'Lord, it was almost as if the world had come to an end' (quoted in Ryan, 1988:77). Professor Selwyn Ryan, the well-known public opinion pollster, reported that after the expulsion of Panday and his faction from the Cabinet: 'Trinidadians reacted with stunned disbelief as they contemplated the possibility that their vaunted rainbow had indeed come to an end and that open racial conflict was imminent' (Ryan, 1988:66).

The breakup of the NAR brought Trinidad to the brink of open ethnic strife. Fears of organised physical confrontation were rife. Ryan noted that 'there were also fears that social unrest might ensue if disaffected politicians mobilised their supporters for a confrontation with those perceived to be responsible for their removal from the government. The example of Fiji and Sri Lanka were uppermost in the minds of many' (1988:66). If it is true that the NAR's accession to power contained the promise of a new dawn for national unity, by the same token, the leadership split 'precipitated one of the most significant political crises Trinidad had faced since becoming independent in 1962' (Ryan, 1988:66). Luckily, the Robinson and Panday factions held their followers under firm control. Panday promised that he would take the matter to the people by way of political meetings. The NAR party appointed an internal group to conduct an inquiry into the dissension. Both Panday and Robinson publicly declared that they wanted reconciliation. It is instructive to examine briefly the report of the NAR internal committee of inquiry which sought reconciliation.

The NAR's own inquiry into the leadership split was chaired by J. Nanga (hereafter referred to as the Nanga Committee) (Nanga Committee, 1988). Its terms of reference required it to seek out evidence from all NAR sources to determine the cause of the leadership rift and to make recommendations. It is useful to remember here that basically Robinson's official reasons for expelling the Panday faction pertained to points of procedure, that is, the use of public fora by Panday to vent his grievances. Panday, on the other hand, felt that as deputy leader of the NAR and leader of the Indian communal section which provided the majority for the NAR's electoral victory, he should have been consulted in decision making made by Prime Minister Robinson. This was Panday's expectation, but it was not a written agreement.

The Nanga Committee discovered that after the NAR acceded to power, practically all of the party's internal organs had fallen into disuse. It further found that the Panday-Robinson division had permeated all structures of the party membership so that a major chasm divided the organisation: 'It is correct to say that when we examine the party structure, unity has been replaced with division. This division is present at almost all levels. Some party units are in a state of dormancy ... The party machinery is disunited, frustrated and lacks the motivation and political will to ... impact ... on ... the government' (Nanga Committee, 1988:11). The Nanga Committee paradoxically concluded that although the party institutions were not operating, 'failure to give due recognition and failure to utilize party institutions to settle problems and air differences are indeed serious and unpardonable' (Nanga Committee, 1988:15). In the light of the dormancy of the party organs and the emergency nature of the dispute, the committee recommended that a special forum be established to handle problems such as occurred between Panday and Robinson.

On the issue of Robinson's consultation of his partners in the NAR in governmental decision making, the Nanga Committee observed that orthodox Westminster parliamentary procedures did not oblige the Prime Minister to consult anyone. Panday, however, had charged that Robinson, in the spirit of the NAR's multi-ethnic coalition structure, and in the light of the fact that he was leader of the Indian section, should have been consulted on major decisions. To Panday, Robinson's lack of consultation indicated that Robinson 'did not respect him or give him his due as a deputy leader' (Nanga Committee, 1988:33). Further, Panday alleged that 'Robinson had treated him with contempt and disrespect in failing or neglecting to consult with him ...'(Nanga Committee, 1988:33).

Robinson had a special interpretation of the reason, however, why Panday had taken his complaints to the public instead of the party. According to the Nanga Committee: 'Mr Robinson felt that Panday's behaviour in speaking out resulted from the cult of opposition politics and was a direct challenge to his authority' (Nanga Committee,

1988:33). Robinson, as Prime Minister, further felt that he needed a unified party in support of his leadership of the country which was in deep economic crisis. He is known to be a keen observer of formality and parliamentary protocol. On this score the Nanga Committee pointed out that although Robinson was acting within his formal rights on the issue of consultation 'having regard to the manner in which the NAR was formed' (i.e. a coalition of parties), Robinson should have consulted Panday (Nanga Committee, 1988:32).

Behind the outward issues of correct procedure and lack of consultation, though, lurked more fundamental issues of power and ethnicity. It would have been useful if, at the founding of the NAR, some sort of explicit consociational formula had been adopted to depoliticise these issues. To the press and in public places, the two leaders would speak out openly and in so doing gradually reveal the underlying tensions which marked the relationship between them. In this regard, the Nanga Committee condemned both Robinson and Panday for 'political immaturity' in dealing with the problems. It concluded that 'all the leaders must share the blame for the current situation' (1988:34). The committee recommended that 'reconciliation should be pursued amongst the leaders' (1988:35).

In the end, as days became weeks and months, the leadership split festered and grew worse since the underlying issues were not addressed. It is useful here to describe briefly these problems as seen by Panday and Robinson. For Panday, the fundamental issue of his evictions pertained to his attempts to rectify the grievances of the Indian constituents whom he represented. The charge was racial discrimination and institutional racism. He, however, cast the charge of inequality within the larger framework of the country's quest for development. According to Panday:

> Only the most callous and insensitive in our society would argue that the Indo-Trinidadian has no cause to feel discriminated against. That means that half of our population has no enthusiasm and no motivation to make sacrifices for a country that has persistently marginalised them.
>
> That is the most debilitating national factor in our effort to progress economically, socially and politically. As a small country with a population of a mere 1.3 million souls, our most valuable resource in any plan or programme for economic development is not our oil and sugar, but our human resource.
>
> It follows that the most urgent task confronting us is how to mobilise our human resources to the task of nation-building

if large sections of the population are alienated because they feel that they are being discriminated against because of their race (Raphael, 1990:5).

After the leadership split Panday explicitly charged Robinson with being a racist (Raphael, 1990:5). However, Robinson's alleged racism was seen as a device for him to grab power away from his coalition partners who had contributed towards building the multi-racial NAR. Robinson was depicted as having deliberately manipulated his position as Prime Minister to eliminate Panday from the joint leadership of the NAR and the sharing of power. Again Panday alleged:

> The *raison d'être* of the NAR, its campaign thrust and its goal was to end racism in Trinidad, that had debilitated our society for so long. On 15 December 1986, when we won the election we demonstrated that we had succeeded in uniting this country as it has never been before in its entire political history.
>
> The population was ready to undergo the most serious sacrifices in the task of nation-building. Robinson smashed that unity when he sought to exclude the former ULF element [Panday's previous party] from power, first by dismissing us as ministers and then by engineering our expulsion from the NAR (Raphael, 1990:5).

The evidence adduced by Mr Panday to support his claim of Robinson's alleged racism pointed at three sources of conflict apart from the expulsion of the Panday faction from the cabinet. First, on coming to power, the ethnic imbalance in the government bureaucracy was only temporarily rectified. Panday argued:

> When we went into government in 1986, we discovered what the PNM government had done – there were 4 per cent of Indians on state boards, and what explanation can one give than that was the result of deliberate racism.
>
> So when we got into Cabinet we said the time had come to redress this imbalance. Because of my [faction's] activities, the percentage of Indians on the state board rose to 22 per cent. Then Robinson fired us and fired the 22 per cent.
>
> His removal of several Indians from Boards of State Corporations is evidence of racism. He has refused to redress the imbalance in the public sector created by the PNM (Raphael, 1990:5).

The second source of conflict that allegedly pointed to Robinson's acts of racial discrimination referred to the issue of the Indian Cultural

Centre. In this case the government of India had agreed to give a gift of a Cultural Centre to Trinidad as an act to assist Indians in celebrating their ancestral identity. The Indian government had contributed similar centres to the governments of Fiji, Guyana, and Mauritius – where Indians are resident in large numbers. However, in Trinidad, the gift caused a rift in the NAR cabinet along racial lines. Creole cabinet members saw such a gift as a factor that would retard Indian assimilation into Trinidad's culture. Some even saw the Centre as a Trojan horse, a way by which the Indian government could interfere in Trinidad's affairs. Panday felt that he had an undertaking from Robinson and the NAR prior to the general election to accept the cultural Centre, which had been practically refused by the previous Creole-dominated PNM government. However, Panday, who was Minister of External Affairs in the NAR government before his expulsion, proceeded to sign the necessary protocol papers in accepting the Cultural Centre from the Indian government. He was sure that Robinson was consulted and agreed to his official action. However, after the signing of the agreement, the NAR cabinet, dominated by Creoles, voted against the Cultural Centre until such time as the last detail on the site and land of the Centre had been agreed upon. To Panday this smacked of Robinson and the NAR reneging on their solemn promises. Hence Panday concluded: 'His [Robinson's] refusal to accept the gift of a Cultural Centre from the Indian government was motivated by racist considerations' (Raphael, 1990:5).

Finally, Panday saw in Robinson's actions a larger plan to manipulate power similar to the sort of undisputed control the towering late leader of the PNM, Dr Eric Williams, exercised over the government from 1956 to 1981. The item in particular that Panday pointed to as evidence of Robinson's motive referred to two newspaper articles which were headlined in one of the country's major newspapers, *The Express*. The two articles proclaimed the 'Indianisation of the Government' and the 'ULF Grasp for Power'. These articles purported to portray a surreptitious design, a 'hidden agenda', or a 'game plan', by the Panday faction in the NAR government to utilise their position to staff the government public bureaucracy with a majority of Indians. Since Indians were discriminated against in the past, the articles claimed that Panday's faction (the old ULF) in the NAR cabinet sought to take their turn in overcompensation. One of the articles said:

> By their turn they did not just mean that it was the turn of the Indian population, nor even of the Hindus, who they felt had always been excluded from government. It was their personal turn. And while putting forward a set of arguments

based on discrimination and injustice, they proceeded to make an immediate grab for power (Ryan, 1988:94).

The articles reversed the charge of racism and power-grabbing which Panday had levelled against Robinson. They charged that the Panday faction sought to 'Indianise the government' with a view to seizing power. The articles further counter-argued that the Creole and mixed-race dominance and over-staffing in the public service was more than offset by 'the African's disadvantage in areas of business, agriculture, medicine and law' (Ryan, 1988:94). The articles, signed anonymously by 'Technocrat', concluded that it was not Robinson but Panday and his faction who were power-hungry:

> ... the men involved do not represent the true feelings of the Indian community. They really do not care about the welfare of the Indian population, nor Hinduism nor Cultural Centres as they are about gathering power into their own hands for their personal aggrandisement and profit. The danger for the country is that in their greed, stupidity and selfish ambition they will light a match that will blow this whole country sky high (Ryan, 1988:94).

The charge that the Panday faction sought to 'grab power' through appointments was quickly squashed when a survey showed that of the 198 persons assigned to government statutory boards, only 34, or 17 per cent, were Indians. However, it would be difficult to gainsay the contention by the anonymous articles that in the absence of a pre-arranged formula to share the benefits of office, the factions in the victorious NAR government were conducting an intense behind the scene struggle over 'patronage, power and the spoils of office and it has strong racial overtones' (Ryan, 1988:94). The articles clearly portrayed a population polarised around ethnic interest even within the 'one love' and 'rainbow' bosom of the multi-racial NAR government.

Consociationalism and the NAR experience: an evaluation

In this final part, I look briefly at the causes of the NAR's dissolution – which led to its demise at the polls in December, 1991 – from the standpoint of what consociational advocates might consider deficiencies in the multi-ethnic arrangement. To begin with the NAR did meet, however approximately, certain criteria for success in establishing a stable multi-ethnic government. Most noteworthy was the coalition structure of the NAR. Here, the leaders of four groupings joined forces to form a single party. Among those groups was the major representative of the Indian communal section, Basdeo Panday. He was able to mobilise over 80 per cent of the Indian vote for the NAR. In effect, he enjoyed the confidence and trust of his own ethnic section. The other three leaders – Robinson, Hudson-Phillips and Best – were all Creoles. None of these was separately capable of mobilising the political loyalty of the Creole communal section. However, together they obtained about 45 per cent of the Creole vote for the NAR. The powerful French Creole and Syrian white section of the population withdrew their support from the PNM and moved *en bloc* over to the NAR via Hudson-Phillips's ONR organisation. Hudson-Phillips was able to attract the French Creole representative, Clive Pantin, to the ONR ranks and he more than anyone else symbolised the shift of French Creole loyalty to the NAR. Overall, then, the Creole section apart, the NAR contained the overwhelming majority of votes from Indians, French Creoles, and mixed races. The Creole section was split almost 50-50 but this division was enough to give a number of critical traditional PNM constituencies in the strategic East-West corridor to the NAR. For all practical purposes, then, the ethnic mix of the NAR broadly conformed to the coalition pre-requisites of the consociational model.

If the coalition structure was the main achievement of the NAR in establishing a broad-based legitimate multi-ethnic party for the first time in Trinidad's history, the other structural features of the consociational model were lacking in the NAR. These include mutual veto, proportionality, and decentralisation. With regards to 'mutual veto', this provision empowers each of the leaders in the coalition to veto any decision that goes against a vital interest of its community. Succinctly, this feature of consociational democracy points to joint decision making. Clearly, this was sorely lacking in the NAR. It was on this point, 'lack of consultation', which was confirmed by the Nanga Committee, that the NAR floundered. The NAR's leader, Robinson, it must be recalled, construed his leadership in accordance with correct Westminster protocol. He, as Prime Minister, was the leader who had the traditional prerogative to consult if and only if he so wished. However, the NAR party structure fitted into the model of a federal system which meant that each constituent leader of the NAR was equal to the other and that decisions had to be collective as well as consult-ative. In a unitary pyramidal organisation such as the PNM, the leader is paramount. In a *de facto* federal coalition the leader is in a consultative relationship with the other leaders. Without this, the union is likely to fall apart. The lack of this compulsory consultative feature in the

NAR's decision making while in power accounts in part for the NAR's internal strife and disintegration.

With regard to 'proportionality', this factor, like the lack of consultation, featured centrally in instigating and sustaining the ethnic strife in the NAR. 'Proportionality' refers to the 'method of allocating civil service appointments and scarce financial resources in the form of government subsidies among the different segments. It can be contrasted with the winner-take-all principle of unrestrained majority rule' (Lijphart, 1977:38-9). For Panday and the Indians the salient political issue revolved around the ethnically-oriented discriminatory practices of the PNM government. Conversely, the NAR was seen as the vehicle to override and rectify this system by some new concept of proportionality. It may be recalled that Best, the leader of one of the four component units (Tapia House) that constituted the NAR, had suggested for the 1986 elections that the NAR work out an agreement on 'proportionality' to share jobs and projects. This was ignored in the heat of the campaign. To Panday there was an implicit understanding, however, that the NAR would introduce new principles of equity in the allocation of jobs and projects. However, Robinson did not seem to share this view. It is also quite conceivable that the Pandayite faction in the NAR started to press too early for the restructuring of representation in the public service. Whatever the causes, the fact of the absence of an explicit policy of proportional sharing of the values of government led to the reassertion of Indian alienation in Trinidad.

Finally, with regard to 'segmental autonomy' or decentralisation, this part of the consociational scheme was scheduled for implementation by the NAR government under its policy of 'decentralisation'. In terms of resolving ethnic conflict by separating cultural communities so that they may govern their affairs autonomously, this device did not apply in the Trinidad context. Although a small island, Trinidad is fairly densely populated and urbanised. Most towns are mixed. Even rural areas which tend to be marked by predominantly uni-ethnic settlements and villages tend to be not far from similar ethnic clusters of another ethnic group. The growth of the island's population, the rise of urbanisation, especially by Indians leaving their traditional rural residence, and the open access to lands and houses for the purchase by anyone, have all made the concept of autonomous ethno-regional autonomy irrelevant to Trinidad. Even idle talk of separating north Trinidad, meaning in particular Creole-dominated Port of Spain, from south Trinidad, referring to the plains where the Indians used to live in dense concentrations, cannot make sense where it takes a maximum of 45 minutes to move physically from north to south. The small size of Trinidad constrains any meaningful experiment in geographical decentralised local government as a means to alleviate ethnic contact and tensions.

What would have made more sense and had more bearing on decentralisation was cultural autonomy functionally and associationally expressed. That is, a policy which provided state funds and subsidies to permit each of the ethnic groups to celebrate its own festivals and rituals. Under the Creole-dominated PNM government that preceded the NAR regime, large sums of state funds had been allocated for carnival and calypso festivals. An official commission was actually created to disburse state funds for these occasions. Indians as a whole, partake minimally, if at all, in these activities which they regard as Creole culture. With the arrival of the multi-ethnic NAR on the political scene, Indians had come to expect equitable treatment of their cultural traditions and identity. More specifically they wanted to acknowledge their cultural traditions and identity by receiving the Cultural Centre which was offered by India and state funds to subsidise such festivals as Divali Nagar. On the issue of the Cultural Centre, as pointed out, the NAR cabinet split racially. Creole members who outnumbered Indians two to one were against the Cultural Centre, viewing it politically as a cultural foothold and a preliminary act aimed at interfering in Trinidadian affairs. It was the Cultural Centre affair that triggered the split in the NAR's leadership ranks, causing Panday to feel betrayed. After Panday and his faction were evicted from the NAR, it is rather ironic that the residual NAR government has offered large subsidies and even lands to Hindus and Muslims to conduct their cultural festivals. Moreover, belatedly, the Cultural Centre was accepted by the NAR after Panday left. In the end, the NAR did practise a variation of 'decentralisation' by offering to recognise and fund the religious festivities of the Hindus and Muslims but this came too late, after the split had already occurred.

Looking, then, at the main pillars of the Lijphartian consociational model, it is clear that the NAR embodied only one of these structures, namely, 'grand coalition'. Clearly without being reinforced by the 'proportionality principle' and 'mutual veto', the co-operation and sharing feature in the coalition structure could not be sustained. Certainly, decentralisation in the distribution of funds to different cultural organisations would have aided the coalition to keep together. However, unless political will, especially goodwill, accompanies a multi-ethnic accommodation structure such as a consociationalism, the experiment in sharing will likely collapse.

The collapse of a multi-ethnic, cross-communal government can have serious consequences in a segmented society such as Trinidad.

The immediate crisis that ensues usually pertains to legitimacy of regime rule. A shattered legitimacy is often an invitation to anti-government anomic behavior, ranging from violent acts of insurrection to non-violent acts of discontent such as emigration. The broken legitimacy leaves a power vacuum often offering an invitation to acts of non-compliance and rebellion coming from any quarter of disgruntled citizens. Such an event occurred on 27 July 1990 when a band of Muslims called the Jamaat-al-Muslimeen, led by Imam Yasin Abu Bakr, attempted to overthrow the Robinson-led NAR government (cf. Ryan, 1991; Yelvington, forthcoming).

The insurrectionists were eventually suppressed but not before they pointed to aspects of popular discontent which alluded to the broken legitimacy of the NAR regime and the resurgence of inter-communal racism. Bakr sought to justify the insurrectionary challenge to the government by saying:

> . . . we call God to witness, and we pray that He will give us an opportunity to unite this country once more, that He will remove the racialism, the hatred, the bigotry . . . [1]

Importantly, the Bakr-led Muslimeen insurrectionary action was not condemned by the new Panday-led opposition party, the United National Congress (UNC). Instead, the UNC inquired sympathetically into the written promise of the NAR captives which had included Robinson himself to offer amnesty to the insurrectionists. The critical point relates to the sorts of challenges that are likely to follow when a consociational consensus breaks down. Legitimacy is lost and a continuing crisis in confidence erodes the national will, destroying the very basis of long-term development.

Note

1 Taken from the television script on 27 July 1990 when Bakr addressed the people of Trinidad and Tobago.

References

Barry, B., 1975, 'The Consociational Model and its Danger', *European Journal of Political Research*, Vol. 3, No. 4.

Daalder, H., 1974, 'The Consociational Theme', *World Politics*, Vol. 26, No. 4, pp. 607-9.

Lijphart, A., 1977, *Democracy in Plural Societies*, New Haven: Yale University Press.

Lustick, I., 1979, 'Stability in Deeply Divided Societies', *World Politics*, Vol. 31, No. 3, pp. 325-42.

Milne, R.S., 1982, *Politics in Ethnically Bipolar States*, Vancouver: University of British Columbia Press.

Nanga Committee, 1988, *Report of the Committee Appointed by the National Council of the National Alliance for Reconstruction to Investigate and Make Recommendations for Solving the Problems Affecting the Party and Government*, mimeo, March, 1988.

Premdas, R., 1981, 'Ethnic Conflict Management', in Lal, B. (ed.), *The Politics of Fiji*, London: Allen and Unwin, pp. 107-38.

– 1986, 'Politics of Preference in the Caribbean', in Nevitte, N. and Kennedy, C. (eds), *Ethnic Preference and Public Policy*, Boulder, CO: Lynne Reinner Publications.

Premdas, R. and Hintzen, P., 1983, 'Guyana: Coercion and Control in Political Change', *Journal of Interamerican Studies and World Affairs*, Vol. 24, No. 3, pp. 1-19.

Raphael, C., 1990, 'My Brother is *Dougla*', *Sunday Guardian*, 25 March 1990, p. 5.

Rothchild, D., 1986, 'State and Ethnicity in Africa: A Policy Perspective', in Nevitte, N. and Kennedy, C. (eds), *Ethnic Preference and Public Policy*, Boulder, CO: Lynne Reinner Publications, pp. 15-62.

Ryan, S., 1972, *Race and Nationalism in Trinidad and Tobago*, Toronto: University of Toronto Press.

– 1988, 'One Love Revisited', *Caribbean Affairs*, Vol. 2, No. 2.

– 1991, *The Muslimeen Grab for Power: Race, Religion and Revolution in Trinidad and Tobago*, Port of Spain: Imprint.

Smith, M.G., 1969, 'Institutional and Political Conditions of Pluralism', in Smith, M.G. and Kuper, L. (eds), *Pluralism in Africa*, Berkeley: University of California Press, pp. 26-63.

Smooha, S., 1980, 'Control of Minorities in Israel and Northern Ireland', *Comparative Studies in History and Society*, Vol. 22, No. 2, pp. 256-80.

Yelvington, K.A., 1987, 'Vote Dem Out: The Demise of the PNM in Trinidad and Tobago', *Caribbean Review*, Vol. 15, No. 4, pp. 8-12, 29-33.

– forthcoming, 'Trinidad and Tobago, 1989-90', in Malloy J.M. and Gamarra, E.A. (eds), *Latin American and Caribbean Contemporary Record*, Vol. 9, New York: Holmes and Meier.

CHAPTER 7

Afro-Trinidadian identity and the Africanisation of the *Orisha* religion

James Houk

Introduction

We have seen in earlier chapters that Trinidad over the last 150 or so years can be roughly characterised as a pluralistic society consisting of two primary components, Afro-Caribbean and East Indian. Of the two groups, East Indians have managed to perpetuate significant aspects of their 'Old World' culture, especially in the areas of religion and domestic customs. In the past, these manifestations have served as a cultural buffer between Africans and Indians in Trinidad. There are signs, however, that the ethnic boundary separating the two groups is gradually eroding – major political parties are now multi-ethnic, and popular calypsonians, at one time exclusively African, now include Indians among their number. This trend is reflected in the Nigerian-derived *Orisha* religion as well.

The *Orisha* religion in Trinidad ostensibly began as a transplanted African religion, but gradually took on selected religious elements drawn from Catholicism and Protestantism, and some *Orisha* worshippers are involved in the Kabbalah as well. More recently, during the last 30 or so years, Hindu deities and paraphernalia were borrowed by *Orisha* worshippers and incorporated into their shrines and their worship. This has been accompanied as well by a significant influx of Indians into the religion. While it is true that *Orisha* worshippers have a great respect for Hinduism and tolerate Indian involvement, this relatively recent development has been met with passive resistance in the form of a nativistic revitalisation that seeks to 're-Africanise' the *Orisha* religion by emphasising its Nigerian roots.

The setting

Trinidadians enjoy a temperate climate, a productive agricultural complex, and copious oil reserves that have combined to give them one of the highest per capita incomes in the area. American movies, Cable News Network, and American soap operas have all become part of the cultural fabric of the island and the general flavour of daily life is decidedly Western.

Imbedded in this Westernised context, however, are bits and pieces of 'traditional' lifeways that are more than simply vestigial remnants of Old World lifestyles, but, rather, significant components of a complex socio-cultural system. This is especially noteworthy in the religious life of Trinidad which includes Catholicism, Hinduism, Islam, Anglicanism, Protestantism (including Pentecostals, Seventh Day Adventists, Jehovah's Witnesses, Presbyterians, Methodists and others), and Afro-American religions (the Spiritual Baptist and *Orisha* religions).

While many Trinidadians might share a general way of life, when it comes to religion there is a distinct parting of ways – there are Hindu temples, the Muslim mosques, Catholic churches and *Orisha* shrines. Thus, in a general sense, 'Trinis' carry out the affairs of daily life in the context of a complex, mutable and malleable socio-cultural system. But, complex, mutable and malleable give way to homogeneous, stable and unpliable when the discussion moves to religion.

There is, however, one glaring exception to this general 'rule', and it is the 'Afro-American religious complex' in Trinidad. Those who are affiliated with all or part of this 'complex' participate in a form of worship that is actively syncretic, borrowing religious elements from a number of traditions.

If we were to break down this 'complex' analytically we would find the following 'parts': the Spiritual Baptist religion, the *Orisha* religion, and the Kabbalah. At this most general level we have three basic parts that combine to form a whole, what I am referring to here as the Afro-American religious complex. In reality, however, the situation is much more complicated.

The Spiritual Baptist religion is comprised of what I will refer to as 'orthodox' and 'non-orthodox' groups – orthodox Baptist worship is highly 'Protestantised' and non-orthodox worship is somewhat 'Africanised'. These different forms of worship fall somewhere on a continuum of the relative degree of presence or absence of Protestant or African elements.

The *Orisha* religion, as was noted above, is an African-derived religion that includes the beliefs, rituals and material culture of Catholicism, Protestantism, Hinduism, and the Kabbalah in its worship complex. I estimate that well over 50 per cent of *Orisha* worshippers in Trinidad are also Spiritual Baptists and participate in the activities of both religions on a regular basis.

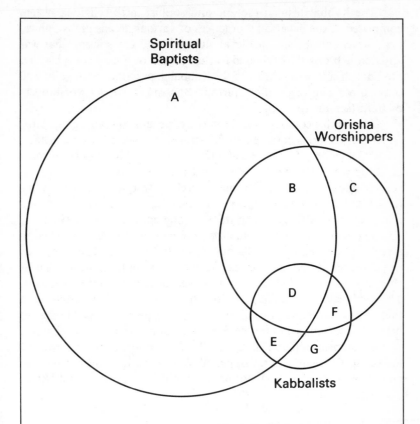

The area inside the circles represents the members of the religion(s)
designated by the corresponding letter. The three primary groups
represented here are the Spiritual Baptists (the largest circle), *Orisha*
worshippers (the next largest circle), and the Kabbalists (the smallest
circle). The circles have been superimposed on one another resulting in
seven categories:
A = Spiritual Baptists only; B = Spiritual Baptists and *Orisha* worshippers;
C = *Orisha* worshippers only; D = Spiritual Baptists, *Orisha* worshippers,
and Kabbalists; E = Spiritual Baptists and Kabbalists; F = *Orisha*
worshippers and Kabbalists; and G = Kabbalists only. 'Orthodox' Spiritual
Baptists would belong to category A, and the 'nonorthodox' to category B
or D.

Figure 7.1:   The affiliation distribution of worshippers in the Afro-American
religious complex.

The Kabbalah is an esoteric and sophisticated religious system comprised of the beliefs and practices of various arcane philosophies, e.g., Jewish mysticism, medieval alchemy, and Gnosticism, that was apparently brought to Trinidad by the Spanish or French, or, possibly, the English colonisers. Most of the Kabbalah practitioners (again, well over 50 per cent) are either Spiritual Baptists or *Orisha* worshippers or both (see Figure 7.1).

All possible combinations of the three groups comprising the Afro-American religious complex are illustrated in Figure 7.1 but, in fact, E and G have very few empirical referents. I should point out that some of those who affiliate themselves with the Afro-American religious complex also attend the Catholic church. In a questionnaire sample (N = 42) of *Orisha* worshippers, for example, ten (23 per cent) stated that they were affiliated with the Catholic church in some way.

The Spiritual Baptist and *Orisha* religions have been involved in a reciprocal exchange of religious elements for years. This has given rise to the non-orthodox Spiritual Baptists. Most of the Spiritual Baptist churches (the orthodox faction), however, have resisted this influence. The Kabbalah has remained virtually distinct as a religious system since there has been very little, if any, exchange of beliefs and practices between the Kabbalah and the Spiritual Baptist and *Orisha* religions.

The *Orisha* religion[1] is by far the most eclectic and syncretic of the three. It began as a transplanted West African (Yoruba) religion and through time gradually took on Catholic, Protestant, and Hindu elements in roughly that order.

Historical development of the Orisha religion in Trinidad

Very little is known about the early developmental period of *Orisha* worship in Trinidad. Early travellers' accounts (e.g., Day, 1852; Kingsley, 1871) describe religious ceremonies involving what they perceived to be African drumming and singing, but it is not clear whether or not those involved were *Orisha* worshippers. The early history of Trinidad has been researched by a number of scholars (e.g., Black, *et al.* 1976; Williams, 1964; Carmichael, 1961; Wood, 1968; and Brereton, 1981), but, perhaps because of the sheer lack of data and documentation, they have little or nothing to say concerning the origins of African folk religion in Trinidad. Thus, a discussion of this topic will be necessarily speculative.

There was virtually no African presence to speak of until about

1790 when the sugar plantations became salient part of the socio-economic landscape of Trinidad. A significant portion of the plantation slaves came from southern Nigeria and the surrounding area, but only about 1 per cent of the African-born slaves in 1813 were Yoruba (John, 1988). There was, however, a significant influx of Yoruba into Trinidad beginning in the 1830s and lasting until 1867 (Trotman, 1976). We have, then, for the first time, a significant presence of Yoruba in Trinidad during the 1830s. This immigration coupled with the complete emancipation of slaves in Trinidad in 1838, probably led to the establishment of the *Orisha* religion on the island during that time.

We will, perhaps, never know just when Catholic elements were incorporated into *Orisha* worship, but, beginning in the early nineteenth century, the Africans in Trinidad were exposed to the teachings, beliefs and practices of Catholicism. This included instruction every Sunday where the Africans 'were taught the Lord's Prayer, the Belief, [and] the Litany' (Ottley, 1974:60). Harricharan (1981) writes that their participation in church activities was generally 'peripheral' and 'limited', but nevertheless notes their involvement in several church activities.

Another indication of the Africans' affiliation with the Catholic church at this time is the large number of slave baptisms that were conducted. According to Ottley (1974), almost 15,000 of the approximately 17,000 slaves in Trinidad in the 1820s were baptised Catholics. Of course, many of these baptisms were done *en masse*, and were probably not an indication of the quality of the African slaves' involvement in the religion.

The African/Catholic syncretism that is such an integral part of Afro-American religions in the New World no doubt began sometime during the first half of the nineteenth century in Trinidad, and its most salient result is the pairing or associating of Yoruba gods and Catholic saints that is still evident today.It appears likely that the Catholic aspect of *Orisha* worship was firmly in place by the end of the nineteenth century. A short time later, however, there was to be another period of change and adjustment as the Spiritual Baptist religion became popular among Africans in Trinidad.

It is not known whether the Spiritual Baptists in Trinidad can be traced to African, Caribbean or American roots, although it appears as though the argument for a St Vincentian provenance is the strongest (see, for example, Henney, 1974; Bourguignon, 1970; and Williams, 1985). It is possible that an African form of Christianity (the 'Shouters' according to some of my informants) merged with a New World Protestant form of worship to form the Spiritual Baptists. Nevertheless, it is quite clear that by 1920 the Spiritual Baptists were firmly established in Trinidad.

There is little or no historical information regarding the relationship between Spiritual Baptists and *Orisha* worshippers, but, given the similar socio-historical backgrounds of their respective members this inter-relationship is not surprising.

The followers of both religions have been, until recently, exclusively African, and, thus, have shared a similar historical tradition and socio-economic class affiliation. The two religions endured a long period of state oppression whereby their practices were banned, resulting in their respective members going 'underground' to worship. Even today, despite some acceptance, both religions are not generally considered to be serious and legitimate forms of religious worship by the general public.

The important factors contributing to this interrelationship are, perhaps, almost exclusively social since the two religious systems, one primarily Protestant the other primarily African and Catholic, appear to have little in common. And, in fact, virtually no syncretism involving the two religious systems has occurred – any mixing, be it on the level of ideology or practice, involves a juxtaposition of the two rather than a blending. The strong influence with regard to ritual, belief and paraphernalia of each religion, however, cannot be denied.

The Kabbalah has apparently been practised in Trinidad since early colonial times, but only in the last 20 or so years has it become openly associated with *Orisha* worshippers. Two prominent Kabbalah practitioners explained that before 1970 Kabbalah banquets were generally private and closed affairs. Because of its diabolical overtones and the fact that most *Orisha* worshippers themselves consider this practice to be evil, even today, so I am told, much of this activity is secretive. Each year, however, there are ten to twenty 'banquets' that are open to the general public, but, of course, only those aware of such activities actually attend. The probable colonial presence of the Kabbalah notwithstanding, Kabbalah ritual, flags, shrines and other paraphernalia have only recently become a prominent and salient part of *Orisha* worship in Trinidad.

Various components of Hinduism have also recently been incorporated into the *Orisha* religion. This has been accompanied by an increase in the number of Indian *Orisha* worshippers. This issue, involving as it does the two primary ethnic groups on the island, will be addressed further below.

The most recent change in this complex and highly dynamic religion involves the expurgation of Christian and Hindu elements from *Orisha* worship in an attempt to return to a liturgy and practice that is exclusively Yoruba. (As was explained earlier, Kabbalah worship is supplemental to *Orisha* worship and, thus, does not directly affect it. Hence the emphasis on the Christian and Hindu components.)

The *Orisha* religion, then, is a complex and eclectic blend of elements drawn from five different religions or religious traditions. Not surprisingly the religion today is quite variable when viewed as a whole and can differ significantly from shrine to shrine.

Heterodoxy and the Orisha religion

Group structure

The *Orisha* religion has traditionally been a loosely organised folk movement, but there have been attempts to consolidate and organise the religion in the last ten years or so. At this time there are two organisational bodies, the *Orisha* Movement and the *Shango* Belief System. The former is recognised by the government and the latter has filed a constitution with the government and should be sanctioned in the near future.

Neither group appears to have much influence at present, although the *Shango* Belief System practises and endorses a broad, eclectic philosophy and has been successful thus far in its attempt to incorporate a number of shrines in Trinidad into one unified body. One of the most knowledgeable and respected *mongbas* (*Orisha*, priest), Mr Clarence Ford, is the spiritual head *(babaorisha)* of the *Orisha* religion, and is affiliated with the *Shango* Belief System, thus lending considerable credibility to the group.

These attempts at organisation notwithstanding, the group as a whole is still only loosely organised at best. The *Orisha* religion remains a very personalised religion as the large variety of shrine designs and worship practices indicate. Many shrines are established as the result of dreams and visions, or instructions received while 'mourning' (a ritually controlled trance-state). Often, however, the inexperienced worshipper will seek the help of elders when constructing his shrine or holding a feast.

Each shrine is an independent entity with its own core members. The random and unstructured makeup of the feast season is an indication of this. Since there are probably more than 150 *ebos*[2] (feasts) held during any given year, and the feast season generally lasts only about 36 weeks or so, there is often more than one *ebo* per week. In fact, during one particular week I counted seven. During some weeks of the feast season, however, no *ebos* are held. Another problem is spatial distance. On some occasions, two *ebos* occurred in close proximity thus resulting in a split of worshippers and resources in the area. During the third week of October 1988, two *ebos* were held within a short walking distance from one another. The attendance at one of the feasts appeared to be affected by the presence nearby of an *ebo* directed by a popular *mongba*, Aldwin Scott.

Given the lack of consolidation and organisation on an island-wide basis, with the exception of the *babaorisha* and the *iyaorisha*, the recognised male and female spiritual heads, there are no officially recognised positions in the religion, the result being that the structure and hierarchy of the religion has been formed primarily by consensus.

The shrine

An *Orisha* shrine is a compound that contains *Orisha* flags and/or stools, which serves as the site for the annual *ebo*. There are approximately 156 'open air' or public shrines on the island.

The eclectic nature of the religion is reflected in its material culture, as the data in Table 7.1 will illustrate. These data are based on a sampling of 37 *Orisha* shrines. (The samples discussed in this work are generally opportunistic, although special care was taken to avoid obvious biases.) The incidence of occurrence (IOC) of the more popular *orishas* (Yoruba-derived gods or 'powers') in the form of external or exposed flags and/or stools (small shrines) in the compound is given in both raw and percentage form (rounded off to whole numbers), and the flag colours and their incidence of occurrence is also noted.

Table 7.1: Material culture of 37 Orisha shrines

Orisha	IOC	Flag colour(s)	IOC
Ogun	37 (100%)	red/white	24 (65%)
		red	11 (30%)
		red/green	2 (5%)
Osain	34 (92%)	yellow	27 (79%)
		yellow/brown	5 (15%)
		yellow (triangular)	2 (5%)
		no flag	1 (3%)
Shakpana	32 (86%)	red	28 (88%)
		red and other colours	1 (3%)
		green/yellow	1 (3%)
		brown	1 (3%)
		grey	1 (3%)

Table 7.1 (cont'd.)

	IOC	Flag colour	
Mama Lata	22 (59%)	brown	11 (50%)
		no flag	7 (32%)
		brown plaid	3 (14%)
		pink	1 (4%)
Oshun	21 (57%)	pink	11 (52%)
		blue	5 (24%)
		no flag	4 (19%)
		white	1 (5%)
Peter	17 (46%)	no flag	7 (41%)
		white	3 (18%)
		blue/white	2 (12%)
		yellow/white	1 (6%)
		purple/white	1 (6%)
		mauve/white	1 (6%)
		yellow/blue	1 (6%)
		purple	1 (6%)
Emanje	15 (40%)	blue	12 (80%)
		blue/white	2 (13%)
		blue with white dots	1 (7%)
Erele	12 (32%)	blue	4 (33%)
		blue/white	4 (33%)
		blue/yellow	2 (17%)
		brown/white	1 (8%)
		green	1 (8%)
Oya	10 (27%)	green	8 (80%)
		green/white	1 (10%)
		pink	1 (10%)

IOC = incidence of occurrence

The remaining *orishas* had an IOC of less than ten (27 per cent).[3] Eleven of the shrines in the sample had anywhere from one to seven different *orishas* not noted here that are known only to a handful of worshippers.

While there are a few general tendencies here in regard to prevalence and colour(s), there is also considerable diversity. It must be noted here that certain subtle differences were left out, e.g., light and dark shades, and in cases where two colours are given, which is closest to the bamboo pole.

The *chapelle* is a small, enclosed religious sanctuary in which small stools or shrines of particular *orishas* are located. The *chapelle* shows similar characteristics in that there are a few general tendencies, e.g., the presence of *Shango* and *Oya* in practically all cases, but, again, there is considerable diversity.

In addition to the primary religious structures that one generally finds in an *Orisha* compound, there may also be a Spiritual Baptist church, a Kabbalah room, or Kabbalah flags and/or stools present as well. Data were collected from a survey of 51 shrines (most of which are included in the shrines that were sampled for the information noted above) and the IOC in both raw and percentage forms was found to be as follows: Spiritual Baptist church: 18 (35 per cent); Kabbalah: 16 (31 per cent); and Hindu: 23 (45 per cent). The category 'Kabbalah' includes rooms as well as flags and/or stools. I have also included the category 'Hindu' for the purpose of comparison. IOC in this case refers to the presence or absence of flags and/or stools for at least one Hindu deity.

The annual *Ebo*

The *ebo* or annual feast is without question the most important ceremony in the *Orisha* religion. It is basically a celebration of food, dance and song during which the *orishas* manifest themselves and interact with worshippers in a variety of ways. On a very general level the ceremony is somewhat similar from compound to compound, but there is no set or standard programme that a feast giver must follow thus allowing for considerable liturgical freedom.

For example, while a typical feast night at many shrines begins with Christian prayers, some *mongbas* or *iyas* (priestesses) prefer to recite Yoruba prayers instead. Such shrines are often exclusively African and contain no stools for Catholic saints or Hindu gods, and no Christian or Hindu paraphernalia. The Catholic counterparts of the *orishas* are not recognised at such shrines. These properties all reflect the recent trend towards 'Africanisation' of the religion and are discussed further below.

The sacrifice of animals is also not practised at all shrines and fruit is offered instead. This might be done for moral reasons since some object to the spilling of blood or at least to the sheer number of animals that are offered, or for financial reasons since fruit offerings are relatively inexpensive. This type of offering is not practised on a large scale, but it is considered to be a proper and appropriate ritual practice.

Since the traditional feast season extends from the Tuesday after Easter Sunday to the beginning of Advent (four Sundays before Christmas Day), a period of approximately 36 weeks, and, since each year 150 or so *ebos* are held, there is often more than one feast in any particular week, as noted earlier. Not all shrine heads, *mongbas* and *iyas* recognise the traditional feast-giving period – three in a sample of 76 were not held during this time. Thus, worshippers have the opportunity to visit many different shrines during the feast season, often during the same week. More importantly, the large number of feasts, some of which are in close proximity to one another, encourages competition among shrine heads as each seek to draw as many worshippers and ranking heads to their *ebo* as they can. This competition is no doubt at least partly responsible for the high degree of variation one finds at the level of the shrine as each shrine head seeks to personalise his or her worship pattern.

There are also additional processes at work in the religion that make it amenable to change. Perhaps most significant in this regard are the mechanisms of information exchange.

The transmission of religious knowledge

In the *Orisha* religion, the most influential individuals are the *mongbas* and *iyas*. This relatively small group of individuals (35 or so) will have more impact during their lifetime on the religion than any other group. These high-ranking individuals transmit religious knowledge both directly and indirectly.

There are two primary ways in which *mongbas* and *iyas* have a direct impact on the information exchange process. *Mongbas* and *iyas* will transfer selected bits of their religious knowledge to particular individuals, especially biological and spiritual sons and daughters, but they will not pass on their religious knowledge *in toto* to anyone. This fact was confirmed a number of times by rank-and-file worshippers and *mongbas* and *iyas* themselves. The reason for this partial secrecy can apparently be attributed to the intense competition among *mongbas* and *iyas* (one would not knowingly assist another in attaining as much or more knowledge than he or she has), and the fear that the student might use this knowledge against the teacher.

Mongbas and *iyas* will also be called upon to instruct those who are relative newcomers to the faith but have been 'instructed' (through 'mourning', visions or dreams) to carry on an *ebo*. When functioning in this capacity, the *mongba* or *iya* can fashion the proceedings to his or her liking. The resulting worship pattern is, thus, a highly personalised one based as it is on the dictates of one individual.

Finally, by virtue of the fact that these priests and priestesses guide and direct *ebos* throughout the year, which are attended by as many as 200 or more worshippers in some cases, they also play a role in the indirect transfer of religious information.

This 'one-to-many' mechanism of information transfer obviously has quite an impact on the nature of religious knowledge in the *Orisha* religion, but there are other mechanisms at work as well. For example, one only has to be present at an *ebo* to learn which *orisha* takes which implements, the sacrificial foods of the *orisha*, Yoruba prayers, drum rhythms, and songs. Proper ritual behaviour can be elicited from the actions of those actively participating as well.

The final mechanism of information exchange is a trance-state ritual referred to as 'mourning'. Mourning is a Spiritual Baptist ritual but given the interrelationship between this religion and the *Orisha* religion, many *Orisha* worshippers have mourned in a Spiritual Baptist context. Of the *Orisha* worshippers sampled by questionnaire (N = 42) 50 per cent noted that they had mourned, in most cases more than once.

Mourning is an important source of knowledge for *Orisha* worshippers. Equally significant, however, is that the mystical and existential nature of the mourning ritual allows the worshipper to interject knowledge gained during his or her own personal experience into the general body of religious knowledge. It is, thus, an important source of change and variation.

If this process were to continue unabated, the beliefs and rituals of the religion would become diffused to such an extent as to render it unviable. Perhaps in response to this possibility, a 'policing' or 'tempering' mechanism has been developed to control this process. The Leader, Mother, or other 'officers' of the church can discern the truth or falsity of mourners' statements, and can evaluate the legitimacy of their experiences. Mourning, then, is not totally subjective and personal, but it is, nevertheless, an important source of knowledge and change.

In summary, the transmission of religious knowledge in the *Orisha* religion is the result of primarily three processes:

(1) *Mongba/iya* ⟶ rank and file worshippers. This is an example of one-to-many/oblique transmission when the *mongba* or *iya* is from an older generation than the worshipper, one-to-many/horizontal transmission when both parties are of the same generational age, and one-to-many/ vertical when there is a biological relationship between the two parties.

(2) Feast context ———➤ rank and file worshippers. This is an example of many-to-many/vertical, horizontal, and oblique transmission forms since anyone might be considered a transmitter or transmittee in this case.

(3) Mystical/psychological/metaphysical realm ———➤ individual. The complex, secretive and mysterious character of the mourning ritual makes it virtually ineffable. The three terms chosen here to designate the transmitting 'party' are drawn primarily from worshippers' descriptions. In cases such as these when there is a lack of data to substantiate otherwise, the worshippers' explanation, the 'cognised model' (Rappaport, 1968) is as valid, or more so, than others since it is obviously an important determinant of behaviour. In regard to transmission type, we could call it one-to-one/ (intra-)horizontal, although, since the mourning process apparently draws from the religion's knowledge as a whole, it could also be designated many-to-one.

The eclectic nature of *Orisha* worship and the high degree of variability that exists on the level of shrines and on the level of the individual can now be at least partly explained as a result of the manner in which religious knowledge is exchanged. The one-to-many transmission type, perhaps the most important mechanism here, can potentially produce the most rapid cultural change of all the various transmission types (Hewlett and Cavalli-Sforza, 1986), since one individual is directly affecting a number of individuals. The somewhat existential and personal nature of the mourning ritual can potentially bring about change and variation on the level of the individual and, subsequently, on the group level. If we combine the two processes, i.e., one-to-many transmission where the transmitter mourns regularly, the potential for change and variation is even greater than is the case with only one of these mechanisms at work.

There are, then, several mechanisms at work in the *Orisha* religion that make it vulnerable and amenable to change. Illustrative of this point is the fact that Indians are becoming increasingly involved in the religion, and Hindu paraphernalia can now be found in many shrines.

Indians, Hinduism and the Orisha *religion*

The *Orisha* religion has long been almost exclusively African. As late as the 1950s the involvement of individuals who were not of African descent was almost non-existent (Mischel, 1958). Today, however, the

Indian presence in particular is significant. Head counts at a number of feasts (N = 18) revealed that approximately 10 per cent of those in attendance were Indian. While many of these were only interested bystanders, some were quite active. One Indian, for example, is a popular and respected drummer. Another Indian is one of the most prominent and respected figures in the religion and is himself a shrine head who annually holds one of the most popular feasts on the island.

Sometime after 1950 selected Hindu gods and rituals were incorporated into *Orisha* worship. Leader Scott, a well-known and respected *Orisha* priest and Spiritual Baptist leader, and other worshippers noted that it was not until 1960 or so that they began to notice Hindu elements in *Orisha* compounds. In the sample of 37 Orisha compounds discussed above, it was found that 10 or 27 per cent contained Hindu flags and shrines for up to six different Hindu deities.

In this case, unlike that of the *Orisha* and Spiritual Baptist religions, we are dealing with two groups who do not and did not share a common historical or ethnic heritage, but did practise religions that were similar in some respects. Most significant here are the rich and complex pantheons of both the *Orisha* religion and Hinduism replete with anthropomorphised deities.

Just why this curious association involving African and Indian culture has occurred is difficult to say. Some of my informants noted that the workers' rebellions of the 1930s temporarily united the two ethnic groups under the banner of anti-colonialism, thereby assuaging inter-ethnic hostility, resulting in increased contact between members of the two religions. It was also noted that during the Black Power movement of 1970, Indian and African workers united, at least temporarily, in a similar way. It should be pointed out, however, that the late 1950s and early 1960s were marked by ethnic-based party politics and heightened racial tension (e.g., Ryan, 1972; Oxaal, 1982). Given the general atmosphere of distrust and resentment that has existed virtually since the arrival of the Indians, I think that it is unlikely that the incorporation of Hindu elements into the *Orisha* religion can be explained by political factors alone.

It is probably no coincidence that the recent incorporation of Hindu elements has been accompanied by the influx of Indians into the religion. While it is true that it is the predominantly African shrine heads, *mongbas* and *iyas*, that have actively engaged in this borrowing, the fact that the Hindu religion and *Orisha* worship have been displayed and discussed as religious counterparts has not been lost on Indian worshippers.

The 'Africanisation' of the Orisha religion

It has been suggested that this Yoruba-derived religion which was initially ostensibly solely African, has gradually been transformed into an eclectic and highly variable religious system consisting of a variety of components borrowed from other religious traditions. While many worshippers have passively assimilated the extraneous elements into their worship, there has also been considerable resistance to change. In what can be interpreted as an attempt to assert and emphasise Afro-Trinidadian identity, a strong movement towards the 'Africanisation' of the *Orisha* religion is taking place, quite possibly partly due to a revitalistic response to the significant Indian presence in the religion. Additionally, this movement benefits from a favourable socio-political climate in which the religion is no longer oppressed as it once was.

Never before has the *Orisha* religion in Trinidad enjoyed the degree of freedom and self-determination that it now has. Legal persecution came to an end in the 1950s, and the Black Power movement of the early 1970s ushered in a new African consciousness that gave rise to an increased awareness of things African. The *Orisha* religion has apparently flourished during this time. Of 35 shrines which were sampled in regard to age it was found that the ages of 25, or roughly 71 per cent of the sample, were less than or equal to 20-years-old.

During this time there has also apparently been an increased emphasis placed on the African aspect of the religion at the expense of the Catholic and Hindu. This 'Africanisation' of the *Orisha* religion is at present only a 'grassroots' level movement, but there are indications that it is increasing in popularity.

The two primary ethnographers of the *Orisha* religion in Trinidad, Mischel (1958) and Simpson (1965), conducted their research in the 1950s and early 1960s and their writings include no mention of this Africanising tendency. In fact, they seem to emphasise the Catholic component. My older informants also note that 'old time' or 'long time' *Orisha* worship was highly Catholicised. In my sample of shrine ages, only five were found to be older than 30 years, but all five were significantly Catholic, e.g., pictures and statues of Catholic figures were prominently displayed and, more often than not, Catholic terminology was used to refer to the deities. This is, of course, a small sample, but it does support the contention that the *Orisha* religion was Catholicised to a higher degree than at the present time. The Hindu component has only recently been incorporated into the worship pattern of the religion so a similar comparison cannot be made.

As was noted above, this Africanising trend appears to be only incipient at the present time, but there are signs that it is on the increase as a few examples will illustrate. Traditionally, much of the liturgy was recited in languages other than Yoruba, e.g., French *patois* and/or English. Today, however, many worshippers are emphasising the Yoruba language and consider it to be the proper language of *Orisha* worship. Whereas earlier it was only the *mongbas* or *iyas* who could conduct worship in the Yoruba language, the goal of some worshippers is to popularise a Yoruba liturgy. Perhaps the individual who has been most involved in this movement is Jeffery Biddeau, an elder and *mongba* in the religion. He has drawn on his knowledge of the Yoruba language to create an exclusively Yoruba liturgy for *Orisha* worship. He has personally typed and distributed copies of this liturgy for others to use. Another *mongba*, a young Rastafarian named Gock, has distributed copies of *Orisha* songs written in the Yoruba language.

It is not uncommon to hear worshippers complain of the Catholic prayers that are said during an *ebo*. Some *mongbas* and *iyas* do their best to limit such prayers. As was noted earlier, not all feast nights begin with a session of Catholic and Baptist prayers and singing. I attended three *ebos* in which each feast night began with Yoruba prayers and drumming and singing for the *orishas*. Additionally, in a number of others, the Christian session could be described as perfunctory at best.

A list of five questions was drawn up and at least one feast night at 30 different shrines was sampled in order to assess the degree to which the religion has become Africanised. The five questions were as follows:

(1)   Does the ceremony begin with a session of Christian prayers and singing?

(2)   Are Christian prayers cited at all once the African part begins?

(3)   Are Catholic statuettes and iconography used to mark shrines or stools in the *chapelle* or elsewhere?

(4)   Is a Bible or rosary present either in the *chapelle* or the *palais*?

(5)   Are the names of saints invoked or cited during the service?

In 18 of the 30 cases there was at least one 'no' answer to the above questions. If we add the question 'Is there a Spiritual Baptist church in the compound?', we get at least one 'no' in 25 of the 30 cases. There are, perhaps, a number of ways that this issue could be tested, but my results are at least suggestive of this tendency towards Africanisation especially when one considers the highly Catholicised flavour of the religion in the past.

My research also revealed that the Hindu influence is being countered as well. Many of my informants explained that the *Orisha* religion is perfectly capable of standing on its own and that the Hindu and Christian components are simply New World additions to the religion. A handful of shrines that have been built only recently contain no Hindu shrines or paraphernalia. Additionally, 28 of 51 *Orisha* compounds sampled contained no Hindu components. This is noteworthy especially when one considers that Hinduism has been present in Trinidad for approximately 150 years.

The incorporation of three of the four 'extraneous' components, i.e., the Catholic, the Spiritual Baptist, and the Kabbalistic, did not involve the subsequent assimilation of non-African peoples. In fact, the borrowing and subsequent integration of various aspects of Catholicism and the Kabbalah had no demographic impact on the religion. Spiritual Baptists were easily absorbed into the group given the fact that they shared a common ethnic, cultural, social, and political background with the *Orisha* worshippers. In the case of the Hindu component, however, the incorporation of religious elements subsequently gave rise to the addition of new converts from an ethnic group that had little in common with Afro-Trinidadians.

This attempted expurgation of all of the non-African-derived components from the *Orisha* religion can be interpreted, in part, as a response to the influx of Indians into the religion. While the religion has a long tradition of eclecticism and tolerance in Trinidad, it has always been solely an Afro-Trinidadian organisation. During the last 30 or so years, however, the hegemony and self-determination of Afro-Trinidadians in the *Orisha* religion has been seriously threatened. This recent attempt at Africanisation is, no doubt, a revitalistic response to that threat.

Conclusion

It has been argued that the *Orisha* religion in Trinidad has long moved away from its 'unicultural' origins, and through time has incorporated 'extraneous' elements from a variety of religious traditions. The reasons behind these syncretic episodes were not discussed, however, while this syncretism took place in both directed (forced) and non-directed (unforced) historical contexts, the incorporated elements remained integral parts of the religious system up to the present time.

It has also been shown that there are various mechanisms or structural components built into the *Orisha* religious system that are conducive to and make it amenable to change. These include the loose organisational structure, the individualistic or personalised flavour of the annual feasts, and the mechanisms of knowledge transmission, both horizontal and vertical. Data were given to demonstrate the variability of the religion both in regard to liturgy and physical setting.

This eclectic religion appeared to be on a course of increasing complexity and syncretism, but recently these tendencies seem to have been countered or at least tempered by the movement towards Africanisation. Of the four extraneous components that have been integrated into the religion over the last 150 or so years, only the most recent episode, that involving Hinduism, actually involved the incorporation of non-African peoples.

It is argued here that the Africanisation movement is quite clearly a response to this 'demographic threat' since Afro-Trinidadian self-determination regarding the affairs of the religion is now being threatened from the 'inside' for the first time.

This particular issue is a small part of the more general problem concerning Afro-Trinidadian identity in Trinidad, but it is an important one involving as it does one of the few socio-cultural institutions on the island that is predominately African in form and which is apparently destined to stay that way.

Acknowledgements

During my two visits to the island I came into contact with many Trinidadians who graciously offered their time and hospitality. I cannot possibly name them all, but the following people, because of their singular contribution, should be mentioned: Jeffery and Lydia Biddeau, Henry White, Aaron Jones and Carli. Finally, I would like to thank Aldwin Scott and his wife, Joan, for their endless patience and boundless hospitality. The project on which this chapter is based was funded by a Fulbright Fixed Sum Grant.

Notes

1   In deference to my friends and informants in the *Orisha* religion, it should be pointed out that the religion in its original, African, form is quite capable of functioning independently of Catholicism, Hinduism, Protestantism and the Kabbalah. The Yoruba religion has a long and rich history and probably pre-dates all the above traditions.

2   An *ebo* is an annual religious ceremony involving the beating of drums, singing of songs, recitation of prayers, and the offering of food for the particular *orisha*.

3   They are listed here with their IOC and the number of different colour schemes used for the flags: *Gurum:* seven (19 per cent), two, one with no flag; *Elefa:* seven (19 per cent), two; St Anthony: five (14 per cent), two; *Eshu:* five (14 per cent), one; St Raphael: four (11 per cent), two, one with

no flag; *Shango:* two (5 per cent), one; *Ajaja:* two (5 per cent), one; and *Vigoyana:* two (5 per cent), one.

References

Black, J.K., Blutstein, H.I., Johnston, K.T., and McMorris, D.S., 1976, *Area Handbook for Trinidad and Tobago*, Washington D.C.: US Government Printing Office.

Bourguignon, E., 1970, 'Ritual Dissociation and Possession Belief in Caribbean Negro Religion', in Whitten, N.E. Jr., and Szwed, J.F. (eds), *Afro-American Anthropology: Contemporary Perspectives*, New York: The Free Press, pp. 87-101.

Brereton, B., 1981, *A History of Modern Trinidad 1783-1962*, London: Heinemann Educational Books.

Carmichael, G., 1961, *The History of the West Indian Islands of Trinidad and Tobago, 1498-1900*, London: Alvin Redman.

Day, C.W., 1852, *Five Years' Residence in the West Indies*, 2 vols., London: Whittaker, Treacher & Co.

Harricharan, T., 1981, *The Catholic Church in Trinidad, 1498-1852*, Vol 1., Port of Spain: Inprint Caribbean Ltd.

Henney, J., 1974, 'Spirit-Possession Belief and Trance Behavior in Two Fundamentalist Groups in St Vincent', in Zaretsky, I.I. (ed.), *Trance, Healing and Hallucination*, New York: John Wiley and Sons, pp. 1-111.

Hewlett, B.S. and Cavalli-Sforza, L.L., 1986,'Cultural Transmission Among Aka Pygmies', *American Anthropologist*, Vol. 88 No. 4, pp. 922-34.

John, A.M., 1988, *The Plantation Slaves of Trinidad: A Mathematical and Demographic Enquiry*, Cambridge: Cambridge University Press.

Kingsley, C., 1871, *At Last: A Christmas in the West Indies*, New York: Macmillan & Co.

Mischel, F.O., 1958, 'A Shango Religious Group and the Problem of Prestige in Trinidadian Society', unpublished Ph.D. dissertation, Ohio State University.

Ottley, C. R., 1974, *Slavery Days in Trinidad: A Social History of the Island from 1797-1838*, Port of Spain: C.R. Ottley.

Oxaal, I., 1982, *Black Intellectuals and the Dilemmas of Race and Class in Trinidad*, Cambridge, MA: Schenkman.

Ryan, S., 1972, *Race and Nationalism in Trinidad and Tobago*, Toronto: University of Toronto Press.

Simpson, G.E., 1965, *The Shango Cult in Trinidad*, Rio Piedras: Institute of Caribbean Studies, University of Puerto Rico.

Trotman, D.V., 1976, 'The *Yoruba* and *Orisha* Worship in Trinidad and British Guinea: 1838-1870, *African Studies Review*, Vol. 19, No. 2, pp. 1-17.

Williams, E.E., 1964, *History of the People of Trinidad and Tobago*, London: Andre Deutsch.

Williams, M.R., 1985, 'Song from Valley to Mountain: Music and Ritual among the Spiritual Baptists ('Shouters') of Trinidad', unpublished M.A. thesis, Indiana University.

Wood, D., 1968, *Trinidad in Transition: The Years after Slavery*, London: Oxford University Press.

CHAPTER 8

What is 'a Spanish'?: Ambiguity and 'mixed' ethnicity in Trinidad

Aisha Khan

Man No. 1: 'My father is mix with white and Portagee. Trinidad is such a mix country, Spanish, French, white, Indian. My mother is from Arima, a Spanish. If you see she hair! *Straight* and jet black'.
Man No. 2: 'Women in Arima are all mix'. ·
(Conversation overheard in taxi, Trinidad, 1987)

The problem of 'mixed' in perspective

Recent anthropological work on ethnicity, nationalism, and trans-nationalism has emphasised that social identities are constructed – that is, are composite and multivocal, and that multiple identities can be activated in different combinations depending on the contingencies in question. Furthermore, these combined constructions, particularly categories of ethnic identity, are not necessarily isomorphic or without ambiguities. This is not to say they are ambiguous in the sense that persons have trouble comprehending or applying particular ethnic categories in any given social situation. They are ambiguous in that they are 'capable of being understood in two or more possible senses' *(Webster's New Collegiate Dictionary,* 1975), in that these categories are frequently equivocal: contingent upon individual perception (though obviously not entirely) and upon varying and not always predictable emphases of combinations of attributes. Categorisations of ethnic identity that marshall a variety of historical, social, and cultural dimensions in their construction may also encompass apparently contradictory images, since traits, qualities, stereotypes, and the like are not self-contained or mutually exclusive. Indeed, the very fact of combination and ambiguity foregrounds the fluidity of ethnic identity.

In Caribbean research the fluid and protean nature of ethnic and racial identities has been evident for some time. In these studies the units of analysis tend to be distinct *racial* categories (such as 'African' or 'East Indian' or 'Chinese') and *colour* terms (such as 'black', 'brown', 'white', 'red', etc.) involving pliable meanings, designations, and significance. An important issue to emerge from this literature was that so-called intermediate categories – that is, combinations lying between the extremes of 'black' and 'white' – signal important questions about the nature of ambiguity and the significance of the relationship between appearance (phenotype) and background[1] in social relations, and more broadly, between social identity and social stratification, and ultimately between ideology and power. Sidney Mintz observed early on that perceptions of colour (and I would add appearance in general) are not merely 'a matter of observed phenotype but of observed phenotype taken together with many other factors' (1957); that perception of appearance is variable not only with context but within a dialectic between *self*-consciousness and perception of an Other (1957); and that the social meaning of an intermediate category 'may depend upon the indefiniteness with which its boundaries are drawn, and the difficulties people experience in trying to draw such boundaries ...' (1971:443). Also recognised in the literature is that in mediating appearance, background does not simply connote position in the social hierarchy but descent as well, in the form of alleged cultural history and traditions and in the notion of family pedigree. Moreover, although appearance can attest to background, it can belie background as well, because it is negotiable, situational, and to a degree observer-specific. In other words, looks can be deceiving, as we saw in Chapter 4.

The phenomenon of 'mixing' – often referred to as 'miscegenation' – has always been a key issue for colonial and post-colonial societies (e.g., Stoler, 1989), and in the Caribbean ever since European master and African slave produced socially problematic offspring – that is, slave or free; and if free, with an uncertain place in the social structure. When intermediate categories (that is, 'mixes') are taken up in studies of the Anglophone Caribbean, discussion is by and large couched in terms of the rubric 'coloured' or 'brown', mixtures of 'black' and 'white' that either subsume or overshadow other categorisations of 'mixed' possibilities. In the literature, 'mixed' and 'coloured' often stand for each other, implicitly calling forth variations on a 'black'-plus-'white' theme. Hence, Trinidad has been characterised historically as a social class-colour pyramid consisting of three strata: upper/'white', middle/'coloured' or 'brown', and lower/'black'; a social pyramid more or less incorporating subsequent influxes of foreign (e.g., East Indian, Chinese, Portuguese) immigrant labourers (cf. Braithwaite, 1975 [1953]; Brereton, 1979). Discussions of racial or ethnic 'mixing' tend to be placed within a larger agenda of race relations research.

In this chapter I want to explore the notion of 'mixed' in Trinidad on its own terms, as an overarching rubric for glossing ethnic or racial combinations, and to analyse the importance of ambiguity for defining, sustaining or resisting hierarchy in systems of social stratification – a subject not of primary interest to researchers until relatively recently (viz. Cancian, 1976).[2] I do this by focusing on one of its specific manifestations, that of 'Spanish'. I also want to raise a related issue of critical importance not yet thoroughly studied in Caribbean literature. Since all ethnicities are somehow 'mixed' (i.e., 'pure' and 'impure' are social constructs, not biological facts), how and when is 'mixed' ('combined', 'impure') socially emphasised as the primary identity marker and how and when is an ethnic identity principally perceived as a socio-cultural 'whole'? My premise is that in polyethnic New World societies such as Trinidad, 'mixed' is more than 'coloured', beyond 'black'-plus-'white', and should not be confined within implicit assumptions – scholarly or popular – of distinctly bounded categories of 'race'.

In exploring the concept of 'mixed' ethnicities, it is instructive to consider Ardener's (1982) notion of the simultaneous process of classifying an event and the 'event' itself (1982:11). Applying this idea of simultaneity to analyses of 'mixed' ethnicities broadens our appreciation of these categories as windows into understanding ethnic identity as being both structural and processual (Chapman *et al.*, 1989:9). Ambiguity can be seen as a nexus, if you will, between classification/definition and action. More than a continuum of categories (viz. Chapman *et al.*, 1989), 'mixed' ethnicities are fluid in the sense of consisting of a *dialectic* between boundary and content rather than as shifting boundaries that encompass interchangeable attributes. In other words, once the attributes are exchanged, the boundary itself that separates 'who are' from 'who are not' is transformed. Barth's (1969) landmark turn away from the content ('cultural diacritica') of ethnic groups toward a focus on ethnicity in action through boundary shifts was critical for understanding ethnicity as process. Problematic, however, was that content tended to be construed in rather static or secondary terms (viz. Fox, 1990:6). In order to better understand situations where, simultaneously, boundaries are negotiable and their content is plastic, and where ethnic categories may function as mediators that modify other ethnic categories, we must analyse the operation of ambiguity and its functions and role in 'mixed' ethnicity, as it is central to the manipulation, contingency, and idiosyncracy of ethnic identity. Ambiguity both reveals and negotiates the extant system of social stratification and the power relations upon which it rests. That is, ethnic category constructs possess diverse qualities, meanings and uses in social action and at the same time form, maintain, and challenge hierarchical structures.

The notion of 'mixed', accepted as both empirical reality and metaphor, is multivalent in local Trinidadian ideology. For instance, one of my informants could recite without hesitation (and with dubious sincerity) what he conceived as appropriate nationalist rhetoric: 'Over time, a few generations, with mixing the future wouldn't have race consciousness'. And in grappling with the issue of defining a Trinidadiari, Merle Hodge (1975:31) suggests that 'perhaps the epitome of a Trinidadian is the child...with a dark skin and crinkly plaits ... decidedly Chinese eyes ... [named] Maharaj'. Although the child, symbol of a heterogeneous identity, is a 'mixed', every attribute in this composite is disaggregated and identified. Yet 'mixed' is not *necessarily* one concrete end result of a prior act of mixing, precisely measurable, an always exact set of specified attributes that are 'situationally' activated. While 'mixing' does not necessarily mean haphazard, since most attributes are accounted for – recollected, traced, and thus defined – in some way, 'Spanish' indicates a 'mix' whose attributes may or may not be unanimously acknowledged or verified.

It is not merely that one may choose to be or not be 'a Spanish'; 'Spanish' itself as a ('mixed') designation fluctuates. By this I do not mean that 'Spanish' is not a clearly understood ethnic designation in a particular individual's reckoning; rather, many of its constituent attributes are ambiguous and variable, as are the ways it is meaningful in Trinidadian society. For example, the definition and function of what 'a Spanish' *is* depends on a number of variously selected criteria such as colouring, hair texture, area of origin (e.g., Venezuela or locales in Trinidad with historical Spanish and/or Amerindian populations such as Arima, Santa Cruz, or parts of southern Trinidad), lineage (i.e., individual forebears), class position, and what is generally associated with class as one of its markers: presentation of self – behaviour, comportment, and speech.[3] Also critical are the specific reasons for their attribution to particular individuals, the moment in which the designation is made, and by whom. Therefore, 'Spanish' is both a malleable category and a negotiable identity for individuals who may differentially promote a variety of criteria. It can conjure up different associations to different people. Thus while 'mixed' is also a generalised rubric, the attributes of specific kinds of 'mixed' come together in various numbers and combinations and, as in the case of 'Spanish', can be again sub-categorised. 'Mixed' constitutes both a fluid ethnic category and an individual's negotiable membership. In fact, as will be discussed, certain kinds of 'mixed', such as 'Spanish', are terms describing individuals (rather loosely designating an aggregate) and emphasise cultural and phenotypic characteristics rather than social – i.e., jural, political – dimensions. As a 'mixed' category, 'Spanish' lets us get at these various processes as it: 1) identifies or emphasises particular qualities and their combinations; 2) reveals how various kinds of 'ethnic'/'racial'/'cultural' combinations are valorised; and 3) throws into relief actual or putative historical events and relationships. While some of these issues arise in connection with more clear-cut race and colour categories in Trinidad (all of which are, of course, social constructs and hence to some extent malleable), more multivalent and thus potentially ambiguous 'mixed' classifications such as 'Spanish' permit even less to be assumed or taken for granted.

'Spanish' is certainly a label that is used by some Trinidadians to describe themselves. In this chapter I will not refer to self-referential statements of 'Spanish' persons.[4] Rather, my intention is to underscore the significance and sharpen the concept of ambiguity in 'mixed' ethnicities through the example of Trinidad's 'Spanish'. I am dealing with the idiomatic usage of ethnic categories, conceptualisations of 'mixed' persons, and the ideological construction of kinds of groups. I do this by considering two distinct yet connected domains: 1) historical evidence taken from secondary sources, and 2) contemporary ethnographic data gathered during fieldwork undertaken in Trinidad (1984, 1987-89). While my interpretation of the historical material is somewhat speculative, I think it can stand as a provisional attempt to elucidate some of the antecedent dimensions underlying the current significance of a 'Spanish' ethnicity among the general population in Trinidad. The ethnographic data offered here, however, emphasises Indo-Trinidadian perception and use of the construct 'Spanish', rather than those gleaned from a cross-section of the society. The focus of my field research in Trinidad did not specifically address 'Spanish' ethnicity but ethnicity among Indo-Trinidadians. Moreover, my research was conducted in a relatively small, semi-rural area, traditionally perceived – with some degree of accuracy – as a particularly conservative (both politically and culturally) region of the country. For these reasons my observations in this chapter should be seen as exploratory and provisional. Due to the nature of ethnic group relations in post-colonial Trinidad, however, especially between the two demographically most significant ethnic groups – Afro-Trinidadians and Indo-Trinidadians – Indo-Trinidadians' conceptualisations can provide a useful window through which to view the meanings and social significance of both 'Spanish' and, by extension, 'mixed' as ethnic categories.

A number of my informants referred to 'Spanish' in three senses: 1) as a distinct ethnic category, 2) as occupying a particular symbolic space in Indo- and Afro-Trinidadian relations, and 3) as a form of 'African' or 'black' identity – a diluted or 'softer' variation that in a sense upgrades the person designated 'Spanish' in an ethnic hierarchy where elements of colonial ideology have relegated Afro-Trinidadians and Indo-Trinidadians to the bottom, where both struggle against being last. To a significant extent my informants' perceptions of 'Spanish' discussed in this chapter act as what I will call an ethnic modifier, (cf. Alexander, 1977:421). By this I mean a category of ethnicity that modifies other ethnic categories, indicating a positive condition which improves another ethnic referent into something more highly valued, at least by certain sectors of society. While the constructions of 'Spanish' discussed here are *by no means* Indo-Trinidadians' *exclusive* conceptualisation of this category, as ethnic modifier, 'Spanish' functions *in part* to affirm an ethnic hierarchy where 'softened' or ambiguous 'African' or 'black' convey and confer a higher status that modifies the perceived stronger or more clear-cut expression of 'African' or 'black' attributes.

Yet it is also significant that because of the particular history and social use of the colour 'black'/concept 'African' in Trinidad, the category 'Spanish', in this capacity as ethnic modifier, has not been a focal point in local discursive traditions avowing a positive image of 'blackness' or 'Africanness'. Examples of the latter include philosophical treatises from the turn of the nineteenth century such as J.J. Thomas' *Froudacity* or social movements like the Pan-African Association; Trinidad's Black Power movement of the 1970s; contemporary political bodies such as the National Joint Action Committee; or that evinced in aesthetic expression, particularly in some calypsoes and cultural competitions such as Best Village.[5] Labour unions and political parties (such as the Oilfield Workers' Trade Union, the former Workers and Farmers Party and United Labour Front) that embrace notions of class unity in rejection of ethnic (and other) factionalism fostered by colonial ideology have also subscribed to cultural equality and pride. While 'blackness' or 'Africanness' is not today a principal theme in everyday discourse among the majority of people, these examples are all clear illustrations of the positive associations and imagery of 'Africanness' and 'blackness' in Trinidadian society. Moreover, in individuals' personal estimations, 'Africanness' or 'blackness' can certainly be emphasised. For example, an acquaintance remarked to me that although his Trinidadian wife 'is a Spanish', she refers to herself as 'Afro-Trinidadian', emphasising her African heritage and identity.

From both a national Trinidadian perspective and that of my informants, the category 'Spanish' illustrates that categories of ethnicity are ways of talking about power that reveal the tensions around the nature and construction of ethnic boundaries and the cultural contents they enclose, within structures of group conflict and competition. The category 'Spanish' also allows us a means to explore how people use multiple and contrastive *ideas about* ethnicity, history, and culture to understand their place and/or create places for themselves in society.

Before discussing the foundations and contemporary significance of the category 'Spanish', I will briefly sketch the historical context of Trinidadian social structure and then locate the concept of 'mixed' within it.

Ethnicity and politics in Trinidad

The development over time of particular world views and definitions of social identity is part of a broader question of how material conditions are experienced and expressed as particular ideologies. The nature of colonial society is, in most cases, that economic and social boundaries are made to correspond with racial, ethnic, religious and other communal groups, which are differently incorporated into the stratification system of the society (Hintzen, 1989:6). Through this unequal incorporation, which fosters conflictual political and economic interests, adversarial relations can develop between the communal groups *(ibid.)*. In Trinidad's origins as a colonial society, a system of stratification based on a class-race-colour hierarchy – beginning with slavery and continuing through emancipation and indenture – laid the foundations for a post-colonial society whose hallmark has been ethnic group competition fostered by class inequalities and state control of certain resources. While an analysis of the genesis of all salient Trinidadian categories of ethnicity is beyond the purview of this chapter, noting the historical context in which ethnic identities evolve, are evaluated and contested clarifies how ethnic hierarchies become salient in social life. Labour deployment and its associated standards of value and prestige helps shape the way people classify their world – and each other – as well as the rationalisations marshalled that ratify these classifications. (See Chapters 1 and 2 for a more detailed look at the social organisation of nineteenth-century Trinidad.)

After the abolition of West Indian slavery in 1838 a cheap and ready labour supply was still needed to continue the colonial production of sugar. Under an indentured labour project between 1845 and 1917, the British brought East Indians to Trinidad from India to work on sugar estates. Mid-nineteenth century Trinidadian society was permeated by '. . . the whole intricate experience of the Afro-European encounter since the Renaissance, the stereotypes formed by slavery, the legacy of the master and servant relationship, and, equally important, the growing dogma of the superiority of European culture and technology' (Wood, 1968:248). To this we can add another critical influence, noted by Brereton (1979:193ff.), the development of British and European concepts of racial types and the 'natural' inequalities between them. These ideologies and their institutionalisation formed the context within which the various sectors of the Trinidadian population interacted and into which the East Indians entered.

As a 'segmented society' divided by occupational hierarchies, status groups of colour and race, and class levels partly determined by race/colour and differential access to key resources (such as land or employment possibilities), nineteenth century Trinidad had clear lines of demarcation among a population 'conscious of belonging to definite and separate groups' (Brereton, 1979:205). Constituting these groups were, according to Ryan (1972:19-20): a) whites, subdivided between 'principal whites' (wealthy European and creole planters and merchants, and British officials), 'secondary whites' (wage-earning employees of 'principal whites'), and Syrian, Lebanese, Portuguese, and Jewish small business people; b) coloured persons, of whom the middle class was mostly comprised; and c) at the lowest point, blacks and the indentured labourers.

Such a complex social structure as this assuredly produces diverse, cross-cutting, ambivalent and ambiguous ideologies of social place and privilege. While elite whites asserted racial (and class) superiority, there were other (lesser) whites who could not make the same claims. Moreover, as Brereton (1979:208) points out, an emergent 'Creole identity' participated in by both whites and middle-class coloureds and blacks was evident, creating a unity that contrasted with the feelings toward British representatives and indentured immigrants. Within the coloured and black middle class itself, many scholars of the Caribbean note that to an extent the analogy between 'whiteness' and 'superiority' had been accepted (e.g., Ryan, 1972; Patterson, 1975; cf. Brereton, 1979). It is a familiar characterisation in the literature that many of this group 'accepted and internalised' notions of black inferiority (Ryan, 1972:20) and '. . . compensated to some extent for the negative racial self-image . . . by turning it against those lower in the shade hierarchy . . .' (Patterson, 1975:317).

For the mid-nineteenth century Wood (1968) and Brereton (1979) assert that there was little conflict between the indentured East Indians and blacks, separated to a great extent by regional distance and occupational concentration. After the early 1880s, however, when increased recruitment of indentureds within a depressed economy exacerbated the competition between lowest rung East Indians and blacks, the latter increased their perception of East Indians as an 'economic threat' (Brereton, 1979:189-90). In this vein the coloured and black middle class articulated a 'systematic critique' of immigration and these immigrants, and 'a whole collection of unfavourable stereotypes was built up' against them throughout the nineteenth century *(ibid:*186) from various sectors of the society. According to Wood (1968:136-7), even by the 1850s Negro Creoles '... who had been at the bottom of the social scale now had an easily recognizable class beneath them'. Feeling similar pressures, the East Indians in turn imbibed local Trinidadian stratification and elaborated upon traditional forms of bias, particularly regarding their nearest competitors.

Beginning from a largely separate existence, as constraints in the economy tightened, Indo- and Afro-Trinidadians increasingly – though not exclusively – began to voice their interests in communal terms, reflecting their interests as ethnically segregated workers. This process was encouraged and made more complex after World War II by the needs of the state and the efforts of political leadership that mobilised support through platforms of race/ethnicity.

The strength of communal politics derives from the implementation of voting in Trinidad, where 'the most important, visible, and salient dimension of political cleavage is race ...' (Hintzen, 1989:20). As Hintzen (1989:3, 39) succinctly explains, by the 1950s the appeal to race was a principal aspect of mass political mobilisation. The notion of majority rule required aspiring leaders to amass the support of the largest voting blocs. With little overt class mobilisation, this pointed to the black and East Indian populations (1989:39). However, through the significance of the black and mixed populations, 'majoritarianism' gave rise to a black political party (the People's National Movement) 'which relied on communal mobilisation to gain control of the state' (Hintzen, 1989:3). Reliant on communal politics, the state became synonymous with 'black' and opposition parties largely with 'Indian'. While the ruling National Alliance for Reconstruction from 1986 up to December 1991 rested on a self-conscious (if not entirely successful) platform of multi-ethnic representation, the previous PNM regime's strategies of racial politics fomented ideologies of interests based on ethno-cultural identification rather than that of class (Phillips, 1990; Hintzen, 1989). Although today there is also a local discourse of ethnic group harmony regarding Afro- and Indo-Trinidadians, in many social and political contexts it is largely rhetorical.

We have seen so far that a curious combination of forces is at work in Trinidadian society: a ready acknowledgement of its multiple cultural influences and the 'mixed' quality of its history and population, along with an apparently clear ethno-political division into Afro- and Indo-. This local characterisation of Trinidad as having experienced its entire history as a 'callaloo' (literally, a kind of multiple ingredient stew, and designated a national dish) or 'mixed' society, the presence of large

numbers of variously 'mixed' persons in Trinidad,[6] and the existence
of a formal as well as informal ethnic category 'mixed' (evident, for
example, in the official census listings[7] and in everyday parlance) pose
an interesting, if submerged, conundrum for Trinidadians. On the one
hand, an image of cultural, religious, and ethnic heterogeneity and
amalgamation is evoked – a 'cosmopolitan' nation with Amerindian,
African, Spanish, French, Portuguese and English influences (from
centuries of colonial endeavours), flavoured with subsequent 'foreign'
ethnic cultures, such as East Indian or Chinese. On the other hand,
in the competition for scarce, state-dispensed resources, ethnic groups'
cultural legitimacy, distinctive historical roots and separate-but-equal
representation form the discourse through which political claims are
made. In other words, the degree of cultural presence is deemed
commensurate with the degree of political efficacy, since the social and
political voices of competing ethnic groups are framed in an essentially
cultural idiom (cf. Williams, 1989, 1990). As Williams (1989:420) points
out, '... when cultural distinctiveness becomes a criterion of group
identity formation in a single political unit it is certainly a product of
the power relations existing among citizens of that unit'.

   The popular local credo 'unity in diversity' exists simultaneously
with a socio-cultural 'callaloo'; both serve as key metaphors for national
unity and ethnic group harmony. In other post-colonial societies,
nationalist ideology has taken 'miscegenation' – putatively resulting in
a particular kind of person – as a symbol of national identity (cf.
Morner, 1967; Stutzman, 1981; Wright, 1990). Williams' (1989:433)
comment on works dealing with these issues applies here:
'[i]n short, creating a new race through such mixed union would
[ostensibly] eliminate the inevitable conflicts assumed to be the
consequence of racially distinct groups' struggle to maintain their purity
and a "homeland" for their culture'. Trinidad, though a self-proclaimed
'callaloo' society, cannot *unequivocally* or *uniformly* embrace an
ideology of a 'mixed' national identity, given the concern over potential
cultural oblivion that competing ethnic groups allegedly risk. In
Trinidad it is the concern over the assumed intrinsic relationship between
racial/ethnic assimilation (mixing) and acculturation (cultural change or
demise) that makes for a 'callaloo' society that remains unamalgamated
(cf. Morner, 1967:5); it is synchronously 'mixed' and distinctive (cf.
Alexander, 1977). It is this, in part, that allows 'mixed' to be both a
formal and informal ethnic category.

   This dual quality figures in the question of how a particular 'mixed'
designation is socially meaningful. As Alexander (1977:429) points out
for Jamaica, '... the notion of union between persons of different races
has an air of illegitimacy around it'. In Trinidadian society these unions

have many possible social interpretations. By embracing a 'callaloo' identity, Trinidadians modify and broaden any implicit suggestion of 'illegitimacy' within the category 'mixed'. Although not necessarily overtly denigrated, all types of 'mixed' are not deemed, *vis-à-vis* each other, equally desirable or distasteful. What makes any given 'mixed' category positive, negative, or somewhere in between depends on how and by whom the constituent attributes are valorised individually, assessed in composite, and seen in relation to the wider ethnic arena. Two brief examples illustrate this.

First, the modification (mixing) of socially devalued racial traits, is ironically and disapprovingly commented upon by a character in Merle Hodge's *Crick Crack, Monkey*: '... Mrs Harper muttered about the 'lil 'Panol prostitute down in the Place-Sainte who had a chile o' every breed God make and couldn' tell yu which Yankee sailorman she make that pissin'-tail runt for – what these people wouldn' scrape-up outa the rubbish-truck to sharpen they gran-chirren nose, eh!' (1970:139). Second, the category *'dougla'* (East Indian and African mix) is, at least among some Indo-Trinidadians, an at times tacitly avoided and to a certain extent disapproved identification, in large part because ultimately it symbolises the potential engulfment of a minority[8] or subordinate ethnic group. In a letter to the editor in the *Sunday Guardian* newspaper (24 June 1990, p. 11), there is a call for 'conservation' of pure Indian and African races, lest the proliferation of *douglas* result in a 'homological' [*sic*] Trinidad that ultimately loses the 'beauty' of distinct 'races, cultures, and religions', who need to 'develop their language, religion, culture, economic and political power *now*'. Given the nature of Trinidad's ethnic politics, this letter reflects the concern over establishing the possibility of Indo-Trinidadians', and other 'distinct' ethnic groups', political and thus cultural demise.[9]

The meaning and significance of *'Spanish'* are as complex as the examples of other 'mixed' categories. In this chapter we will see that, for differing yet related reasons, on both a national and community (i.e., Indo-Trinidadian) level one important connotation and use of 'Spanish' is that which is socially acceptable, a positive condition.

What is 'a Spanish'?: historical context

In determining *what is* a 'Spanish', we must first consider *who were* the Spanish, for this historical population of colonisers provides a heritage symbol that functions as a key image in the ideological construction of the *category* 'Spanish'. Claimed by Columbus for Spain at the turn of the sixteenth century, Trinidad offered no significant caches of precious minerals or vast numbers of indigenous inhabitants to be harnessed in large-scale labour schemes. Trinidad's most important role for Spanish colonialism was as a military base to launch expeditions to El Dorado (Newson, 1976:235). Consequently, Spanish colonisation and settlement was very limited. As Laurence (1980:214) puts it, the Spanish colonial era was one in which Trinidad lay in a '... state of neglect ... for almost the entire period it remained a Spanish colony'. This situation had significant consequences for the path of Trinidad's development as an increasingly populated, revenue-producing colony. But more significant for our purposes, the peculiar nature of the Spanish occupation likely had repercussions for retrospective assessments of Trinidad's history. I suggest that the Spanish colonial experience holds a qualitatively different kind of place in contemporary estimation than that of the British, rendering the Spanish a more or less neutral, if not benign, coloniser.

This hypothesis is based on four possibly contributing factors: first, the Spanish are sufficiently far back in Trinidad's history not to be seen as leaving detrimental legacies felt in contemporary times, contrary to British colonialism. Perhaps contributing to this view is that, as Hintzen (1989:21) points out, unlike the British, 'who considered themselves colonial expatriates, the [nineteenth century] French and Spanish creoles developed a special pride in their Trinidadian identity'. Second, Trinidadian perceptions of European identity are not uniform. There is a difference between 'white' (most notably the English) and 'Trinidad white' – those Europeans alleged to be variously if minutely 'mixed' with non-Europeans (notably Africans) or Europeans assumed to be 'darker' than northern Europeans. These can include French Creoles, Portuguese, and Spaniards. Moreover, from their arrival, the Spanish were interacting with the indigenous Amerindians on sexual as well as other terms.[10] This resulted in the Hispanicisation of Amerindian culture and society (Laurence, 1980:220-1) and undoubtedly to some extent the Amerindianisation of Spanish life in Trinidad. Hence, the Spanish identity carries with it vestiges of Trinidad's original, 'authentic', and somewhat romanticised past, in the form of aboriginal Amerindian 'blood' and cultural survivals.[11]

Third, the eighteenth century saw an influx of wealthy colonists into Trinidad who 'tended to displace the original Spanish inhabitants down the social scale' (Newson, 1976:193). Furthermore, Spain was defeated by England (who annexed Trinidad in 1802). History records that in 1802 Governor Picton observed that there were 'only six or seven Spaniards of "any respectability" in Trinidad' (Newson, 1976:194). These factors potentially enable Spain to be rendered, with hindsight, an underdog of sorts, or at least potentially more sympathetic.

Finally, it can be provisionally suggested that the debated and largely dismissed but influential claim in histories of the colonies that the supposedly paternalistic and benevolent nature of slavery among the Spanish and Portuguese, compared to the harsher attitude of northern European countries, has influenced perceptions of Spanish colonisation *vis-à-vis* that of the British. Thus, Ottley's (1955:86) comment:

> The free people of colour and the Negroes found in Trinidad [after the Cedula of 1783] a Spanish government which gave them liberty to indulge in, to the fullest extent, and to expound on, and glorify the new Republican doctrine of liberty, equality, and fraternity . . . . These exponents of the new order . . . were in no way different from the other free society of nobles and semi-nobles, although the two groups lived in complete isolation. Both were rich, in money and in quality.[12]

Although Brereton notes that Spanish slave *laws*, if not *practice*, 'were generally more humane and paid more attention to the slaves as individuals with human and religious rights' (1981:26), she provides a more realistic assessment than Ottley's eulogistic reconstruction. However, she also acknowledges that many historians subscribe to this unfavourable comparison between Spanish/Portuguese and northern European colonisers. While it is not possible to speculate to what extent popular sentiment or scholarly information is imbibed by the mass population over time, we can assume that some of these issues found their way into local wisdom through such avenues as oral tradition, the educational system, and the media.

Over the eighteenth and nineteenth centuries more waves of Spanish emigrated to Trinidad. A small number of wealthy Venezuelan *émigrés* assimilated into Trinidad's white elite (Brereton, 1979). From 1802 on, political refugees arrived from the Venezuelan mainland. Furthermore, large numbers of *peon* labourers were brought to Trinidad from Venezuela during the nineteenth century as immigrant workers for 'specific tasks for which they were considered particularly well suited – wood-cutting, stock-rearing, and labour on cocoa estates' (Laurence, 1980:219; Wood, 1968:33-4). Known as *payoles* or *cocoa-pañoles*, the *peon* labourers were identified with these rural pursuits and some (likely Amerindian-derived) craft production, e.g., basketry (Laurence, 1980:223). Significantly, they arrived in Trinidad as 'mixed' people – African-Amerindian-Spanish.[13] Along with the larger black and coloured labouring population, they 'were rigorously excluded from political or civic life, their most characteristic cultural forms tended to be despised by the upper and middle classes, and they were in a low economic position . . .'(Brereton, 1979:110). Rather than assimilating into the then predominantly French population, they were inclined toward the extant Spanish population (Laurence, 1980:219). The latter were predominantly relegated, along with the fast-disappearing Amerindians, to the interior, far from existing centres of population and social amenities (Brereton, 1981:80). It would seem that now 'Spanish' necessarily takes on an association with marginality, labouring classes, and lack of social privilege, possibly particularly exacerbated by their relationship with the defeated Amerindians.

However, a contradiction becomes evident in the ethnic category 'Spanish', since nineteenth century observers also deemed the *peons* important contributors to the island's cultivation and settlement, as well as being 'the most industrious class' in the Montserrat district (Brereton, 1979:131-2ff.). According to accounts of the day, cited by Brereton, they were depicted as 'honest, active, God-fearing, law-abiding, and hard-working', 'a peaceful people', 'the original clearers of the forest', 'doing [much] for the future development of the Colony . . .' and being 'the most valuable of all pioneers' (Brereton, 1979:131-2). Moreover, the small-scale cocoa farming undertaken by *peon* labourers rose dramatically throughout the century, and, by 1900, cocoa was Trinidad's primary agricultural export (Wood, 1968:34). As Wood (1968:34) notes, 'the *peons* prized their freedom and were scornful of field labour on sugar estates during the time of slavery'. The imagery of this population as skilled, proud, and worthy contributors to the nation and its ascendance (cf. Williams, 1990), albeit within the confines of contemporary class restrictions and ethnic prejudices, added to the complexity of the panoply of dimensions of 'Spanish' identity, in such a way as to preserve significant positive associations with this population.

Thus, by the turn of the century a figurative and literal transformation of the Spanish population must have occurred, in terms of the construction of 'Spanish' as a category of identity. First, as an ambivalently assessed (rather than uniformly decried) coloniser, the category gradually comes to refer to a very different, and largely dependent, population, called in general terms 'Spanish' and encompassing through historical metaphor[14] a number of ethnic groups, characteristic attributes, and class associations. While we must be careful in considering historical evidence in retrospective interpretation, I think it can be posited that the conceptualisation of 'Spanish' has gone from denoting foreign and essentially homogeneous nationality – Spain/Spaniard – to connoting localised 'mixed' ethnicity – 'a Spanish', one among other 'mixed' kinds of persons. But it is best to view this gradual transformation in identity as an accretive mosaic that gives rise to multivalence and ambiguity rather than as a linear falling away of *a* prior identity to *a* subsequent one. The question, then, is what is the nature and role of this mosaic: why has 'Spanish', as a contemporary 'mixed', maintained in current times a critical function as socially acceptable ethnic modifier?

What is 'a Spanish'?: contemporary context

As Hodge (1975:33), among others, asserts, in Trinidad 'Spanish influences are abundant' – in the form of the language which can be heard in certain parts of the island, through its proximity to South America, and, importantly, in the Christmas folk music called *parang*.[15]

We can consider *parang* at some length here, as it figures as one of the principal symbols of Trinidadian national identity, evidence of the 'callaloo' composition of the society. Although it is performed by persons from a variety of ethnic backgrounds in addition to those who are 'Spanish', *parang* implicitly and explicitly draws a focus on the Spanish presence in Trinidad, evoking notions of local *history*, 'Spanish' *culture* as part of the 'cosmopolitan' nature and 'plural' heritage of Trinidad, and the image of the ambiguous 'Spanish' *phenotype* that can blur the boundaries of (and among) such socio-politically distinct ethnic categories as 'African', 'Chinese', and 'East Indian'. *Parang* begs the question of the distinction between cultural traditions that are considered embodied in and exclusive to certain groups or collectivities, and cultural traditions that are not so contained.

'Culture' or cultural identity is harnessed in different ways and toward different ends. Creating or reinforcing an ethnic *category* is a distinct process from determining the boundaries and function of an ethnic *group*. Ethnic categories are not always isomorphic with ethnic groups. Indeed, this distinction is illustrated in one university professor's rhetorical question to me: 'Why is *parang*, which is sung in Spanish, a national symbol, yet [East] *Indians* must give up his [*sic*] language to be "national"? The language of the coloniser was, after all, also Spanish'. The underlying issue here is that *parang*, and other 'Spanish' cultural traditions, are not necessarily 'owned' by or located within one, specifically demarcated ethnic group, in the same way as, for example, the Hindi language or *bhajans* (Hindu hymns) would be for East Indians. *Parang* serves as part of the symbolic imagery of what makes Trinidad 'cosmopolitan'. *Bhajans* or Hindi are to many non-Indo-Trinidadians[16] a symbol of what makes Trinidad society parochial.

Moreover, conceding a prominent place in the national arena for Indian culture is a problematic act, since cultural representation and political competition are often synonymous. Conceptualised as a different kind of ethnic category, 'Spanish' and its constituent cultural traditions pose no such politico-cultural threat. Furthermore, while *parang* was a dying art form until it began to be promoted in the 1960s, it was revived as something that had been previously integrated into Trinidadian society and already known (Gordon Rohlehr, personal communication, 1988) – i.e., as an authentic part of Trinidad's original cultural repertoire.[17] *Parang*, as a definitive representation of 'Spanish', can serve as a legitimate, unproblematic national symbol because: 1) it is a different *kind* of ethnic identity from those that are politically salient and whose boundaries are more exclusively defined; and 2) it has a priority of claim, a putatively extensive history of integration as part of the 'original' fabric of Trinidadian society. No other ethnic group (except the partially 'reinvented' Amerindians) can make this kind of claim about their traditions for the *local* context.[18]

Given the plethora of scholarly attention to Trinidadian ethnic and race relations and national identity, and given Laurence's (1980:228, fn. 63) observation that despite a degree of creolisation,

> within the Creole structure the *payoles* have always main-
> tained, and continue to maintain their own traditions e.g.
> music, dancing, songs, food, *oraciones* [prayers], super-
> stitions, and, above all, language,

one would think that there would be more investigation of the contemporary 'Spanish' as one of the ethnic segments in Trinidad's 'plural society'. Laurence *(ibid.)* goes on to suggest that 'this subculture has doubtless helped to create a sense of group identity which has contributed to the persistence of this minority group and its traditions'. However, this 'minority group' is being defined by its 'subcultural' traditions and only secondarily – if at all – by power relations. Critically important is that this 'minority group' of 'Spanish' subculture is not as clearly bounded (defined) as Laurence's comment might imply, given that the *political* dimensions of their corporate identity are unclear and that both phenotypical and genealogical claims to being 'a Spanish' are made by and levied at a significant variety of people.

Ethnographic data

In answer to my queries about their designations of a particular individual as 'a Spanish', my informants were not suggesting a strict genealogical line of descent from the original Spaniards. To do so would contradict the idea of 'Spanish' as a 'mixed' category that recognises various streams of influence: Spaniards from Spain, Amerindians from Trinidad, 'mixed' Spanish from Venezuela, and African, Indian, Chinese, and European aspects.[19] Offering a Jamaican example, Alexander (1977:420) states that 'Spanish persons are generally regarded as being of darker complexion than north west Europeans. Nevertheless Spanish persons are classified as white'. In the Trinidadian context, 'Spanish' is not a colour term *per se* but a term signalling putative 'background' and 'appearance'; contemporary 'Spanish' persons are decidedly not classed as 'white'; and 'Spanish' entails a significant ambiguity in the establishment of another's ethnic identity.

My informants, and contemporaries such as Vidia Naipaul (below), use the category 'Spanish' as a descriptive device for different kinds of messages. In what follows I present some examples, grouped to illustrate the ambiguity and hence symbolic depth of the category 'Spanish'. I will discuss each section in order to shed light on the significance of 'Spanish' in current ethnic relations.

I   This section shows various perceptions of possible criteria for 'Spanish' identity.

   (a)   ' "Spanish" is white Negro mixed with Indian. It also have red Negro and black Negro. White Negro is fair, clear, with straight or straightish hair' (Indo-Trinidadian woman).

   (b)   'My daughter-in-law is "a Spanish". She have a [East] Indian mother and a Spanish father, [he is] a red [very light-skinned Afro-Euro mix], with kinda curly hair' (Indo-Trinidadian woman).

   (c)   'We went through purely mulatto villages where the people were a baked copper colour, much disfigured by disease. They had big light eyes and kinky red hair. My father described them as Spaniards' (V.S. Naipaul, *The Mimic Men*, 1985 [1967]:121).

   (d)   'If I see the hair is straightish I will say Spanish, and if it is more curly I will say red .... I look for skin colour, hair, and what not. I say mixed if they seem more whiteish, and Spanish or Spanishy if they seem more Negro' (Indo-Trinidadian woman).

In these statements each person offers an idiosyncratic perspective on what particular attributes constitute a 'Spanish' identity. What recurs in all, however, is the notion of 'Spanish' as a kind of 'mixed'. The two principal constituent qualities of 'Spanishness' refer to appearance: hair texture and skin colouring, which derive from African, East Indian, and/or European background. Interestingly, cultural characteristics are not what is salient about 'Spanishness' to these respondents. In this sense the delineation of 'Spanish' as an ethnic group is ambiguous, and renders 'Spanish' an applicable term to whatever an observer is describing, of course within general parameters, for a particular person or situation.

Colour terms, hair texture, and other appearance diacritica transcend the *cultural* boundaries of ethnic identity and are not dependent upon commonly claimed ethnic group ideologies such as a sense of community, a shared history or traditions, a feeling of kinship, and so on. Naipaul's comment comes closest to indicating a community, but primarily in the literal sense of co-residence and secondarily in physical resemblance.

The diversity of qualities or attributes in these four statements aid us in perceiving 'Spanish' ethnicity as not only a social construction like (all) other ethnic categories, but as having greater capacity as an ideologically charged symbol. Its ambiguity and more or less generalisable applicability find relevance where other, more precise ethnic categories do/can not. However, although ethnic categories may be couched in the language of phenotype, the driving force of their significance is not phenotype itself. The meanings derived from perception do not reflect 'objective' phenomena, particular attributes *per se*. Rather, meaning is derived from social relations – including those of class, politics, and history.

II The quotes in this section illustrate historical and class dimensions of 'Spanish' in inter-ethnic relations and its consequent use as an ethnic modifier.

(a) 'Spanish people [have been] with the Hindu people since long time [the far past]. Spanish have a peaceful history with Indians' (Indo-Trinidadian man).

(b) 'Only the old midwives with Spanish [descent] does with the babies like we do, probably because they intermingled with the Indian people long time, the Hindu people. Long time we had no differentiation, there was no racialism then. Neighbours lived close together, not like now, where you become more aware of South Africa and all them kinda things ...' (Indo-Trinidadian woman).

(c) 'When [an Afro-Trinidadian person] not mix with anything, you must know both they mother and father is *nigger*, they not mix with anything. When I say 'a *Negro*' I mean a mixture, Spanish, Chinee, Indian. They just act different, you see it right away in them. You see the kind of *softness* into

> it, the softness in their personality. The Spanish or the Indian is coming out in the personality ... They mighn't be clear, clear [very light-skinned] ... Basically, the colour have nothing much to do with it. But their *personality* is different, a mix of qualities gives a complete different way [manner]' (Indo-Trinidadian woman).

(d) Indo-Trinidadian woman: 'My boyfriend is a Spanish – Indian and Negro'.
 AK: 'Isn't that a *dougla*?'.
 Woman: 'Well, I doesn't use that word, I calls it Spanish. He have grey eyes, like, and soft hair. I doesn't say *dougla*'.
 AK: 'How about if he had dark eyes and hard hair?'.
 Woman: 'Oh! Then he'd be *dougla*, not Spanish'.

These comments demonstrate that 'Spanish' can be used when the African/'black' element is being made ambiguous or diluted. When Indo-Trinidadians employ it, this can suggest a smoothing out of otherwise omnipresent racial antagonisms. The 'Spanish' are portrayed here as having a pacific and co-operative history with Indo-Trinidadians, learning (thus implicitly valorising and legitimising) aspects of Indian culture and not symbolising group conflict, such as is deemed an intrinsic part of the ethnic politics of Afro-Trinidadians and Indo-Trinidadians. 'Spanishy' Negroes can be less of a threat, elicit easier camaraderie, and seem more sympathetic than *'real'* ('pure'?) Negroes, who have had in Indo-Trinidadian perception a putative, culturally homogeneous, precisely defined identity as the allegedly materially envious, politically competitive, sexually covetous, sometimes threatening Other. 'Spanish' seems to efface antagonisms rather than represent them. In the ability to do this, its capacity as ethnic modifier does not render 'Spanish' as a *category* less ambiguous, because the very condition of ambiguity makes possible its appropriation in one direction or another. Furthermore, the function of ethnic modifier is just one of its aspects.

The reference to South Africa (IIb) – the epitome of Black oppression and struggle – 'and all them kinda things' implicitly points to what this speaker sees as a relatively recent schism between local ethnic groups, where the present politically derived ethno-racial 'differentiation', and hence acrimony takes the place of a past harmony of cultural exchange. Politics divides, and divides along ethnic lines, or boundaries, but these boundaries apply to specific ethnicities with particular histories and qualities – i.e., African, Indian, but not 'Spanish'. She seems to imply that political boundaries that create ethnic identity are artificial, and that the genuine differences between groups are cultural and therefore not problematic.

In the use of the term 'Spanish' we can see the association of class and culture personified, insofar as behaviour and comportment (sometimes glossed as 'personality' or 'ways') modifies so-called 'ordinary' *black* (Hodge, 1970) into a higher social category of *'Spanish'*. The speaker of these remarks (IIc) clearly communicates her ideas about the relationship between (physical) appearance and (cultural) background, and the consequences for social position. In her statement, a 'mixed' identity is far superior to a 'pure' or clear-cut African ethnicity, which she labels with an epithet; mixing, in her estimation, improves the personality (or formation and presentation of self) by blurring stark boundaries. (In contrast, this reasoning would likely not, however, be the case with regard to Indian ethnicity – ideally to remain 'pure'.) Action or behaviour is more important than colour *per se*, and 'personality' is expressed in behaviour, which in turn is often assumed to be indicative of status in the social hierarchy. Proper comportment (respectability, manners, 'living good' with people) and the equation of being 'civilised' with being 'cultured' are implied, and seen as the province of the middle (or upper) class. A 'nigger' is low(er) class; a 'Negro' and, even better, a 'Spanish', are high(er) class. As an ethnic modifier, within a rubric of 'mixed', 'Spanish' can alter the meaning (if not the designation) of an original constituent attribute. While this is potentially applicable to any ethnic group, since the very nature of ambiguity in the notion of 'mixed' renders it protean, given the nature of ethnic politics in Trinidad it is here notably Afro-Trinidadian-associated when used by this Indo-Trinidadian.

The sub-text of (IId), in what was at the time self-conscious distinction between *dougla* and 'Spanish', reveals the complex nature of 'Spanish' ethnicity. The 'grey eyes' and 'soft hair' of her 'Spanish' boyfriend allows this speaker to tag *dougla* as a less preferable identity, whose greater association with ostensibly non-white qualities, 'dark eyes' and 'hard [kinky] hair', would mean downward status mobility for her. Her obvious embarrassment during our conversation reveals a reluctance to assign what she considers an adverse label to a 'mixed' individual: he becomes 'a Spanish' by virtue of his ambiguous 'ethnic' qualities – *grey* eyes as opposed to light or dark, and *soft* hair as opposed to hard (but, significantly, not 'straight').

As the well-known turn of the century West Indian politician, journalist, and author A.R.F. Webber wrote in his novel, *Those That Be In Bondage*, 'His features were *soft* tinted as may be so frequently met with in those creoles of Trinidad who can trace their ancestry back to the Spanish occupation' (Webber, 1988 [1917]:140, emphasis added) Also compare Alexander's (1977:419) Jamaican informant's racial category 'Spanish-dark'. The informant explains: 'that means *soft* darkness with pretty black hair ... Spanish-dark and Indian-dark imply straight hair, and not Negroid features. I mean it could be straight nose and not very thick lips, sort of thing' (emphasis added).

In reference to comments about 'Spanish', the various associations made between the word 'soft' or 'softness' and 'Spanish' leads me to suggest that this word may be understood as conveying what social scientists sometimes refer to as the 'blurring' of ethnic boundaries. The opposite of 'soft' is 'hard', which has many meanings in local Trinidadian usage. One implication is, I think, *definitiveness* of *quality*: for example, 'hard' hair is kinky hair; 'hardened' disposition is wilful (that is, overtly expressed as opposed to the blurring or 'softness' of acquiescence or co-operation). Hence, with reference to 'Spanish', 'softness' can be read as a positive (enhancing) ambiguity.

III   The following statement exemplifies the place of 'Spanish' in the contemporary politics of the 'plural society':

> 'Spanish is people from Venezuela mix[ed] with Negro, with straight hair until they mix with Negro. Most Spanish like [desire] Creole [Negro] people. Is a natural thing for them. In Venezuela Creole and Spanish get along just like natural. Venezuela people aren't racial like we [Indo-Trinidadians] are. The Spanish and Creole even here live good, because the Creole have the jobs. Spanish girls looking for security. Our ancestors made us racial in the beginning, and [former Prime Minister] Eric Williams gave the Creoles all the jobs' (Indo-Trinidadian man).

In this text the speaker communicates two ideas of particular interest. He straightforwardly avers Indo-Trinidadian 'racialism', which he construes as inherent or at least ancient ('in the beginning'). Juxtaposed are the 'Spanish', who have proclivities for amicable relations with Negroes, either through natural sexual compatibility and the smooth interrelations that derive from this, or through the pragmatic affinity caused by economic dependence. Regarding the latter, 'Spanish' are equated in this comment with Indo-Trinidadians, who often say they have been less successful than Afro-Trinidadians in securing the benefits, rewards, and patronage of party politics. Yet the 'Spanish' simultaneously have natural fraternity with Africans and are in a sense forced into it through social inequality, i.e., the unequal dispensing of resources. The ambiguity of 'Spanish' is thrown into relief here: they are 'mix[ed] with Negro' yet akin to Indo-Trinidadians in their material condition; they are sexually associated with Negroes, but in a way that is both 'natural' and pragmatic ('looking for security'); they are, by contrast with Indo-Trinidadians, not 'racial'; yet circumstances and history rather than intrinsic essence dictate this to a degree. In Trinidad ethnic groups do not 'live good' naturally, since social inequality is paramount; it is in Venezuela that 'people aren't racial' and so can interact more naturally.

Conclusion

The category 'Spanish' is multivalent, and simultaneously refers to both one ethnic rubric, and many, diverse individual members who qualify, as it were, through various means. Thus there is more than one way to get to be called 'a Spanish': for example, through various combinations of appearance (phenotype); background (ancestral lineage, name, locales of origin, cultural traditions); social class; personal comportment or behaviour; self-identification; assessment and attribution by others; and so on. The category 'Spanish' also underscores the extent to which ethnic identity is socially constructed and based on perceptions of history. History simultaneously lends authenticity and confers legitimacy, yet threatens cohesiveness of descent through transformations in traditions and practices. Since there is not a uniform ideal model that encompasses the precise qualities that constitute its distinctiveness, attributes defining 'Spanish' as an ethnicity are perhaps even more fluid and contingent than in other, more delimited ethnic 'group' examples in Trinidadian society, such as 'African'/'Negro', 'East Indian', or 'Chinese'. I am certainly not suggesting that any of these categories are uniform or static, only that 'mixed' may offer a greater possibility for the creative use of ambiguity in social relations.

'Mixed' may also act as an ethnic modifier in the suggestive place it holds in local discourse about racial hierarchies. Alexander (1977:427) comments on the ambivalence with which racial hierarchy is conceived in Jamaica: 'This ambivalence is expressed in the touchiness with which the subject is discussed ... race is a subject people do not discuss freely and openly; it remains understood'. This 'touchiness' is similar in Trinidad, even though 'the making of ethnic [and racial] distinctions is an enthusiastic concern of most Trinidadians' (Lieber, 1981:100). What becomes evident is that a two-dimensional discourse is operative, reflecting notions of hierarchy and egalitarianism. That is, showing too much cognisance of, and hence interest in matters of *race* veers too closely to being *'racial'* – attributing validity and legitimacy to the intrinsic inequality of racial hierarchies (and, by implication, other social hierarchies), thereby going against the egalitarianism of both the credo, 'unity in diversity' and the local wisdom of 'living good' with people by not 'showing them a bad face'. As one of my informants (a 'mixed' but not 'Spanish' woman in her mid-40s) stated it:

> In my generation no one looked for ethnicity, no one felt it was important, but if you *had* to put a category on someone, you'd go by surname, what they look like, and culture, like wearing a *sari* on special occasions or the girl who'd bring *won ton* to all our school parties. But even now ethnicity isn't important in Trinidad, because of all this callaloo [mixing] we have ...

There exists a fine line between accepting the apparently self-evident and commonsensical structure of ranked social and cultural attributes (the colour-class-ethnicity hierarchy) while not appearing to contradict (fundamentally preferable) democratic, universalistic ideals. Perhaps one of the means of negotiating this fine line is through the employment of various 'mixed' categories of ethnic identity, such as 'Spanish', where historical authenticity, contemporary ambiguity, and yet categorical distinctiveness permit both the construction and rationalisation of social place. However, it must be noted that the use of 'Spanish' certainly *does not necessarily* suggest the user is deliberately being racially hierarchical. Yet in its function as ethnic modifier discussed here, this implication in a sense serves to buttress the system of stratification. It does this partly through redefining the perceived competitor/ oppressor in terms of creating distinctions and imbuing these with different statuses, and stipulating ostensive allies in an antagonistic environment.

But evaluating the ethnic 'background' of competing ethnic groups and their presence in the national mainstream is a different process from evaluating the ethnic 'background' of 'Spanish'. As a body, 'Spanish' are not competitors in the usual sense for state-defined and state-dispensed resources meted out in post-colonial societies. At the same time it is a buttressing phenomenon, 'Spanish' is a buffer as much as (if not more so than) a clearly-bounded, single-descent, same-traditions, collective voice kind of ethnic construction. It is a buffer in that it exemplifies (though not solely and not deliberately) a solution to a major issue in post-colonial nation-states: it simultaneously affirms and negates ethnic heterogeneity; a symbol of a kind of ethnic compromise in antagonisms between distinct, and competing, ethnic groups. As one kind of 'mixed', 'Spanish' allows recognition of Trinidad's empirically undeniable population diversity deriving from centuries of colonial labour schemes; it establishes Trinidad's historically deep and culturally authentic past; it symbolises a homogenised and 'typical' Trinidadian ethno-cultural group, and in its latitude remains outside the contested terrain of ethnic group competition and conflict.

Acknowledgements

This chapter benefited greatly from helpful comments by Bridget Brereton, Stephen Stüempfle and Percy Hintzen. Special gratitude is due Allyson Purpura and Leith Mullings for their insightful critiques. Also much appreciated were Allyson Purpura's editing suggestions. The fieldwork on which this paper is based was part of a larger research project funded by Fulbright, Wenner-Gren Foundation, and Sigma Xi Society grants.

Notes

1   I conceive 'background' as encompassing related dimensions of social identity such as class position, locale of origin, marriage and sexual relations, cultural heritage, and the like – criteria that can readily be translated into socially meaningful ranked classifications.
2   A well-known exception is Martinez-Alier's (1974) analysis of social stratification that recognises the importance of ambiguity in definitions of rank and their manipulation.
3   By 'speech' I mean manner or style of speaking English. While research shows that Spanish as a spoken language survives to a degree in Trinidad today (Lipski, 1990; Laurence, 1980; Moodie, 1973), I did not find it a significant criterion in people's designations of 'Spanish' identity.
4   My continuing research on this topic will include narratives to be gathered from self-identified 'Spanish' persons, and from Afro- and other non-Indo-Trinidadians. Preliminary data suggest that the term 'Spanish' as used by non-Indo-Trinidadians does not necessarily carry the same symbolic resonance as it does for my Indo-Trinidadian informants quoted here.
5   Best Village is an annual competition for local communities, involving folk music, dance, and drama. It began in the mid-1960s under the auspices of former Prime Minister Eric Williams of the People's National Movement (PNM) ruling party, as a vehicle for fostering national identity and community pride. An implicit objective was to strengthen PNM support within the communities. Historically Best Village has been dominated by Afro-Trinidadians (see, for example, Stuempfle, 1990).
6   According to the 1980 census, Trinidad and Tobago registered 172,285 'Mixed' persons, out of a population total of 1,079,791. Further breakdown within this 'mixed' category is not provided.
7   The other census categories are 'Negro', 'White', 'East Indian', 'Chinese', 'Syrian Lebanese', and 'Other'. 'Spanish' is an informal if commonly accepted ethnic designation; it is not to my knowledge an official (i.e. statistical or census) category. Another example of occasional differences in officially and informally devised categories of ethnicity is taken from an

announcement in the *Trinidad Express* newspaper (10 October 1988,
p. 11): a San Fernando City Queen Pageant beauty contest was held,
featuring nine women representing the nine electoral districts of the
borough. They paraded 'the traditional wear' of nine ethnic groups in
Trinidad: 'Syrian Lebanese'; 'African'; 'Arawak-Maltese'; 'Chinese';
'Carib'; 'French'; 'Spanish'; 'Caucasian'; and 'East Indian'.

8   I mean 'minority' in the political, not demographic sense. An interesting
example of the ambivalence toward the label *'dougla'* is evident in the
following statement. In June 1991 I had the following conversation with
a (male) bank teller:

> Teller: My father is a Indian, Hindu, and my mother is Negro.
> I call myself Indian.
> AK: You can be a 'mix' and an Indian at the same time?
> Teller: Yes. You see, it is the [sur]name that tells you exactly
> the nationality you come from. The seed is from the father, what
> *he* is.
> AK: But isn't a Negro and Indian mix a *dougla*?
> Teller: Well, I don't receive it, I don't accept *dougla*.
> AK: Why not?
> Teller: It's a kind of negative, like. I am a *Indian*. It is the seed,
> you see.

9   On the other hand, some categories that include 'mixed' persons have other
factors that take precedence in their social evaluation, such as considerations of class. For example, the category 'French Creole' contains both
'whites' and those seen as the historical result of combined African and
European colonial, particularly French, relations (at times classified as
'Trinidad white'). It is associated in contemporary usage with the nation's
economic power brokers, the capitalist class of elites whose own interests
are seen by others as not always corresponding with those of the rest, the
nation. As such, 'French Creoles' are admired as enviable for their privilege
and success, yet they are also often identified by working and middle-class
Trinidadians of various ethnic identities as unjustly having more than a
fair share of society's resources and rewards.

10   Such as, for example, the convents and schools organised by Spanish
religious orders, particularly the Capuchins (Lipski, 1990).

11   As recently as 1988, a national newspaper (*Trinidad Guardian*, 14 August
1988, p. 7) had the following to say about the complex construction of
'Carib' ethnicity in Trinidad:

> ... the [post-eighteenth century] ethnic and cultural fusion
> among Spaniards, Africans and Carib descendants was the basis
> for the initiation of a slow and steady disappearance act among
> Trinidad's 'aborigines'. In the emerging gens d'Arime [people
> of Arima] of those days, the genetic endowments and cultural
> retentions by a people with a distinctive personality, are said to
> be unmistakably evident among present day Arimians ... [Arima
> is] still distinguished as the living quarters of an ethnically distinct
> group, shy and reticent, yet no [*sic*] fully a part of Arima's mileu
> [*sic*], in spite of apparently strong Hispanic characteristics ...
> With hardly more than 300 descendants of the past two centuries,

the Carib heritage fails to attract the focus and interest of its young 'liberated tribesmen and women'. The integration with the Arima population appears almost complete ... [a] self-styled leader and 'President', is himself a living example of the total emasculation that insidiously undermines his efforts 'to survive as recognised ethnic entity', stubbornly refusing to be labelled [*sic*] and treated as 'a relic of the past'. [He] remains committed to the utmost, to revive Carib traditions still known, and to rejuvenate the glorious cultural trappings that distinguished the early Amerindian inhabitants.

12 Thanks to Sabiyha Prince for reminding me about this debate as a possibly contributing factor.

13 See Wright (1990). Wood (1968:34) provides a partial illustration of the heterogeneity of *peon* heritage: 'From the Spaniards they had inherited their language and their religion; from the Amerindians they had derived the art of weaving baskets and cassava-strainers ... and slept in bark hammocks like the Indians of the Orinoco'.

14 That is, history serves as a *symbol* as well as the *means* of the emergence of 'Spanish' as 'mixed'.

15 *Parang* (from *parranda* [Lipski, 1990]) was brought to Trinidad by Venezuelan immigrants, but has absorbed influences from Trinidad's other musical styles, such as calypso and forms of Indo-Trinidadian popular music (see Khan, n.d.).

16 And, indeed, to some Indo-Trinidadians as well.

17 Interestingly, 'Spanish' enables being 'authentic' without needing to be 'pure'.

18 Stephen Stuempfle (personal communication, 1991) points out that many Trinidadians perceive calypso as having deep roots in Trinidadian society, and is thus also an 'authentic' national symbol. However, the time depth is still more recent than that of the Carib/Spanish presence.

19 Bridget Brereton (personal communication, 1991) points out that families deemed to be of 'pure' Spanish descent are classified as 'French Creole' and are not included in the 'mixed' 'Spanish' referred to here.

References

Alexander, J., 1977, 'The Culture of Race in Middle-Class Kingston, Jamaica', *American Ethnologist*, Vol. 4, No. 3, pp. 413-35.

Ardener, E., 1982, 'Social Anthropology, Language and Reality', in Parkin, D. (ed.), *Semantic Anthropology*, London: Academic Press.

Barth, F. (ed.), 1969, *Ethnic Groups and Boundaries*, London: Allen and Unwin.

Braithwaite, L., 1975 [1953], *Social Stratification in Trinidad*, Mona: Institute of Social and Economic Research, University of the West Indies.

Brereton, B., 1979, *Race Relations in Colonial Trinidad 1870-1900*, Cambridge: Cambridge University Press.

– 1981, *A History of Modern Trinidad 1783-1962*, London: Heinemann.

Cancian, F., 1976, 'Social Stratification', *Annual Review of Anthropology*, Vol. 5, pp. 227-48.

Chapman, M., McDonald, M., and Tonkin, E., 1989, 'Introduction', in Chapman, M. *et al.* (eds), *History and Ethnicity*, ASA Vol. 27, London: Routledge.

Fox, R., 1990, 'Introduction', in Fox, R. (ed.), *Nationalist Ideologies and the Production of National Cultures*, Washington, D.C.: American Anthropological Association.

Hintzen, P., 1989, *The Costs of Regime Survival: Racial Mobilization, Elite Domination and Control of the State in Guyana and Trinidad*, Cambridge: Cambridge University Press.

Hodge, M., 1970, *Crick Crack, Monkey*, London: Andre Deutsch.

– 1975, 'The Peoples of Trinidad and Tobago', in Anthony, M. and Carr, A. (eds), *David Frost Introduces Trinidad and Tobago*, London: Andre Deutsch.

Khan, A., n.d., 'Survey of Indo-Trinidadian Musical Forms', report for Smithsonian Institution Folklife Programs, Smithsonian Archives, Washington, D.C.

Laurence, K.M., 1980, 'The Survival of the Spanish Language in Trinidad', *Nieuwe West-Indische Gids*, Vol. 54, pp. 213-28.

Lieber, M., 1981, *Street Scenes: Afro-American Culture in Urban Trinidad*, Cambridge, MA: Schenkman.

Lipski, J., 1990, 'Trinidad Spanish: Implications for Afro-Hispanic Language', *Nieuwe West-Indische Gids*, Vol. 64, Nos. 1 and 2, pp. 7-47.

Martinez-Alier, V., 1974, *Marriage, Class and Colour in Nineteenth Century Cuba*, Cambridge: Cambridge University Press.

Mintz, S., 1957, 'Review of *A Framework for Caribbean Studies* by M.G. Smith', *Boletin Bibliografico de Antropologia Americana*, Vol. 8, No. 1, pp. 189-94.

– 1971, 'Groups, Group Boundaries, and the Perception of "Race"', *Comparative Studies in Society and History*, Vol. 13, No. 4, pp. 437-50.

Moodie, S., 1973, 'The Spanish Language as Spoken in Trinidad', *Caribbean Studies*, Vol. 13, No. 1, pp. 88-94.

Morner, M., 1967, *Race Mixture in the History of Latin America*, Boston: Little, Brown.

Naipaul, V.S., 1985 [1967], *The Mimic Men*, New York: Vintage.

Newson, L., 1976, *Aboriginal and Spanish Colonial Trinidad*, London: Academic Press.

Ottley, C.R., 1955, *An Account of Life in Spanish Trinidad*, Port of Spain: College Press.

Patterson, O., 1975, 'Context and Choice in Ethnic Allegiance: A Theoretical Framework and Caribbean Case Study', in Glazer, N. and Moynihan, D.P. (eds), *Ethnicity: Theory and Experience*, Cambridge, MA: Harvard University Press, pp. 305-49.

Phillips, D., 1990, 'Race and the Role it Plays in National Life', *Caribbean Affairs*, Vol. 3, No. 1, pp. 186-98.

Ryan, S., 1972, *Race and Nationalism in Trinidad and Tobago*, Toronto: University of Toronto Press.

Stoler, A., 1989, 'Making Empire Respectable: The Politics of Race and Sexual Morality in Twentieth Century Colonial Cultures', *American Ethnologist*, Vol. 16, No. 4, pp. 634-60.

Stuempfle, S., 1990, 'The Steelband Movement in Trinidad and Tobago: Music, Politics and National Identity In a New World Society', unpublished Ph.D. dissertation, University of Pennsylvania.

Stutzman, R., 1981, 'El Mestizaje: An All-Inclusive Ideology of Exclusion', in Whitten, N.H. Jr. (ed.), *Cultural Transformations and Ethnicity in Modern Ecuador*, New York: Harper and Row, pp. 45-93.

Webber, A.R.F., 1988 [1917], *Those That Be In Bondage*, MA: Calaloux Publications.

Williams, B., 1989, 'A Class Act: Anthropology and the Race to Nation Across Ethnic Terrain', *Annual Review of Anthropology*, Vol. 18, pp. 401-44.

– 1990, 'Nationalism, Traditionalism, and the Problem of Cultural Inauthenticity', in Fox, R. (ed.), *Nationalist Ideologies and the Production of National Cultures*, Washington, D.C.: American Anthropological Association, pp. 112-30.

Wood, D., 1968, *Trinidad in Transition: The Years After Slavery*, London: Oxford University Press.

Wright, W., 1990, *Cafe Con Leche: Race, Class, and National Image in Venezuela*, Austin: University of Texas Press.

CHAPTER 9

Stuctures of experience: Gender, ethnicity and class in the lives of two East Indian women

Patricia Mohammed

Introduction

There comes a time in the work of a sociologist when one begins to lose sight of the fact that sociology is about people; that all of the classes, genders and ethnic groups are comprised of people who are engaging with the world and its problems and living their ordinary lives. And while all of these structures – class, ethnicity, gender – may influence a person in this or that direction to make this or that decision, the simple fact that must not be forgotten is that the process of living is also one of gaining experience and, hopefully, learning from that experience.

Debates on ethnicity and class have long preoccupied scholars of the region. Lately gender has also been acknowledged as an important concept which can help us to analyse and understand our societies. Gender is added on as another sociological concept, another prism through which we can view the historical process of growth and change. The challenge which gender analysis puts to mainstream academia is to examine how 'gender' works in human social relationships. Analyses of class and ethnicity have attempted a similar exercise, usually focusing on the aggregate societal level. Class, gender and ethnicity are themselves intricately related. Seen through the lens of gender analysis, concepts like ethnicity and class also undergo change in perception and analysis. Gender is not just another 'additive' concept: 'Like race, it is a conceptual understanding of a social reality which transforms our very perception of class' (Reddock, 1988:3).

Statements such as these are no doubt revealing about the conceptual relationship which exists between the constructs ethnicity, class and gender. One is still left, however, wanting to understand how the dynamics of ethnicity, class and gender operate in the real life experiences of men and women. A point made by Sheila Rowbotham comes to mind: 'It is worth remembering every time we use words like "class" and "gender" that they are only being labelled as structures for our convenience, because human relationships move with such complexity and speed that our descriptions freeze them at the point of understanding' (Rowbotham, 1981:365). As sociologists, when we use these external constructs to analyse human lives, we sometimes ignore the existential dilemma which all human beings face: while they may be born into a certain set of social arrangements not of their choice, their lives can be viewed in terms of how they use these arrangements to get the best out of them; to fight against them or be defeated by them; how they may use parts and reject others. For instance, within the constraints of ascribed norms which they must observe, some men and women choose, or circumstances may force them, to redefine the culturally accepted notions of their gender, class or ethnicity, but, presumably at all times attempting to satisfy their basic physical and psychological needs. In other words, what do they make of their 'experience'?

'Experience' is itself an ambiguous term. On the one hand it denotes 'passing through any event or course of events by which one is affected' and on the other, common sense usage suggests also learning from such events or course of events and subsequently altering or modifying behaviour. Writing on *The Poverty of Theory*, E.P. Thompson makes an important observation. 'Experience', he says, 'is a necessary middle term between social being and social consciousness'. But at the same time 'for any living generation, in any "now," the ways in which they "handle" experience defies prediction and escapes from any narrow definition of determination' (Thompson, 1978:363). People experience 'experience' both as a feeling and also as ideas in a collective consciousness, be it of class, ethnicity or gender. Class consciousness may be described as the way in which experience is handled in cultural terms, through traditions, values, ideas and institutional practices. There are two additional factors, however, which are equally important in understanding 'experience'. First is the notion of history – the moment in which an incident occurs. What are the economic, political and social considerations which will predispose consciousness and action? The second is the age of the individual when it occurs. At what point are they in their life cycle, what previous experiences do they draw on, and what are their options as a result of both age and experience? Ethnicity and gender are determined by birth, class by circumstances at birth, but how these are shaped in subsequent years is perhaps a complex mix of experience and collective consciousness, the latter being itself modified by experience and so on.

In trying to understand the gender, ethnicity and class dialectic from this perspective the questions we might begin to ask of an individual for instance are: How does the fact of being born female to a poor working class African or East Indian family influence a woman's life? How does this affect the decisions she makes about marriage and family? What factors influence the jobs she takes? What is her relation to other ethnic groups in the society at different points in her life? The subjects of this chapter are East Indian women simply because, as a starting point, I can draw on my own experience of being East Indian and female. I propose to look at the life experiences of two Indian women of Trinidad as gleaned from taped interviews with them. The choice of subjects is deliberate. The first interview was carried out with Mrs Droapatie Naipaul, mother of the authors V.S. and Shiva Naipaul, primarily because of my interest in the works of V.S. Naipaul and also because she is by birth a member of one of the oldest and most prestigious Indian families in Trinidad. My second interview was with Mrs Dassie Parsan, whose life story, class and caste position contrasted sufficiently with Mrs Naipaul's, thus allowing further insights. The two women are now deceased. Mrs Parsan died in May 1990 and Mrs Naipaul in December 1990. This chapter is written in the present tense in order to emphasise the relevance of their lives in contemporary times, and the continuing salience of gender, ethnicity and class in Trinidadian society.

Mrs Droapatie Naipaul

Mrs Droapatie Naipaul lives in the small two-storeyed house in St James, a suburb of Port of Spain. Her house is white both inside and out. The drawing room is spotless and all around the room clean white lace curtains hang from the top of the windows to the floor. An oil painting of her late husband dominates the room; on her dining table a covered *Bhagavad Gita* rests on a carved sandalwood book stand; polished miniature brass Indian vessels and ornaments, intricately filigreed, rub shoulders with red cushioned Morris chairs and a vase of red plastic poinsettias; they give the room its peculiarly Trinidadian aesthetic of a blended culture. At first glance, Mrs Naipaul's house epitomises the Trinidadian idea of the traditional old East Indian woman. She is dressed simply in a white cotton dress, with three little bows down the bosom, the hemline of the skirt reaching almost to her ankle; her almost white hair is pulled into a small bun at the back of her head. Her manner, however, belies this traditional appearance of simplicity and passivity; at age 75 she lives alone and carries out her daily chores briskly and independently. Her answers are always alert, sometimes aggressively so; she is a confident and self-assured woman.

In 1926, when Droapatie was 13 years old, her father Pundit Capildeo made his second visit to India. He died during this visit leaving Droapatie fatherless and Mrs Capildeo with the responsibility of looking after the rest of her family. She was lucky though. Pundit Capildeo, besides being a well respected Hindu priest, was also a businessman and the family possessed some land and a commercial enterprise in Chaguanas, the small town located in central Trinidad where they lived. There was no need for any of the family to work in the fields, the regular occupation of most Indian men and women at the time.

Pundit Capildeo was one of the more than 144,000 Indians who were brought to Trinidad from India between 1845 and 1917 under the system of indentured labour. He had come, like the others, for five years, bound to the sugar cane estates during this time. Like many, he did not return to live in India, choosing to remain instead and marry a young Trinidad-born East Indian girl. He had been an educated man in India and of Brahmin stock – belonging to the highest and most revered caste, class and occupation in India. The Brahmins were the priestly caste and their lives were regulated by a collection of rules and restrictions. They were either the priests or intelligentsia in the Hindu community, their food had to be prepared by Hindus of a particular caste. As with all Hindus they were obligated to marry into their caste.

Droapatie's childhood days, spent with nine sisters and three brothers, were ruled by expectations of her caste and gender. She recalled:

> We were under strict Hindu parentage and we were not allowed to go anywhere. Anywhere you want to go, you have to go with an elder person or sister or if your mother is taking you and you only go to family if you going.
>
> Even when you go to school she is counting the minutes when school is over and you should be home, and you better be home on time. Sometimes you find yourself running home.

Until she was 12 years old Droapatie could mix with the other children at school. She was sent to the Canadian Mission school in Chaguanas which was established since the late-nineteenth century by the Presbyterian missionaries and catered primarily for the Indian population. Without this provision the majority of Indian parents would have been reluctant to send their children to the government or Catholic primary schools for fear of them mixing with non-Indians. The other children in the school were all Indians – either Muslims or Hindus and they would mix indiscriminately. But this was always restricted to school time alone: when school 'broke off' each went their separate ways.

It was unusual during those years for East Indian parents to agree to educate their daughters, even at primary level. Perhaps it was because Mrs Capildeo was Trinidad- and not India-born that she insisted her girl children as well as her boy children be given at least the benefit of a primary school education.

> PM: Why did they allow you to go to school?
> DN: My mother tell my father we must go to school. He said no school, but she wanted all of us to go to school. She went to school as well, though. All of my sisters and brothers went to school. You see we had the store and my mother wanted us all to work in the family business 'till we get married. You had to learn to sign your name at least and to count. But you had to stop school at age 11 or 12 years. Then the girls have to get married and the boys went to college.
> PM: Why did your mother decide to send only the boys to college?
> DN: Don't ask me that question. Don't ask me that question again. She decided to educate them and I think she was very correct in educating them.

She agreed with the correctness of this view just as she accepted that the next stage in her life would be a marriage arranged by her elders.

> PM: What did you feel about entering an arranged marriage?
> DN: It's a routine you have to follow. You don't see nobody before you get married. And after you leave school everybody know in a year or so you have to be married – it was just that routine.
> PM: Why did you feel in a year's time you had to get married?
> DN: Don't ask me that question again.

I realised by now that it wasn't that she was offended by my questions as much as astounded at the idea that one could challenge these traditions. She added:

> I didn't have to feel anything. As I said you have to do that you are told. That was their opinion, this is what we have to do and we were children in the age when you could not ask questions, but just obey and listen. You felt that was the

routine of life, because all the sisters elder than me were married at the same age or younger even.

By 1928, at age 15, Droapatie's marriage to Seepersad Naipaul was arranged. Seepersad also came from central Trinidad from a poor Brahmin family. He was a sign painter by occupation but being a Brahmin by birth he was qualified to be the spouse of a young Brahmin girl even though she came from a prestigious and wealthy family. Pundit Capildeo had always provided well for his family. In fact they were one of the more privileged and respected Indian families in Trinidad. The large and imposing house in which they lived in Chaguanas was known far and wide as the 'Lion House', nicknamed after the stone statues of lions which guard the two sharp front corners of the building. One of her brothers Rudranath, went on to college, and having won an open island scholarship, on to university in London, becoming an internationally known mathematician. He was also to become the leader of the Democratic Labour Party in Trinidad, a primarily East Indian party which opposed the People's National Movement (PNM) for many years.

Droapatie recognised that the circumstances of her life were different to that of many other East Indian women around her:

We never really had to work in the fields, we had a lot of lands. My father find he could maintain us because we had no right to work in the fields. Anybody who had enough to maintain their wife and children didn't let them go to work.

Seepersad had married a young girl who had clear notions of her role as a wife, and the importance of her high class and caste status in Indian society in Trinidad. Unlike her sisters though, she did not move into her in-laws home after marriage. Instead the young couple migrated to Tunapuna where Seepersad was a sign painter with the bus company.

PM: So you had to rent an apartment in Tunapuna after you got married?
DN: *He* had to rent all of these things darling, not me. *He* had to rent it, *he* had to furnish it, I only have to move in. I make my life very comfortable.

They continued to live in Tunapuna for several years. The town itself grew up around the Pasea Estate which was not far from the Tacarigua and Golden Grove Estates. Its population was a mixed one comprising some whites and French Creoles, Indians and Africans. During the years of World War II they moved to Luis Street in

Woodbrook, to a house owned by the Capildeo family. Seepersad Naipaul had by this time changed his profession as well, and Mrs Naipaul had given birth to six of her seven children. She had decided that all of her children must receive a sound education and the older ones had to attend college in Port of Spain.

Woodbrook was one of the several districts within the wider Port of Spain area and attracted a different kind of inhabitant. Shiva Naipaul, her youngest son, recollects the district to which the family had now moved:

> Woodbrook with its quiet streets, its sprinkling of tiny squares, its neat wooden houses fronted by verandas with fretted eaves from which were suspended orchids and ferns in wire baskets, was definitely more respectable, more desirably 'residential' in every respect than was St James. Lighter-skinned folk, families of clerkly status, schoolteachers, they all showed a marked preference for Woodbrook. Not surprisingly it was also a favourite haunt of Presbyterians. There must have been more pianos per square acre in Woodbrook than in any other district of Port of Spain .... It had, predictably enough, many fewer steelbands; while the Hispanic bias of its street names – Luis, Carlos, Alberto, Cornelio, Rosalino – further emphasised its pretensions (S. Naipaul, 1985:29).

Moving to Woodbrook, therefore, the family lived surrounded by upwardly mobile neighbours from all ethnic groups – Africans, Chinese, Portuguese, Syrian and East Indians.

All these changes – from childhood to womanhood, from semi-rural Chaguanas in Central Trinidad to semi-urban Tunapuna in the east and urban Port of Spain in the north – must have begun to change her awareness of the society around her and theirs toward her. East Indians had entered Trinidad society on peculiarly disadvantageous terms, as indentured labourers replacing slaves, and a mutual antagonism had developed between them and the rest of the society. Bridget Brereton writes that:

> The essential reality was that the Indians came to a society that was hostile to them, a society whose attitudes ranged from fear to contempt to indifference. They reacted defensively. Geographical, residential and occupational separation was reinforced by the Indians' protective use of caste, religion, village community and traditional family organisation to cushion them from contacts with a hostile society. This would

be the pattern of race relations long after the system of indentured immigration was ended in 1917 (Brereton, 1981:115).

East Indians were seen as occupying the lowest status jobs, and had been stereotyped as overly thrifty if not miserly, a condition borne out of their need during indentureship to save their meagre wages and sacrifice present comforts for future security. This way of life contrasted greatly with the lower-class Creole population of the day who were reputed to be profligate whenever they had money. Many Indians continued to dress and eat differently so that much of this stereotyping persisted. Some movement out of the failing estate agriculture, the development of a small elite of Indians through the influence of the Presbyterian church and the general movement of Indians into occupations such as teaching, had begun to create changes in the relations between East Indians and the other major ethnic group, the Africans.

'Did you get along well with your neighbours?', I asked. I was searching for something of this change.

'I had nothing to do with anybody I don't know', she replied. 'Because my home, my life was very filled with work – I had to take care of my children and my house and that was a lot of work to do. I got a little help to do the washing and ironing but I alone have to do my cooking ... they can't cook for me, their food is tasteless'.

I persisted again. 'Do you remember who were your neighbours in Woodbrook though? What were they like?' By this time I was not surprised at the characteristic response:

> Don't ask me anything about other people, ask me nothing about other people. I cannot answer anything about other people. The things that they would do – the gossip in the street – I can't do those things. I never could, and furthermore my husband can't come home and see me gossiping on the street neither. He will find 'what happen' if anybody come they must come and sit down inside and talk.
>
> PM: Did you find any change in your lifestyle because of moving?
> DN: No, no. I never changed my lifestyle. I didn't change it at all because I copy nobody, because I believe that what I am doing is the best. I copy nobody lifestyle because I find that their lifestyle *cyar* [can't] be as good as mine. They could never be a good example.

By the late 1930s, Seepersad was no longer a sign painter. He had changed jobs and had entered one which was very unusual for a male Indian of his time – journalism.

PM: How did your husband's new job affect you?
DN: It did not bother me at all. I had nothing to do with his work. He was writing for the Trinidad Publishing Company. I am a housewife. I am doing my duty as a wife and as a mother and that is where I draw my line.

There was nothing to suggest that she valued the role she had undertaken in life in her duties as wife and mother as in any way inferior to that of her husband's. There was a clear and unequivocal acceptance of this role. Was there something in the socialisation of Indian girls which prepared them for this role? Mrs Naipaul said:

Well, they always tell you you have to be obedient and do your duty, and not too much as the people say 'backchat'. If you feel sometimes something offend you, you go in your room or something and you sit down and cry and give vent to your feelings and then you come out.

You see a woman has a place in this world and when she abuse that place, she has lost the thing they call woman-hood because she is no more that woman. She is something else because a woman should always think very great of herself, she must always feel that I am a woman and must live to the name I have. I must do everything which uplifts womanhood and not degrade it ... decide I would never fail in my duty. That is something very important and not every woman has that in them. I could afford to tell you – if they have it they wouldn't be as slack. I talking about Indian people, forget about the others. My sisters all felt the same way about their duty as wife and mother. It was an honour to me – everyday practice meant that I have a duty to do everyday and I must fulfil my duty everyday and that was a very important duty which people fail to do now.

The next and last move Mrs Naipaul was to make with her husband was from Woodbrook to St James where they had bought the small two-storeyed white house. She has lived here for the past 42 years. They moved to this house in 1946 and her husband Seepersad died in 1953. Two of their children had already gone to university abroad – her eldest daughter, Kamla, had gone to India on a scholarship, and her second child, a son Vidiadhar, had gone to Oxford having won an open island scholarship as well – a most prestigious acclaim in the country. Although most of them were grown, there were still two children at home to educate at college first and then at university.

By the time of her father's death, Kamla had completed her scholarship abroad and returned to Trinidad. She found a job easily and helped Mrs Naipaul support the rest of the family at home. Droapatie looked after the last two until they were also independent of her. In 1962 she defied the previous pattern of her entire life so far – as daughter, wife and mother. Her brother offered her a job of managing his quarry for him – a quarry which employed 49 people. Mrs Naipaul had never worked outside her home before she was married nor during the 26 years of her marriage.

'I said I would try', she explained. 'I hadn't managed a quarry before. Not even thinking of quarry. Quarry is an unusual thing for you to think of going to.'

She managed the quarry, however, for 22 years and kept the books successfully. The years of bringing up seven children on a limited budget had proved a useful experience. She retired in 1985.

She lives now as she had lived with her husband and children, never bending her will to anyone. She never remarried. Her first thoughts were for her children, especially her girls. While it was still not possible for a Hindu widow to undergo a second religious marriage, the accepted practice was that widows could co-habit with another male partner. Often, women with children chose to live a life of celibacy, however, rather than introduce a new male into the household for fear that her children would be mistreated or abused.

Mrs Naipaul is still a devout and practising Hindu, does not eat food cooked by anyone other than herself, and goes to the *mandir* (Hindu temple) every Sunday. In some ways she has changed very little from the confident young woman who got married over 60 years ago. In others, though, she has had to change:

> How could you change – I am so old fashioned that I can't change – it don't mean that I can't mix. But you see, if you don't have confidence in your life, when everybody is married and gone, your husband is dead, tell me who you want to lean on. Not me – I want to lean on nobody.

Mrs Dassie Parsan

Mrs Parsan is generous in the way of older Indian women, plying you with food and drink at every visit. Her house is always clean and well 'put away'. She views this business of housekeeping very seriously. It shows in the clean white lace tablecloth always draped over the dining table, in the ornaments placed carefully on crocheted doilies on side tables, in her healthy collection of plants which brighten up the front and back porch of the comfortable three-bedroom house. She is a short and slightly plump woman with a full head of wavy black hair. She is easy to talk to and willing to disclose her life story. Some memories are not easy to relive though and an anxious expression often lines her unwrinkled brown and pleasant face.

Ruth Dassie Singh was born in El Socorro on 16 May 1930. Both her parents were Trinidad-born. Her grandparents on her mother's side were also born in Trinidad. They were from 'Cane Field' on the Tacarigua estate and were estate workers. Her mother Sumintra, worked briefly on the estate before she married Mahadeo Singh from El Socorro. His parents were India-born and were also agricultural workers all their lives.

Tacarigua lies to the east of El Socorro along the Eastern Main Road – a road which links Trinidad's main city – Port of Spain – to a string of small towns all of which grew up around market centres, agricultural estates or railway stations at the foot of the Northern Range which itself spans the northern breadth of the island. El Socorro is an interesting town because it is both an active commercial centre and a very colourful and at times violent working class urban district comprised of both East Indians and Africans. It adjoins some extremely fertile agricultural land which belongs to the Arranguez Estate, once a thriving estate as well.

Before the years of World War II, El Socorro was a swampy land mass with plenty of coconut trees. In 1941, when Dassie was around ten years old, the Americans began constructing the Churchill-Roosevelt Highway through El Socorro, thus extending the available land for housing, agriculture and commercial development. Estate lands from the Arranguez Estate and land from the El Socorro area were parcelled out to farmers who specialised in small crops such as cabbages, cauliflower, sweet peppers, tomatoes and so on. It was rich agricultural land and attracted a large number of East Indian farmers who settled and worked the land. The town of San Juan which abuts on to El Socorro and Arranguez was one of the railway stops for the train which linked the towns along the eastern strip. El Socorro and the surrounding areas were therefore densely populated and with a very mixed population. Apart from the large proportion of East Indian farmers and their families, there was also a significant working class population of African descent, many of whom worked in Port of Spain. Mahadeo Singh, Dassie's father was one of the farmers who worked on leased estate land from the Arranguez Estate. He built a small two-bedroomed house for his family in El Socorro.

He was not a very healthy man and suffered from 'wheezing' (chest ailments) as far back as she could remember. Her mother Sumintra at first sold the vegetables he grew in the market at San Juan but when he became too ill to work full-time in the garden, she took over, and with the help of her older children looked after her family, worked in the garden and still sold produce in the market. When he died, aged 45, she continued doing this until she herself died at the age of 55, leaving only three of her nine children unmarried. According to the hierarchy of the Hindu caste system, Mahadeo Singh was displaced in his occupation for although he was a gardener he also belonged to the second highest caste – the Chatriyas or the warrior caste – as his last name Singh denoted. Being a sickly man, however, he was dependent on his wife and children.

Despite his illness and dependence on them, Mahadeo Singh seemed to have exerted a remarkable amount of control over his family. Dassie recalled this with a great deal of sadness:

> When my mother had four children, my mother and my father they couldn't get along well. So then my mother break up with my father and we went up to Tacarigua to live. I went to school in Tacarigua.

> PM: Why couldn't she get along with him?
> DP: You see the sickness had him so irritable that sometimes he used to be cruel. He used to beat her sometimes. She come out from a very nice home, I would say, my grandparents they were very nice people and when she get married she didn't know about working hard and so on.
> PM: You said that she couldn't get along with your father, this is the same father that died at 45? She had four more children with him though, so this means that she returned to him?
> DP: Yes, they made back up and she came home.
> PM: When they made back up you find the relationship was better?
> DP: No, it wasn't better, it wasn't better at all. What she used to say is that seeing that she had all these children she have to try and make it because she wouldn't like to leave the children and go. And she try and make it with him. Although he was sick he used to still beat her.
> PM: What did you all do about that?
> DP: We couldn't do anything at the time because we were still small and at home – so we had to abide and stay with her and feel sorry for her and try to help her out in whatever way

we could. I find that he was a little too cruel knowing that she had to work so hard.

Her childhood freedom was also very restricted

We used to play with the children around, but my father were a very strict man. He never allow us to go to the neighbour's home. We have to stay in the house all the time and then we used to thief little chance when they not at home and go and play with the neighbour children.

PM: He was strict with the boys too?
DP: Yes, with the boys and girls also. And when six o'clock you can't go nowhere at all.
PM: You used to go out at all, what kind of things you used to go to if you were going out?
DP: Well only theatre, to Ritz Cinema in San Juan. Theatre once in a while, not all the time.
PM: The boys go more often?
DP: Yes, the boys go more often than the girls.
PM: What you used to go and see?
DP: Well, we never used to go and see English pictures. Once in a while we used to go and see an Indian picture because as I tell you my father were a very strict man and he never want us to go. When anyone of the elder heads going well then so we used to get to go with them.
PM: But you never used to go into town at all?
DP: No, I only know between San Juan, Tunapuna and Tacarigua. I only know that when you take a bus in San Juan it used to stop in Tacarigua – we used to take a bus or the train.
PM: But Port of Spain was not very far – you didn't know Port of Spain as well?
DP: No, even though we were so close I didn't know Port of Spain – only when I get married that I started going. Is only the older heads like when they wanted to bank money or pawn their jewels if anything crop up and they have to pawn their jewels they have to go to Port of Spain – we had no bank in San Juan here.

Her father's illness and consequently their poverty created other problems for the family as well.

PM: Did you and your brothers and sisters go to school?
DP: We went to school but as I tell you poverty again – we couldn't make it to go to school for too long. We went to

San Juan Presbyterian school. The teacher who teach me, his
name was Ramkissoon.

PM: For how many years ...?

DP: Well, I wouldn't say years, eh, because sometimes when
you go to school you have to go to school like four times for
the month, five times for the month, and then you stay home,
you help out, and then next month you go four or five days
for the month again and it's like that. We grow up in the hard
way, we grow up knowing that my father was a sickly man.

Despite their relatively high caste status, Dassie's parents were
hardly devout Hindus. Perhaps this fact, coupled with the influences
of El Socorro with its semi-urban mixed population, allowed a certain
flexibility in her religious practice.

PM: Your parents were Hindus? Were they practising
Hindus?

Dassie laughed as she started recounting the religious practices of
her family:

I'll tell you, my parents were never practising Hindus. They
used to have *'howan'* prayers – and we will go and join with
them. That is the Arya Semajes – my father was a Singh but
he was an Arya Semajes also and every Wednesday the Arya
Semajes used to have a little prayers and sing *bhajans* and
so on and I used to go to that, my mother used to go
sometimes, my father – he was a different kind of man, he
never really go. And I remember too that when we were small
we used to go to the Catholic church, and we used to go to
the Presbyterian Sunday school.

The Arya Semaj movement was an alternative Hindu sect being
introduced into Trinidad by missionaries from India. It was a new
movement and brought in more progressive ideas. It was especially
critical of the ritualistic practices of orthodox Hinduism and its
unquestioning observance of a rigid caste system. Time and distance
from India had eroded the memory and need for the rituals traditionally
practised. It was understandable, perhaps, that some members of the
Hindu population would respond to new ideas emerging out of India.
Simultaneously, the Presbyterian church had directed its attention to
converting and saving the souls of the East Indians whom they tended
to view as pagans. But why did she go to the Catholic church as well?

Well, I used to go to the Catholic church because we had a
neighbour next door and they used to go to the church. They

had bought my grandparents property and since they come there to live I always used to be with them and whenever they go to church I used to go with them.

PM: So you were more Catholic?

'Yes', she replied, laughing once again. There was no contradiction, no embarrassment or reservation in her response, just amusement as if laughing at herself. 'Catholic, Presbyterian, Hindu – a mixture'.

I was curious none the less about who the neighbours next door were and why, in the face of her father's strict upbringing, she was able to go to church with them. It turned out that they were Negroes. 'How did you live with them?', I asked, trying to get from her a sense of relations in the mixed community.

DP: The Indians and the Negroes, they used to live like one family in those days. You see if they have anything they would give you, and if you have anything you would give them. If you cook you will give them what you have, and if they know you not eating certain things they will not give you.

Their next door neighbour whom she knew quite well was a woman of African descent whose husband had died. She was bringing up her children single-handedly while working in an hotel in Port of Spain.

El Socorro was also well known for its large and devout Muslim community. What did she know of them? Her picture was again an optimistic one:

The Muslim people always keep up to their religion. El Socorro had a lot of church. Every Friday the Muslim people would go to church. And they used to live very, very nice with even the Hindus. They used to have prayers and invite them.

Despite her generous attitude and openness towards her African-descended neighbours and the Muslims in the community, it was clear that when it came to marriage, both Dassie and her parents had very strong preferences. She was married at 18 in 1949, three years after she left school. During those years she had stayed at home and helped her parents in the garden, sometimes selling in the market with her mother, sometimes at home taking care of the house and the younger brothers and sisters.

She did not have an arranged marriage. 'Who decided you should get married?', I asked. She had chosen to discontinue school as she felt sorry for her mother and preferred to stay at home and help her. For most Indian women marriage was a crucially important event in their lives as this was what they were groomed for from childhood.

Dassie could recall the memories of her courtship and eventual marriage in great detail:

> I went to the garden one day with my eldest sister, she went to help pick some string beans and there is where I met my husband Gobin. He was talking to my big sister and I didn't say nothing because I don't know the person and he said to her 'What happen, your sister like she don't speak to people?' Well I turn 'round and say that I don't talk to people who I don't know. My father was not there at the time. He [Gobin] did know my parents, not my mother, I think, but he had known my father. Then he started to come home to visit my father and he told my mother that he liked me and he want to get married to me. I didn't approve of it. I didn't want to get married to him.

'Why is that?', I prodded gently. She began to think aloud, sounding almost as though she was reflecting and analysing that part of her life for the first time:

> I don't know. I just feel that he was from a higher bracket and I was from a lower bracket. I think that we were very poor, and they were living right near the theatre on the Eastern Main Road, and I always had the feeling that they on top and I kind'a didn't know whether if that relationship would work. I told my mother no I didn't want to get married to him but I say to myself if I had to get married I want to get married to somebody who would be on the same bracket with me. And then my mother say no he is a nice person, he is a nice boy, he come out from a nice home and so on and I should think about getting married and I told her no. Before he, somebody had asked for me and he were a farmer also and I think to myself that that was the right person for I to get married to because seeing that he is a farmer and my father was a farmer I think that we would get along better.

PM: When you say Mr Parsan was from a higher bracket – he wasn't also a farmer?
DP: He was a farmer also but what I mean, they own more land you know, they had this big house, I always had the feelings that they are very wealthy people, not knowing them so good, and a person like me to get married to him, I say to myself I don't think that it is right really, I should get married to somebody poor like myself. And my mother told me no, and she used to leave and go, and she know the time

when he would come, only for us to talk and so on. And still I would just step aside, I don't want to see him at all and eventually he start coming and start talking and then my mother she encouraged me and I get married to him.

PM: Why you felt so strongly about him being of a different bracket – that means you didn't have anything to do with caste?

DP: Good thing you bring up that, that had a lot to do with it too, because we was from a higher caste – Singh – and they were from a lower caste. And my father, I heard him say them is from a lower class and we was from a higher class and that he don't think that I should get married in that home. But my father didn't know that I hear he say so, you see – I think all that too ....

PM: So even though you weren't practising Hindus you still thought the caste was important?

DP: Yes, and when I get married to him, my parents and his parents never meet you know. When I wanted to get married to him my father say that he will go but Gobin, knowing that my father from a higher caste and they from a lower caste, never wanted my father to go and so they never meet. He never wanted my parents to go and meet his parents – he say no that he would marry me.

PM: That would have been wrong for your father to have to go and meet his father because he was from a higher caste?

DP: Yes, but my father still wanted to go knowing that his daughter was going to get married and go in that home, but Gobin never really wanted it - and that is why they never really go. They never met, but the day I went to buy my clothes my mother drop in there and she met my mother-in-law and they talk and so on and we get married.

They were engaged for nine months before they got married. During the courtship period, however, Gobin Parsan, Dassie's future husband, had to prove to her father that his intentions were perfectly honourable: 'He had to go and write my father a solicitor letter before he could'a enter and come there. The only time he could come there in that house is when my parents at home. He couldn't come any and any time'. She did not question this request or in fact any of the restrictions imposed on the courtship. I pursued the point though.

PM: Why he had to write a solicitor's letter to them?

DP: Because my father was a very strict man and my father told him he had to write a solicitor letter before he could enter in this house and come, a solicitor letter promising that he would marry me and promising that he wouldn't come while they were not at home.

I didn't think of asking her if he ever broke his promise and visited when they were not at home. I wondered, however, whether they had been out together during the nine months.

'Only once', she confided. 'We went to the cinema to see an Indian picture'.

PM: And did you go alone?
DP: No, we went with my cousin.

Dassie and Gobin were married first at her parents' home according to Arya Semaj rites. She likens it to the Muslim ceremony where 'you sign up and say a few words and it is over'. She underwent the entire ritual of the traditional Hindu marriage ceremony again when she went to her husband's home. Her parents were not invited to this ceremony. The new couple lived with her husband's parents for a while and she had her first two children over the next three years. These living arrangements did not work out well for the families. Too many people were living in the four-bedroom house on the Eastern Main Road, San Juan. When she had the children there was no place to put them. So they moved to Barataria in 1951.

Barataria is further west and nearer to Port of Spain and was now becoming populated and developed. It was close enough to San Juan though for Mr Parsan to rent lands from the Arranguez Estate, the land which he still cultivates with celery and other seasonings to this day. Barataria was populated predominantly by Indians in those days, most of them working on leased estate lands. Later, with the coming to power of the PNM, more people of African descent moved in as a result of jobs being given out by the new government. Being just outside of the Port of Spain district, it attracted those who wanted to work in the main city but could not afford the rents there or those who could find no place to live in the already overcrowded town. Barataria therefore developed as a curiously mixed semi-urban district, with East Indians and Africans, rural dwellers and urban folk, who among them held a wide range of occupations, from civil servants to bus conductors, sales clerks to gardeners. The latter were still mainly East Indian men who planted vegetables which their wives marketed in the nearby San Juan market. It was the Barataria described by Samuel Selvon in *A Brighter Sun* (1979 [1952]), where Joe Martin and Rita moved in next to Tiger and Urmilla, the former an African couple from 'town' the latter an East Indian couple from the 'country'.

'The men and women used to co-operate a lot?', I asked.

DP: Some of them yes, but some used to beat their wives
a lot.
PM: Why they used to beat their wives so much?
DP: Because they used to drink their lil' liquor; but I think
now it is frustration.
PM: Why frustration?
DP: Because in those days they working for 25 cents a day.
Money not circulating then as it is now you see and they
couldn't get work.

There was no questioning why this frustration had to be taken out
on the women who were themselves workers and also poor. Although
her own marriage had not been formally arranged, Dassie felt that such
marriages, which many of the East Indian men and women had at that
time, did work out well. Why did she feel so?

You see long ago, it wasn't like nowadays. Long ago, even
though you get married, no matter what you meet with your
husband you have to put up with it. Even though you go to
your parents' home, they will take you and bring you back.
And you have to stay, you have to remain. Whatever your
licks you have to stay.

Unlike many women in her neighbourhood who had to 'take licks',
Dassie was one of the more fortunate. Mr Parsan was a good father,
he provided well for her and their seven children, did not beat her, and,
unlike most men at the time, he helped her out with the housework
and children. She feels very fulfilled now about her family but knows
that she has given up a lot for them:

I sacrifice my whole life for my children. I never used to go
nowhere at all, at all, at all. I never give nobody no problem
with my children. Now that they get big I now start to go out.
When they was young, if I go, I taking them with me. All
the people from the district here, they used to dress and go
to carnival, see Hosea [Hosein, a Muslim celebration] and
so on but I used to stay at home.

The family is no longer a Hindu family. When did this happen?

DP: When the children were small I used to send them to
the Catholic church but then it was a problem to get them
to go there. Not even a problem to go there but I think the
Presbyterian church had some kind of thing and they invited

the children and myself and we went and we find that they all were Indians there and everybody talk well and we find it was a nice place where we could be with the children too, you know.

PM: So you prefer the Presbyterian church because more Indian people were there?

DP: Yes, just because everybody were there and they welcome we and everything, it was so different. The Catholic church it was nice too but then I go tell you in those days the Catholic people they used to pray in Latin and then I find with the Presbyterian church everything in English so you could'a understand. So I think through the children we really leave our religion you know – like leaving the Hindu to go over to the Presbyterian. Because then we say that the children can't be one way and we the other way.

PM: But they didn't have any kind of Hindu schools or churches nearby?

DP: Not in those days, no.

PM: Barataria was always very Presbyterian?

DP: No, no, I wouldn't say so. Barataria was more Hindu. But seeing that probably before I get married I used to go to church and so on and I had that in me. When I was having the children I used to read the Bible and all this kind'a thing so although we were Hindus and I think the children look like they take that from me.

She feels very fulfilled by the successes of her children now. One daughter has recently completed a doctorate in England and she is very proud of her achievement. One son has chosen to work with his father in the garden while the others have moved into professional or skilled jobs. Some of her children are married and she has several grandchildren as well.

From a childhood of poverty and an overly strict father she considers herself to be lucky in life. Her marriage continues to be a happy one despite her earliest misgivings.

PM: Did the caste difference make any problems in your life?

'I never bothered with it', she said. 'The marriage was going well, and we never had anything. He never brought it up, I am the one to make it a problem and I didn't find it was a problem so I never did.'

Mitigating circumstances

Mrs Naipaul is over two decades older than Mrs Parsan. Their lives have varied, not only as a result of the circumstances of their birth – one is Brahmin and born into a wealthy and prestigious family, the other has known great poverty and deprivation – but also because they were born and grew up in different parts of Trinidad and at different times. The similar features are that they are both of East Indian descent and female. In disentangling the relationship between class, gender and ethnicity in the lives of these two women we are presented with baffling contradictions.

Take their respective class positions. Commenting on the impact of the development of an East Indian community on class society in Trinidad from 1870 to 1900, Tikasingh writes:

> The development of that community had serious consequences for Trinidad society in that it made this society intractably divided and segmented. Hitherto, the society was stratified along the lines of race, colour, class and caste (between the upper class and the other classes) so that the society may be described briefly as a three-tiered system: the white upper class, the predominantly coloured middle class, and the predominantly black lower class ... an Indian community added a totally new dimension to the basic three-tiered social structure and may even be said to have established a structure outside the main structure (Tikasingh, 1973:46).

In 1953 Lloyd Braithwaite observed that immigrant groups, which included East Indians, Portuguese, Syrians and Chinese, remained largely outside the social system and were considered by the rest of the population to be on the lowest scale. Retaining their own culture and customs, he recognised that they constituted 'a social system within the social system, (Braithwaite, 1975 [1953]:47).

In fact, according to the *West Indian Census* (1951), by 1946 Chinese comprised 1.01 per cent of the total population; Portuguese, who were not separated from the wider group of mixed or coloured, made up 14.15 per cent; blacks comprised 46.86 per cent; whites 2.74 per cent; and East Indians 35.08 per cent – over one-third of the total population of 557,970. Relatively speaking, we are therefore talking about a very significant number of migrants who, under the conditions of their indentureship and later settlement, were able to recreate, both spatially and culturally, a social system within a social system. The fact is that they were largely set apart from the rest of Trinidad at this time: they intermarried, lived in separate villages or settlements, and reintroduced various aspects of their religion, popular culture, and their social structure. Thus East Indians in Trinidad could conceivably have also reproduced a stratification system within their own ethnic group, one which initially at least did not conflict with the wider class system, and which was based on criteria internal to this group.

What were these criteria? They were mainly to do with the system of caste hierarchy which operated among the Hindu section of this ethnic group. Of East Indians in 1946, Hindus constituted 64.5 per cent, Muslims 16.7 per cent, Presbyterians 10.3 per cent, and other Christians 8.5 per cent. Much has been written and speculated about the opportunities provided in the new society to change or altogether relinquish the notion of caste. Of the four major divisions which denoted caste hierarchy, the Brahmin caste was the highest, followed by the Chatriyas, the Vaishas and the Sudras. Clearly there were opportunities to tamper with caste positions, but what is not generally discussed is the way in which a new caste system of one sort or another was in fact reproduced, and how much this was still adhered to well into the twentieth century. Within this system, such features as 'untouchability' may have been jettisoned, but the idea of hierarchy remained deeply embedded among the Hindu population. Shifting one's religion or sect within Hinduism did not completely do away with the notion of caste. For example, a Chamar Presbyterian may have achieved higher status among the members of his or her church group, or his educational status may have increased his, or her, respectability among the wider village population. S/he remained, none the less, a Chamar – a 'low nation' as it was referred to disparagingly in the eyes of the Hindu community. One qualification here, though, is that Muslims tended to remain indifferent to the caste system since years of conversion to Islam in India itself had eroded its importance to them. In so far as class among Indians was concerned in the first half of the twentieth century, they had retained among themselves a viable notion of hierarchy and privilege due to the highest castes. This situation was clearly not a static one for it coexisted unevenly with the class system and values of the wider society which were still based on criteria of race, colour, wealth and education, and with each increasing decade the values and traditions of one would clash more and more with the more dominant Western and increasingly Afro-dominated culture.

A subconscious awareness of this coexisting class/caste system is conveyed in the life histories of both women. For instance, note Mrs Parsan's use of class and caste interchangeably when she says ' . . . because we was from a higher caste – Singh – and they were from a lower caste. And my father, I heard him say them is from a lower *class* and we was from a higher *class* and that he don't think I should get married in that home'. Her hesitancy in the first place to marry Mr Parsan was based not on caste, but on the higher economic standing which his family had over hers – which she also referred to as being of a higher class than hers. Similarly, in the case of Mrs Naipaul, we see another aspect of the class/caste consciousness among Indians. Mrs Naipaul's move to Woodbrook and later St James with its mixed population, her husband's occupation as a writer in the local press, the concerns to educate both her sons and daughters, are all circumstances which force on her an awareness of the values important to Trinidad society, some of which were different to those she had known in the wealthy and respected Brahmin family from which she came. What is remarkable, though, is the way in which she retains the distance of her Brahmin caste position, despite the twists and turns her own life has taken, while also confronting the demands posed by the wider society. We also see the nuances of class/caste relations among Hindus as well. Mrs Parsan, who has agreed to a marriage with a lower caste man, and whose father belonged to the sect of Hindus which reduced the importance of caste, appears to have greater flexibility than Mrs Naipaul, going so far as to change religion as well. In her life story we see more clearly the loopholes through which the values of the wider class society entered.

Let us now consider gender and ethnicity. We find that gender and ethnicity are closely interlocked structures, barely separable during the earlier part of both women's lives. A strictly demarcated gender role is rendered by both these women, the responsibility of a girl child to parents, the obligations to both parents and husband, the duties expected of a woman and wife, the role of mother. The imagery of gender – that is the expectations, roles, responsibilities and so on of men and women – is firmly rooted in the ethnic consciousness of the women of this group. It is a consciousness that both women share despite caste differences: 'My sisters all felt the same way about their duty as wife and mother. It was an honour to me . . .', as Mrs Naipaul says. Or, as Mrs Parsan says, 'Long ago, no matter what you meet with your husband you have to put up with it. Even though you go to your parents they will take you and bring you back.'

I would argue that in the case of East Indian women, gender was unmistakably defined by ethnicity. The scarcity of women in the earlier phase of indentureship led to their increased importance since it was not the habit for East Indian men to marry out of the group. They were a scarce resource at first and a necessary ally in reconstituting an East Indian community in Trinidad. Thus East Indian women were viewed as embodying the values of the group, primarily because of their role in procreation, but also because the bedrock of gender relations inherited from India appeared to be built on the primacy of the male role to that of the female in matters of religion, marriage and a sexual division of labour. To shift this would be to endanger the survival of the entire group. As can be seen in the life stories of both women, in an effort to retain the harmony of the group's concern, and alternatives being unthinkable at the time, women colluded equally with men in reinforcing a particular gender and ethnic identity as observed by this group. Thus one would find the stereotypes of East Indian women who were thought to be passive and subservient and East Indian men, thought to be patriarchal and dominant.

The life stories of both women show as well that, while there are expectations of both sexes, actions very often go against the grain of these expectations. Both women have very strict parents who guard their daughters zealously. 'Patriarchal' control is not only exerted by the father, clearly, but is rather a system of values entrenched in the East Indian family itself. Mrs Naipaul's father died when she was 13, yet her mother, and possibly brothers and elders, ensured the same control over her life – they determined the level of education she should receive and when and whom she should marry. Similarly, when her husband died and she was forced to provide for her family, she chose to work and support them rather than rely on the income of another man. Mrs Parsan's father did not provide for his family, yet his authority was unchallenged. She found herself in a very contradictory position. Conscious of her higher caste status and lower (economic) class situation, she was unsure about marrying Gobin whose family was from the lowest caste but who came from wealthier circumstances. She was also troubled by her father's disapproval of the match. Nevertheless, it was her mother who persuaded her and sanctioned her marriage to Gobin despite his lower caste status. Her mother's response was a pragmatic one. She had had to work hard and endure poverty because her husband could not provide for his family; she did not wish the same fate for her daughter. One could argue that Mrs Singh was also able to defy her husband's decision, not only because he was a weak provider, but also because the changes from India would have allowed her a greater flexibility in redefining gender roles in Trinidad.

The relationship between class and caste is itself interesting and integral to this chapter. High caste, like high class, predisposes certain patterns of behaviour and possibly preservation of an elite culture. Their caste differences by birth seemed to have lent themselves to a variation in class consciousness of Mrs Naipaul and Mrs Parsan. From their life stories and their personalities, one gets the impression that the two women emerged in their 50s with different perspectives and awareness of the same society. For instance, Mrs Naipaul is very rarely aware of people from other ethnic groups, even those who are her next door neighbours. Her concerns are primarily with her family. Mrs Parsan, on the other hand, is constantly aware of the relations between different ethnic groups, people of different religions, and of class differences which exist within the society. In Mrs Parsan's case, this awareness is articulated in many ways, as for instance her class/gender empathy of why men would beat their wives in the old days and not as much now: 'Because in those days they working for 25 cents a day. Money not circulating then as it is now you see and they couldn't get work'.

Throughout their lives both Mrs Naipaul and Mrs Parsan have retained 'the thing they call womanhood' as defined by their ethnic group. Perhaps the circumstances of their lives, supportive husbands, responsibilities for home and family, and so on, have guaranteed that their understanding of gender from early childhood did not undergo traumatic shifts, as for instance a situation in which an Indian woman enters a racially mixed relationship and is forced to contend with competing or at least differing cultures and values. This is also facilitated by the period of their childhood and early womanhood in which there is still a considerable distance between East Indians and other ethnic groups in the society. They may have lived side by side but there were few intermarriages and very little social mixing or knowledge of East Indian festivities or religions. In the triad of gender, ethnicity and class, class is the variable which would most likely influence changes in either gender or ethnicity. Only with the adoption of another set of values would East Indians begin to develop different ideas of ethnicity and consequently different notions of what constituted male and female roles in the society.

The growth of a peasant proprietary East Indian class, the benefits to be gleaned from adopting Christian and Western values, the importance of education from the early twentieth century, were among the significant factors which slowly but surely pervaded the East Indian community, factors which made them participants in the wider class society. But changes which these wrought were to be observed more so in the younger generations – note the trajectory of the lives of both families and the incremental break with tradition and custom which each new generation was able to make. Clearly one cannot generalise about the entire society on the basis of two life stories nor am I attempting to do so. What is perhaps more germane to an understanding of gender, ethnicity and class among East Indian women in Trinidad is the way in which second and third generations of women and men would be influenced by intruding class concerns and thus be forced to confront and shape new gender and ethnic identities. Their experiences from birth would lead to changes more readily than the experiences of their mothers and fathers who cling to the known and familiar, or whose options were limited. This chapter has merely pointed to some of these mitigating circumstances.

There is, however, a message in the tale of the two women's lives, that we need to take account of as sociologists and feminists engaged in the reinterpretation of women's and men's realities. Mrs Naipaul and Mrs Parsan have both forged a happiness out of a given set of social circumstances. They maintain that they have no regrets of unfulfilled ambitions for themselves but have found satisfaction in loving their husbands and families, the gender role assigned them within their ethnic group. They took pride in carrying out what they saw as their responsibility. They have not been passive actors in all of this, at times making a virtue of necessity, at others determining their own goals. Each woman is clearly still the product of her ethnicity and class and assigned gender role. But they show us in their life experiences that they defy our expectations of them as stereotypes of a specific ethnic group, class and gender; that none of these categories are static but in real life are constantly being negotiated and re-negotiated.

Acknowledgements

At the first writing of this chapter, which was a paper done for the Second Disciplinary Seminar in Women and Development Studies, University of the West Indies, held in Barbados, 1989, Mrs Naipaul and Mrs Parsan consented to the use of their names, having also read the interviews before its presentation. Parts of the paper have been altered for publication but the original text of the interviews retained. It is dedicated to the memory of both of these women.

The suggestion to carry out interviews with East Indian women and to explore the relations between class, race and gender through life histories came from Kim Nicholas Johnson. My gratitude to him as well for discussions and ideas during the writing of the paper.

References

Braithwaite, L., 1975 [1953], *Social Stratification in Trinidad*, Mona: Institute of Social and Economic Research, University of the West Indies.
Brereton, B., 1981, *A History of Modern Trinidad 1783-1962*, London: Heinemann.
Naipaul, S., 1985, *Beyond the Dragon's Mouth*, New York: Viking.

Reddock, R., 1988, 'Race, Class and Gender: Gender Issues and the Future of the Caribbean', St Augustine: Institute of Social and Economic Research, University of the West Indies, mimeo.

Rowbotham, S., 1981, 'The Trouble with Patriarchy', in Samuel, R. (ed.), *People's History and Socialist Theory*, London: Routledge and Kegan Paul.

Selvon, Samuel, 1979 [1952], *A Brighter Sun*, London: Longman.

Thompson, E. P., 1978, *The Poverty of Theory and Other Essays*, Harmondsworth: Penguin.

Tikasingh, G.I.M., 1973, 'The Establishment of the Indians in Trinidad, 1870-1900', unpublished Ph.D. thesis, University of the West Indies, St Augustine.

West Indian Census 1946, 1951, Kingston, Jamaica: Central Bureau of Statistics.

CHAPTER 10

An evaluation of the 'creolisation' of Trinidad East Indian adolescent masculinity

Niels M. Sampath

Introduction

This brief discussion of the way the potentially complex notions of 'creolisation', 'adolescence', and 'masculinity' combine to assist transformations of cultural identity, is derived from data collected during a total of 20 months of fieldwork carried out in a south Trinidad sugar cane, rice, and vegetable farming community I call Indian Wood.[1] Somewhat unusually, the village is inhabited almost entirely by Hindus of varying degrees of faith who are the descendants of indentured sugar estate workers brought from India to replace African slave labour. I shall apply the term 'Creole' as it is used by the villagers, meaning someone of African descent.

In the village, behaviours and attitudes regularly occur which are not locally attributed. This is a situation which increased with material gains made during Trinidad's oil boom over a decade ago. One has, for example, the type of person that Angrosino (1972:242) has labelled the 'Indian Portnoy', i.e., someone who works for the high-paying oil company instead of the sugar plantation. This person is 'guilty of the greatest betrayal of his heritage at the very moment he is attaining the highest goal of that heritage'.

In other words, the job is no longer part and parcel of the inter-connected relationship of labour, morality, and family/material needs. But this somewhat romantic illustration of high achievement is hardly representative of most younger rural men facing unemployment in Trinidad's presently depressed economy. Their machismo cannot be reinforced through the respectability of a powerful career. How does one begin to interpret their non-traditional behaviours and attitudes?

Village creolisation: its meanings and contexts

The *Concise Oxford Dictionary* (1982:223-4) includes among its definitions for the word 'Creole'(n): 'descendant of European settlers in W. Indies', 'person of mixed European and Negro descent', and for 'creole', (adj.): 'of local origin or production'. For 'creolise' it states: 'make [the] (language of [the] dominant group, in [a] modified form) into [the] sole language of dominated group.'

These dictionary definitions suggest, in the colonial context, the values of domination (and by implication, submission), racial purity, and the fixed nature of local origins and notions of tradition. However, the hierarchical nature of these values remain quite germane in the post-independence scenario, and while the terms 'acculturation' and, indeed, its close relative 'creolisation', have fallen out of fashion within orthodox anthropology, the fact that these notions are now included in the discourse of the people once studied for this attribute (e.g., Crowley, 1957), warrants a new examination.

Suffice it to say that, despite egalitarian proclamations and national mottos (e.g., 'Together we aspire, together we achieve'), colonial-type attitudes in Trinidad towards race and class continue, albeit in an altered and/or transformed mode as social and national conditions have changed.[2] For example, both Indo- and Afro-Trinidadians will often use the white colonial terms of 'coolie' and 'nigger', respectively, on members of their own ethnic group to insult certain behaviours considered too parochial and unfit for what they perceive as 'modern' Trinidad. Even though they are subject to many of the same tensions and stresses generated by modernity, Indo-and Afro-Trinidadians approach this state from different angles.

For example, local efforts to construct/reconstruct an 'African' identity in Trinidad have been plagued by the ongoing West Indian conundrum of proving equality with Euro-American culture by emulating its supposedly 'superior' characteristics. One may speculate briefly here whether the growth of Afro-American influence in imported popular (or so-called 'mainstream') culture may partly ease the kind of tension generated by this problem. At this point one can say that, to the creole population of Trinidad, an ideal of 'modernisation' continues to mean a relative emulation of disciplined Euro-American development while ironically trying to maintain a supposedly 'relaxed' West Indian lifestyle. Hence, in the 'land of carnival', a popular 1986 calypso complained about the 'rat race' of society.

In contrast, much of the pride inherent to the majority of Hindu Indians' identity rests with a popular, if slightly distorted, belief that their religious and cultural practices are seamlessly continuous with what they perceive is 'the oldest religion in the world'. Social change influenced by either Afro- and/or Euro-American culture is, rather unequally, tested before being accommodated within the values of the perceived Indian/Hindu continuity.

However, one cannot suggest that the collective rural Indian psyche has emerged in an entirely healthy and balanced 'postmodern' condition as compared with Creoles. To Indians acceptable 'modernisation' seems to be a question of acquiring technology and fashion which is perceived to be benign or strengthening to their notions of transcendent heritage (cf., Miller, 1990a). Along with this technology and fashion come associated values which are not always clear at the outset. As a result, unorthodox behaviours are particularly susceptible to criticisms, with women in particular coming under suspicion if they act too bright (or 'modern').[3]

Despite suspicions about 'how nasty white people does get on' and agreeing that British colonialism was late in ending, most villagers believe that 'creole-style' modernisation, as has been developed under the post-independence Afro-Trinidadian-dominated governments, is far too disruptive to what they perceive is the ethnic Indian status quo. This invokes the class aspect of creolisation. There is an on-going competition for resources throughout the social spectrum but, with special reference to the lower-classes, it tends to pit Indians against Creoles politically. This spills over and can prejudice situations dealing with individuals (Vertovec, n.d. [a]:18-19, following Despres, 1975). In other words, class struggles among Indians are also affected by those who seek to maximise their individual stature through conciliation with what are perceived to be creole values. Such status-seekers can then be perceived as being creolised, usually negatively. To quote one village informant in his late 30s:

> I feel some Creole does get on like they living in New York or some place where there is too much freedom and too many strange kind'a people mixing. People in *Trinidad* [my emphasis] ain't supposed to get on like that. And Indian getting on bad too. What is wrong with Trinidad is that there is too much freedom. A man could say 'I free to go out and drink and give people a bad drive'. A woman could say 'I free to go out and have an outside man'.

This reactionary view of modernisation incorporates the local historical and comparative perspective and is fuelled by a perception, gained from 'foreign' imagery, that clear and supposedly secure moral divisions between the domestic and extra-domestic domain may become blurred as 'too much freedom' comes from 'too much mixing'.[4]

Simultaneously, one younger informant by the name of Freddy also represents village views when he interprets non-traditional actions as: 'not how my father or his pard'ners would have behaved, but kind'a like how them Creole does get on'; an affective process Freddy and his 'pard'ners' actually call 'creolisation'. Similarly, the way his 'father or his pard'ners' behaved is known locally as 'traditional'. The reference to class made above, and Freddy's allusions to generation, ethnicity and gender imply that comparisons are being made concerning these local cultural constructs.

In Indian Wood opportunities for villagers to interact with members of other ethnic groups are far less common than in more urbanised areas. For example, in heavily-mixed urban San Fernando, Clarke (1986:133-4) found a ratio of 1:7 for friends of Hindus being Creole, and 2:13 for Creoles having East Indian friends. Interestingly, one of Clarke's major conclusions (*ibid*: vii) is, in fact, that urban mixing does not *necessarily* lead to any greater intimacy, similarity, or commonality.

Among school children and adults in the village, it is the boys and men who make the majority of the sustainable contacts with people, excluding family, outside of the village. Such contacts still tend to be treated somewhat superficially and/or businesslike. In other words, the superficial nature of the majority of contacts between Indians and Creoles seems to have a reinforcing tendency with regards to customary racial stereotyping. Although there is some acknowledgement that there are 'good Creoles' in Trinidad,[5] many descriptions are summarised by the local adage: 'You know how Negro people is'.

Although this sort of judgement is applied (almost) equally to Chinese and whites on the even rarer occasions that contact is made, in Indian Wood itself the undesirable images of creole life are reinforced by the meagre day-to-day contact there is with the only two Creoles who are occasional residents in the village (population 853 Indians in 1989).

One young fellow, in his mid-20s and known as Binko, plays barefoot football (soccer) in the street and drinks with some of the youths. Despite some sympathy for his hard work for a dry-goods wholesaler in the village under whose house he sleeps, when Binko is not around the acerbic comments emerge. These stem from his apparent tolerance, or even a perceived preference, for what is known as stink conditions: 'That family treats Binko like a dog you know. Like a pet you does kick and still it don't run away. I feel Creole strange, yes? Like they does enjoy living that way'.

The second man is in his late 50s, slightly frail, and in local terms is a *dougla*.[6] Known as Creole Bob, he is a self-employed taxi driver. The remarkable thing about him is that he has a total of five concubines, all Indian women, four of whom are in the village, including one pair of sisters in one house (both having borne his children) and a mother and daughter pair in another house (only the mother having had children 'for' him, as is said in Trinidad). All the women know about all the other women. The villagers tend to shrug their shoulders: 'That is how Creole does move. Dem ain't easy at all'.

Although Creole Bob's case raises many points beyond the scope of this chapter, the key to the apparent tolerance shown by the villagers is that all the women concerned had already had partners desert them before Creole Bob 'friended them', that he had inherited land in the village long ago, and also that Creole Bob 'never *limed* this side' (meaning he was never part of the social scene enough to be excluded from it). Both Binko and Creole Bob were too unusual and were pre-excluded from social integration. At the same time, no 'normal' villager is forced into intimate relations with them.

Other oddities are also regarded as potential problems allocated to Creoles and 'creolised' behaviour. These include having 'too much vice', 'going off' (forms of mental illness), living a life of near vagrancy,[7] spending too much time in 'Town' (Port of Spain), or consistently eating creole food, e.g. pumpkin pie, red beans, or too much meat of any kind, but especially beef and pork.

Thus, rather than being just a rhetorical example of uninformed racism, Indian Wood begins to illustrate the way in which many of the so-called creolised behaviours and attitudes found among Indo-Trinidadians are both legitimised and discouraged, from within the ethnic boundary, to use Barth's (1969) terminology. This is reflected in both subtle and direct masculine power struggles.

Adolescents accommodate creolisation

With Trinidad suffering from what has been termed 'the absence of an image of the people at large' (Segal, 1987:173), it is not surprising that creolisation has been described, with reference to East Indian women, as 'a troublesome but useful term' (Mohammed, 1988:381), meaning 'acculturation, commitment to one's country of birth, reactions against external cultures and interculturation'(*ibid*:382).[8]

In contrast, modernisation is considered (*ibid*, following Naipaul, 1985 [1962]:48-9) as both the intrusion of external and metropolitan Euro-American influences and the readiness to accept them. Nevertheless, Mohammed (*ibid*:393) correctly notes that 'the creolisation process becomes interlocked with modernisation as new values are formed and are shared between and among the various groups' and that 'to speak of the "creolized" [*sic*] Indian woman at present, is to employ both concepts [creolisation and modernisation] at the same time'. Apparently, the modern Trinidad Indian woman is 'selective' in her acculturation (*ibid*: 395), which suggests that the elements of control and, therefore, power are changing (see below).

This clarification is an important point and illustrates that the analytical value of deconstructing creolisation from modernisation is questionable, since this would suggest that there is no 'modern' element in the attractions of 'commitment ... to a new society' and would deny any authenticity to the power of either Indians or Africans in applying aspects of modernisation. Furthermore, maintaining a conceptual rift between creolisation and modernisation would encourage the unwanted reification of ethnicity,[9] a process which thrives on presumed delineations of foreign and local. While Naipaul (1985 [1962]) may have derided the way in which Trinidadians succumbed to modern Euro-American advertising techniques, who is prepared to say that this human reaction should be any less or more a part of the identity of either Trinidad Indians or Africans?

This leads to the question: if, as discussed above, modernisation is tested by, and in some cases incorporated into, Indian ethnic identity, can it encourage a denial of, or a resistance to, historically traditional ethnic values? Berreman describes an extreme case for individual identity in India (1973:23):

> Whether resistance to stigmatised ethnic identity be subtle or
> spectacular, covert or overt, effective or disastrous, continuous
> or sporadic, it is an intrinsic and inescapable feature of systems
> incorporating such identity.

Although Berreman defines 'stigmatised ethnic identity' as implying 'deprivation, denigration, subjugation, and exploitation' (*ibid*:12), descriptions which are, perhaps, too severe to be applied, *ad hoc*, to East Indians in Trinidad today, he then goes on to say that 'any system of birth-ascribed stratification ... includes by definition one or more stigmatised groups'. Certainly most ethnographies of Trinidad would define the overall society as having a large degree of ethnically-based, 'birth-ascribed stratification'.

It is, therefore, not unreasonable to assume that East Indian men in Trinidad also attempt to resist what they may perceive to be the negative aspects of their own 'Indian' identity, and that they do so by developing positive/negative self-images, which by contextual definition are ostensibly masculine. The recent phenomena of an oil boom/bust socio-economic phase, political changes, and the introduction of widespread cocaine addiction to an already high degree of alcohol consumption (Yawney, 1979; Angrosino, 1972) and local notions of 'vice' (Littlewood, 1987, 1988), have created a new mixture of references which have a much more ambiguous delineation of positive/negative.

Before broaching the topic of masculinity it is thus necessary to return briefly to the question of identity at the village level.

While most Indian youths feel relatively secure with the 'Indian' portion of their identity, there is a recognition that this heritage is not as continuous as some of their elders would make it out to be. To quote one younger informant:

> Yeah, well, we is Indians. We say we is lamera Indian. You know how when you plant seed, later you cut the rice, and some remain back and grow again? That is lamera. Not the pure original 'ting. All ah we is damn lamera Indian.

Not being 'the pure original thing' allows many younger Indians a claim to freedom from what they often mock as stigmatised 'old time' or 'coolie' values which include being tied to agriculture[10] and extremely vague notions of caste/class endogamy with arranged marriages. Such values are seen to clash with what their post-colonial education has stressed: namely, the 'modern' construct of social equality, again, as expressed by national and common Trinidadian mottoes and slogans such as 'Where every creed and race, finds an equal place' and 'All ah we is one'. Adolescent sentiments associated with creolisation, which are favourable towards it, are thus much more palpable to the older generation of the village than what is perceived to be any 'opposite' process, i.e., some sort of 'Hinduisation' (Singer and Araneta, 1967).

As an illustration, the entire topic of creolisation has come to the fore in recent Trinidad Indian consciousness as part of a reaction to the consideration by the National Alliance for Reconstruction (NAR) government of a national service programme.[11] Led by elements of the Sanatan Dharma Maha Sabha (the orthodox Hindu theocracy) and in free association with sections of the opposition United National Congress party, the rallying cry of the opposition to the programme can be paraphrased as, 'the government is out to creolise the Indian youth'. One reaction to this public commentary by Indian leaders was a somewhat surprising joint declaration by both the Roman Catholic and Anglican archbishops of Trinidad. The Christian clerics were headlined in the *Trinidad Express* newspaper (15 April 1990) as saying 'Let There Be Douglas'. Most conservative villagers were quite surprised by the suggestion that more inter-racial marriages should take place.

While in practice, village masculine adolescence means being unmarried and apparently uncommitted to reinforcing the status quo social and domestic organisation, there is a tacit understanding that until such a commitment is made, the individuals concerned would seem to have choices for their future. On the basis of gender there are differing social consequences. Harsher judgement is accorded to young women who have either not been 'lucky', or who have not co-operated with relatives' suggestions or influence in finding a marriage partner. In this regard, young women increasingly find themselves in a double bind.

Supposedly, 'modern' parents who say they are not forcing their daughters 'to do something she doesn't want to do' are often disguising the fact that they have made unsuccessful attempts in locating securely-educated, well-off grooms who are both modern and respectable: again the local deconstruction of creolisation from modernisation. At the same time daughters are unable to take matters into their own hands and they develop reputations as 'thinking they are too high'. All things considered, such a daughter's only hope, as the villagers say, is for her to meet 'some fella from Town', ironically the prime source of perceived creolisation.

Somewhat in contrast, adolescent men can be accepted as 'normal' in their teens, 20s, or early 30s. Thus, being immersed in neither male childhood nor male adulthood, village male adolescence has an interstitial and liminal nature. Because of this, and despite the more neutral judgements when compared with unmarried younger women, it is sometimes considered a 'problem'. But it can be distinguished from the Euro-American 'problematic' construct of adolescence by its relationship with the general Trinidadian social and ethnic atmosphere, whereby the notion of creolisation can assume some responsibility for the problematic aspects of adolescence.

In this way, the traditional Hindu ideals of fitting specific behaviours to specific periods of life do not necessarily produce an outright clash with the influence of non-Hindu/non-Indian ways upon the children of the community.[12] There is a recognition which comes with most local interpretations and/or rationalisations that there is a time for adolescent experimentation which need not produce a person having little or no moral standing. As an example, this is reflected in the heightened sense of social prestige for a pundit to announce at a *yagna*[13] that 'when I was a young fella, I was bad too bad. My father would only give me endless licks ...' The pundit then would go on to describe what sorts of mischief he would get into on visits to San Fernando. This would always be correlated with the bad influences which are claimed to be even more present in the society of today.

On more than one occasion it was made plain by informants that, although people might occasionally appear to criticise a pundit by saying that he was once a Bad John,[14] or that his family background was questionable, there was something to be admired in the obvious improvement in the intentions and actions of the man. He had conquered temptation. In this sense of potential improvement there has always been an acceptable form of male 'adolescence' in Indian Wood, but with rapidly changing economic circumstances and longer periods of bachelorhood, what happens during these years may now be considered more crucial. This is important when one concedes that people can still develop negative attitudes towards former Bad Johns. For the moment it can be said that these sorts of prejudices are highly situational and personal, and along with such notions as skin colour, caste/varna, and sources of wealth (not necessarily in that order), are usually brought out only as ammunition for argument once a conflict or dispute has already begun.

The experimental aspects of (male) adolescence take on a *de facto* symbiotic role which, in effect, helps shape the fluid boundaries of what is acceptably Indian and what is not. They not only allow the members of the adolescent generation to test themselves, both literally and in relation to society, but also provide members of the older generation with suitable contrasts with which to justify, and to test, a moral superiority.

To elaborate on these points: once contrasts involve foreign/ creolised images they can prove not only a mere generational superiority of old over new but, as with the quotation above dealing with Trinidad becoming like New York, also an apparent cultural superiority of Indian over foreign/Creole. Countering this, if the experiences of the adolescent male become less foreign, and essentially more creolised, as part of, for example, a senior secondary school in San Fernando, the cultural superiority of his parents' generation becomes somewhat suspect to him. The schoolyard is as much his reality as is his village and reactions will vary with the situation as to whether an individual accommodates 'creolised' values or maintains a steadfast ethnic identity.

'Reality', in this context, is taken to mean that different interpret- ations can be made depending on the differing ideals of the informants providing the focus of study (cf., Holmes, 1987 viz. Mead, 1981 [1928] and Freeman, 1983). Thus, in Indian Wood, some informants may at one moment suggest the existence of (an implied ideal of) *brahmacarya*, while they may later advocate a 'year-round carnival'. In the same sense, once a young man tests himself successfully against the previous generation, the generational superiority which has been shattered can also affect any perceived cultural superiority.

Though it might not be agreed with by any particular Hindu pundit, this analysis of (male) village adolescence is not as cynical as it might appear. The net result is that the transition period between male childhood and adulthood can sometimes be considered a cultural transition as much as a generational one. It is a time where decisions are made as to the viability of the old as well as the new.

The problem of masculinity

Discussing the dynamics of the 'generation gap' introduces the notion of creolisation as an instrument pertaining to masculine power. Creolisation is seen by many as a threat to an already tenuous hold men have over women and, just as importantly, over other men. To Indians, becoming creolised is to forgo many of the local notions of honour and shame and to become ripe for *tabanka*, an Afro-Trinidadian conceptualisation of reactive depression which, in effect, socially belittles sexual/moral shame. Despite, or because of, this danger, there is prestige to be gained. Ironically, a high suicide rate for Indians as compared with Creoles (Ministry of Health and Environment, 1984; Littlewood, 1985) indicates, among other things, that while Indian morality may differ from that of Creoles, behavioural practice may be somewhat more coincidental.

Because of the linkages between identities mentioned above, (ethnic, gender-based, and generational) local situational ideas about masculinity become very important in that they can dictate salient features about ethnicity and adolescence.[15] The 'youth of the nation' are consistently portrayed and fought over as both the vanguard of progression (usually defined in masculine terms) and as the sanctuary of tradition (usually illustrated by traditional femininity under threat). Such apparent ambiguity leads to controversy.

In the case of the national service programme, the anxiety would seem to stem from a belief that the government is no longer 'we own', in marked contrast to what was believed when it came to power in 1986 (Yelvington, 1987). In fact, the disillusionment (Ryan, 1989) and alienation, or re-alienation considering the marked Indian distaste for the former PNM government, was a leading contributing factor to the malaise which launched the 'refugee' migration, in 1988-9, of East Indians to Canada (Sampath, 1989). At that time Canadian immigration officials were given a litany of complaints about racial discrimination (against men) and physical/sexual intimidation (against women but thereby affecting men's honour) as reasons for requesting asylum in Canada. In other words, most of the dreaded consequences of a forced integration into the society that the NAR government was perceived to be creating.

In rural Trinidad, for example, the 'selectivity' by modern Indian women mentioned above (Mohammed, 1988) is often entirely precluded by the general male domination ideology, or 'masculinism' as Brittan (1989) has recently called it. Simply put, this encompasses not only power over women and other men, but also support of this ideology throughout society. Hence, extra-domestic communication of the values of other cultures is also affected. In fact, a general focus of successful Trinidad masculinity is to be empowered with a selectivity as regards domestic and extra-domestic commitment. As one educated village informant crudely contrasts the resulting classical double-standard: 'A woman in Trinidad who does try to move like a fella? She may be a nice place to visit, but, man, you wouldn't want to live there!'.

Masculinity, in Trinidad as in other cultures, can be said to suffer from the 'taken for granted syndrome' as Gilmore has recently described it (1990:2). Following Western sociology, the first focus for academics commenting on Indo-Caribbean gender has been on women's issues generally, dealing with women's struggle for some form of emancipation when faced with both domestic and extra-domestic economic and moral demands (cf. Reddock, 1984; Poynting, 1987; Mohammed, 1988; Williams, 1988; Seapaul, 1988). Particularly in the case of rural Indo-Trinidadians, implicit local definitions of manhood have tended to revolve around patriarchal domestic roles and often stereotypical views of ethnicity, rather than being open to more explicit examination.

Gender role has been defined by Pleck (1987:36, following Money and Ehrhardt, 1972) as 'the extent to which individuals have the traits, attitudes and interests culturally expected of their sex'. It should be distinguished from gender identity: 'the individual's awareness of and satisfaction with being a male or female' *(ibid.)*. Thus, considering that a major aspect of adolescence is its importance to the individual in securing a cultural gender identity, there is ample room for a continuing appraisal of masculinity from the adolescent viewpoint.

One cannot help but adapt Wilson's (1969, 1973) ideas on reputation and respectability. In the case of Indian Wood, a secure reputation involving creolised behaviour represents Indian manhood's power and macho security relative to that afforded by the perceived respectable traditions of Trinidadian Hinduism as maintained by women in domestic ritual and practice. But with adolescents who, as we have noted, are acutely aware of pressures to be 'modern', one is often dealing with greater fluctuations of emphasis on either domestic or extra-domestic security within a short period of time. It is largely in this sense that creolisation becomes, to paraphrase Herdt's (1981) terminology, an idiom of adolescent masculinity.

Superficially, male adolescence in the village is an adopted Western construct which has developed in parallel with the average age for marriage, becoming more distant from the end of a dependent childhood. It assumes a variety of ostensibly positive guises when associated with comments such as 'being modern' and 'in a free society'.

'Adolescence' thus becomes 'adolescences' which, in situational terms, is utilised by young and old alike either to reinforce, defy, contrast, or synthesise gender and other cultural constructs.

Sometimes there is confusion in the individual concerned which illustrates the way adolescence is not simply a clear-cut phase of rebellion against conservative values. This is evident in the following quote from Romeo, a 25-year-old bachelor, and hence still a 'youth', who contributes to his family by 'garden work' and occasional carpentry. Here he describes how his values of pride and power apparently differ from those of his father's.

> Sometimes I don't know what to say about my father, yes? I mean, sometimes I feel he does move real good. He stays quiet, don't bother with no stupidness [referring to cuss ups on the road], he doesn't drink again. Boy, he could drink too bad you know. At least now he don't really take a drink again.
>
> But other times I feel he does go too far with this kind'a quietness 'ting. Take his nephew Chit, right there two houses away. Every year that man does take away another inch, or a foot, or sometimes even a yard of we own [rented] land by moving his fence or planting a bigger bed for his tomatoes or whatever. I mean to say there are times when you have to stand up a bit and keep what's yours. But he stays quiet-quiet, like he's ashamed to say anything. Another thing he likes now is to always keep himself pampered. You know? Aftershave, new razor blades every day. New combs. And he knows how my mother has to save to buy the girls their school books. But we can't tell him nothing. I mean to say, is only he who have any regular work.

Yet, Romeo does not seem too happy with the younger generation following him either:

> I can remember when I was going up to Junior Sec, Senior Sec, five, eight years ago, once somebody a little older than you self ... five or 10 years ... come to you if you *liming* here and playing a game? And them tell you go up to the shop and come back? Don't say you ain't going because you getting some good wood [in this sense, 'wood' refers to physical abuse]. And if you go home and report it you getting more wood again. So you have to go up the road quiet and come back.
>
> Now let we say I tell a fella seven years old now; 'Here take this money and go up the road to the parlour and get me

a [soft] drink'. He might tell me 'haul your mother-arse something and something'. Back then the parents had the children real quiet. If you were 18 years you can't walk out on the road after 7:00 [p.m.] you know. You had to be inside your house. Now them fellas, real young, going to see 'blues' [pornographic films] in San Fernando, or going with [a disc jockey] to Tobago. Things changed plenty. And I talkin' about the last five, 10 years.

No respect. Now them fellas cussin in front of an old woman. I mean to say, it have some people you could cuss, but it have people you have to respect too. Now them fellas don't even watch. I mean you might cuss, but you'd watch to see. You know who you show respect to, that is who you show respect to.

What does ambivalence of this sort mean? Why is being quiet and not bothering with 'stupidness' good, while putting up with land encroachment is bad? Apart from personal motivations behind such actions, or inactions, one must also consider a relative contentment, and in this case a slight withdrawal, of the older generation in the face of changes beyond their control. Although Romeo admires the peace and quiet, he cannot admire the tolerance aspect. To him this is indicative of a loss of power and, but for a few words left unsaid to his father's nephew, an unnecessary loss at that. On the other hand, one can also suggest that Romeo has yet to face the full implications of upsetting the balance of respect towards family and neighbours. His father's occasional 'doh [don't] give a damn for anyone but himself' attitude illustrates the situational judgement which intrudes on perceived creolised behaviour. When undertaken by the older domestically-established generations it can actually maintain the status quo in the village masculinity power balance between notions of honour (Indian) and reputation (Creole).

Rural Indian men flirt with a two-fold danger from creolisation: firstly, the degree to which men are individually free to mix in the wider society and, secondly, an implicit support of those women who are outside, or who supposedly have access through domestic boundaries. Successful creolisation either enhances, or is at least benign towards, the attainment of 'Indian' domestic patriarchal power. It sanctions 'living in a free [post-colonial] country' without undermining the traditional sources of domestic security. This produces two ramifications to be dealt with in turn.

The immediate corollary is that female power must be reduced or at least left unenhanced by 'successful' creolisation. In addition, there is an implicit hierarchy in place over those men, especially the younger ones, who are not successful at this process. A brief example can illustrate and introduce these ramifications.

Pertaining especially to young village men is *tabanka*. As suggested above, it occurs among Afro-Trinidadians when a woman's affections are lost to another man (Littlewood, 1985). But since Indian adolescents have few real opportunities to engage in active heterosexual relationships in the first place, the term *tabanka* has been extended by them to describe a state of unrequited love, where a macho reputation has been prevented, rather than lost. In this respect, the effect of the mocking which customarily accompanies it is different for the adolescent.

A 24-year-old individual known as Pastor, who was once an enthusiastic Christian convert and who had mocked Hindu idolatry, found himself longing for, though not speaking to, a young woman in the village who was rumoured to have broken off with a boy from elsewhere. Pastor gave up liming with his 'pard'ners' so that he could walk back and forth in front of her house, hoping for something spontaneous to occur. His 'pard'ners' in turn intensified their acting as they saw fit for his *tabanka*: by belittling his situation (and the woman) and telling him to 'make a move on de chick man, she's an ole cat'. Instead, Pastor sought solace in watching Indian films on videos where, for example, after years of separation, the hero and heroine might finally speak to each other before a painful death. He also began re-attending Hindu prayer meetings. If he went shopping people asked him if he was going to buy 'Gramazone', a defoliant commonly used as a suicide potion.

While Pastor's ex-'pard'ners' quickly became true-true Trinis and made light of his situation, Pastor attempted to console himself with the relative security of 'Indian culture'. Lack of 'modern' masculine success and not 'moving well' can be indicated by a reversion to fatalism and a relative over-concentration on traditional sources. To quote Pastor's 'pard'ners':

> Poor Pastor. He does want to make a move on the girl but he ain't getting nowhere. He used to mock them star-boys in Indian pictures and now he suffering just like they. Well, that is what does happen. Once you does lose courage to take action, bang, *tabanka* does take hold and you back sitting and scratching, doing nothing.

Pastor, it seems, could not be blamed for being attracted to the girl, but he could not successfully broker the cultural values for himself. According to his 'pard'ners', had he not mocked Indian values in the first place and partly retained their security he might have had the courage he sought to establish successfully a modern masculine identity. Instead of becoming a master of creolisation, he became a victim of it, and this is essentially the problem of masculinity in the village.

Conclusion

Creolised behaviour in Indian Wood is not exclusive to adolescent males but it is the significant part of their own expansive quest for power and identity. Peters (1972) has described how adolescents can mediate the moral ambiguities which a small community may have to face. While it might seem possible to expand directly on this, following Barth (1984 [1966]), to include direct brokering of creolised behaviour and sanction allocation, Paine (1974:27, following Bailey, 1969:167-8) has pointed out that the purpose of such intermediaries is to bridge a certain gap in communications and that once communication across this gap occurs, the intermediaries are then out of business. One must suggest, however, that continuous social change demands continuous communications.

Although I have highlighted some cases of apparently unsuccessful creolisation in terms of satisfaction for particular individuals and mentioned certain negative effects on women, there is a varied matrix of acceptable and unacceptable masculine behaviours and attitudes in Indian Wood. These can be bridged by either what is locally perceived to be non-traditional or traditional values, depending on the situation and the parties involved. While such an outline may sound somewhat schematic, it reflects much of rural Trinidadian thinking on concepts of 'good' and 'bad'. Rapid social changes and the extra choices afforded by Trinidad's 'global mass consumption' (Miller, 1990a, 1990b) encourages new forms of communication, acceptable modernity, modernity that is perceived to be creolised, and hence, adolescent male flirtations with creolisation.

The distinction between gender role and gender identity lends support to the idea that non-traditional behaviours in men can become self-justified in the sense that long-term role expectations, and (some of) the associated perceived 'traditional' values, may be forfeited for shorter-term gender, i.e., adolescence (hence its culturally-determined quality), identity satisfaction. Sometimes role and identity may clash, but even an occasional coincidence should produce a cultural transformation. In Trinidad the dominant ideology of masculinism provides the ideal social conditions for such coincidences, without seriously compromising what is perceived to be 'tradition'. This is especially important when one considers, for example, the apparent ability of traditional institutions to adapt to accommodate the wishes of some

Hindu youths to organise themselves into revival-style groups (see Vertovec, 1990).[16]

'Problems' of adolescence and creolisation may continue to arise, particularly when individuals make tacit differentiations between creolisation and modernisation on the basis of gender effect. With the control of acceptable modernity apparently 'engendered' by masculinity,[17] there does not seem to be any 'modern' respite for rural Indian women in sight in the near future. Nevertheless, it can be suggested that because of a mediation effect between creolised village adolescence and commonly accepted Indian cultural history, some Indo-Trinidadians may be able to avoid the standard West Indian culture conundrum of over-aspiring to self-defeating 'foreign' imagery.

Acknowledgements

I would like to thank Marcus Banks, Aisha Khan, Dan Segal, and Kevin Yelvington for their comments and criticisms of previous versions of this paper. Any mistakes or nebulous characteristics of this paper are strictly of my own making.

Notes

1   Indian Wood is a fictitious name to protect the confidentiality of informants. The pun on the word 'wood' which, in Trinidad, is a common vulgarity for 'penis', remains valid to the real village in question, and so I choose not to avoid it. Regular usage of the word is just as common.

2   The qualification is important. It would be incorrect to suggest, as M.G. Smith does (1984:35), that 'the basic components of the colonial society and political order persist below the surface of social life and party politics'.

3   The 1990-1 controversy over the popularity of 'Chutney singing' and its associated dancing, best described (and often criticised) as 'Indian bacchanal', illustrates the ambivalence that is present in Indo-Trinidadian society.

4   The ultimate consequence of creolisation would be *dougla*isation, as Afro-Indian miscegenation is sometimes termed locally. With all of these definitions, however, it is important not to lose track of the underlying issue of gender and generation.

5   For example, young Indians judge Rastafarians on economic terms. 'Good' Rastas sell sandals and cassette tapes on city pavements with loud rockers music playing from a radio.

6   Often spelled as *dooglas* (the way it is pronounced), it means 'of African and East Indian parentage'.

7   This contradicts Lieber's (1981:22) description of urban Trinidad. In fact, most of the urban 'down and outs' are Creole and not Indian. As Stewart

(1989:21) points out, the Indian poor are left behind in the villages, i.e., spiritual ascension equals material ascension equals [physical] urbanisation. Stewart's emphasis on Indians consistently views Creoles as being over-materialistic in terms of their self-image.

8 I do not believe Mohammed intends to use these terms (acculturation and interculturation, the latter following E. Brathwaite, 1974) in the negative sense of ignoring 'social, economic and political structures of dominance or of ethnic interaction', and the strategic use of cultural elements in contact situations' (Seymour-Smith, 1986:1). This chapter uses such terms as touchstones, because their usage reflects the discourse within Trinidad.

9 A. Khan and K. Yelvington, personal communications.

10 Disdain for agriculture need not extend to land ownership or tenure.

11 A brief consideration of the impact this type of program had on East Indians in Guyana is to be found in Poynting (1987:242-3).

12 Re: 'the four *asramas*: *brahmacarya*, the period of disciplines and education, *garhasthya*, the life of the householder and active worker, *vanaprasthya*, retreat for the loosening of bonds, and finally *sannyasa*, the life of an [ascetic] hermit' (Sen, 1984:22, italics addedl). Significantly this book was quoted from by a 'creolised' Indian Wood geologist (i.e., said to be creolised by the local population) at a Divali celebration.

13 An important social/religious event in either *mandirs* (temples) or private homes lasting seven or nine days.

14 Bad Johns are, as implied, quarrelsome and anti-social.

15 It may be suggested at this point that the reverse postulate is also true; that ethnicity (and adolescence) also shape masculinity. I would argue that at this point in time, ethnicity studies and ethnographies in general have not attempted to deliver adequate treatment to this relationship. It is as well that gender studies take the initiative and perhaps offer a momentary diversion, if not relief, from the identity puzzle which, as it has been presented in the literature so far, is best illustrated by Selvon's description of 'East Indian Trinidadian Westindians' [*sic*] (1987:21).

16 In Indian Wood these groups were occasionally mentioned by visiting pundits but there was no direct participation in them.

17 I am grateful to Dan Segal for this insight.

References

Angrosino, M.V., 1972, 'Outside is Death: Alcoholism, Ideology and Community Organization among the East Indians of Trinidad', unpublished Ph.D. dissertation, University of North Carolina, Chapel Hill.

Bailey, F.G., 1969, *Stratagems and Spoils*, Oxford: Basil Blackwell.

Barth, F. (ed.), 1969, *Ethnic Groups and Boundaries*, London: Allen and Unwin.

– 1984 [1966], *Models of Social Organization*, Occasional Paper No. 23, London: Royal Anthropological Institute.

Brathwaite, E., 1974, *Contradictory Omens*, Monograph 4, Mona, Jamaica: Savacou Publications.

Berreman, G.D., 1973, 'Self, Situation, and Escape from Stigmatized Ethnic Identity', in Brogger, J. (ed.), *Management of Minority Status*, Oslo: Universitetsforlaget.

Brittan, A., 1989, *Masculinity and Power*, Oxford: Basil Blackwell.

Clarke, C., 1986, *East Indians in a West Indian Town: San Fernando, Trinidad, 1930-1970*, London: Allen and Unwin.

Concise Oxford Dictionary, 1982, Oxford: Oxford University Press.

Crowley, D., 1957, 'Plural and Differential Acculturation in Trinidad', *American Anthropologist*, Vol. 59, No. 5, pp. 817-24.

Despres, L., 1975, 'Ethnicity and Resource Competition in Guyanese Society', in Despres, L. (ed.), *Ethnicity and Resource Competition in Plural Societies*, The Hague: Mouton, pp. 87-117.

Freeman, D., 1983, *Margaret Mead and Samoa: The Making and Unmaking of an Anthropological Myth*, Cambridge, MA: Harvard University Press.

Gilmore, D.D., 1990, *Manhood in the Making: Cultural Concepts of Masculinity*, London: Yale University Press.

Herdt, G, 1981, *Guardians of the Flutes: Idioms of Masculinity, A Study of Ritualized Homosexual Behaviour*, New York: McGraw-Hill Book Company.

Holmes, L., 1987, *Quest for the Real Samoa: The Mead/Freeman Controversy and Beyond*, Massachusetts: Bergin and Garvey.

Lieber, M., 1981, *Street Scenes: Afro-American Culture in Urban Trinidad*, Cambridge, MA: Schenckman.

Littlewood, R., 1985, 'An Indigenous Conceptualization of Reactive Depression in Trinidad', *Psychological Medicine*, Vol. 15, pp. 278-81.

– 1987, 'Pathology and Identity: The Genesis of a Millennial Community in North-East Trinidad', unpublished D. Phil. thesis, University of Oxford.

– 1988, 'From Vice to Madness: The Semantics of Naturalistic and Personalistic Understandings in Trinidadian Local Medicine', *Social Science and Medicine*, Vol. 27, No. 2, pp. 129-48.

Mead, M., 1981 [1928], *Coming of Age in Samoa*, Harmondsworth: Penguin.

Miller, D., 1990a, 'Fashion and Ontology in Trinidad', *Culture and History*, Vol. 7, pp. 49-77.

– 1990b, 'The Young and the Restless in Trinidad: An Example of the Global and the Local in Mass Consumption', seminar paper presented at the Institute of Social Anthropology, Oxford, May.

Ministry of Health and Environment, 1984, *The Health Situation – Epidemiological Analysis: Trinidad and Tobago*, Port of Spain: Ministry of Health and Environment.

Mohammed, P., 1988, 'The Creolization of Indian Women in Trinidad', in Ryan, S. (ed.), *Trinidad and Tobago: The Independence Experience, 1962-1987*, St Augustine: Institute of Social and Economic Research, University of the West Indies, pp. 381-97.

Money, J. and Ehrhardt, A., 1972, *Man and Woman, Boy and Girl*, Baltimore: The Johns Hopkins University Press.

Naipaul, V.S., 1985 [1962], *The Middle Passage*, Harmondsworth: Penguin.

Paine, R., 1974, *Second Thoughts about Barth's Models*, Occasional Paper No. 4, London: Royal Anthropological Institute.

Peters, E.L., 1972, 'Aspects of the Control of Moral Ambiguities', in Gluckman, M. (ed.), *The Allocation of Responsibility*, Manchester: Manchester University Press.

Pleck, J.R., 1987, The Theory of Male Sex-Role Identity', in Brod, H. (ed.), *The Making of Masculinities: The New Men's Studies*, Boston: Allen and Unwin, pp. 21-38.

Poynting, J., 1987, 'East Indian Women in the Caribbean: Experience and Voice', in Dabydeen, D. and Samaroo, B., (eds), *India in the Caribbean*, London: Hansib, pp. 231-63.

Reddock, R., 1984, 'Women, Labour, and Struggle in Twentieth Century Trinidad and Tobago: 1898-1960', unpublished Ph.D. thesis, University of Amsterdam.

Ryan, S., 1989, *The Disillusioned Electorate: The Politics of Succession in Trinidad and Tobago*, Trinidad: Inprint.

Sampath, N.M., 1989, ' "De Country Gone Through": Trinidad East Indian "Refugees" to Canada', paper presented to the 88th Annual Meeting of the American Anthropological Association, Washington, D.C., 15-19 November.

Seapaul, O., 1988, 'Hindu Women in Today's Society', *Caribbean Affairs*, Vol. 3 No. 1, pp. 90-5.

Segal, D., 1987, 'Nationalism in a Colonial State: A Study of Trinidad and Tobago, unpublished Ph.D. dissertation, University of Chicago.

Selvon, S., 1987, 'Three Into One Can't Go: East Indian, Trinidadian, Westindian [*sic*]', in Dabydeen, D. and Samaroo, B. (eds), *India in the Caribbean*, London: Hansib/University of Warwick, pp. 13-24.

Sen, K.M., 1984, *Hinduism*, Harmondsworth: Penguin.

Seymour-Smith, C., 1986, *Macmillan Dictionary of Anthropology*, London: Macmillan.

Singer, P. and Araneta, E., 1967, 'Hinduization and Creolization in Guyana: The Plural Society and Basic Personality', *Social and Economic Studies*, Vol. 16, No. 3, pp. 221-36.

Smith, M.G., 1984, *Culture, Race and Class in the Commonwealth Caribbean*, Mona: Extra-Mural Unit, University of the West Indies.

Stewart, J., 1989, *Drinkers, Drummers, and Decent Folk: Ethnographic Narratives of Village Trinidad*, Albany: State University of New York Press.

Vertovec, S., 1990, 'Religion and Ethnic Ideology: The Hindu Youth Movement in Trinidad', *Ethnic and Racial Studies*, Vol. 13, No. 2, pp. 225-49.

– n.d., 'East Indians and Anthropologists: A Critical Review', unpublished manuscript.

Williams, C., 1988, 'The Role of Women in Caribbean Culture', in Ellis, P. (ed.), *Women of the Caribbean*, London: Zed Books, pp. 109-14.

Wilson, P.J., 1969, 'Reputation and Respectability: A Suggestion for Caribbean Ethnography, *Man*, Vol. 4, No. 2, pp. 70-84.

– 1973, *Crab Antics*, New Haven: Yale University Press.

Yawney, C., 1979, 'Drinking Patterns and Alcoholism in Trinidad', in Marshall, M. (ed.), *Beliefs, Behaviors, and Alcoholic Beverages*, Ann Arbor: University of Michigan Press, pp. 94-107.

Yelvington, K.A., 1987, 'Vote Dem Out: The Demise of the PNM in Trinidad and Tobago', *Caribbean Review*, Vol. 15, No. 4, pp. 8-12, 29-33.

CHAPTER 11

Ethnicity and social change in Trinidadian literature

Patrick Taylor

Ethnic plurality provides Trinidadian society with a reservoir of symbols and traditions which can make a vital contribution to the building of a dynamic multicultural nation. From a modern, secular perspective, however, ethnicity may amount to no more than the murky, enveloping waters of outmoded tradition and communal exclusion. Trinidadian culture has been fashioned by India, Africa and Europe. Though many different ethnic groups make up each of these traditions, colonial society was defined primarily in terms of race with the result that ethnic difference, as the cultural specificity of particular groups, tended to be reduced to racial difference. Ethnicity provided the basis for communal identity and resistance to colonialism: Africans and Indians maintained aspects of their own cultures, distinguished themselves from their European overlords, and challenged colonialism.

Trinidadian authors have focused both on questions of ethnic identity and on the processes of social and political transformation in the society. Sam Selvon and Earl Lovelace are two authors whose novels stand out because of their ability to represent Trinidad as an ethnically-plural, modern society, subordinate neither to stultified and conflictual notions of tradition nor to Eurocentric expressions of national development. In their own unique ways, each writing in a different historical period and from a different ethnic perspective, they capture the dynamics of ethnic particularity as it relates to social and political change in twentieth-century Trinidad. Their works can be contrasted with those of other Trinidadian authors who find themselves trapped in ethnic perspectives when they address the project of building the new nation.

Pluralism, nationalism, and Trinidadian reality

More than other analyses of Caribbean society, the pluralist school, associated particularly with the work of M. G. Smith, captures the reality of ethnic differentiation and social conflict in Trinidad.

According to Smith, Caribbean societies are hierarchically structured and institutionally segmented in terms of ethnic difference. The primary ethnic differences are articulated in racial terms. In the basic model of the plural society, Europeans have authority over Africans; in the complex model, Africans, Indians, and other ethnic groups are culturally and socially differentiated from each other and from Europeans in a complex of hierarchical relationships. Whereas Lloyd Braithwaite stresses the process of acculturation through which subordinate groups accept the values of the dominant group, Smith emphasises the conflictual nature of plural societies in terms which echo Frantz Fanon's analysis of the colonial contradiction: because subordinate groups do not accept the racial claims of the dominant group, these societies must be held together by force (Smith, 1960:767, 773; Smith, 1984: 28-30, 138-40; Braithwaite, 1960:822-5; Fanon, 1968:37-40). Though Smith's model makes some explanatory sense of Caribbean societies, it privileges ethnic and racial segmentation, difference, and conflict over processes of community formation, nation building and development. It is unable to provide an analysis of the forces of unity and the struggles for social justice in the society.

There are many aspects of Trinidadian literature which appear to sustain a pluralist reading. White colonial images of Africans and Indians penetrate early Caribbean writing, and Kenneth Ramchand has commented on the common tendency even of later Caribbean writers to appeal to racial stereotypes. In his study of Indian-African relations in Caribbean fiction, Jeremy Poynting has argued, more emphatically than Ramchand, that Caribbean fiction tends to reproduce existing ethnic polarities. Works by non-Indians either exclude Indians or relegate them to the status of a minority depicted as different, as 'Other'. Indian fiction likewise tends to avoid dealing with Africans in the community, or stereotypes them negatively. Poynting notes a difference, however, in attitudes to racial mixing: whereas in *Green Days by the River* the African writer Michael Anthony portrays the *dougla*, the person of mixed African and Indian ancestry, as an attractive female, in *The Chip-Chip Gatherers* the Indian writer Shiva Naipaul depicts the abhorrence of racial mixing that is felt by an Indian character (*dougla* is from a Hindi word meaning 'bastard') (Ramchand, 1983:41; Ramchand, 1985:18-19; Poynting, 1986:15-16, 18).

In contrast to the pluralist reading of Caribbean society, historians such as Edward Brathwaite argue that emphasis must be placed on the process of creolisation through which different ethnic and racial groups were incorporated into plantation society. African slaves were forced to adopt the language and culture of the master on the plantation. In the process of doing so, however, they reworked European cultural patterns in terms of their own traditional African cultures (Brathwaite, 1971:306-7). When other cultures came to the Caribbean they were incorporated into this African-European cultural matrix (see, for example, Mahabir and Maharaj, 1989). Through creolisation, a popular culture was created which was distinct from the dominant colonial culture and often dared to call the dominant culture into question.

The idea that unique creole societies were formed in the Caribbean is consistent with the dominant ideas of the nationalist movement of the mid-twentieth century: the building of a unified, independent nation. According to Eric Williams, leader of the People's National Movement, the party with its mass support 'had released the latent capacities and pent-up energies of the people of Trinidad and Tobago and was leading them inexorably on the road to independence'. He emphasised that the new nation could look to neither Mother Africa, Mother India, nor Mother Europe. The old colonial divide and rule policies would be replaced by a single Mother, Mother Trinidad, 'and Mother cannot discriminate between her children' (Williams, 1964:248, 279). With the informal motto 'All o we is one', the nationalist movement led the new nation to independence in 1962. The irony of this new era of unity and progress, however, was that a new middle class, primarily African in origin, appealed to the rhetoric of national community to sanction its own ascendancy. An emphasis on development and modernisation, following European and American models, displaced the concern for social justice and cultural authenticity (see LaGuerre, 1988:195-8 and Ryan, 1972:370, 374-82).

Michael Anthony is one example of a nationalist author who writes from the experience of the creolised African community in Trinidad. The characters in his works are members of the community engaged in everyday activities: human interrelationships, the quest for respectability, the discipline of self, popular celebration. In *The Games Were Coming* (1977 [1963]) the mystique of respectability is pierced by the exuberance of carnival as the spirit of the community triumphs over bourgeois pretensions. Anthony's work, however, is haunted by the society's colonial residues. The language and popular traditions in the novel are tame and an aura of creole respectability remains. The national community is viewed from an African middle-class perspective. Vishnudat Singh argues that in presenting the relationship between Mohansingh and Sylvia the novel moves towards 'an understanding of a relationship across the ethnic lines' even though Mohansingh is not a fully realised character (Singh, 1989:152). However, the relationship might be better characterised as one of mutual manipulation. Indians play minor roles in the novel and are stereotyped negatively. Mohansingh is an outsider, an exploitative shopkeeper, a 'snake in the grass' waiting to eat Sylvia (Anthony, 1977 [1963]:56, 58). Nor does the community jettison its patriarchal baggage. It is Leon and Mohansingh who determine the events in Sylvia's life, and even though she manages to define a space for herself, she defines it in terms of their world.

Anthony's work contrasts with that of the female Trinidadian writer Merle Hodge, who could more clearly discern the limits of the nationalist generation and who writes from a female perspective and presents a female genealogy. Hodge's *Crick Crack, Monkey* (1981 [1970]) uses irony to call into question the triumph of light-skinned, middle-class respectability. Reflecting the colonial values of church and school, Aunt Beatrice centres her understanding of life around the photograph of 'The White Ancestress'. From this perspective it is necessary to avoid mixing with 'niggery people' and 'coolies'. Cynthia confronts herself as a shadow of her double, of Helen, the imaginary white, female heroine of a distant land. Hodge creates a model of colonially-imposed, racial and ethnic conflict in relation to which the young girl Cynthia must discover herself. Her Tantie links her to African traditions, her friends to Indian ones. Unable to leave Aunt Beatrice's house, she longs for salt fish and roti; she wants to attend the wedding of her Indian friend Moonie: 'I thought of Moonie mysteriously transfigured into a startlingly pretty and fragile doll smothered in folds of delicate cloth and flowers ...' (Hodge, 1981 [1970]:78). Hodge's book is incomplete, Cynthia does not quite reach adulthood, and the perspective on Indians remains external. However, the contradictions are exposed, and there are implications for the reconstruction of a community free of the manipulative values of a Europeanised middle class.

The tension between pluralism and nationalism was at the centre of the new quest for social transformation in Trinidad initiated by the Black Power movement. The movement challenged Trinidadians to overcome the shadowy, colonial mentality characteristic of the new ruling class by recovering a distinct black identity. With its appeal to African ethnicity and its call for social change, Black Power can be situated in the tradition of African Caribbean resistance to white colonial domination. Garveyism had been influential throughout the Caribbean, and the United Negro Improvement Association, very active in Trinidad in the 1920s, had strong ties with the Working Men's Association and the early nationalist movement on the island (see Martin, 1986). The Black Power movement renewed Garvey's themes of racial identity and development from a Marxist perspective. Walter Rodney, one of the main ideologists of the movement in the Caribbean, defined Black Power as a struggle against White Power, that is,

Imperialism. Both Indians and Africans were exploited as 'Blacks' and should unite to overthrow both the old white and the new black elites. Once a socialist society was created, as in the case of Cuba, categories of black and white would disappear (Rodney, 1969:24-5, 28, 31). In Trinidad, the Black Power demonstrations organised by the National Joint Action Committee (NJAC) won some support from Indian workers. When NJAC marched out from Port of Spain to join striking Indian sugar workers, the Williams' government feared African-Indian unity enough to declare a state of emergency (Nicholls, 1985:68-9).

The Black Power movement in Trinidad was spontaneous rather than organised and lacked a full programme of social change. Despite attempts to include Indians, the movement emphasised African cultural symbols and the need to recover an African identity. Africans remained suspicious of Indians, and most Indians did not see Black Power as particularly relevant to their own situation (Nicholls, 1985:65, 70-1, 75-8; see also Ryan, 1972:454-68 and Bennett, 1989:135-9). While the rhetoric and symbols of Black Power excluded Indians, the continuing influence of the Indian subcontinent on Indian culture in Trinidad put limits on Indian commitment to Black Power. Brinsley Samaroo has argued that Indians derived a vital sense of pride and dignity from ongoing contact with learned men from the subcontinent. However, because of this contact, Indians in Trinidad were denied the opportunity to find their own solutions to the problems encountered in their new environment (Samaroo, 1987:55).[1] Smith points to the failure of the Black Power movement in order to support his pluralist analysis of the society. Race and ethnic disunity took priority over class or national unity (Smith, 1984:96-7).

The fragmentation of the national project evident in the Black Power events has been at the centre of much of Trinidadian literature. This is particularly true of the writings of the internationally-acclaimed Trinidadian author, V.S. Naipaul. Naipaul presents Trinidad and other post-colonial societies in tragic and conflictual narratives which conform in many respects to the pluralist model. Colonialism left a tense legacy of ethnic allegiances and racial mythologies. Naipaul's well-known comments in *The Middle Passage* (1969 [1962]) set the tone for the critique of nationalism in his work. Following the nineteenth-century English novelist Anthony Froude, he describes Indians and Africans as 'monkeys pleading for evolution', both appealing 'to the unacknowledged white audience to see how much they despise one another'. Slavery and the plantation created only 'grossness' and 'futility'; 'nothing was created in the West Indies'. Ironically, Naipaul himself is hardly immune from that very racism which he identifies in the society.[2]

If in Naipaul's works the national project was destined to failure, so too was the Black Power movement. In the profoundly disturbing novel, *Guerrillas*, Naipaul reduces the themes of the Black Power movement to rape, murder, and madness. His essay, 'Michael X and the Black Power Killings in Trinidad', while correct in pointing out the millenarian limits of the movement, goes on to reduce it and every other quest for social change in the Caribbean to 'jargon', 'sentimental hoax', and 'deep corruption' (Naipaul, 1981:73). The pathology of Jimmy (Michael X) is Naipaul's rather than the society's, Selwyn Cudjoe has concluded. Ramchand argues that *A House for Mr Biswas* dissolves the myth of Indian self-sufficiency. But Naipaul's subsequent works go on to dissolve any possibility of human reciprocity. The irony is that Naipaul ultimately attempts to avoid the emptiness of his own position by locating himself firmly in Imperial mythology. He arrives at the centre of empire, the bastion of culture, as Derek Walcott remarks about *The Enigma of Arrival*, 'grateful to the vegetation of an English shire. Not to India or the West Indies, but to the sweet itch of an old wound' (Cudjoe, 1988:178; Ramchand, 1985:18; Walcott, 1987:29).

The writings of Neil Bissoondath belong to the tradition of V.S. Naipaul, his uncle and mentor. A comparison of Naipaul's *Guerrillas* and Bissoondath's *A Casual Brutality* suggests that uncle and nephew share a lack of respect for Third World peoples and their cultures, reduce social and political change to absurdity, and depict women as objects to be murdered. Bissoondath's alienated narrator, a male Indian professional of Hindu background, measures his maturity by his ability to see the 'reality' obscured by nationalist myths: 'Blacks we wrote off as lazy, Chinese dirty, Muslims malicious, mulattoes impure .... Only the tourists mixed; only they ignorant of our estrangements, brought truth to our pieties'. The reality of Casaquemada is the 'impossibility of possibility'. The narrator finds his salvation in Toronto: 'I go, like my forebears, to the future, to the challenge that lies elsewhere of turning nothing into something, far from the casual brutality of collapse, far from the ruins of failure, across thousands of miles of ocean'. And so the real irony: betrayal represents itself as expiation (Bissoondath, 1989 [1988]:313, 268, 378).

Creolisation and social change: Sam Selvon

The tragic vision of ethnic conflict and social disunity is not, however, the only alternative to the nationalist romance. In contrast to Anthony's myths and Naipaul's realities are the possibilities presented in the works of Sam Selvon and Earl Lovelace. Selvon, in some of the earliest and most insightful treatments of community life in Trinidad, shows from an Indian Trinidadian perspective how ethnic differentiation is transformed through creolisation in the creation of a uniquely Trinidadian society. In this respect, his writing can be linked to the nationalist movement. However, Selvon's work also goes beyond the limits of Trinidadian nationalism to subvert its modernising and Europeanising strategies and address the formation of new inter-ethnic relationships. Lovelace is of a later generation and his work is written from an African Trinidadian perspective. Like Selvon, however, he is concerned to portray the community in its depths, its cultural base, ethnic conflicts, its new possibilities. His work focuses on the independence period, and the need for cultural, political, and social renewal.

Selvon's first novel, *A Brighter Sun* (1952), and its sequel, *Turn Again Tiger* (1958), are written from the point of view of the experience of the Indian popular classes in a Trinidad in transition (Selvon, 1979a [1952], 1979b [1958]). The process of modernisation and the quest for national independence underlie both novels. In *A Brighter Sun*, modernisation comes to the East Indian peasant village of Barataria in the form of the new Churchill-Roosevelt Highway, built by the Americans during World War II. Sookdeo, a former indentured worker who dies with the coming of the road, symbolises the passing away of the old colonial system. Many indentured workers who had become small farmers were transformed into wage workers: Tiger gives up his plot of land to work at the American base. At the same time, an indigenous professional middle class is in formation, local elections are held, and there are indications that independence from Britain is coming. Pointing forward to this new era of modernisation and national independence, the novel hints at the possibility of a future of betrayal by Indians and Africans of a professional class indifferent to the needs of the popular classes, interested only in its own self-advancement. Tiger tells the crowd: 'these damn people who have money and moving in society ... does laugh and spit on we poor people' (pp. 188-9).

The failure of the middle-class nationalist movement and the modernisation process is the ironic centre of *Turn Again Tiger*. The story of the old Indian, Soylo, symbolises the harshness of the plantation system: as foreman, Soylo had ordered the burning of canes to facilitate the harvest only to discover that his own child was playing in the now burning field. Soylo and the other villagers left the canes behind when they moved to Five Rivers. A new estate was established in their valley, however, using modern agricultural techniques and new varieties of cane. Tiger and his father come to the valley to be the sole supervisors of the estate and found that there was a white supervisor, an Englishman, already in charge of the estate. The old plantation system had not entirely disappeared as Tiger becomes particularly aware once he is promoted by his father to the position of trusted house boy working for the supervisor's wife.

Issues of race and ethnicity are central to the social order portrayed in both novels. The colonial system is based on the distinction between white (privileged) and non-white (exploited). Even on the American road building project and the modernised plantation, social position is defined by race. Tiger is promoted but remains subordinate to white overseers and employers. At the same time, gender relations are subordinated to racial divisions: though he can abuse his own wife, Tiger finds that he must submit to a woman, to the overseer's wife. Ethnic difference is politicised and the culture of the oppressed is constructed as both exotic and inferior to European culture. When the American supervisors come to supper at Tiger's house, they announce that they want to 'feast like gods' on 'Oriental dishes'; they insist on using their fingers and squatting on the floor in 'true Indian fashion' (*Sun*, pp. 167, 169). In playing native, however, they simply affirm their own sense of supremacy. Pressuring Urmilla to come in from the back room to drink with them, they degrade wife along with husband.

In Selvon's works, the basic social conflict between the coloniser and the colonised, between white and black, is complicated by ethnic difference and racial conflict between persons of African descent and those of Indian descent and, to a lesser degree, Chinese descent. If Indians work on the land as small farmers or estate workers as Tiger does in Barataria and Five Rivers, Africans tend to have working class positions in town or, like Joe, at the American base. The scattered Chinese characters such as Tall Boy and Otto have found their place as shopkeepers. Persons of each ethnic group differentiate themselves from persons of other ethnic groups. In *A Brighter Sun*, Joe announces that he 'don't like dis business wid coolie people', and Tiger's father asks Tiger if 'is only nigger friend' he has made. 'Indian must keep together', he advises (pp. 45, 47). School children are quick to taunt Tall Boy's 'Chinee' children about their 'chinky eyes'; they quickly retort with rhymes about how 'niggers' 'stink' and 'coolies' eat with their hands (pp. 55-6).

The colonial legacy of difference undergoes transformation through the process of creolisation. This process is one of the focal points of Selvon's work. The African teacher who straightens her hair so that she will look 'like white people or Indian people' is trying very hard to erase the colonial legacy of difference (*Sun*, p. 54). Joe's job with the Americans brings him into closer contact with an American lifestyle and makes it possible for him and Rita to have a stove, electricity, chairs, knives and forks, and more. That creolisation should be distinguished from Westernisation, however, is indicated by the failure of the assimilationist project. Joe is creolised, but he knows that he is not accepted as an equal by the Americans: in the United States, he points out to Tiger, niggers 'does catch dey royal arse' (*Sun*, p. 196). Despite a desire to absorb American money and ways, Trinidadians ultimately differentiate themselves from the Yankees and conflict develops between them and the soldiers stationed on the island.

The term 'Creole' is used by characters in Selvon's novels to refer primarily to African Trinidadians. However, the process of creolisation has also affected the Indian population, though the members of the older generation see themselves as Indian rather than Creole. The process of creolisation for Trinidadian Indians occurs in a double movement, a movement towards African Trinidadians (Creoles) and a movement towards Europeans or Americans. In *A Brighter Sun*, Boysie has a Creole girlfriend and eventually moves to the United States. Tiger and Urmilla begin to develop relationships with their neighbours Joe and Rita; through contact with their Creole neighbours and Tiger's American employers, they begin to adopt some Western ways.

The relationship between Urmilla and Rita shows how women separated by ethnicity and race, but unified by male-centred systems of oppression, can provide a nucleus for a creolisation process through which community is constructed. Rita and Urmilla are able to establish a relationship of trust across their differences and against their husbands' wishes. The relationship climaxes when Rita gives her own bed to a pregnant Urmilla, protects her from Tiger's abuse, and, finally, delivers her baby. A new, national foundation is encoded in a unifying, female principle. But there is no romanticism in this mothering relationship. The baby is the victim of the conflicts and tensions at the heart of the creolisation process itself: tensions of gender inequality, racial exclusivity, and exploitative relationships. The baby is born dead. Like it, the independent nation is a fiction, and history is the reality of difference, struggle, and new possibility.

Tiger's own creolisation can be seen in the contrast between him and Sookdeo, an older Hindu man, and his informal teacher and adviser. Whereas Sookdeo is an Indian-born, practising Hindu, Tiger grew up in a Christianised Indian community, with little knowledge of Hindi or Hindu divinities. The plantation experience has reduced Sookdeo to a tragic alcoholic, but he is still able to help Tiger learn to read. He advises him to educate himself, go to the city, and get a good job off the land. Paradoxically, it is the old Hindu, Sookdeo, who pushes Tiger in his drive for creolisation. Tiger then has the problem of dealing with his desire for the type of white lifestyle he sees on a visit to Port of Spain. His self-education helps him to advance in his job with the Americans and Tiger seems to be fully on the path to Westernisation.

However, Tiger must also be contrasted with Bunsee, another older Indian who has become completely Westernised, like some of the Port of Spain Indians. Bunsee's desire is to rise above his lowly people and be like the white American officers in charge of the road. For Tiger, the process of creolisation is full of ambiguities and transformations and cannot be understood as a linear process from Indian identity through creole to Western identity. If Joe has no illusions about American racism, Tiger also comes to an understanding of colonial racism and the limits that it places on any dream of Westernisation. After Tiger has come face to face with white power in Trinidad, Boysie explains to him what it means to be 'black' rather than Indian (p. 95). Tiger later uses the same term 'black' to identify what Indians and Africans in Trinidad have in common, a history of opposition to 'white' oppression (p. 189). 'Ain't coolie does live good with nigger?', he asks Joe, 'Is only wite man who want to keep we down, and even so it have some good one among them'. Tiger recognises that he has grown up as a Trinidadian rather than as an Indian; nor, he also recognises, is he an American. Joe, too, finally comes to the realisation that Tiger is Trinidadian, like him: 'Ain't yuh creolize? Wat yuh worrying bout?' (*Sun*, pp. 194-5).

The irony is that Tiger should indeed worry: as the men engage in political discourse, the son that Tiger so much wanted is born dead. If Joe recognises Tiger as a creolised Trinidadian, does he also recognise him in his difference, as an Indian? Tiger's doubts about his identity remain, particularly his self-doubts as an Indian Trinidadian: he wonders if he should begin to wear a *dhoti*. An estranged Urmilla returns to join Tiger at the end of the story and is wearing her *sari* 'with a touch of pride' (p. 208). The novel hints at the need to go beyond the idea of sameness, of reducing Indians and Africans to 'blacks'. At the same time there are clear, insightful warnings that a politics of difference may be manipulated politically to produce renewed oppression. Tiger is worried by patterns of communal politics and clientelism summed up in Jaggernauth's slogan: 'Indian must come first' (p. 203).[3]

In *Turn Again Tiger*, Tiger's relationship with his white overseer's wife on the modern plantation provides another focal point for self-understanding in a racially determined social system. More Lazy (an African Trinidadian) entertains the men with a dream he has had about a destructive American giant whom he has been able to defeat. The dream rewards him with the white woman accompanying the giant. Working on the plantation, Tiger tries very hard to prove to himself that he can resist the temptation of being seduced by Doreen, the overseer's wife. With lust and hate, he eventually abandons himself to what for the white woman is a seduction and for him a rape. This act is decisive for Tiger for it brings him out of his self-destructive alcoholic state. What at first appears to Tiger to be a failure, a breakdown in self-control, becomes a personal liberation: he feels '[n]o triumph, no satisfaction, no extension of desire to make him want to do it again. Just relief, as if he had walked through fire and come out burnt a little, but still very much alive' (p. 181). At a personal level, Tiger has overcome his phantasm and is now ready to face the real; in his relationships with his wife, Tiger is able to accept her in terms of her own integrity; at a socio-political level, he has confronted the system of oppression and can now work towards the building of the new nation. The *diablesse* that haunted him has been vanquished.[4]

Selvon's latest novel, *Those Who Eat the Cascadura*, switches the focus away from the Indian male's fixation on the mistress to the European male's fixation on the Indian woman. Whether Indian or African, the Caribbean woman has been victimised by the white man's rape. Roger, the owner of the estate, ritually enters Kamalla's hut and plunges on top of her. The relationship between the master's English friend, Garry, and the Indian woman, Sarojini (the master's daughter, it turns out), seems to break with the colonial norm for it is presented as one of mutual fulfilment. However, through parody, irony, and humour, Selvon's novel subverts its own romantic presentation of this loving relationship. As the African Obeahman, Manko, points out, 'good is good with white people, and is a different thing with black people'. What Manko constructs as the contradictory relationship between white and black, coloniser and colonised, Sarojini reconstructs in more complex terms: 'I not black, Manko ... I is *Indian!*' (Selvon, 1990:23). However, as Indian, Sarojini does not escape the colonial relation: Garry leaves the pregnant woman to return to his home in England. Nor does she escape from the frustrated Indian overseer, Prekash, who attempts to rape her. Though Sarojini is hopeful that Garry, having tasted the legendary Cascadura fish, will return to her, the novel leaves the reader unconvinced that her fantasies will ever be fulfilled. The project of Westernisation is forever deferred. Rather, the end of the novel is the point at which a new beginning must be constructed out of colonial difference.

In a presentation on ethnicity in Trinidad, *Three Into One Can't Go – East Indian, Trinidadian, West Indian* (1987), Selvon makes a strong plea for the recognition of the fundamental unity of Caribbean society. Reflecting on his own creolised background, he states that one of his grandfathers was a Scotsman. Selvon's mother spoke Hindi, but his father and other relatives avoided it. His family 'only ate curry once a week – the other days it was creole food, souse and black pudding on Saturday night, and stew beef or chicken and callaloo for Sunday lunch'. At the same time, Selvon is fully aware that creolisation did not give birth to a unified national identity. The lesson of creolisation was 'that the Indian was just a piece of cane trash while the white man was to be honoured and respected'; Indian customs were an embarrassment. Even so, Indians felt 'that Indians were "better" than Negroes, (pp. 14-15). When Africans began to assert their own identity and to call for Black Power, they excluded Indians.

How is Caribbean unity possible when creolisation and attempts to build national unity have only fostered difference? Selvon holds on to a vision of national unity which would exclude power relations based on racial difference or ethnicity. At the same time he recognises that the history of difference cannot be imagined away: 'the quest for identity remains, and the right to live by one's own creed peacefully in a mixed society such as we have in Trinidad'. It is important to remember and recognise the sacrifices and contributions Indians have made and 'to put our house in order', but at the same time Indians in the Caribbean 'must work together for the benefit of the people of the Caribbean' (pp. 23-4). This vision is consistent with that in Selvon's novels. It can be rephrased using some of the terms of contemporary cultural theory: if superimposed on the historical specificity of the 'Other', a universal narrative of freedom becomes little more than a colonial imposition. But Selvon retains in his work a quest for human community which assumes difference as a creative reality, a point which is sometimes lost in the contemporary rejection of universal values (see, for example, Lyotard, 1984:81-2).

Cultural specificity and social renewal: Earl Lovelace

Whereas Selvon writes from the point of view of a nationalist generation, however critical his perspective, Lovelace belongs to the later generation which witnessed the disappointments of independence and the resurgence of the national movement expressed in terms of Black Power. The process of modernisation and the anti-colonial movement remain as central features in Lovelace's *The Dragon Can't Dance* and *The Wine of Astonishment*, but both texts emphasise the need to move beyond the failures of the nationalist regime with its slogan 'All o we is one' (Lovelace, 1981, 1983).

Lovelace, like Selvon, is very careful to depict the complexity of racial and ethnic factors as they relate to the socio-political processes transforming twentieth-century Trinidad. The old colonial order and its racial system lie below the layer of events presented in *Wine* and *Dragon*. In *Wine*, an old plantation house overlooks the village, the descendants of generations of Richardsons now back in England. According to Eva, 'It like a old Church with God gone from it that nobody want any more to worship in' (p. 8). In the colonial period, God was white and the white man was like God. African Trinidadians were not permitted to follow their own cultural traditions. Prince, the black police sergeant in the village who has internalised white colonial values, delights in breaking up the Spiritual Baptist meetings. The Baptist community finds itself marginalised even in relation to other marginal groups: Buntin is loaned no money to enlarge his shop, whereas 'Portuguese, Syrian, Chinee, okay' (p. 6). In *Wine*, as in *A Brighter Sun*, American soldiers appear on the scene with World War II and attract Trinidadians to work for them, men by day, women by night. Despite social and economic transformation, the colonial racial structure continues to exert its influence.

The nationalist movement ushers in new forms of colonial relationships in Lovelace's novels. Ivan Morton, the black village boy whose mother had washed the Richardsons' clothes in order to see the boy through school, becomes an elected politician and takes over the Richardsons' estate house. Ivan's metamorphosis is similar to that of Slime in George Lamming's Barbadian classic, *In the Castle of My Skin*. Having first had to convert to Catholicism in order to gain entry into the educational system, Ivan succumbs to the programme of Westernisation. As he tells Bee, leader of the Baptist community, 'We can't change our colour ... but we can change our attitude. We can't be white, but we can act white' (p. 13). Unable to change his race, Ivan envisions Trinidadians adapting to a new ethnic identity. As a nationalist politician, Ivan finally ensures that Baptist religious services will be legalised, but only after he has neutralised the Baptist community.

Issues of race and ethnicity likewise enter *Dragon* as the ever present remnants of the colonial order. Guy is the well-dressed rent collector who must compensate for his colour by ensuring that people can say about him: 'He black, but he never dirty' (p. 108). Cleothilda is the good-looking, mulatto shopkeeper who joins the yard community to play queen every carnival: 'You hear rhythm, Miss Olive? You hear song? Carnival! ... Bacchanal! Trinidad! All o we is one' (p. 19). But the yard understands the masquerade: Cleothilda must be queen in order to assert a superiority based on the lightness of skin; once carnival is over, everyone who is blacker than her is treated with disdain. Philo is a black man and is treated as such by Cleothilda; he himself remains enchanted by what she represents. When he becomes a successful performer and, like Ivan Morton, begins to erase his own ethnic background, Cleothilda finally accepts him. Philo turns calypso against the Hill and wins the calypso king competition with the lyric, 'Hooligans in Port of Spain messing up the place' (p. 163). Once carnival is over the police launch a campaign against the 'hooligans'. Like *Wine, Dragon* depicts the rise of the new middle class with the appearance of the People's National Movement. The Party wins popular support and is elected on an anti-colonial platform. From the point of view of Fisheye and the Bad Johns from Calvary Hill, however, little has changed with independence.

While Indians appear as very minor characters in *The Wine of Astonishment*, they play important roles in *The Dragon Can't Dance*. Lovelace places Pariag and his family firmly within the network of social relationships which constitute the yard. Pariag is perceived as being an outsider, a 'spectator'. At the Queen's Park Savannah, he is a 'country Indian', or simply 'Channa Boy'. In the yard, where the same people see him and his family on a daily basis, Pariag fares no better. He is not invited to join in the card games or carnival festivities. His wife reminds him of the reality of ethnic and racial difference in Trinidad: 'You don't see that you is Indian and they is Creole'. Yet Pariag feels a need either to belong to the Creole community or, at least, to be seen, to be treated as more than a spectator.

Lovelace shows how the Creole middle class and those aspiring to belong to this class, manipulate the sense of racial and ethnic difference characteristic of Trinidad's complex plural society. When Pariag decides to buy a bicycle which he can use both to sell barra and doubles (Indian snacks) and to make himself visible, it is Cleothilda and Guy, the ones closest to the norms of the Creole middle class, who are particularly threatened. Invoking her favourite motto of oneness, Cleothilda murmurs that the egalitarian philosophy of the yard has never before been so threatened. She expects that Pariag will soon open his own shop. Guy takes this one step further: soon Pariag 'will take over the whole Hill, the whole town' (p. 108). The irony of the situation is not missed by Aldrick, who remarks: 'Is like nobody remember what life is, and who we fighting and what we fighting for .... Guy and Cleothilda ain't fooling me. The Indian is a threat to them, he ain't no threat to me .... Guy and Cleothilda trying to protect what they own' (pp. 110-11).

Whereas Selvon emphasises the problematic of creolisation and its limits (unity with difference), Lovelace focuses on the issue of difference and the possibilities of the nation reconciling itself to its differences (difference with unity). Lovelace's novels are about the assertion of African identity and, by implication, of Indian identity. In a situation where skin pigmentation has historically been associated with class and where Euro-American culture is dominant, what role does ethnicity play in the struggle for human dignity?

In its basic structure, Creole culture as presented by Lovelace is African; creolisation is a process in which Western culture is Africanised. At the same time, Creole culture is a culture of resistance against colonial domination. Ethnicity provides a means of preserving the individual and uniting the community in the struggle against oppression and exploitation. Practice of the Baptist religion is banned by the colonial government in *Wine*, but the community decides to go ahead with its Africanised Christian ceremony: 'and all over the church people was getting up with their Spirit on them and we meet there in the centre of the church and we hold hands and salute one another'. The Baptists sing their song of resistance: 'The Lion of Judah shall break every chain/And bring us to victory over Satan again' (p. 62).

The African Trinidadian culture of resistance is symbolised by the stickfighters in Lovelace's works. In *Wine*, Bolo enters the stickfighting competition every carnival 'so as to keep alive the warrior in them, in us' (p. 92). Likewise, Fisheye in *Dragon* is the stickfighter and Bad John who wants to bring out the warrior spirit which formerly accompanied the steelbands as they competed against each other. Aldrick's dragon mask also captures the spirit of resistance that erupts during carnival: through it he demands that 'others *see* him, recognise his personhood, be warned of his dangerousness' (p. 36).

With the process of modernisation and the growth of the nationalist movement, this culture of resistance gives way to a politics of co-optation. The warrior dies and the scholar, such as Ivan, becomes 'the way to win the battle to be somebody' (*Wine*, p. 46). For the new middle class, African ethnic identity gives way to Euro-American identity. The Baptist community finds itself without any Spirit. Carnival loses the resistance which was its centre: the steelband is no longer a site of battle and the calypso is reduced to Philo's songs of male sexual prowess: 'I am the axe man cutting forests down'. Aldrick, impotent in this new world, begins to see only surrender in the abandonment that is carnival; his Dragon becomes a tortuous masquerade (*Dragon*, pp. 112-14, 150).

The focal point of both *Wine* and *Dragon* is the relinquishment of the spirit of resistance. How is it possible to recover personal integrity in this dehumanised, post-colonial world? Lovelace's work suggests that it is only possible through an ethnic recovery in an historically concrete politics of recognition. In *Wine*, it is Bolo's mad and self-destructive act that becomes the sign of the community's need to recover its own identity in the new historical context. As the warrior in the community, he had wanted to respond to the repression of the Baptist church by killing Prince. The community opts instead to support Ivan and work through the legal system. No longer having any role in the community, Bolo turns into a Bad John, destroys property, and kidnaps two young women. Bolo's death at the hands of the police becomes a sign of the crucifixion for Bee and Eva, the voices of the Baptist community: 'it was easier for Christ to bear the sins of the world than for people to take upon their own self in their own life the burden that is theirs from being human in the world'. Bolo's death challenges the members of the Baptist community to reclaim their own dignity in the struggle against oppression.

By focusing on the Spiritual Baptist tradition in *Wine*, Lovelace is able to represent the historical vitality of the African tradition in Trinidad. However, Lovelace does not privilege ethnic identity over human responsibility. Bee is contemptuously unresponsive when Mitchell states that they have to support Ivan in the upcoming elections, despite the fact that he has betrayed them, or else 'de Gannes or the Indian will come in' (p.138). The book makes no call for a return to the past, to traditional ways, to Africa. African ethnicity is situated within a changing, historical trajectory. The Spiritual Baptists are creolised in the sense that they have adapted aspects of Christianity. They participate in the changing national culture and are being co-opted by that culture. Bolo's death does not suggest a literal return to a past of ritual, warrior-hood, and resistance. It suggests instead a reclaiming and renewing of the spirit of struggle in the new situation of national politics. Bee, as Baptist leader, comes to a new understanding of the need to take responsibility for history, but the spirit has left his church. Eva takes note of its rebirth in another cultural form: in the steelband tent. It has also entered into the realm of 'high' culture, into the book we read.

The Wine of Astonishment, like Lovelace's society, has patriarchal overtones: is it just another story of the male warrior hero, his demise, and the need to reclaim him? Once again, it is the human depth of struggle, the spirit, that takes priority over masculine behaviour as such. Bolo is ultimately an anti-hero, a Bad John who goes so far as to abuse innocent women. The narrator of *Wine* is a woman, and it is she who helps us to put the events together. Along with Bee, she recognises the deep implications of Bolo's act; even before Bee, in faith and hope, she trusts that the 'Spirit will come back'; it is she who acknowledges its return in the steelband players (pp. 145-6).

In *Dragon*, carnival itself is problematised. National politics brings about a transformation in the community as the spirit of resistance gives way to accommodation to the new post-colonial order. However, Aldrick and Fisheye, the dragon of carnival and the stickfighter, join a small group of rebels in a desperate attempt to recover the lost spirit of the warrior. Playing with the 1970 Black Power events, the novel presents the rebels driving around Woodford Square, waving guns and making speeches, calling for liberation and justice. Crowds gather and applaud, but nothing happens. Like carnival, the spontaneous rebellion exhausts itself; unlike carnival, the rebels are marched off to prison. Aldrick comes to a full realisation that he and the rebels were playing mas' and that the population was responding to the rebellion as it would to a masquerade: 'We coulda do more than play a mas' .... We wasn't ready to take over nothing for we own self' (p. 188). In sharp contrast to Naipaul or Bisoondath, Lovelace takes a sensitive, yet critical look at the rebellion and seeks to discern its deeper meaning.

Dragon is a novel about coming to grips with one's responsibility in a changed post-colonial situation. As in *Wine*, there is no call to return to a heroic past. Rather than being a symbol of an African past, the warrior is the African Trinidadian as a responsible agent acting in the present. What then of the Indian Trinidadian? More than any other Trinidadian novel, *Dragon* has been praised by critics for the way in which it presents, from an African Trinidadian perspective, the dignity of the Indian Trinidadian (Ramchand, 1985:20, 23; Poynting, 1986:20; Singh, 1989:155, 158). The racial conflict generated in the yard by Guy and Cleothilda climaxes with the destruction of Pariag's new bike. The event is critical for it marks the depth of an insidious racism. It is the point at which Pariag fully assumes his difference and wins respect for so doing: like a captive soldier who holds on to his integrity, he marches the bike through town 'with head held high and that attitude of undefeat that challenges the whole meaning of war' (p. 140). Fisheye and Aldrick are impressed and begin to acknowledge him in his difference; later they will shout to him from the circling Black Power jeep: 'Power to you, Brother!' (p. 147).

Pariag is not a peripheral character in the novel. Lovelace places him squarely in the middle of the yard and deals with the problems that arise when a 'country Indian' tries to fit into a creole world. The incident with the bike marks a turning point for Pariag because he now assumes his own Indianness.' He no longer tries to fit in; he sees an Indian movie with Dolly and feels the call of India, the loneliness of being away from his family. Paradoxically, however, a visit to his family reveals his distance from them and his unwillingness to be dependent on a wealthy uncle. Pariag has broken out of traditional ethnic loyalties, but racial prejudice thwarts his possibilities and he recognises this. Fisheye and Aldrick finally recognise him as his own person, though they remain apart; he wants to embrace them, but it pains him that they only recognise him just as he is drawing away. Perhaps he should have joined them in the steelband yard with a flute or a sitar, he thinks to himself. It is the interplay between recognition and difference, possibility and failure, that gives the encounter its depth. The tragedy is that the yard is not able to realise the unity that can sustain these differences: 'We didn't have to melt into one' (p. 210). However, through self-understanding and recognition of the Other, a fundamental human unity has begun to articulate itself, and on the basis of it difference can be creative.

As in *Wine*, it is male heroism and its demise that is most prominently depicted in *Dragon*. What then of the female African or Indian Trinidadian trying to find herself in this changing world? A character such as Cleothilda is presented more for her social status than her gender: she represents the unitary ideology of a middle-class nationalism. In contrast, Sylvia is presented in terms of her own development, though as seen through Aldrick's eyes. When Aldrick sees in Sylvia's carnival dance a scream for a life beyond dragon and carnival, he begins to recognise his own failure. When he reaches out, as he thinks, to help her find herself in this new life, he touches only himself. Sylvia, it turns out, can take care of herself; she already has her 'man' (p. 128). Aldrick goes away with a new respect for her, and is on the way to a new understanding of himself. Sylvia will return, but only when Aldrick has found himself. Dolly, Pariag's wife, is presented for the most part as a subservient female voice warning her husband about the dangers of moving beyond ethnic lines. However, even she comes into her own when she points out to Pariag that a person is more than what is seen by the other, more than an ethnic other and more than a gender other: 'You is more, Boya. More than what you show them. I is more than what I show you, not so?' (p. 212). Compared to Hodge, Lovelace's novels, like Selvon's, position female characters, regardless of their ethnicity, primarily in relationship to male characters. Compared to the works of Naipaul and Bisoondath, however, Selvon and Lovelace preserve a space for human relationships which go beyond patriarchal and other exclusions, and, in this respect, their works can enter into dialogue with the work of female authors such as Hodge.

In the article, 'The On-Going Value of Our Indigenous Traditions', Lovelace calls on Trinidadians (and Tobagonians) to acknowledge the importance of the African base of Caribbean society. Unlike Europeans and Indians, Africans were 'forced to address the Caribbean landscape with radically new eyes'. The language may appear exclusionary: an African Caribbean narrative of freedom becomes the basis for understanding the totality of Caribbean experience, difference is erased, and Indians and Europeans excluded from political participation. However, Lovelace does not argue for the recovery of traditional African society, and he insists that the fundamental issue is the struggle for dignity and humanity. In their 'struggle for recognition', Africans 'were forced to transcend certain things African' and came 'to see the country not solely in terms of their group but of all who share the space with them' (Lovelace, 1988:336, 340-3). Read through *The Dragon Can't Dance*, Lovelace's point is that the colonial reading of the Caribbean experience must be deconstructed, and a history of human creativity and struggle reconstructed on the basis of a notion of human dignity. The challenge is to start from one's cultural base in a way which opens up to others, to place culture in the service of human dignity. This does not exclude the contribution of Indians or even Europeans, for if human dignity is respected and creativity in history is the point of departure, then the acceptance of difference becomes a necessity. Whereas contemporary cultural theorists tend to lose the moment of reconstruction, Lovelace takes a stand as a Third World writer who insists on a new vision of history and humanity which is both constructive and open-ended.

In a situation such as that of Trinidad, where there is a colonially imposed legacy of ethnic conflict, literature either reproduces that conflict or confronts it in a way that renders it historically comprehensible as an imposed and lived past, a contemporary issue, and a future to be shaped. Some authors find themselves caught by the primary ethnic stereotypes of the society and either reproduce them or contemptuously condemn both Indians and Africans from a white, colonial perspective. Selvon and Lovelace stand out as major Trinidadian authors who challenge stereotyped visions of Trinidadian society and realistically open up some of the possibilities for building a more just society. Each writes from a different historical situation and ethnic perspective, and each has a different sensitivity to the cultural issues and creolisation process in the society. However, in a sympathetic presentation of separate ethnic groups and the problems of their relationships, they relinquish cultural traditionalism but not cultural difference, and they contribute to the very essential educational work that Lamming has called 'the reciprocal sharing of cultural histories' (Lamming, 1989:51). Though they write from a male perspective, they also begin to explore the reality of female difference. Their task as writers is not to reflect or reproduce the contradictions of the society but to explore, from the point of view of that reality, the fundamental human concern for mutual respect and dignity. Only from that perspective is it possible to talk about meaningful social change.

Notes

1 At the time of the Black Power movement, Samaroo was himself sympathetic to its aims but did not feel fully involved (see Nicholls, 1985:73).
2 See the summary of the critical discussion of racism in Naipaul's work in Cudjoe (1988:8-9). Derek Walcott's review of *The Enigma of Arrival* (Walcott, 1987) is particularly trenchant.
3 See Poynting's criticism of Ramchand for his dismissal of Tiger and of Selvon's early works: Tiger does not confront his own 'Indianness'. (Ramchand, 1985:19; Poynting, 1986:16-17).
4 See the *diablesse* motif in Walcott's *Dream on Monkey Mountain* (1970:316-20).

References

Anthony, M., 1977 [1963], *The Games Were Coming*, London: Heinemann.
Bennett, H.L., 1989, 'The Challenge to the Post-Colonial State: A Case Study of the February Revolution in Trinidad', in Knight, F.W. and Palmer, C. (eds), *The Modern Caribbean*, Chapel Hill: University of North Carolina Press, pp. 129-46.
Bissoondath, N., 1989 [1988], *A Casual Brutality*, Harmondsworth: Penguin.
Braithwaite, L., 1960, 'Social Stratification and Cultural Pluralism', in Rubin, V. (ed.), *Social and Cultural Pluralism in the Caribbean*, Annals of the New York Academy of Sciences, Vol. 83, Art. 5, pp. 816-31.
Brathwaite, E., 1971, *The Development of Creole Society in Jamaica, 1770-1820*, Oxford: Oxford University Press.
Cudjoe, S., 1988, *V.S. Naipaul: A Materialist Reading*, Amherst: University of Massachusetts Press.
Fanon, F., 1968, *The Wretched of the Earth*, translated by C. Farrington, New York: Grove Press.
Hodge, M., 1981 [1970], *Crick Crack, Monkey*, London: Heinemann.
LaGuerre, J.G., 1988, 'Race Relations in Trinidad and Tobago', in Ryan, S. (ed.) *Trinidad and Tobago: The Independence Experience*, St Augustine: Institute of Social and Economic Research, University of the West Indies, pp. 193-206.
Lamming, G., 1989, 'The Indian Presence as a Caribbean Reality', in Birbalsingh, F. (ed.), *Indenture and Exile: The Indo-Caribbean Experience*, Toronto: Toronto South Asian Review.
Lovelace, E., 1981, *The Dragon Can't Dance*, Harlow, Essex: Longman.
– 1983, *The Wine of Astonishment*, London: Heinemann.
– 1988, 'The On-Going Value of Our Indigenous Traditions', in Ryan, S. (ed.), *Trinidad and Tobago: The Independence Experience*, St Augustine: Institute of Social and Economic Research, University of the West Indies, pp. 335-44.
Lyotard, F., 1984, 'Answering the Question: What is Postmodernism?', in *The Postmodern Condition: A Report on Knowledge*, translated by R. Durand, Minneapolis: University of Minnesota Press.
Mahabir, N. and Maharaj, A., 1989, 'Hindu Elements in the Shango/Orisha Cult of Trinidad', in Birbalsingh, F. (ed.), *Indenture and Exile: The*

Indo-Caribbean Experience, Toronto: Toronto South Asian Review, pp. 191-201.

Martin, T., 1986, 'Marcus Garvey and Trinidad, 1912-1947', in Lewis, R. and Warner-Lewis, M. (eds), *Garvey: Africa, Europe, the Americas*, Mona: Institute of Social and Economic Research, University of the West Indies, pp. 52-88.

Naipaul, V.S., 1969 [1962], *The Middle Passage*, Harmondsworth: Penguin.

– 1981, *The Return of Eva Peron*, Harmondsworth: Penguin.

Nicholls, D., 1985, *Haiti in Caribbean Context: Ethnicity, Economics and Revolt*, New York: St Martin's.

Poynting, J., 1986, ' "The African and the Asiatic Will Not Mix" (A. Froude): African-Indian Relations in Caribbean Fiction: A Reply', *Wasafiri*, No. 5, pp. 15-22.

Ramchand, K., 1983, *The West Indian Novel and its Background*, 2nd. edition, London: Heinemann.

– 1985, 'Indian-African Relations in Caribbean Fiction', *Wasafiri*, No. 2 (Spring), pp. 18-23.

Rodney, W., 1969, *Groundings with My Brothers*, London: Bogle-L'Ouverture Publications.

Ryan, S., 1972, *Race and Nationalism in Trinidad and Tobago: A Study of Decolonization in a Multiracial Society*, Toronto: University of Toronto Press.

Samaroo, B., 1987, 'The Indian Connection: The Influence of Indian Thought and Ideas on East Indians in the Caribbean', in Dabydeen, D. and Samaroo, B. (eds), *India in the Caribbean*, London: Hansib/University of Warwick, pp. 43-59.

Selvon, S., 1979a [1952], *A Brighter Sun*, London: Longman.

– 1979b [1958], *Turn Again Tiger*, London: Heinemann.

– 1987, 'Three into One can't go – East-Indian, Trinidadian, West Indian', in Dabydeen, D. and Samaroo, B. (eds), *India in the Caribbean*, London: Hansib/University of Warwick, pp. 13-24.

– 1990, *Those Who Eat the Cascadura*, Toronto: Toronto South Asian Review.

Singh, V., 1989, 'The Indian in the Trinidadian Novel', in Birbalsingh, F. (ed.), *Indenture and Exile: The Indo-Caribbean Experience*, Toronto: Toronto South Asian Review, pp. 148-58.

Smith, M.G., 1960, 'Social and Cultural Pluralism', in Rubin, V. (ed.), *Social and Cultural Pluralism in the Caribbean*, Annals of the New York Academy of Sciences, Vol. 83, Art. 5, pp. 763-77.

– 1984, *Culture, Race, and Class in the Commonwealth Caribbean*, Mona: Department of Extra-Mural Studies, University of the West Indies.

Walcott, D., 1970, *Dream on Monkey Mountain*, New York: Farrar, Straus and Giroux.

– 1987, 'The Garden Path', *New Republic*, 13 April 1987, pp. 27-31.

Williams, E., 1964, *History of the People of Trinidad and Tobago*, London: Andre Deutsch.

CHAPTER 12

Ethnicity and the contemporary calypso

Keith Q. Warner

Although by 1990 Denyse Plummer, a white woman born in Trinidad who sang calypsoes after having sung popular ballads on the nightclub circuit,[1] would be crowned calypso queen, she had not always been accepted by all sections of the Trinidad and Tobago public. Indeed, a short few years before Plummer had the misfortune of being pelted with rolls of toilet paper and orange skins while performing before a traditionally unruly crowd in San Fernando during the semi-finals of the Calypso Monarch Competition. To her credit, this performer did not allow the very partial crowd to chase her from the stage, and she reacted to its treatment of her with good-natured repartee. Plummer had performed well, delivering her songs with commendable art and gusto. Her only problem that day, for some still unexplained reason, was the fact that she was seen as intruding in a domain that was the reserve of those of another race, of another ethnic group. She was a white woman venturing into what is virtually a black man's territory, and she did not fit.

A few years prior to this 1987 incident, similar scepticism, if not similar hostility, had greeted the entry into the calypso arena of the Mighty Trini, a member of a prominent Syrian family. He apparently chose this sobriquet as a reminder to his listeners that he too was a son of the soil, and was thus entitled to sing calypsoes just like any other Trinidadian. Why, one is led to ask, would these two artistes meet with such an attitude in the country of their birth, a country whose national anthem proudly boasts that every creed and race find an equal place? Why would a public made up of such a mixture of races even think of excluding any one of its sons or daughters from practising the country's universally recognised art form?

The answer to these questions lies in the fact that, although over the years there have been calypsonians of other races, there has long been the feeling that calypso is the exclusive province of the black section of the population. This feeling has been legitimised by the fact that, for some researchers, the calypso came from Africa, though it is probably not a carbon copy of some African original.

The authoritative Mitto Sampson, in an article on calypso legends of the nineteenth century, maintains that:

> when African slaves came here [Trinidad] they found a form of singing. They took up the local songs and of course they sang their own songs too. They introduced more pep, more vigour, more liveliness and more animation. Singing under extremes as a form of escape from conditions abhorrent to them, it is natural that they should carry a greater intensity into their singing. Consequently, the Negro enriched the calypso but did not originate it (Pearse, 1956: 257).

The local songs involved were by the Caribs, and Sampson's source was himself a Carib called Surisima, so there may have been a touch of chauvinism in the account. Still, Sampson seems to give some measure of credit to his source, though conceding that the African input changed the tempo and the tone of the songs. It is conceivable, therefore, that the African not only enriched the Caribs' songs he heard on arrival in a new land, but proceeded to absorb them completely, to the point where the adopter, the adapter, and the owner were all fused into one.

Andrew Pearse, the editor and arranger of the Sampson article, does not, however, give much credence to the Surisima account. 'If the claims of Surisima to a Carib origin of calypso could be taken seriously', he writes, 'if they had less of the aura of misty Ossianic nostalgia, then it might be proper to give them priority' (1956:252). In place of this account of the origin of the calypso, Pearse prefers the other one given by Sampson, which he terms 'a realistic starting point at the beginning of the nineteenth century' *(ibid.)*. This other account held that a planter from the French-speaking island of Martinique, one Pierre Begorrat, lived on an estate in the north-west section of Trinidad with many African slaves, some of whom were singers of 'cariso' or 'caiso', a source of entertainment for his guests (1956:253). This account, if true, clearly shows that the African slaves were the ones to have started the singing of calypsoes, or at least of songs that later came to be called calypsoes.

Other researchers have documented the African origin of calypso. Gordon Rohlehr (1990) cites Maureen Warner-Lewis' (1984) study of Yoruba songs from Trinidad in which she states: 'the *picong* (provocation) and *mépris* (scorn) modes of so many of these Yoruba songs, whether sacred or secular, indicate one source, no doubt a reinforcement, of that satire-cum-boast tradition within the calypso' (Rohlehr, 1990:xviii). He then goes on to affirm that her pioneering works:

provide us with our first bits of real evidence in support of
the strong hypothesis that the African element was a major
matrix out of which the calypso developed; and that it was
in the process of the adaptation of the African matrix to the
wide and various elements of creole society in the West Indies
(French, Hispanic, English, Hindu, Muslim, *et al.*) that the
calypso assumed its various shapes (1990:17).

In other words, from the very beginning, calypso had a certain
'Africanness', a certain 'blackness' about it, and the fact that the
overwhelming majority of calypsonians were, and still are, of African
descent has led to a situation in which calypso is seen by the Trinidad
and Tobago public as first and foremost 'a black man's thing', and this
despite the very cosmopolitan make-up of the society. Consequently,
a great deal of what calypsonians have said, a great deal of the positions
they have taken, has been from a decidedly black perspective, even when
such a perspective has been negative and self-deprecating. Further, in
instances where race has apparently not been uppermost in their minds,
calypsonians have steadfastly taken an ethnic position, blending race
and culture, pitting, for instance, all Trinidadians and Tobagonians
as a group against their Caribbean island neighbours.

There can, of course, be no doubt that calypsonians mirror to a
very large extent what is going on in the society. This does not mean
that everything they say is always to be taken at face value, for they
have been known to be notoriously two-faced, but, by and large, they
provide accurate assessments of what makes Trinidad and Tobago
society tick. For this reason, therefore, it is reasonable to assume that
what appears in the contemporary calypso concerning race and ethnicity
is an accurate reflection of prevailing attitudes, at least among the
members of the group represented by the singers.

Not only do contemporary calypsonians reflect the mores of their
society, they are part of a long tradition, as Rohlehr's exhaustive study
(1990) so admirably demonstrates, and to which the reader is referred
for detailed accounts of calypso and society in pre-independence
Trinidad. Indeed, all of the demonstrably ethnic themes treated by
contemporary calypsonians were already present prior to the so-called
modern era, except for those that dealt with independence or situations
stemming from actualities of local or international significance.

Let us, for the purpose of this chapter, define 'contemporary' as
over the past two decades, thus from approximately 1970, although
there is nothing absolute about this date. We could, for example, just
as easily have set it at 1956, another arbitrary but convenient cut-off
point. The year 1956 marked the coming into power of the People's

National Movement (PNM) under Dr Eric Williams, a leader of African descent whose first cabinet included blacks, Indians, a Chinese, and a 'Trinidad white'. The 30 years this party remained in power saw some of the most significant moments in the country's modern history. The year 1956 also saw the emergence of the Mighty Sparrow, who was to have a major and enduring influence on contemporary calypso. Finally, 1956 marked the beginning of a renewed political education of the electorate, as the PNM drew the masses to the 'University of Woodford Square' in downtown Port of Spain.

Yet another possible cut-off date for a study of the contemporary calypso could be 1962, the year Trinidad and Tobago achieved political independence. It was only natural that the entire population, regardless of ethnic affiliation, would see political independence as an opportunity to set right all the perceived wrongs of the past. Nevertheless, as D.V. Trotman indicates:

> Despite the fact that the leadership of that political movement considered themselves children of the spirit of Bandung, and committed to a multi-racial society, the movement could not help but be considered both by Africans and Indians as an African party with its political leader as a living symbol of African vindication (1991:386).

A black leader (as opposed to a white expatriate governor) was firmly in control. In addition, this leader was perceived as capable of doing nearly anything. The Mighty Striker sang:

> Annabella stocking want patching
> She want de doctah help she wid dat
> Johnson trousers falling
> He want de doctah help he wid dat
> . . .
>
> Now Dorothy lose she man
> She want to complain to Doctah Williams.

Annabella, Johnson, and Dorothy were clearly Afro-Trinidadians, who saw in this new black leader someone who could, and would, do for them what an insensitive white colonial regime never did. What did not emerge in this calypso, but what was definitely fermenting below the surface, was the fact that the Indian population was quietly wondering what the country would be like under an Indian Prime Minister, a question that would continue to nag the entire nation even as it faced the polls in the early 1990s.

Williams himself, as noted in the last chapter, had sought to neutralise the difference in the races in the conclusion to his hastily-written *History of the People of Trinidad and Tobago* (1962):

There can be no Mother Africa for those of African origin, and the Trinidad and Tobago society is living a lie and heading for trouble if it seeks to create the impression or to allow others to act under the delusion that Trinidad and Tobago is an African society. There can be no Mother England and no dual loyalties; ... There can be no Mother China, even if one could agree on which China is the Mother; and there can be no Mother Syria or no Mother Lebanon. A nation, like an individual can have only one Mother. The only Mother we recognise is Mother Trinidad and Tobago, and Mother cannot discriminate between her children (p. 281).

One can only assume that omission of any reference to Mother India in Williams' list was an oversight due to hasty writing. Needless to say, Williams' exhortation, later reinforced by his call for the nation to ban the words 'coolie' and 'nigger' from its vocabulary, fell on deaf ears, though calypsonians too, like Valentino, urged the nation to 'forget the nigger and the coolie grouse'.

Sparrow had already noted the impending change for blacks, in particular with his 'Ah tell you soon in the West Indies/Is please, Mr Nigger, please', a back-handed compliment at best, since it did not completely remove the term of denigration. Be that as it may, there was every reason for blacks to feel that a new day had indeed dawned, and for Indians, for example, to hope that the generally negative stereotyping to which they had been subjected would come to an end. The upbeat note of Sparrow's 'Model Nation', his popular though not prize-winning contribution to the independence calypso competition, would not be maintained:

The whole population of our little nation
Is not a lot
But oh what a mixture of races and culture
That's what we've got
Still no major indifference
Of race, colour, religion or finance
It's amazing to you I'm sure
We didn't get independence before.

Clearly, if this was the prevailing mood, then anyone saying anything to the contrary would be deemed the proverbial villain, for it was obviously better to foster the belief that all in the society was perfect, and Sparrow, like Williams, was no exception.

This did not in any way mean calypsonians were not aware of the ethnic imbalance in the society, with the white minority controlling a disproportionate amount of the wealth, and their growing militancy *vis-à-vis* the power structure was grounded in the fact that they saw themselves not being given their fair share. Indeed, Sparrow's leading of the calypsonians on strike in 1957 for better conditions at the annual calypso king competition was rooted in the fact that more attention (and prizes) went to the 'carnival queen' than to the calypsonians. The queen was invariably either a local white or a very light-skinned mulatto.

But the event that forced everyone to revisit all issues of race and ethnicity occurred in 1970, hence my use of this year as a cut-off point for my use of 'contemporary'. This was the year of the so-called Black Power Revolution. According to Herman L. Bennett in his case study of the February Revolution in Trinidad:

> Inspired by [Walter] Rodney's ideas, many young radicals throughout the Caribbean embraced Black Power and raised probing questions about the political order. To the surprise of most observers, the most sustained expressions of Black Power emerged in Trinidad where the ruling People's National Movement (PNM) had been characterized as the best example of black majority rule (1989:131).

Surprise, yes, because those observers would have been like Sparrow in his 'Model Nation'. But one group that was not surprised was the National Joint Action Committee (NJAC), though, as is the burden of all militant groups, its stance was fraught with problems:

> NJAC's Black Power emphasis was somewhat injudicious in a racially heterogeneous society like Trinidad. Given the shrewd manipulation of hostilities between Afro- and East Indian Trinidadians (who respectively comprised 42 per cent and 37 per cent of the population), Black Power only exacerbated a potentially explosive relationship .... Although both [groups] shared similar socio-economic conditions, the years of racial tension and conflict in addition to cultural differences effectively prevented Afro-Indian unity (*ibid*:133).

The 'revolution' propelled race, always lurking just under the surface, to the forefront of the country's economic and political agenda, and many of the changes subsequently effected – more blacks in banks, black carnival queens, etc. – are directly attributable to this 1970 event, which even had the (belated) support of Prime Minister Williams. The

Trinidad Guardian (23 March 1970) reported on his acknowledgement during a televised address to the nation that:

> The fundamental feature of the demonstrators was the insistence on Black Dignity, the manifestation of Black consciousness and the demand for Black economic power. The entire population must understand that these demands are perfectly legitimate and are entirely in the interest of the community as a whole. If this is Black Power then I am for Black Power.

The revolution thus took on a mantle of blackness as a symbol of the plight of a struggling Third World nation, and the Indians found it difficult to throw their full support behind it, viewing the blacks' sudden interest in the East Indian sugar worker with suspicion. 'Overall', writes Bennett, 'the concept of Black Power has little appeal for the Indian population and throughout the period of unrest the majority of participants were of African desent' (1989:139).

The 1970 calypsoes had already been composed and recorded by the time the main events of the revolution took place, so one had to wait till 1971 to hear what the calypsonians, as mirrors of the nation's mood, were going to say. Among the many commentaries from the likes of Sparrow, Chalkdust, Kitchener, and Black Stalin, the one from Valentino tackled the race aspect head on, and even echoed the statement made by the Prime Minister:

> We didn't want them trigger-happy police
> We only wanted to demonstrate in peace
> Yet you hold my people and charge them for sedition
> We was marching for equality
> Black unity, black dignity
> Dr Williams, we didn't want no revolution.

Valentino, soon to be dubbed 'the people's calypsonian', would return time and again during the 1970s and 1980s to the theme of blackness, of Africa, and of the exploited black brother in Trinidad and Tobago, a theme he would share with Black Stalin.

These two calypsonians, or kaisonians if we use the 'purer' name they both purport to prefer, became virtual spokesmen for blacks in the country as a whole, as opposed to being spokesmen for the other races. But they also adopted a decidedly Third World posture, so that when in that context they sang of the 'Trinidadian' they did, technically, include their compatriots of all races, all rolled into a single 'Trini' persona, the way Chalkdust would do in calypsoes such as 'You Can't Beat A Trinidadian'.

Valentino, having examined what makes the Trinidadian (and Tobagonian) tick, came up with 'Dis Place Nice', a bitter-sweet return to the belief that 'Trinidad is nice/Trinidad is a paradise', but one that warned that after the carefree living, fêting, and spreeing, 'the people getting ready for the revolution/fire on the way'. One could not escape the feeling, however, that Valentino was speaking to the black Trinidadian in particular:

> They don't know their worth
> Like they have no sense of values
> They don't know their right
> Even that they cannot argue
> · · ·
>
> They born in a land
> The better part control by the alien
> They fill the pockets
> Of Portuguese, Chinese and Syrians.

As columnist Raoul Pantin commented in the *Trinidad Express:*

> It's the chorus that makes the whole calypso. The voices sing in a slow melodic line 'Trinidad is nice/Trinidad is a paradise.' Between choruses, Valentino sings of the black Trinidadian's persistent stupidity, his passion for consumption, his warped sense of values, his inability as a community to unite for a perceived goal .... It is a savage attack on the old Tourist Board view of the country (9 February 1975, p. 7).

No one, then, could accuse the calypsonian of denigrating one race or ethnic group at the expense of another. His attack was equally devastating, aimed at both the exploiter and the exploited in the society as a whole, although it was clear that the exploited counted an unusually large number of blacks among them.

Valentino's 'blood brother' Black Stalin would achieve even greater popularity with calypsoes that were consistently in the same vein: urging blacks to take stock of themselves, to reject exploitation, to remember their African roots, etc. Unlike Valentino, whose calypsoes were not accompanied by the kind of music one could dance to, Stalin was able to please with both lyric and melody, an unbeatable combination for a calypsonian, and one that on more than one occasion has seen him crowned national calypso monarch.

Stalin won the crown the first time in 1979, singing 'Play One', a tribute to the panman, and 'Caribbean Unity', a calypso that caused an instant furore because of the view it took of the Caribbean man;

indeed, the calypso is more popularly known as 'Caribbean Man'. The overall theme is one of unity among Caribbean people, but it is the chorus that offended:

Dem is one race – De Caribbean man
From the same place – De Caribbean man
That make the same trip – De Caribbean man
On the same ship – De Caribbean man
Is so we must push one common intention
For a better life in the region
Dat must be the ambition
Of De Caribbean man, De Caribbean man, De Caribbean man.

Ramesh Deosaran, a Trinidadian of Indian descent, immediately termed the calypso racist and sexist, and categorised the opening lines of the chorus as 'nothing less that an insult to the vast number of people from other races here who have come in different ships and from different places and who are also struggling to make this unity thing work' (1987:114). He aptly summarises the controversy as follows:

The emotional impact and widespread interest generated by the controversy is evidenced by the fact that it occupied a total of 660 column inches and involved six of the seven national newspapers across the country. The controversy drew in strident contributions from major opinion leaders; among them prominent community leaders, reporters and columnists from the two major ethnic groups – Indians and Africans. As far as responses to the newspapers were concerned, the public debate lasted for two and a half months – 28 February, 1979 to 12 May, 1979. It provided an exciting snap-shot of the social psychology of race relations in the country (*ibid*:81).

There was no escaping the fact that this was a major controversy in a country accustomed to controversy stemming from positions taken by the calypsonians, and Stalin did not help matters when he appeared on television shortly after winning the competition and reiterated that 'his calypso was really confined to men of African descent, that his "Caribbean Man" was of African descent, that Africans here were the ones who developed the Caribbean, and that they were the only ones concerned with Caribbean unity' (*ibid*:87). Deosaran was himself accused by the *Trinidad Express* of reading too much into the calypso, and Selwyn Ryan, University of the West Indies political scientist (and of African descent), thought that Stalin had absolutely nothing to apologise for. Even the normally aloof Eric Williams jumped into the fray several weeks later, and quoted lines from the calypso during his three and a half hour address to the party at its annual General Convention. Williams gave a historical survey of how each of the country's ethnic groups had come to the West Indies, and interjected frequently that 'dem too is one race ... from de same place ... dat make de same trip ... on de same ship'. This was no ordinary calypso, and Stalin would never take back anything he had sung in it.

We are led once more to ask ourselves why such a state of affairs could have developed. Did Stalin compose his calypso bearing in mind that people of African descent comprise by far the largest ethnic group among Caribbean peoples? Did Stalin think, as Selwyn Ryan would later explain in his *Sunday Express* column of 11 March 1979, that 'one of the reasons why blacks believe that they are more integrally Caribbean than any other group is that they alone have completely severed primordial ties with their "Motherland"'? Did Stalin see far beyond the moment to a time when all Trinidadians and Tobagonians, indeed all Caribbean people, would have blended into one race, into one ethnic whole? Is calypso so much of a black product that it automatically presents an exclusively black point of view? Or was it simply a case of poetic license? Would all the fuss have come about if there had been an equivalent calypso about the Indian Caribbean man? And if there were, how would it have played in those islands where the Indian population is relatively small? And finally, where were the Indian calypsonians who could put forward an opposing view?

Of course, to this final question there was one simple answer: there were none, or at least none with similar stature. This has meant that the Afro-calypsonians have taken it upon themselves, or have had it thrust upon them, to speak for and about the entire society, all of which explains the ethnic purity of many calypsoes but also accounts for the ethnic bias and stereotype.

The Afro-calypsonian as spokesperson of his or her race produced calypsoes that purported to revisit the way Africa and Africans at home and abroad were portrayed, though some only managed to perpetuate the caricatural image of the continent and its people already present in Sparrow's 1965 'Congo Man' (reissued in 1990), and reinforced in his 1980 'Love African-style'. Squibby's 'Shango', Superior's 'African', Merchant's 'Umbayao', Stalin's 'Time' and 'More Come', Valentino's 'Stay Up Zimbabwe', Bally's 'Shaka', Duke's 'Uhuru' and 'How Many More Must Die?', and Machel Montano's 'Take Me Back Africa', to give a mere sampling of what was offered, spanned the two decades under consideration with positive images of Africa, and kept alive the question of the Afro-Trinidadians' link to their heritage. Of course, after years of colonial pressure and Euro-centric education, it was not a given that the African descendants would readily identify themselves as African, the way, to their credit, the Indian descendants identified themselves as Indian, a phenomenon that was patently illustrated whenever a touring Indian cricket team played in the Caribbean. As a result, Superior felt it necessary to sing:

> How come if an Indian born in England is an Indian man
> And if a Chinese born in Scotland he is a Chinese man?
> I think is time that my black brothers try to understand
> No matter where you born you still African, yes man.

This was not a political statement. It was one born of ethnic pride.

The fact that Superior could sing such a calypso, and that Smiley could also sing 'What Is Wrong With the Negro Man' meant that despite this ethnic identification there were problems in need of attention. Thus an Afro-calypsonian like Explainer would seek to have his Afro-Trinidadian brother, 'Mr African', liberate himself from the mental slavery under which he was trapped. He directly addressed the African descendants in the society, exhorting them to stop creating their own condemnation for

> As a cosmopolitan nation
> With two race in majority
> The people facing the most frustration
> Is the black man like you and me.

He went on to point out that the 'Indians were prospering', that the 'Chinese were capitalising', and used these goads to prod 'Mr African' to do likewise. He criticised the African's apparent inability to work in solidarity with his brother, whereas

> The Indian man, he thinks differently
> Every Indian for he is he family.

Explainer cleverly played on the fear among the blacks that once Indians are in a position of authority they help one another, a fear that blacks have grumbled about every time there is talk of electing a new Prime Minister.[2] Deosaran (1987:107) cited this calypso as an example of those that 'not only exclude other groups in favour of Africans, but go on to implicate other groups with negative stereotypes'.

The main 'other' group, of course, was the Indians, a group that Rohlehr characterises as one of those that existed 'on the margins of the calypsonian's consciousness. Since the calypsonian generally perceives himself as an insider, a man in the know and at the forefront, groups seen to be on the margins are rarely presented as sanely ordered within themselves, but as eccentric, unsophisticated, weird and comical' (1990:494). This marginalisation would continue in the absence of any conscious attempt on the part of the almost non-existent Indo-calypsonian to set the record straight. The Indian community would sit virtually helpless – save for its vociferous objection *after* the fact – while Afro-calypsonians accused it of clannishness, made fun of its women, of its religion, of its work ethic, of its accent, indeed of its very attempt to be part of the Trinidad and Tobago mainstream, over which blacks seemed unfairly to claim a monopoly. It was not until the emergence of Drupatee in the late 1980s that one heard anything close to an authentic Indian 'voice' in calypso.

The easily recognisable Indo-calypsonian, like Shah, Rajah, Indian Prince, Ricky Jai and Kenny J., did not produce any calypsoes that were the equivalent of those by their Afro-counterparts. In fact, calls for black/Indian unity and solidarity came from the blacks like Valentino and Shorty, who would still capitalise on the perceived quaintness of the Indian woman in his 'Indrani' in 1972. Shorty, who claimed that he had 'grown up with East Indians in Lengua Village' angered sections of the Indian community by appearing on stage decked in *ohrni* and other obvious Indian accoutrements. In addition, he was still then known for his very suggestive, sexually-oriented lyrics, so the calypso was seen as yet another attempt to drag the Indian woman down into the gutter.

Shorty would later (1979) try to redeem himself with 'Om Shanti' but ran into even more trouble because he was seen as desecrating something held in reverence by large sections of the Indian community, specifically the Sanatan Dharma Maha Saba, which supposedly represented some quarter of a million Hindus. A plea for unity and brotherhood among all the country's people, the song was termed a mantra by Shorty:

> This song you hear
> Is an Indian prayer
> From ancient times
> Created to soothe your mind
> In danger, in anger, remember
> Sing this mantra
> This golden mantra from the master
> This song is to enable people
> To struggle against the devil
> In this human jungle
> Is plenty people, yes plenty people.

The music was clearly inspired by Indian melodies and rhythms, giving the entire calypso a feeling of authenticity. However, once again, the calypsonian was seen as degrading 'Indian people thing'. When shortly afterwards the calypsonian fell on hard times that caused him to withdraw from society, to change his well-known image as super stud, and even to change his sobriquet to Ras Shorty I, there were those who felt that he had finally paid the price for having interfered with what did not concern him.

Sparrow's Indian trilogy of the 1980s ('Marajhin' in 1982, 'Marajhin Sister' in 1983, and 'Marajhin Cousin' in 1984) resorted to the now classic references to Indian foods and their preparation, to the supposed strictness of the Indian parents, to Indians' purported penchant for violence, to their clothing, and even to their supposed inability to keep the same time as 'real' Trinidadians ('And jump out of time to sweet pan for carnival'). These were essentially love calypsoes to his Indo-lover from the Afro-suitor, afraid that their cultures were keeping them apart. They were marred, however, by the snide digs the suitor takes at the very culture he wants to become part of ('And gladly trade my toilet paper for some water'). On the other hand, the music, like Shorty's, was a wonderful blend of Indian and African rhythms, and foreshadowed the Indian soca of the late 1980s.

In 1988 an Indian woman, singing under her real name, Drupatee, released a calypso that went a long way toward breaking down racial and gender barriers. She sang about 'Mr Bissessar', inviting him to 'roll up the tassa', and this drum was actually featured prominently in the musical arrangement. What Drupatee captured was the growing interpenetration of black/Creole and Indian music as she made no attempt to disguise her Indianness, even playing to the stereotype of the Indian female who cannot dance ('wine') like the other Trini women.

The following year she sang 'Indian Soca', in which she showed the benefit to be derived from the blend of the Indian and African cultures:

They give me blows
Last year for doing soca
But it shows
How much they know 'bout culture
For the music of the steeldrums from Laventille
Cannot help but mix with rhythm from Caroni
For it's a symbol of how much we've come of age
Is a brand new stage
[chorus]
Indian soca, sounding sweeter
Hotter than a chula
Rhythm from Africa and India
Blend together is a perfect mixture

All we do is add new flavour
Leh we get down to Indian soca.

There followed a veritable explosion of interest in this blend, and
this has resulted in the development of 'chutney singing', the term by
which 'genuine' Indian soca is being called.

Only time will tell whether the primacy of place now held by the
Afro-calypsonian will lose ground. There may come a time when the
Indian section of the population will take full political control, thus
spurring the Indo-calypsonian into action the way his or her counterpart
felt emboldened when the black-controlled PNM was in power from
1956 to 1986.

Part of the problem stems from the ambivalence of Trinidad and
Tobago's position with regard to the international community. On the
one hand the country allies itself with other black Third World nations.
In this respect, it is seen as a black country with black, that is non-
white, people, and its calypsoes reflect this stance. But, on the other
hand, the country boasts of its cosmopolitan make-up, its racial
diversity, and whereas its calypsoes pay lip service to this boast, the
composers often retain the predominantly black stance. It is in this
context that we can understand the dilemma of a Denyse Plummer or
a Mighty Trini: 'Dem too is one race?'.

It is blatantly unfair for any ethnic group to be the butt of criticism
and ridicule in a multi-ethnic setting. As Deosaran (1987:107) writes:

> This matter of ignoring or relegating the presence or
> importance of one or another ethnic group in Trinidad only
> instigates apprehensions by the neglected group which, like
> self-fulfilling prophesy, would then be viewed as 'insularity'
> by those who engineered the relegation. The theme of black
> nationalism in Trinidad calypsoes cannot continue to ignore
> other ethnic groups here without appearing to be quixotic at
> some point.

Such a group in point would be the Chinese, who in calypsoes prior
to 1970 had had fun poked at their names, and at their manner of
speaking, but who were not seen as a problem *per se*. However, Afro-
Trinidadian was silently observing, and Smiley, who felt that he could
legitimately pillory the Chinese because he had done the same to the
blacks in 'What Is Wrong With the Negro Man', sang:

> Them Chinese don't lend
> They don't give, they don't spend
> They don't take part in nutten
> Ah wonder what go happen

According to Mr Guy
They sucking the country dry
Ah want the government to pass a law
And charge them 50 times more.

Smiley's good friend Chalkdust cited this calypso in his comments on the role of the calypsonian in bringing about 'greater unity in the society by singing praises to the Chinese', without mentioning anything about the open attack on this one section of the population (Liverpool, 1986:18). Typically, there was no outcry from the Chinese community.

The 1970s and 1980s saw the emergence of another ethnic grouping that would stake its claim for recognition, that would fight to avoid being subjected to what Rohlehr calls 'ethnic scapegoating'. This group, the Rastafarians, would in the mind of the public at large suffer the same fate the immigrant population had endured at the hands of Blakie in 'Send Them Back', or Sparrow in 'Barbadians'. Explainer sprang to the defense of the rastas:

Everybody hate and scorn a rasta
Most people believe that he is dread
They can't have peace no time
They always linking them with some crime
If you read the daily paper
Any crime committed they say is rasta.

Several calypsonians started to wear dreadlocks (Stalin, Valentino, Ras Shorty I, Rootsman, Struggler), while others, like Explainer, were openly sympathetic and supportive. Stalin's 'Caribbean Unity' even suggested that Caribbean politicians should look seriously at Rastafarianism:

The Federation done dead
And Carifta going to bed
But the cult of the Rastafarian
Spreading throughout the Caribbean
It have rastas now in Grenada
It have rastas now in St Lucia
But to run Carifta you getting pressure
If the Rastafari movement spreading
And Carifta dying slow
Then is something dem rastas on
That dem politicians don't know.

If the rastas were marginalised by a society awash with petro-dollars, they were not marginalised in the calypso, and their natural link with Jamaica's reggae provided another dimension into which contemporary calypso music could expand.

When in 1986 the PNM was finally voted out of office after 30 years in power, the new government, which had campaigned on a theme of 'One Love', tried to build on the coalition of parties and races that had helped it wrest victory. It was soon obvious, however, that the hoped-for harmony was not going to materialise, and that the question of race and ethnicity was going to plague the society for a long time, despite all the facile musings about 'One Love. There were open disputes among the top brass in both party and government, and each year's calypsoes chronicled the unfolding bacchanal.

What has remained clear over the years is the fact that the calypso will continue to mirror the thoughts and feelings of the Trinidad and Tobago public. Its popularity is not about to wane, as each year's crop is eagerly awaited by a public anxious to hear what slant the calypsonian is going to put on a particular event. What is also clear is that the race and ethnicity question will not go away in a society as cosmopolitan as this one, and indeed could deteriorate if those in a position of influence do not manifest the necessary sensitivity. The calypsonian is in an admirable position to go far beyond the politician, far beyond the academics and other social commentators, and to help foster the type of attitude that would have us believe, along with Chalkdust, that although 'culturally we are different/ . . . is right here we will find our identity'.

Notes

1   Denyse Plummer is among a growing number of calypsonians who have chosen not to sing under a sobriquet. Others include David Rudder, Machel Montano, and Eastlyn Orr.
2   Rumour has it that in the hours immediately following Eric Williams' death there was intense debate among his deputies over who would become the new Prime Minister. Kamal Mohammed is alleged to have lost out precisely because of this fear of an Indian leader.

References

Bennett, H.L., 1989, 'The Challenge of the Post-Colonial State: A Case Study of the February Revolution in Trinidad', in Knight, F.W. and Palmer, C.A. (eds), *The Modern Caribbean*, Chapel Hill: University of North Carolina Press, pp. 129-46.
Deosaran, R., 1987, 'The "Caribbean Man": A Study of the Psychology of Perception and the Media', in Dabydeen, D. and Samaroo, B. (eds), *India in the Caribbean*, London: Hansib/University of Warwick, pp. 81-118.

Liverpool, H., 1986, *Kaiso and Society*, St Thomas: Virgin Islands Commission on Youth.

Pearse, A., 1956, 'Mitto Sampson on Calypso Legends of the Nineteenth Century', *Caribbean Quarterly*, Vol. 4, Nos. 3 and 4, pp. 250-62.

Rohlehr, G., 1990, *Calypso and Society in Pre-Independence Trinidad*, Port of Spain: Gordon Rohlehr.

Trotman, D.V., 1991, 'The Image of Indians in Calypso: Trinidad 1946-86', in Ryan, S. (ed.), *Social and Occupational Stratification in Contemporary Trinidad and Tobago*, St Augustine: Institute of Social and Economic Studies, University of the West Indies, pp. 385-98.

Warner-Lewis, M., 1984, 'Yoruba Songs From Trinidad', Mona: University of the West Indies, unpublished manuscript.

Williams, E., 1962, *History of the People of Trinidad and Tobago*, Port of Spain: PNM Publishing Co.

Index

achievements: and colour respectability,
91-3, 94, 102-5 *passim*
and social status, 102
Achong, Tito P., 95
adolescents, male: and creolisation,
239-50
identity, of Indian, 241
African influence: and calypso, 276
in Trinidad culture, 5
Africanisation: and *Orisha* religion,
18, 161, 175-9
Africanness, 102, 185
and calypso, 277
Africans: in colour terms, 82, 88
culture, loss of, 95
enslavement, 33
equality with Indians, 75, 76
identity, 236, 268
image of, 95
mixing with Indians, 96-7
and *Orisha* religion, 161-79
struggle for recognition, 272
Afro-American religious complex,
162-4 *passim*
Afro-calypsonians, 284, 288
Afro-Christian religion, 49-50
Afro-Trinidadians, 184, 188
and creolisation, 236
Afro-West Indians: and culture, 96
Alcazar, Henry, 47
Amerindians, 4, 35, 191, 193
Anthony, Michael, author, 255, 256-7

Best, Lloyd, 146, 147, 156, 157
behaviour: and creolisation, 237-9
passim, 246, 249
Biddeau, Jeffrey, 176
Bissoondath, Neil, author, 259
blackness, 185
Black Power: and calypsoes, 280-1
movement, 13, 20, 126, 174, 175, 185
in literature, 257-9
riots, 1970, 68
blacks: categories of, 87-8, 187
and East Indians, 7-9
identity, 18, 187
nationalism, and calypso, 288
and *Orisha* religion, 18, 161-79
percentage, 124

see also Africans
Black Stalin, calypsonian, 282-4,
289
Borde, P.G.L., 39
Braithwaite, Lloyd, author, 255
brahmacarya, 243
British: influence of, 4, 6, 88, 105

callaloo: and mixed society, 188-90
calypso, 11, 158, 205, 275-81
ethnic politics of, 20, 275-91
calypsonians: *see* kaisonians
Capildeo, Pundit, 211
Capildeo, Rudranath, 140, 141
Caribbean fiction, 255
Carib: and calypso, 276
ethnicity, 204-5
carnival, 11, 50, 158, 243
in literature, 268, 269-70
caste: in Indian society, 42, 51, 76,
227, 229-30
Catholic church, 221-2, 226
and the elite, 45-6
and *Orisha* religion, 165, 175-6, 177
Chambers, George, 145, 146
Chinese, 6, 83, 228
and calypsoes, 288-9
intermarriage, 131
in society, 35, 37, 38
Christian: Indians, 121-2, 126, 229
class: – colour pyramid, social, 181
and economic equality, 76
and ethnicity, 208-34 *passim*
and gender, 208-34 *passim*
cocoa-panoles, 192
colonialism: anti- struggle, 12
in literature, 258
and multi-ethnicity of Trinidad, 136,
186
power of, 64-5
colour: and achievements, 91-3
boundaries of, 89-90
Creole scale of, 87-9, 91, 97, 102
identity within families, 89-90
observed relationship, 91
in pre-independence Trinidad, 18,
81-115
and respectability, 92-3
sensitivity to, 43